A Note on Language and Spelling

The Yanomama have a taboo on uttering personal names which becomes even stronger when an individual dies. Out of respect for this taboo, all Yanomama names in this book have been fictionalized. The spelling of Yanomama names and words has been rendered in a way that most closely approximates their pronunciation. Thus the word *nape* (outsider) is spelled "nabuh," which is approximately how the word sounds in Yanomama.

The name Yanomama itself has appeared in various forms in English language publications, most commonly Yanomami or Yanomamo. The form Yanomami, which regularly appears in newspaper accounts, is a corruption of the phonetic spelling Yanomamï, where the *ï* sounds similar to the *e* in roses. We have used Yanomama here, since the final *a* renders an English pronunciation close to the original.

INTO

the HEART

One Man's Pursuit of
Love and Knowledge
Among the Yanomama

kenneth good

with david chanoff

SIMON & SCHUSTER
NEW YORK   LONDON   TORONTO   SYDNEY   TOKYO   SINGAPORE

SIMON & SCHUSTER
SIMON & SCHUSTER BUILDING
ROCKEFELLER CENTER
1230 AVENUE OF THE AMERICAS
NEW YORK, NEW YORK 10020

DESIGNED BY ERIC ZIMAN

MANUFACTURED IN THE UNITED STATES OF AMERICA

1 2 3 4 5 6 7 8 9 10

LIBRARY OF CONGRESS CATALOGING IN PUBLICATION DATA

GOOD, KENNETH.
INTO THE HEART : ONE MAN'S PURSUIT OF LOVE AND KNOWLEDGE
AMONG THE YANOMAMA / KENNETH GOOD WITH DAVID CHANOFF.
P.   CM.
1. YANOMAMA INDIANS.   2. GOOD, KENNETH.   3. GOOD, YARIMA.
4. ETHNOLOGISTS—VENEZUELA—BIOGRAPHY.   5. ETHNO-
LOGISTS—UNITED STATES—BIOGRAPHY.   I. CHANOFF, DAVID.
II. TITLE. F2520.1.Y3G66   1991
987'.004982—DC20   90-48018
CIP

ISBN 0-671-72874-1

TO THE HASUPUWETERI,
WHO SHOWED ME THE
YANOMAMA WAY OF LIFE,
AND ESPECIALLY TO MY
WIFE, YARIMA, WHO SO
COURAGEOUSLY ENDURED THE
TRIALS OF BOTH HER
WORLD AND MINE

FOREWORD

For centuries the lost world of the Amazon has cast its spell on outsiders, spawning legends and drawing to itself conquerors, adventurers, explorers, and scientists. Greedy, curious, brave, or foolhardy, they have come, beginning with Christopher Columbus, who discovered the Orinoco half a millennium ago, and extending to present-day botanists, biologists, zoologists, anthropologists, and other, less benign, intruders. The Amazon still has places where a good botanist can emerge from a field expedition with twenty or thirty species of heretofore undiscovered plants; for anthropologists, the jungle's remotest depths even now are home to groups uncontacted by the modern world, perhaps the last place on earth that still beckons with such splendid seductions.

From the earliest days of exploration Spaniards, Portuguese, and Germans came, men with names like Orellana, Teixeira, Ursua, Berrio, Aguirre, and Alfinger. By the time the Pilgrims landed at Plymouth rock, expeditions of discovery had been penetrating the

Amazon for almost a hundred years. Yet in 1914 one of the later explorers, Teddy Roosevelt, still called it the "last true frontier" and barely escaped death on his own mapping voyage down an uncharted Amazonian river. Many of Roosevelt's predecessors, and some who came after him, weren't as fortunate. In the jungle's interior death took unpleasant forms: septicemia, starvation, snakebite, fevers, and the curare-tipped arrows of hostile Indians all claimed their share of the intrepid. Some returned on the backs of their friends; some were eaten by cannibals; others, like Colonel Fawcett, surveyor of the Brazilian border, simply disappeared.

But despite the monumental suffering the jungle routinely inflicted on its visitors, they still came. Something about the Amazon breathes mystery and fires imaginations. Within its unknown immensity what might not be awaiting discovery by so-called civilized man? What astonishing and wonderful—or odious and horrifying—places and creatures? What wealth? What knowledge? After Pizarro's conquest of the Inca empire, he forged eastward, sending parties of conquistadors and Indian slaves in search of the fabled land of El Dorado, so rich that its king rolled naked in gold dust each morning and washed himself clean each evening in a lake whose golden sediment deepened by the year. Francisco de Orellana led one of these expeditions. He found no gold, but the Franciscan father who accompanied him reported that they saw women warriors, "white and tall, with long braided hair wound around their heads, and they are very robust and go naked, except with their privy parts covered, with bows and arrows in their hands, fighting like ten men." This was in 1540. Three and a half centuries later the Amazon had lost none of its hold on the imaginative. Sir Arthur Conan Doyle dreamed that in the heart of the jungle a vast plateau rose, an island forgotten by time, where dinosaurs and ape-men battled for survival. His book was called *The Lost World*. One wonders how much he had heard about the *tepui* plateaus of the Guiana shield that rise in sheer walls thousands of feet above the surrounding jungles and are indeed islands in time.

Of all the vast Amazonian jungle, perhaps the least explored region lies in the fastness of Venezuela's Territorio Federal Amazonas, which spreads out from the rough frontier capital of Puerto Ayacucho southward toward the Brazilian border. Through this country of dense rain forest and rugged hills the great Orinoco River curves toward the sea, draining in its sweep more than 350,000 square miles and linking up through the Casiquiare and Río Negro with the even mightier Amazon. When Columbus first discovered the broad mouth of the Orinoco he wrote to Queen Isabella that it seemed "the gateway to Celestial Paradise." Sir Walter Raleigh thought it might lead to paradise, too, though an earthier one, sparkling with treasure. The expeditions he launched in 1595 and 1617 found neither, but they implanted in the English imagination the vision of El Dorado that had already been heating Spanish and Portuguese dreams for decades. Some believed the city lay on the shores of Lake Parima in the far highlands or in the kingdom of Chibcha in the distant southwest. Alexander von Humboldt himself, the great nineteenth-century naturalist explorer, did not reject all of the Amazon legends outright. "Beyond the cataracts [near present-day Puerto Ayacucho]," he wrote, "an unknown land begins."

"The unknown land," Venezuela's Amazonas. Even today the epithet is apt, for much remains unexplored, and, unlike the Brazilian Amazon, the region is still relatively unexploited and unsettled by modern man. Gold and diamond smugglers ply their trade, naturalists and anthropologists do their research, now and then a photographer or filmmaker ventures upriver for a brief stay with the Catholic fathers of St. Francis de Sales or the American Protestants of the New Tribes mission. But few have penetrated above the Guajaribo rapids. Few have heard the chittering of the vampires below Peñascal or seen the print of a jaguar on the sand beside the Orinoquito. The great Sarisariñama *tepui* is known to a small number of Sanema and Ye'kwana Indians whose villages lie near the Brazilian border but to almost no one else. La Neblina, the cloud mountain that rises nine thousand feet out of the Sierra Imeri and is the highest Venezuelan peak outside the Andes, was not even discovered until 1953. Except for the rare adventurer, and the scientists who have found a trove of unusual flora and fauna on its rain-drenched heights, the mountain has been seen only by the occasional band of seminomadic deep-forest Indians.

These seminomads of the Brazil-Venezuela borderlands are the Yanomama. Horticulturalists and hunter-gatherers, they inhabit the remotest interfluvial backlands of the rain forest, a land that until recently has remained closed to outsiders. For the ten thousand or so Yanomama who live scattered through the Venezuelan Amazon it still is. Their brothers and sisters across the border in Brazil have not been so fortunate. During the last decade their forests have been devastated, their rivers poisoned, their game destroyed by the miners, rubber workers, and farmers who make up the wave of immigrants that is relentlessly pushing back the forest and driving its inhabitants toward extinction. But in the meantime, for the Venezuelan Yanomama of the interior, life goes on more or less as it has as far back as they have memory, as far back as anyone can trace.

Many anthropologists believe the Yanomama were part of the second wave of Paleo-Indians who crossed the Bering land bridge into North America some 25,000 years ago. For thousands of years they wandered southward, arriving in their present home as long as 20,000, or perhaps as recently as 12,000 years ago. No one can say with certainty. Today their settlements span only a degree or two on either side of the equator. They live communally in large circular houses called *shaponos;* rarely does a group number more than a hundred and twenty. With the exception of sex and defecation, they carry on all their activities in public.

In terms of their material and technological culture, the Yanomama stand out for their primitiveness. They have no system of numbers; they manage with "one," "two," and "many." Their only calendar is the waxing and waning of the moon. On trek they carry everything they own on their backs; they have not invented the wheel. They know nothing of the art of metallurgy, and interior villages might boast only a few worn machetes and battered tin pots, acquired in trades with groups living closer to the *nabuh,* the non-Yanomama from beyond. Until recently they made fire with fire drills, the efficient rubbing together of two sticks.

Traditionally the Yanomama wear no clothes; they paint their bodies in serpentine and circular designs of red *onoto* seed paste; their thick black hair is cut in a regular bowl fashion, sometimes tonsured. Among men, body hair is sparse; most women have none at all. Girls and women adorn their faces by inserting slender sticks through holes in the lower lip at either side of the mouth and in the middle, and through the pierced nasal septum. Except for this and for their pierced ears, into which women insert flowers and men feathers, they do not practice bodily mutilation.

They are, it is said, a violent, bloody people. According to some anthropologists, Yanomama life is characterized by persistent aggression among village mates and perpetual warfare between antagonistic groups. They are supposedly given to club fighting, gang rape, and murder. This was my understanding when I first read about them in an anthropology course I took as an undergraduate at Pennsylvania State University in 1969, and it was still my understanding six years later when as a graduate student I went off to do a fifteen-month stint of fieldwork among them.

Contrary to all my initial intentions, I did not leave the Yanomama when the fifteen months were up. To my great surprise I had found among them a way of life that, while dangerous and harsh, was also filled with camaraderie, compassion, and a thousand daily lessons in communal harmony. In time I learned to speak their language. I learned to walk in their forest and to hunt, fish, and gather. I discovered what it meant to be a nomad. As more time passed I was adopted into the lineage of my village and given a wife according to Yanomama custom and in keeping with the wishes of the great shaman-headman. My last exit from the Amazon was in 1986, eleven years after I first passed Humboldt's cataracts into "the unknown land." But I have still not completely come out. Since then my wife, Yarima, and I have gone back up the Orinoco once; we are planning to go again. Love does not lessen the need to see other loved ones, most especially for the Yanomama, who pass their entire lives in such close proximity to family and friends.

When I was five years old my own family moved from west Philadelphia to the quiet suburb of Havertown, Pennsylvania. Havertown was a pleasant place to grow up. It was adamantly middle class, a township of single family homes, well-tended yards, and good schools. Like many others, when my family moved we turned our eyes away from the big-city ethnic stew we had left behind. We loved the orderly homogeneity of our new neighborhood; if we looked anywhere, it was toward the even more stable and homogeneous suburbs farther out. I have often thought that I became an anthropologist in part because, having been separated from everything that was exotic and different when I was young, I was inevitably attracted to strange lands and distant peoples as I grew older. My first experience of anthropological fieldwork was in Mexico's Central Valley, where I studied the remains of the Toltec nation, conquerors of Teotihuacan and predecessors of the Aztecs. But studying a people remote in time left something inside me unsatisfied, and eventually I immersed myself in the life of a people also remote in time, but nonetheless vividly alive. How that experience would change my own life was beyond my wildest imaginings.

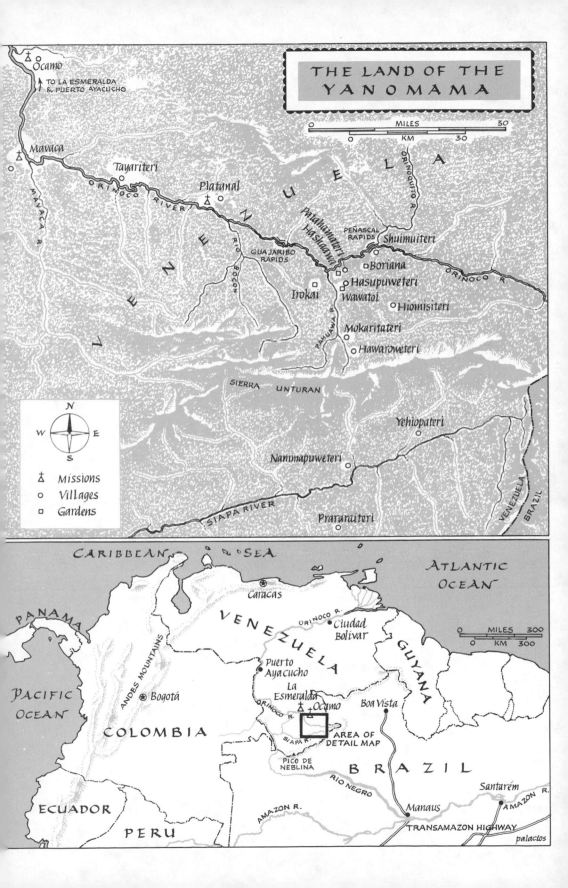

1

With the final shouts of battle ringing in our ears, the six of us boarded a Pan Am flight at Kennedy, bound for Caracas and the heart of the Venezuelan Amazon. First onto the plane was Napoleon Chagnon, the great Yanomama fieldman—whose expedition this was. After Chagnon came Bob Carneiro, South American curator at the American Museum of Natural History, then William Sanders, the eminent Meso-American archaeologist. Following them into the plane were Ray Hames, Eric Fredlund, and myself, the three anthropology graduate students who would be living for the next fifteen months in the deepest recesses of the jungle, primary researchers for Chagnon's Yanomama project.

The Yanomama Indians, the "Fierce People," as they were known in anthropology circles: killers, hallucinogenic drug takers, wife abductors, the last of the world's stone age warrior tribes. They dragged their women through the jungle and raped them. They blew powdered *epene* up each other's noses with three-foot-long tubes.

They fought with curare-tipped arrows and drank the ashes of their dead relatives. These people were going to be our hosts, if that was the right word for it. And since I was a little older and a little more robust than my two fellow students, I had been assigned to the most ferocious of them, the Hasupuweteri Yanomama, whose territory lay near the headwaters of the Orinoco. These people were fierce, the bearded, broad-boned Chagnon had assured me, maybe not quite as fierce as the village where he had done his own doctoral research, but pretty damned fierce.

Of course not everyone agreed that the Indians were innate killers. That was what the battle in New York had just been about. There Chagnon (whose anthropological best-seller on the Indians, *The Fierce People*, had ignited the controversy) had taken on his chief tormentor, Professor Marvin Harris of Columbia University. Harris didn't believe Chagnon's Fierce People thesis for a minute. Man, he argued, was no genetic killer lashed to violence by his DNA. The causes of warfare were more subtle, more complex. There were environmental reasons for it, ecological causes that could be found in the need to defend hunting territories and satisfy the dietary demand for protein.

As the 707 reached cruising altitude I thought about the debate; I had been thinking about it for months now, ever since I had learned that I was the one whose research was supposed to destroy the ecological theories once and for all. With the seat belt sign just off, Chagnon was already in the aisle, standing over me with a Scotch in his hand and starting on a joke. But what he had just told Harris in New York wasn't any joke. The Yanomama killed each other, he said, because they had evolved no social controls to contain their violence. Any other view was nonsense. Their villages split up so frequently because they couldn't suppress their continual fighting and feuding. Anybody who thought differently would find himself eating crow, high-protein crow.

Landing at Caracas's Maiquetia Airport, I quickly found myself negotiating with the owner of a big station wagon to carry our mound of gear into the city. It was a pleasure to find that the last two semesters at Penn State hadn't affected my command of Venezuelan street Spanish. Before that, I had had fun living in Caracas and teaching at Venezuela's Central University. What hadn't been fun was the separation and divorce from my Venezuelan wife, whom I had met and married when we were both undergraduates at Penn State. The divorce was a tragedy that sometimes seemed too much to bear. Anyway, I thought as the driver surveyed six extremely appetizing Yankee victims and named a price that would leave his colleagues gasping with laughter when he told them about it later on, at least one thing survived the divorce: my command of the vernacular that was just the thing for situations like this.

In the end we hired both the wagon and driver for the entire frenzied week we were in Caracas. We had to hit the lumberyards for the doors and other supplies we'd use building our huts. We had to get barrels of trade goods and big sacks of rice. For five days from morning to night, all of us were running off to every part of the city on different errands. We bought axes, machetes by the box, loincloth material by the roll, fishhooks by the thousands. All this was added to the tons of equipment we had shipped down in advance, in addition to what we had brought with us on the plane. It was an incredible operation. I had to admire Chagnon's energy and persistence. The man was driving, driving, driving, all the time.

When we finally mustered the entire mountain of goods and got our Amazon territory permits in order, Chagnon put us all aboard a DC-3 he had chartered. Four hours later we landed at the Ocamo mission, which had the biggest airstrip of the line of missions on the Orinoco reaches. The moment we touched down we started unloading; the pilot had a long flight back, and he had no intention of spending a night in the jungle. We started dumping our things off the plane, a sight that left the little crowd of missionaries and Indians that had gathered wide-eyed with astonishment. There were the fifteen big army trunks bursting at the seams, all of them painted different colors as part of a coding scheme. There were barrels and boxes of clothing and supplies and trade goods. Then four outboard motors came out of the cargo door, all of them packed in wood-framed, protected crates—monstrous things. Fifty-pound bags of rice joined the pile, and crate after crate of other foodstuffs. The knot of onlookers couldn't conceive that such a stupendous accumulation could possibly belong to such a small number of people.

Ocamo was a Catholic mission headed by Padre Coco of the order of St. Francis de Sales. I had been here before—two years earlier, when I was a lecturer in anthropology in Caracas. I was looking for a way upriver then, hoping to make a quick visit to the village of Jacques Lizot, a French anthropologist who had been living with the Indians for almost a decade. I had met Padre Coco briefly then, but I had spent more time with Sor Felicita, a formidable nun whose Yanomama was fluent. She had spoken to a Yanomama warrior wearing only a penis string (at which she had clucked disgustedly) about taking me up in his canoe. But the river had been too low, and after two days fighting rocks we had had to turn back. That had been a real disappointment.

This time Sor Felicita was not at the mission, nor was Padre Coco. Instead there was Padre Bis, a big Polish father who seemed to enjoy driving around on his tractor, pulling a cart loaded with screaming Indian children. It was, they yelled, not an *autobus* (Spanish for "bus"), but a "auto*Bis!*" Fifteen minutes later the good-hearted padre was using his "autoBis" to haul our supplies down to the river, a miracle of sorts, I thought, since the river was half a mile from the landing strip and I couldn't imagine how we might have gotten our mountain of things there by ourselves. Even with the tractor cart it took many trips, and it wasn't until about two o'clock that we had the entire heap on the bank ready to load.

Now we had to make a decision. By rights we should have slept at the mission and left the next morning. But Chagnon was driven. He wanted to get moving immediately instead of wasting the afternoon hanging out at Ocamo. As a result, we loaded our things onto a beat-up little *African Queen* of a riverboat with a tin roof that Chagnon had chartered and headed upriver for Mavaca, the next mission along the line, taking three Yanomama along with us to lend a hand.

On the great, slightly ominous river, the boat seemed almost a toy, dwarfed by the expanse of water and the immense, looming forest that hemmed it in. Despite myself, I was excited. There was something mysterious about this region that hadn't struck me the last time, something eerie and wild. The heavy pure air of the Amazon enveloped us. Except for the whine of the engine there was not a single sound made by civilized man or any of his works.

March was the tail end of the dry season, and though the river here was broad, it was also quite low. But the first rains were on their way. We had flown in under heavy clouds, and all afternoon the skies had been threatening to let go. Fifteen minutes into our trip they did, and we were smack in the middle of a tropical monsoon. A low river makes navigation difficult, with rocks near the surface and channels hard to find. But if the river's low and the weather is clear, at least you can see where you're going. Conversely, in the rainy season it's no fun to be on the river (as I was to find out), but at least the water's high and there isn't much danger. Now we were smack in the middle of a low river and a torrential rainstorm—the worst-possible combination.

From Ocamo to Mavaca ordinarily takes two or three hours by motorized dugout. But groping our way along in the slow, clumsy riverboat, we didn't hit Mavaca until midnight. It poured all the way, and as we neared the confluence of the Mavaca and Orinoco rivers the storm intensified. There, in front of the Mavaca mission, the river widened, and in the dark sandbars and rock formations seemed to appear out of nowhere. We knew that to get to the mission we needed to find a channel that would take us upstream, then we'd have to turn and pull into Mavaca's dock with the current. Even if we had known what we were doing it would have been a difficult job, and Chagnon, who was piloting, didn't. Suddenly, as we were nosing upriver, the boat lurched and growled, then shuddered to a halt fifty yards offshore, stranded on a sandbar like a beached whale.

Everyone at the mission was long asleep, since people in the Amazon all go to bed at eight or nine o'clock. But the noise on the river had awakened them, and soon we could see the swaying and dipping of flashlights along the shore. As they came opposite we started shouting into the rain, trying to make ourselves heard above the storm. The scene had its humor, if we had chosen to look at it that way—six intrepid jungle-going anthropologists sitting on a sandbar at midnight in the pouring rain, like lost tourists, shouting at these sleep-dazed figures with flashlights to please come out and show us how we might get to shore. I wondered what Katharine Hepburn would have said to Humphrey Bogart, as I shouted at the top of my lungs toward a flashlight that seemed to be drawing nearer.

A minute later a priest, a lay brother, and two criollos from the local malaria team came wading out toward us in the shallow waters. I knew there were supposed to be nasty things in the river—piranha, stingrays, electric eels—but when no one seemed bothered by it, we all got to work, manhandling crates and boxes under the boat's tin roof or hauling them through the water to get them out of the rain on the mission's veranda. But the things on the front of the deck, the part without a roof, were already soaked. We knew we were losing a lot of our food, especially rice, which rots quickly after it gets wet. It was chaotic.

We did the best we could with the supplies and equipment, then we hung our hammocks under the veranda roof and, exhausted, fell asleep in drenched clothes. Four or five quick hours later a gray light dawned, and we loaded everything, still dripping, back onto the boat. Then we struggled to push it off the sandbar where it had lodged, and once again we headed upriver, this time bound for Tayariteri, the Yanomama village where Jacques Lizot lived.

Lizot, the French anthropologist I had unsuccessfully tried to visit two years earlier, had made an agreement with Chagnon for us to use his village as our base of operations and depository, rather than the more normal situation of arranging this kind of assistance with a mission. But as we soon found out, Lizot was currently at war with the missionaries, and he didn't want us—colleagues from the anthropological community—to have anything to do with them either. Despite the amiable Padre Bis, the general idea seemed to be, keep the anthropologists on one side and the missionaries on the other.

So Lizot had had his Indians build a little hut and storage place for us, which is where Eric Fredlund and I hung our hammocks the night we arrived at Tayariteri. Ray Hames, our fellow grad student, set himself up in an even smaller hut, and the expedition's senior members were over in Lizot's hut—Chagnon, Carneiro, and Sanders, along with Jacques Lizot and another French anthropologist who happened to be visiting. Eric and I were tired beyond measure and looking forward to sleeping in a dry place as we strung our hammocks and arranged the mosquito netting around them. It had been a very difficult couple of days. In Lizot's hut, though, the camaraderie had been enhanced by a bottle of Scotch broken out to celebrate our arrival. And at some point in the revelries three of our elders decided it was time to have a little fun.

Chagnon, Lizot, and the French anthropologist all knew the Yanomama, and of course their reputation for violence, and having had more than a little to drink, they figured it would be a lot of fun to scare the pants off us. It was, after all, the first night Ray, Eric, and I were spending in a Yanomama village, and who knew what kinds of fears might be racing through our heads. So they decided they would initiate us.

Whatever Chagnon and the others imagined we might be thinking probably wasn't far from the truth. We had landed only an hour ago on a shoreline crowded with Indians shaking bows and six-foot-long arrows in our direction. Their bodies were painted in black-and-red patterns, and brightly colored feathers hung from their ears. None of them had actually threatened us, but if their behavior matched their looks, we wouldn't be far wrong in expecting something very bizarre. These were Lizot's people, of course, and he had lived here for years, so they were probably friendlier than the Yanomama upstream. But still, Chagnon's stories of arrows whistling by his ear and close escapes from ax-wielding warriors were very much in our minds.

Inside our hut, the gloom was relieved by light from a Coleman lantern. Outside, night had fallen. It was pitch dark and silent. The *shapono,* the great Yanomama communal house, was only about a hundred yards away. As big and close as it was, the night seemed unnaturally quiet. As Eric and I were busy working with our hammocks and nets, all of a sudden out of the night two big figures burst into the hut screaming, "Aaaaaaaaaahhhhhhh!" grabbing us, and shoving us toward our hammocks, ripping the mosquito netting. My heart skipped a beat. I heard Eric gasp. Bracing myself against a table to keep from falling, I twisted around and saw in the glow of the Coleman Chagnon and the French anthropologist, both of them completely drunk.

"Jesus Christ," I yelled, clutching a ripped tatter of netting. "Jesus Christ!" My pulse was racing. Eric was sitting on the floor, his eyes like saucers. He looked as if he had had a heart attack.

"Aaaaaaaaaaaaaaaah!" The sound still filled the hut, though by now I realized it was coming from me as well as them. Still screaming, I grabbed Chagnon with one arm and the Frenchman with the other and went stampeding out the door with them. There something tripped me up, and I sprawled on the ground, watching as Chagnon and his friend rolled into the eight-foot-deep pit from which the Indians had excavated clay for the hut.

Lying there panting, I looked up and saw Lizot emerge from the darkness. "*Tranquilo,* Ken, *tranquilo,*" he said. "Take it easy, they were just joking."

"Well," I said, trying to calm down. "Well . . . look at this." I waved the piece of torn netting that was still bunched in my fist, which of course Lizot couldn't see in the dark, but which I was sure would explain everything. By now Chagnon and his friend were crawling out of the pit. They came slowly, helping each other along, not even noticing Lizot and me a couple of feet away in the dark. We watched as they went lurching and stumbling into the night back toward Lizot's hut. The next morning they wondered what had happened, not remembering much about it except that they were a little bruised and sore. I was just as happy they didn't. This was definitely not an auspicious way to start off an expedition in the jungle with your dissertation adviser.

We spent two more days on the river, making camp in the woods one night, then sleeping another on an island just below the Guajaribo rapids. All we could see on both sides was dense tropical jungle—trees, trees, and more trees—the thick, tangled foliage of the Amazonian rain forest. There were no people, few animals other than the herons and an occasional flock of screaming toucans. The forest was vast and silent. Watching it slide by, we felt almost as if we were going back in time. We were approaching the headwaters of the great Orinoco, which had narrowed now to only thirty or forty yards—this second largest of South America's rivers.

At the rapids everything had to be taken off the boat and carried, six of us portaging this mountain of gear. I could hear Sanders mumbling softly to himself as he hoisted an end of one of my trunks, "This is the last damned trunk I'll carry. This one, then that's it." Sanders was fifty years old and one of the world's leading archaeological anthropologists. Chagnon had invited him along just to have a brief look at the Yanomama, and here he was lugging around supplies and equipment for a couple of graduate students. But being the man he was, of course he thought he should help rather than just stand around and watch.

Once we had portaged our things we had to haul the boat through, which meant getting into the water and dragging it to the side, since we didn't know how to shoot the rapids. It took all our strength, even though now we weren't pulling against the fast current of the main rapids. Off in the side channels the water flowed more slowly, though the current was still brisk. Straining at the ropes, we seemed to be making good progress—until suddenly the bottom disappeared under my feet. Treading water, I realized that everybody was struggling to stay afloat and the boat had stopped moving forward. I was at the front, and not knowing what else to do, I put the rope in my teeth and started to swim. Sanders, who was up on the bank, looked at me as if I were crazy.

Eventually we got through—wet, tired, and mosquito-bitten, but through. Five hours above the rapids we rounded a rocky bend in the river, which Chagnon recognized instantly as the place he had visited the Hasupuweteri Yanomama two years earlier. These were the people I was supposed to be living with, but as we scanned the shore there wasn't an Indian to be seen, which meant that they weren't in the area. If the Yanomama are anywhere nearby, they will always come down to the river when they hear a motor. They could, we knew, be on a short foraging trip or perhaps visiting another village. But it could also be that they were out on one of their long treks in the forest or even that they had moved permanently to some other site. Temporarily at a loss for what to do, we decided to continue upriver to the small community where Ray would be living and conducting his horticultural study.

Fortunately Ray's village was there, a small community of only thirty or so people. I was sick with a bad cold I had picked up on the river, and I was happy to be able just to hang my hammock and sleep. Meanwhile, Chagnon took Bill Sanders downriver and made arrangements for him to get out. Ray, Eric, Carneiro, and I stayed put, resting and waiting for Chagnon to return. I wondered what we would do if the Hasupuweteri were really nowhere to be found.

A week later Chagnon was back with the news. He had made contact with the Hasupuweteri a little farther down from where he'd thought they would be. Now they knew I was coming and had already started building me a hut. Carneiro and I should leave immediately, he said. Carneiro would be there for one month. My stay would be open-ended.

2

As Bob Carneiro and I puttered downstream in my motorized dugout, we wondered what we would find. Lizot's village had seemed peaceful enough the night we were there (the Indians, anyway), and Ray's community—not much more than a few extended families living together—hadn't exhibited any aggressiveness either. In fact, I had spent most of our time resting quietly. But the Hasupuweteri were another story—they were enmeshed in the cycle of violence that enveloped the tribes beyond the influence of the outside world. They lived, as the anthropological journals put it, in the zone of intense warfare.

As we came around the bend we saw the Indians on the bank, waiting for us. There were a crowd of them, painted up and armed with their long bows and arrows. From a distance they looked alien and menacing, but as we got closer our anxieties lessened. We could see that they were all smiling and laughing, shaking their bows and jumping around, obviously in a holiday mood. As I stepped onto the bank, smiling myself, I scanned the crowd. There was no one hulking around in an intimidating or threatening manner. Only smiles. And just beyond the smiles I could see where they were starting to erect the corner posts of my hut, right above a little embankment that fell away eight feet or so to the river.

The Hasupuweteri didn't seem at all menacing as they watched us begin to unload the dugout, but they had a wildness about them that was altogether different from what we had seen at Lizot's village. Unlike their downriver cousins, they had no loincloths and no other clothes, just a string that went around the waist and tied up their penises by the foreskin. Their lower lips bulged with wads of tobacco, just as I had seen in the anthropological films. But in life the bulges seemed larger, more protuberant, giving their faces an elongated, primeval look. Pulling a trunk up the bank, I bumped into one of the men whose back was toward me as he stared at Carneiro. Attached to his arrowhead quiver I saw a fire drill, the slim wood shaft used to start fire when another piece was twirled in one of the holes worn into it. Suddenly I realized why they seemed different. For all their exotic appearance, Lizot's villagers were accustomed to foreigners, familiar with at least some of their ways and some of their gadgets and devices. But not the Hasupuweteri. As they gazed wide-eyed at our gear, it seemed to me that they weren't quite sure what to make of us or how to act with us. They had, I thought as we examined each other, an air of innocence about them.

And at that moment it struck me that these were my people, that whatever happened from here on in would be important. What kind of relationship I developed with them would determine how things would go for me during the next fifteen months. And as for the Hasupuwteri, they saw Kenny, the person Chagnon said would be living with them. I could see they were observing me carefully, too— in a friendly and very, very curious way.

The Hasupuweteri's happiness about having me there was, I realized very quickly, absolutely genuine. Not that there was any reason to feel flattered about it. Behind all the excitement was a single, uncomplicated fact. These people understood very clearly what my presence among them would mean. They could see it with their own eyes: the boxes and crates that we had hauled out of the dugout and that were now sitting by the side of the river waiting for the house to be finished so I could put them away. These things, this treasure trove of things, might be mine. But they could also be theirs.

Despite our strangeness, I knew the Hasupuweteri had had sufficient contact with the outside so that Carneiro and I weren't a complete shock to them. An occasional malarial team came to visit them, Chagnon had been there a couple of days, some of the older men had been down to the mission and had seen the priests. They had heard of a strange white man or two (Lizot and Chagnon) who had lived with other groups. So they knew there was such a thing as outsiders. And they also knew what kinds of things outsiders were capable of bringing with them, things they could be induced to part with. So having an outsider come to live with them was regarded as a kind of windfall from heaven, an endless source of trade goods—machetes, cloth, aluminum pots, fishhooks, axes, all the things we had hustled together in Caracas.

Chagnon had made the arrangements with the Hasupuweteri and had told them I was his younger brother, to try to facilitate things for me. But it took about a day for Carneiro and me to realize that no Yanomama was going to reject an outsider. The foreigner—the *nabuh*—brings a large array of goods, evidently for them, and in return all he wants is to live in his little hut and walk around their village and talk. Or maybe take pictures, which some may not like but others will accept. You (the *nabuh*) are not going to bother them. Your presence will not disturb them. They have no problems with you as long as you treat them and their customs with respect and decency.

As all this was dawning on me I began to feel, perhaps not like an honored guest, but certainly not like a fearful stranger, either. On the other hand, everything I was coming to understand was strictly on the basis of my intuition. The fact was, I didn't understand a word that my hosts were saying to me. At Penn State I hadn't learned a single useful thing about the language, and as the days passed I realized that the Yanomama didn't even seem to have the little etiquette words—hello, good-bye, please, thanks—that make it so easy to relate to someone without actually saying anything. Of course there was a good reason for this. Yanomama don't meet strangers. They know everybody in their universe. They see everybody every day, like a big family. So these terms don't make sense to them. "How are you?" What do you mean, "How am I?" Here I am. You saw me ten minutes ago, you see me now. That's how I am. They'll say, *"Eou,"* a greeting, like in native Philadelphian "Yo," with the same intonation. But that's about it. They do have the formalities, of course, but they do it their own way. If someone is down at the river bathing and someone else shows up, he doesn't say, "Hi, how's the water?" That would be nonsensical; the water's the water. It always has been and always will be. Instead he says, *"Eou,* you're taking a bath," a statement of fact that announces, I'm here, you're here.

All this would become clear to me in time, but now the need to learn was urgent. As the Indians crowded around me that first day, and the second, and the third, they were saying, *"Shori, shori, shori."* They were patting me: "Hahahaha. *Shori, shori,* hahaha. *Nohi, nohi, nohi"*—"friend, friend, friend"—then smiles. Smiles are universal. And under pressure I was picking up the words quickly. *Shori*—later I found it means brother-in-law, but they can use it for any unrelated person they meet, too. I didn't know that, but I did know it was a term of recognition—*"shori, shori." "Nohi,"* the same thing, said with a smile. A nice word to call somebody—*nohi,* a friend. *"Yahi,"* they say, and point to the house. *"Eou, shori. Yahi."* "Hey, brother-in-law. How about the house?" *"Matohi,"* they say, pointing at the things you've brought along for them, the trade goods. *"Yahi, matohi."* "House—goods." And that's it, your first transaction in Yanomama.

Almost immediately I got involved in building my house. My dugout was ideal for going across the river to get palm logs (it was the only boat in the village). My tape measure was the only way to measure the slats so the builders would know where to hack them off with their machetes—otherwise they would have cut any approximate length (as they had already started to do). I had to lay out the hut so it would be square, and as I showed them how I wanted it to go, I realized they had no concept of square or rectangular.

Like the roof of their circular communal house, the *shapono,* the roof of my hut consisted of leaves and vines woven together. It peaked at about ten feet and came down to about four feet off the ground. The sides of the hut were made out of slats of palmwood. The outer part of a palm tree is as hard as a rock. I had to split it with a machete down the middle, then split it again and again. Then I cut out the pulpy core and was left with a slat of palmwood. Not having any experience, I had them put the slats up vertically, which was wrong. Laying them out horizontally would have been faster and would have allowed us to seal the cracks and openings more effectively with the claylike mud the Indians dug up from the riverbank.

But with all its defects the hut was ready in three or four days, and Carneiro and I gratefully moved our hammocks and gear inside. There was a problem, though, which I discovered while we were still building. The house was going up on the riverbank, on the spot Chagnon had pointed out to the Indians. But the Hasupuweteri communal dwelling, their *shapono,* was about a third of a mile inland. As a result, I wouldn't actually be living with the community, which would create difficulties with my plan to become a participant-observer in the Indians' activities.

While I was mulling over how to deal with this, I was also discovering another disadvantage of remaining an outsider in the Hasupuwteris' world. Every morning at first light I would hear them pounding down the trail. I'd hear excited talking and laughing in the distance, and opening one eye, I'd squirm a little in the hammock, then try for an instant to fall back asleep. It was the crack of dawn. They came at the crack of dawn, the first day Carneiro and I were in the house and every day after that. Then the panic struck when I remembered that once again I wasn't prepared for them, that the flashlight and my knife were lying on the floor in plain view. How could I have fallen asleep without putting them away, again? After the first day I learned that everything had to be closed up and locked in the trunks. The Hasupuweteri might not have been the violent bullies I had half expected, but their concept of privacy was nonexistent, and their idea of "mine" and "yours" was enough to drive me wild. And once they got inside, their hands were all over everything, touching, stealing, begging, demanding. So I had to be prepared for these people. They showed up at first light and were there until nightfall or many times after nightfall. I never had peace. I never had privacy. I could never get away from the staring eyes and the comments and the demanding and wheedling. I'd want to take a nap at midday, and I'd try to fall asleep, but inevitably eight or ten Yanomama would gather around to make remarks. And I didn't know how to say, "Please leave me alone, I'm trying to sleep." I assumed they'd see what I was trying to do and respect it. But no. They knocked on the slats. They banged on the door. They shook their bows and arrows. They called me: *"Shori, shori. Eou, shori."* They'd want me to come out, talk, show them things, give them things. They'd want me to be there with them. And I was so drowsy with the heat and the humidity that I would have given the world to shut my eyes and just forget about them for an hour. But they would not go away.

And yet I understood them, not that understanding lessened the torment. They had been living undisturbed in the jungle all their lives, and suddenly out of the clear blue sky two strangers showed up to live among them. And the strangers had an incredible amount of material things, most of which they had never seen before, a simply astonishing collection of exotic goods. So of course they came down and stayed. Bob Carneiro and I were the biggest attraction they had ever seen, an attraction that mesmerized them with a constant unfolding of the amazing and improbable.

From morning to night I could see the eyes through the slats in the house, looking at me, watching my every move. I took my shoes off and heard comments, the oohs and aahs and laughing and giggling, the ever-present "hahahaha." And I didn't know why. What can they be thinking? I wondered. Maybe it's the shoes; they've never seen shoes. Look at that, he's got these things on his feet, and he takes them off. Or maybe it's not my shoes that are funny, it's my feet. My toes are all crunched together. Theirs are splayed out, the way our toes would be if we always went barefoot. And our feet are white, white and soft. Theirs are as tough as leather.

Or maybe it's something else, my glasses, maybe—an incomprehensible eye adornment. Months afterward one of the women told me I had very nice eyes, very pretty eyes. But why did I adorn them so foolishly? Of course I didn't want them to know I couldn't see too well without the glasses, so I didn't make much of an effort to explain them. Later when I would be out in the jungle hunting, the glasses would fog up. I'd go to shoot a bird in a tree and I couldn't see it because they would be all fogged over. I'd squint or try to clean them, and my hunting companions would say, "That's your problem, *shori*. If you'd throw those things away, you could see the bird." So, I'd answer, "Well, no, I don't want to throw them away, I like them, they're good."

Inevitably, too, some of the young men, the *huya*, began to test the situation, to see how far they could go. I didn't need the language to know that for a few of the more rambunctious teenagers I was becoming a target. They reminded me of street corner kids getting a kick out of harassing the new guy in the neighborhood. To them it must have seemed they had found the perfect subject, someone who couldn't talk, couldn't walk in the forest properly, who seemed to be just asking to be tricked and teased. And of course they didn't know the reason for my ineptitude. They thought the whole world was an Amazon forest. Wherever it was that outsiders came from, they had to live in Yanomama-type villages in a Yanomama-type setting. It didn't occur to them that there might be anything else. And here's this stranger covered with clothes, sweat running down him all the time (they hardly sweat at all), tripping over vines. He has big boots on to protect his feet, he's clumsy beyond any human being they've ever seen or imagined. His movements seem quick and jerky instead of slow and fluid like theirs. He does everything too fast, then lies down, exhausted by his efforts.

At times I felt almost as if it were circus time in the Amazon, and I was in the center ring. While some of my new friends would come up close to talk and ask questions, others would be rolling on the ground with laughter. I knew the questions were nonsensical, asked only for the comic effect. But of course I couldn't understand, which was the whole point. All I knew was that I was getting an excellent view of the Yanomama teenagers' sense of humor from a victim's perspective. It was hard to know what to do. With everyone laughing, I could hardly take offense and attempt to stand on my dignity. And for the life of me, I couldn't remember reading whether other anthropologists had encountered this situation and had given advice about how to deal with it. So I just grinned and bore it.

But although on one level they knew I didn't understand (which was so hilarious to some), on another level they couldn't quite believe it was true. How was it, after all, that I *couldn't* understand? As a result I would find some of the men sitting down next to me and talking seriously, telling me at length about whatever subject occurred to them—their hunting party last week, a visit they made to some other group, the chances of good fishing—asking me questions, sometimes seriously, sometimes not. All of it just to see how I would react.

One day a number of *huya* were sitting down talking to me, or at me, while I was cleaning my tape recorder. I wasn't paying much attention, but every once in a while I would say, "Hm? Hm?" just to indicate I was trying to understand. Shortly after that they disappeared. A half hour later I went down to the river for some water, and there they were off in my boat fishing. I yelled at them to get back, trying to say, "What are you doing? Why did you take my boat?" (with the irreplaceable motor on it). I understood later that they had asked me if they could borrow it, and that "hm" is one Yanomama way of saying "yes."

At the end of the first month I was just about going out of my mind. The stealing and trickery were a constant bother, but far worse was the endless, utter lack of privacy. I never got over the sensation of having all eyes trained on me, of having every move I made scrutinized and contemplated. I even had to shoo the little kids away when I went into the forest to relieve myself. Celebrities must feel this way about the paparazzi, I thought. But it was worse than the movie star and the paparazzi. The Hasupuweteri did not have any concept of privacy. They had no idea that as far as I was concerned there was a norm they were violating. They didn't know anything about it, they didn't need it, apparently they didn't want it. They themselves lived communally, and absolutely everything they did with the exception of sex and defecation was public. Why I might feel differently was beyond them.

So although the Yanomama didn't seem violent or aggressive, they made up for it by being the most irritating group of people you could ever possibly imagine. Yanomama, the Fierce People? I began thinking that Yanomama, the Pain in the Neck People, was more like it. On the other hand, for all the difficulties, from the moment I got there I never worried about living among them. Underneath the exotic body painting and strange adornments they were just human beings, smiling, laughing, having fun, like people anywhere.

One result of this realization was that I put away the mace. During the yearlong preparation at Penn State, Napoleon Chagnon had painted a dramatic picture of Yanomama ferocity, and he had equipped us with canisters of chemical mace—the kind reserved for police use—against the hostility and treachery we might encounter. Chagnon had acquired it somehow, and I dutifully scraped off the labels (since we couldn't have gotten it through customs), applying others that read, "Center County Dog Repellent." I had felt uncomfortable about it at the time. After all, if I wanted to develop good, friendly relations with the Yanomama, cans of mace were not going to help me.

It was with some relief that I realized I'd have no call for the mace and that I could consign it to the least accessible corner of my footlocker. But since I did have it, I thought, why not at least give it a try—say, on one of the vampire bats that occasionally got into my hut? Small, with mouselike bodies and foot-and-a-half wingspans, the vampire bats would swoop down at night and bite sleepers on their fingers and toes, injecting an anticoagulant that kept blood dripping for hours. So razor sharp were their teeth that the sleeper rarely awoke. The first time I was bitten, I was half-asleep and felt one nip my finger. I hardly felt it, but I panicked and without thinking leaped to my feet. But I was in my hammock, and it twirled over, throwing me onto the floor and waking Carneiro, who sat up with a start and stared at me in bewilderment.

The next time a vampire got into the hut, I decided to mace the damn thing. The bat was perched on a cross stave only about eight feet up, so I took the canister, pointed it up at him, and sprayed. The vampire looked startled, then took off and fluttered around the eaves a bit before settling down on a rafter on the other side of the hut. Meanwhile the mace sank down, and I started gagging and tearing so badly that I had to run out into the forest. There I was, out in the forest at night while the bat was occupying my house. The mace hadn't bothered him a bit.

In reality, of course, bats were nothing but a nuisance. It was the business of learning to live with them and with the rest of our new environment that Carneiro and I found difficult. Getting physically acclimated was also a hard process. The Amazonian heat and humidity exhausted us and made us pay a price for everything we did. At night we would fix a dinner of soup or rice and feel the pleasure of putting warm food in our empty stomachs. But immediately afterward we would begin sweating copiously, the perspiration running down our chests in rivulets and sopping our T-shirts. We would go into the river to take a bath, and when we came out swarms of bloodsucking gnats would cover us. And we'd wonder why we had even bothered.

But despite the problems, Carneiro started his project almost immediately. He had done work previously on indigenous agriculture, and now he was undertaking some very technical museum studies, determining the densities of different trees the Indians had to cut down to make way for their plantain gardens. Carneiro wanted to compare the efficiency of steel axes (which the Yanomama have now) to stone axes (which their ancestors probably had used at the beginning of the century). How long had it taken them to clear land before steel axes from the outside world had revolutionized their agriculture, and what effect had the revolution had on their diet?

While Carneiro was off measuring trees and gardens, I started the job of getting familiar with the *shapono,* the great communal dwelling that circled around a central plaza. Most Amazonian Indians build dark, closed houses with no windows; the only light comes from a hole at the top that lets out some (though not nearly all) of the smoke from their fires. Compared with these, the Yanomama house, the *shapono,* is a marvel of airiness and light. It is built in a large circle anywhere from twenty to fifty meters in diameter around a central open area, the leaf roof sloping from a height of twelve or fifteen feet in the center to two or three feet at the outer perimeter. Inside the roofed circle there are no walls or partitions. Each successive hearth area is occupied by a nuclear family, and the families arrange themselves by kinship and lineage so that the social organization of the families in the village is reflected in the placement of hearths and hammocks. It is within this great, continuous house and its central plaza that nearly all domestic activity takes place: child rearing, food distribution and preparation, trading and feasting, curing and cremation, the drug taking of the men, the singing and dancing of the women.

Because my hut was so far away, I would go up to the village twice a day, in the morning and then again in the afternoon. I wanted to take it easy at first, while I was getting acclimated. I had the idea that I could only get to know the Hasupuweteri little by little. To look at everything, to get a sense of their society as a whole, would take time. The detailed study of protein capture and dietary habits that was the focus of my fieldwork would have to wait a bit. First I had to immerse myself in the daily round of Yanomama life. Becoming fluent in the language would be the key.

At first I would show up and just stroll around the *shapono* and the nearby gardens, watching people at their activities. The impression of wildness I had gotten when the Hasupuweteri men greeted Carneiro and me at the river quickly wore off. Physically, the Yanomama were not imposing. They were, in fact, among the world's smallest people—the men averaging about five feet, the women about four ten. But despite their small stature and slender arms and legs, they had great strength; they could carry hundred-pound loads long distances if necessary and chop away with their axes at enormous trees for hours at a time.

Even when they were working hard, though, they moved gracefully and without haste, in a rhythm that seemed perfectly suited to the languid motions of the rain forest. Their copper-and-bronze coloring blended in with the forest, too, with the buffs of the lianas and the patchwork browns of the fallen leaves. The red *onoto* paint, wildflowers, and exotic bird feathers they often decorated themselves with set off their rich skin tones and lent them a distinct yet delicate fragrance. Their hair was black, straight and coarse; even the elderly people had almost no gray, nor was there any baldness that I could see. They had, though, virtually no body hair at all. In their high cheekbones you could trace vestiges of an Asiatic origin. Their ancestors had crossed the Bering land bridge some twenty thousand years before, taking thousands of years to work their way down to the South American lowlands.

Walking around the interior of the *shapono*, I would pass by all the hearths and watch what was going on. A number of the men, those who hadn't gone out hunting that morning, would be lying motionlessly in their hammocks with their hands over their mouths, just staring. I'd try to figure out what they were doing. Were they looking at me with curiosity or with scorn? Or were they afraid, and was that why they wouldn't speak? I thought they might be reacting to my shotgun, which I always carried to the village, just as the Indians never took a step away from the village without their bows and arrows. No one in the jungle walks around unarmed. You can never tell what you might encounter—a snake, a jaguar, an anaconda, maybe an enemy raiding party. Who knew? But the shotgun didn't seem to bother them, not visibly, anyway. So what were they thinking? "It's okay," I wanted to say. "Take it easy, there's nothing to worry about. I'm a friend."

Other people would smile, particularly the women. They might be chopping wood or preparing food or nursing their babies, and they'd look up and smile. It was a way of establishing contact. Then I'd catch someone's eye and be motioned over, and since we had no words they'd make noises, clicks or clucks or tch-tch's . . . man's universal tongue. And of course the smile, which can have many meanings, some of which vary from culture to culture. But beneath all those things is the basic friendliness the smile conveys.

I'd use whatever words I knew. The way you ask, "What is this?" is *"Weti kete?"* I didn't learn the full phrase at first, just *weti*— "what." So I went around pointing and saying, *"Weti?"* And they'd tell me what—they thought it was cute. Then I'd write it in my notebook. So there I had the beginnings of a vocabulary.

And always in the *shapono* children were all around—beautiful, smiling, laughing children. They were a funny bunch, as curious as the teenagers but without the urge to torment—though at times I'd find them eating the dried clay walls of my house, leaving big holes that were a bother to fix. When I asked them why, they'd say, "It's good!" (I assumed the clay ameliorated intestinal problems, like the kaolin clay in our Kaopectate.) When I sat down to take notes they would come around babbling and laughing, touching my hair and my skin, pinching my nose to see if I was real. I had pictures in books, so I'd open a book and point to an animal. A moment later a dozen childish voices would teach me the word—nouns first, then after a while verbs. Children had the patience, they could repeat everything a thousand times. An adult would never be able to teach me the language, I concluded after several unedifying exchanges. An older man would repeat a word once or twice, then he'd start shouting and looking at me strangely, wondering what kind of an idiot he was dealing with. Then he'd repeat it again, very loudly and slowly and sarcastically. And if I still didn't get it, he'd shake his head and walk away to do something worthwhile. But the kids didn't care in the least. So what if I was an idiot? I was also the strangest, most interesting creature in their landscape.

I was a little girl when I first saw Kenny. I had never seen a nabuh before. We all pulled the black hair on his face. We laughed at his white skin and wondered why his body was so long. He had the biggest forehead I had ever seen. We helped him build a house out of clay to put his things in, away from the shapono where we all lived. But when we ate some of his house he got mad and shouted. He couldn't speak to us, so we called him "Ghost Tongue," like someone who can't speak, or a baby. Or sometimes I called him "Big Forehead." I was just a little girl then, just a little girl.

3

It took Bob Carneiro a month to finish his studies on gardening and energy expenditure. When he did, and his time was up, I accompanied him downriver. At the Guajaribo rapids we met Chagnon and Eric Fredlund, who had planned to be there to help us with the tricky business of maneuvering the heavy dugout through the side channels, holding it back and guiding it with ropes from the bank. One particular spot was especially dangerous, an outcropping that went right out into the whitewater, where the roaring current could take the canoe and rip it loose or pull in anyone trying to keep it in check. Just at the crucial moment, with the four of us straining at the ropes, Eric was stung painfully in the ear by a bee and almost dropped his rope. To shouts of "Hang on, Eric, hang on!" he recovered just in time to save us from being dragged into the current by the lurching canoe.

The rest of the trip down to our depository at Tayariteri was easy, but the incident left me with a healthy respect for the rapids and a certain concern about the need to negotiate them alone on future supply runs. At Tayariteri I said good-bye to Carneiro, who was continuing down to Ocamo mission with Chagnon. Then Eric and I loaded our canoes from our storage hut and went our separate ways.

I stopped first at Platanal mission for a short visit with Padre Gonzalez, the Salesian father in charge; then with two hundred kilos of supplies in the dugout I headed back toward Hasupuweteri, really alone now for the first time. It was sobering going upriver by myself. I had never been an outdoorsman and wasn't comfortable with this kind of thing. I didn't know my way around boats or rivers, and this was an Amazonian river. There were piranha in it, stingrays, electric eels, caimans. It was full of rocks and swift, treacherous currents. What happens, I thought, if I flip, or more likely swamp, which these dugouts were so prone to do? It's not as if I'd be able to just stop at the next town and get the boat fixed up or get myself fixed up. And even if I did manage to get back in the boat after I flipped, I'd have lost all my supplies—my food, clothes, and medicines. There'd be no point in going on; I wouldn't survive if I had to live like a Yanomama. I'd have to turn around and go back; without money for new supplies, I'd have to drop the whole project. All it would take would be one little mishap.

And if there was a mishap, the chances were I'd find myself camping out at night in the forest, contending with all the ground dangers—snakes, scorpions, inch-long ants whose bite can be painful for up to twenty-four hours (in Spanish they're called the *veinte y cuatro*—the twenty-four), and army ants, with whom I had already had an experience in my hut . . . one I would not soon forget.

I had awakened from a deep sleep one night. There had been no sudden noise or movement—just a vaguely anxious feeling. When I flicked on my flashlight everything seemed to be moving: walls, floor, ceiling, everything. As I stared I realized I was seeing ants, a living, undulating carpet of ants. I was shaken. I remembered hearing that army ants don't attack people, but I still didn't know what to do. Should I lie there and hope they would go away, or get up and do something—try to drive them off somehow, maybe crunch through them to get to my cans of insecticide? But what would my two cans of spray do against this horde, anyway? The very idea that I had brought insecticides into the Amazon was laughable (though at the moment, with a light rain of ants falling from the ceiling onto my mosquito netting, I wasn't laughing). Usually when

I was invaded by ants or termites I'd get out my cans and bomb them, but my Indian friends would say, "Why are you doing that? Leave them alone. They're just passing through. They're cleaning your house for you, that's all."

This time I just lay in the hammock and watched them, and slowly the horde moved out of the hut. So I had survived the invasion. But what if one of these living carpets found me sleeping on the ground in the open jungle? I found myself thinking of all the hair-raising possibilities and watching every ripple in the water like a hawk, trying to make sure it wasn't caused by a rock or a submerged tree trunk that might capsize my boat.

By the time I got to Hasupuweteri I was exhausted but also elated that I had accomplished this feat of navigating the river alone. The elation was short-lived. I had expected to find the banks next to my house crowded with Indians joyously welcoming me back. But as I motored up, the shoreline was deserted. Maybe they just hadn't heard the engine, I thought, so I grabbed my shotgun and fired it, thinking that that would draw somebody down for sure. Still no one came.

Although I had only been gone a week, inside my hut tiny saplings had already sprouted on the floor, and the palm slats were white with mold. My equipment and clothes were damp and soggy. I made a small fire that drove away some of the dampness and prepared myself a pot of coffee as the sun set behind a brilliant orange cloud mass that loomed over the river to the west. The silence outside was unnerving. I wondered where the Hasupuweteri had gone and when or if they would ever be back. I had never been so totally alone, in such an alien, menacing night. Suddenly the silence dissolved into the croaking and braying of a thousand frogs, and to this eerie music I fell into a fitful sleep.

Thirteen long days later I was still alone and beginning to think about going back to the Mavaca mission. Being alone among the Hasupuweteri hadn't been easy, but being completely alone in the middle of the Amazon jungle—that got me to thinking. I didn't relish the idea of facing those rapids again, but how long could I just sit hoping for these people to come back from wherever they had gone? On the other hand, I now had six months of supplies in my flimsy hut, and I didn't want to risk leaving them unattended, either.

Late that afternoon as I lay in my hammock writing my journal entry for the day, I heard a voice from outside: *"Shori?"* Accustomed by now to the silence, the sound startled me. *"Shori. Eou, shori."* Looking between the cracks in my palmwood door, I saw two young men in loincloths holding bows and arrows.

"Weti kete?"—"What is it?" I said, trying to sound nonchalant but feeling a surge of emotion.

"It's me," said one of the Indians, as if that should have been enough. As soon as I opened the door, though, I realized that they weren't Hasupuweteri but were from the small community upriver. Their group had been off on a trek and had just returned. The two of them had come to check on me. The Hasupuweteri had been off in the jungle on trek, too, they said, but they were close now. They would summon them for me early next morning.

Dawn had barely broken when I was awakened by the familiar sound of laughter and talk as the Hasupuweteri men and boys headed down the trail toward my hut. The very sound that had driven me almost to despair weeks before was now almost warm and comforting.

And so it started again, as if there had been no interruption. Once more I was the anthropologist caught in what I had begun to think of as the observer-observed paradox. Here I was, the scientist come to study the natives, but it was I who was being studied—obsessively, ruthlessly, endlessly studied. At dawn they would come whooping and hollering down the trail. At midday they'd follow me back to my hut. In the evening they'd come down again. The Hasupuweteri didn't have notebooks or pencils, but they mentally recorded every move I made with all the seriousness of the most conscientious anthropologist. To them, the way I slept, ate, moved, talked, and dressed was nothing less than fascinating.

From my base down on the river, observing the Hasupuweteri wasn't easy. Ordinarily I would walk up to their *shapono* twice a day—morning and afternoon. But since I was not in any way integrated into the village, it was difficult to stay for more than a few hours at a time. By midday I would grow weary of the biting gnats and enervated by the tropical heat. My notebook would be full of language and vocabulary notes, but I'd have more and more trouble concentrating. Needing a nap desperately, I'd head back to my hut, followed closely (to my dismay) by my entourage of men and boys, who would cluster around and stare at me for an hour or two while I tried to relax with a cup of coffee or catch some sleep. Then I would head back up to the village for a few more hours of note taking before the approach of evening sent me packing again—back to my coffee, my food, my writing table, my hammock, all the things to which I had become so attached.

What I did see in the *shapono* and garden area was fascinating and very different from what I had expected. Almost invariably the women would greet me with a big smile, looking up from spinning cotton on their reed spindles or weaving a basket out of lengths of vine. The men, too, those who had decided not to go hunting that day, seemed anything but aggressive. Mothers nursed children as they turned plantains roasting over the fire coals; fathers cuddled their babies or played with them in their hammocks. Out in the garden just beyond the *shapono*, men cleared and planted additional space while women harvested and bundled plantains to bring back to their hearths. To an outsider, the garden appears to be one large undifferentiated area, but in fact each family has its own section where they often grow ocumo, manioc, sugar cane, bananas, and cotton in addition to the staple plantains. It struck me that while the Hasupuweteri lived communally, they carried on their gardening and most of their other activities too, not communally, but as individual family units. But I knew that the observations I was making were only partial and that if I wanted to see everything, I'd have to find a way to become much more a part of what was going on.

Older brother said that some other nabuh *had visited our village when he was a little boy. He said that they liked to point their black boxes at people. He said the black boxes take your* noreshi. *He said they know how to make things like machetes and fishhooks. Maquina made them, he said. I wondered who* maquina *was. I wondered if* maquina *was a person or a thing. I wondered if* nabuh *could die. Maybe they lived forever. Would Kenny live forever? Kenny couldn't talk like a person. He could only say a few words, so we laughed at him. He laughed, too. But I thought he would make evil magic on me. He would make me sick, and I would die. I was frightened of him. He had big things on his feet that made a funny print on the trail. He had shiny things on his eyes. Older brother said he could see great distances.*

I soon saw that the only way to make myself less of an outsider would be to integrate myself as much as I could and so become less of an alien, foreign phenomenon. The more they saw of me, the less of a spectacle and a disruption I would be. What I needed was to build another house right next to their community.

I had already made up my mind to do that when one morning in mid-April I thought I heard a noise on the river. I was still in my hut, getting ready to go up to the village, surrounded by the usual collection of men and boys who had gathered at dawn for another day of observing the *nabuh,* when suddenly it grew quiet, everyone listening intently. Then half a dozen voices shouted, *"motoro."*

Five minutes later a yellow, motorized canoe with two men in it rounded the bend. The *huya* from the village, the young men, came stampeding down the trail, as they always do if they hear a motor. "DDT, DDT," they yelled, by which they meant the malaria control teams that visited them from time to time. The antimalaria teams were made up of local people hired by the government to distribute preventative medicines to whatever Yanomama groups could be reached. Often the malaria workers were half Indian themselves, not much more educated than the tribal Indians.

The head of this particular team was a short, fat, beady-eyed criollo who introduced himself as Blanco. His boat driver was a young man named Francisco Valero, whom I had heard about. Francisco Valero's father was Yanomama, and he spoke the language fluently. He had the dark skin and straight black hair of his father's people. When he smiled he showed a mouthful of small, perfectly white teeth, another Yanomama characteristic. His mother was Helena Valero, a Brazilian woman who had been abducted as a child and had lived with the Indians for almost twenty years before being rescued.

Blanco and Francisco accepted a cup of coffee from me, but Blanco was tired from the journey and decided not to walk all the way up to the village. It was rainy, the trail was muddy, and it was just too much trouble. Instead he told the young men to call the villagers down to the river.

I knew the team was supposed to go up to the village and distribute chloroquine tablets to everyone in the community. They were also supposed to see that the people took the pills, to make sure they were swallowed and not thrown away. The chloroquine was very bitter, and the Yanomama didn't see much sense in taking medicine if they weren't sick. They didn't grasp the idea of a preventative.

"Why don't you go to the village?" I said.

"No," answered Blanco, glancing at the mucky path. "Maybe next time."

"Well, what about the women? They're not going to come down to the river, and they get malaria, too."

"Ah, don't worry about it," came the answer, "we'll get them next time."

"Come on," I entreated.

"Nah," said Blanco. "Besides, they never have any water up there to take the pills with." It was true, they didn't keep much water around the *shapono*.

"Look, I've get a jerrican. Take the water up with you."

"No, no, let them come down here; they'll come down."

Meanwhile the *huya* had gone up and had gotten all the men. I could already hear them in the distance. But suddenly the familiar babble of voices on the trail turned into screams and shouts, and a moment later the Hasupuweteri were storming toward me yelling, "Come on, *shori,* come on! Bring your shotgun and come on."

Something was happening, but I wasn't exactly sure what. Francisco Valero understood. *"¡Enemigos!"* he said, his voice shaky. "Raiders."

Coming down the trail, the men had been ambushed by a raiding party from another village. The last one in line had been shot. One young teenager stood next to me trembling; the rest seemed to be in a panic, yelling at me to get my shotgun. But I said no, I wasn't coming. There was no way I was going to get involved. When they saw I wouldn't be any help, the Hasupuweteri took off up the trail toward their gardens in hot pursuit.

I didn't know if they would catch the raiders, but I wasn't expecting any pitched battles. The Yanomama, I knew, never engage in anything like open warfare. They think it's absurd to risk your life that way and possibly get a lot of people killed. Instead, a raiding party will sneak up on an enemy village and hide in the bushes overnight, maybe on the trail leading to the village gardens. Then next morning they will wait until someone passes, shoot him, then run off. No heroics, no single combat, no massed battles. Just hide, shoot, and run. You accomplish your purpose, and you don't get yourself killed in the process.

About half an hour later the Hasupuweteri came back, excited and angry. I was only picking up phrases, but Francisco Valero translated. Someone had indeed been hit, shot twice as the men were coming down to see the DDT. He was up at the village now, and they wanted us to come see him. When we got there, the wounded man was in his hammock with the shaman chanting over him and a group of women sitting on the ground crying. It was Takawe, a young man of eighteen or nineteen whom I knew well. His right arm had been slashed open by an arrow, but the second arrow in his stomach was the real problem. The arrowhead on this one had been barbed, and when they pulled it out a section of Takawe's intestines had been yanked out with it. A loop of large bowel was hanging out of the wound.

The men said a few words to Valero, then he turned to me. "Okay, Kenny, they want you to fix him up." They were all looking at me. The poor soul obviously needed major surgery, but I thought I could at least push his intestines back inside, though clearly that wasn't going to help matters much. I put a roll of gauze bandage around Takawe to keep off the flies and control the bleeding a little. Then I bandaged his arm. But it didn't take a doctor to know that he was a goner. He was still alive, moaning, but weak and at death's door.

Meanwhile the Hasupuweteri were talking a mile a minute among themselves, extremely agitated, the speakers slapping themselves hard on the back and sides to emphasize their points. They gestured with their bows and arrows, pointing down the trail and off into the forest and sometimes at us. This was a volatile, angry situation, not one I was anxious to be around. When Valero and I walked down to the river together, I asked what they were saying, and a little nervously he told me that they were talking about him and Blanco. They weren't angry at me, he said, and they didn't seem to be blaming him, either. At least that was the general opinion. But Blanco was another story. Blanco was the one who had refused to go up to the village and forced them to come down the trail and fall into the ambush. Most of them seemed willing to let him leave—this time. But if he ever came back, they swore to kill him.

They were also talking about the raid and vowing revenge. Valero had only gotten a small part of it—the raiders were from Kasharaweteri, a community that lived downriver near the rapids—and it wasn't clear to him why they had attacked. Later I found that until recently the Hasupuweteri and Kasharaweteri had traded and visited with each other, enjoying friendly relations. But then the Hasupuweteri had invited the others to a feast where there was supposed to be a large quantity of smoked fish and plantains. Some of the visitors had come up in canoes, while others walked the long distance. But when they arrived it turned out there wasn't nearly as much food as had been promised. Fishing hadn't been good, and the feast was sparse.

As guests, the Kasharaweteri were upset about this. They had traveled a long distance to get there, and the visit of course had a purpose. Yanomama never simply visit each other just to say hello. It's always for trade goods, or to acquire something, or to make good on a past trade agreement. And to eat. But with food so meager, the visit hadn't gone well. Before long the young men in the two groups had started arguing and insulting each other. Some of the Hasupuweteri *huya* got so angry, they hid their guests' canoes. The visitors went home incensed—so incensed that they decided to raid the Hasupuweteri. This first raid would undoubtedly elicit revenge, which would elicit revenge and more revenge. None of these raids would be open battles where one side won decisively and the other lost. They'd all follow the pattern of the encounter I had just seen. One group would shoot someone, then run home. Three or four months later the others would sneak up and return the favor. And on it would go, sometimes for years, even decades. Some groups could hold grudges for generations.

The next evening Takawe died and was cremated. I was only six hundred yards away, and I missed it. I didn't know when he was going to die, of course. And although I knew that the Yanomama cremate their dead and drink the ashes, I did not know when it was that they performed these ceremonies. As it happened, Takawe died in the evening and was cremated that night—all of this after I had called it a day and gone back to my hut. The next morning I went up to the village and he was gone. The only thing left was the remains of the fire.

That accelerated my plans to build a new house next to the community. I simply could not spend my precious time off by myself in a hut a third of a mile away. I got to work and hired some Hasupuweteri men to build me a new house. This time I would make use of all the lessons I had learned when we had built the first. It would be tight, with no spaces for vampire bats to get in; there would be one horizontal, screened window, but above a man's height, so no one could peer in; it would be bigger, big enough for me to build some sturdy writing tables where I could organize my notebooks and journals. Best of all, I sited the hut only forty yards from the *shapono*.

It took more than a month before my new home was ready. But

when it was, my quality of life took an instant turn for the better. Down on the river I had been a visitor. Now I was much more a part of the flow of life. Even if I was in my hut, I was virtually inside the communal structure (eventually I did move inside). I could hear everything, and I could be there instantly to see whatever was going on. The house was nicer, bigger. I set up my working tables and finally started getting seriously into my studies.

By this point I had the fundamentals of the Yanomama language down and was working hard to acquire a basic conversational ability. Most of my effort in the first months had gone into learning the language, an essential element in my conviction that the best way to study the Yanomama was to understand the entire cultural context, rather than concentrate solely on the quantitative measurements I'd need for my protein studies. There was an alternative to this, a methodology that would involve spot-checking the village at regular intervals, recording what each family was doing at those times. With that type of data collecting it was possible to do quantitative analyses, extrapolating from the numbers to determine how many hours a day a person spent hunting, how many hours gardening, and so on. It was an efficient procedure—not necessarily valid, but efficient. And I did think about doing it that way. For fifteen months, I told myself, I could put up with that kind of mechanical reporting. I could do the spot checks, make the measurements, get the data, and complete my study. On the face of it that was the purpose of this whole experience.

On the other hand, I was living with a group of people, and spot checking would never give me the intimate knowledge I was looking for. Although I never lost sight of the fact that I was supposed to be studying the Yanomama in order to report on them, I was here, living with them and interacting with them, I wanted to understand them—and I wanted them to understand me. Only that way, I thought, would I be able not simply to record what they were doing, but to comprehend what it meant in the context of their lives.

And there was certainly a lot to comprehend about their lives. I was seeing the most striking activities, especially now that I was living up at the village and spending so much more time with them. I watched and took notes on everything, often without having a good idea of what it was I was witnessing.

One afternoon shortly after I moved into the new house, I walked into the *shapono* while the shaman was chanting over someone who was sick. He sang and shouted hoarsely. He had taken the *epene* drug and was being assisted by five or six other men who had also taken the drug and were painted and decorated with feathers. Suddenly the helpers jumped up and ran frantically around the *shapono*'s central plaza. Then, just as suddenly, they fell over, as if they had been struck dead. People came up and carried their inert bodies back to the shaman, who started chanting over them, to revive them while they groaned, "Water, water," which was the one thing in this whole performance that I clearly understood. Then without warning the shaman ran from the central plaza to the roofed circumference of the *shapono* and began scrambling on all fours through the family areas, knocking household items every which way, trampling through hearth fires, upsetting kettles, and spreading clouds of ash behind him. As I stood there documenting everything with my camera, tape recorder, and notebook, I wondered exactly what was going on. I understood that this was a curative ritual— the shaman was drawing the sickness out of the patient, transferring it to the others, then reviving them. But my lack of the language forced me to guess and conjecture, so I taped and photographed it, thinking that maybe someday I'd find out what it was all about.

In the weeks that followed I went about learning the language, filling notebook after notebook and making vocabulary cards by the hundreds. It was hard. Learning an unwritten language among a native population with whom you have nothing in common linguistically can be painfully slow. Yanomama words are run together and spoken quickly. Getting a Yanomama to say a word slowly is difficult. It's even more difficult to get him to say it syllable by syllable. They don't understand what you're after; they never speak like that. You've got to train an informant to do that.

In Yanomama the word *obisi* means both "slow" and "soft." So in the beginning I would say, "*Obisi, obisi,*" meaning "Slowly, slowly." Instead they'd begin to whisper whatever it was they were telling me. I'd say "No, no, no," and try to imitate the way I wanted them to say it, slowly and syllabically. But they'd just laugh. I found myself envying Chagnon and Jacques Lizot, who had both started at mission stations working with Spanish-speaking Yanomama. Sometimes I wondered if I wouldn't have been better off living at the mission myself for three months or so, working closely with a bilingual Indian. It would have saved me a lot of frustration and a lot of time. But it hadn't happened that way.

Instead I learned the language by total immersion, word by word and phrase by phrase. In this process the children helped the most. Not only did they have the patience to teach me words, they even played around with the concept. I would ask them, *"Weti kete?"*— "What is this?" But then they'd reverse it. If they saw an ant, they would come to me and say, *"Weti kete?"* And I'd say in Yanomama, "I don't know," and they'd break up in laughter. How in the world could I not know what an ant is—not thinking that it was the word I didn't know, not the creature. Can you just believe this *nabuh* doesn't know what an ant is? Or a grasshopper, or a tree? Every child there knows the name of every tree and every variety of ant (in fact, there is no single word for ant). They'd just laugh and laugh. I'd ask them, then they'd ask me, and all of us would have tears in our eyes from laughing so hard. But I was learning. Slowly but surely I was learning.

As I learned to communicate I began to grapple seriously with my studies, the core of which was the question of protein capture. I wanted to measure how much game the Hasupuweteri consumed per capita; how much time they invested in catching it; what distances they had to cover; how much territory they needed to supply themselves with adequate amounts. I wanted to understand what the relationship was between the number of people living in a given place and the amount of territory they needed to give them a sufficient protein supply. Was there, after all, any validity in Marvin Harris's theory that war among the Yanomama was a way of keeping communities dispersed to insure that the population density in a given area would not outgrow the availability of game? Or was Napoleon Chagnon on solid ground in assuming that Yanomama warfare had nothing to do with scarce protein resources and everything to do with the Indians' ferocity?

To answer these questions I was going to have to find out everything I could about the Hasupuweteri's food-gathering and eating habits. I would accompany the men on hunts, carefully observe the men and women as they gathered the wild foods and fished the streams, and closely document their gardening activities. I would also have to meticulously measure the food they consumed.

The idea of measuring someone's food consumption might sound reasonable enough in a classroom discussion, but it is another story in practice. To do it accurately you have to weigh every morsel people put in their mouths. No intellectualization here, you just have to be brazen enough to go and do it. So that's what I did.

One day Kenny came into the house with a strange thing. He hung it on a rafter when older brother and some others came back from hunting. The thing was black and had a big hook. Then Kenny picked up a peccary that Abami's husband had brought back, and he stuck it on the hook. When we saw the peccary hanging from the house, we started to laugh. No one had ever seen a peccary hanging like that. I was laughing so hard, my side ached. But Abami's husband was not laughing. He asked Kenny why he had done that to the peccary. Kenny said, "Heavy?" Then we really laughed. Abami's husband started laughing, too. He had carried the peccary all the way from the Rahuawe River. Then Kenny took down Abami's husband's peccary and hung up Yoama's husband's spider monkey. It was so much fun that after that whenever someone killed an animal we would run to tell Kenny. We wanted him to come and see if it was heavy.

Initially, because I didn't have an adequate command of the language, I couldn't even ask. When I saw the men come in from a hunt I would go over with my big scales, pick up an armadillo or an anteater or a peccary that they had just dropped to the ground, and weigh it—regardless of how annoying or embarrassing it was. And while I weighed the animal everyone stood around laughing, no doubt wondering just what in the world I thought I was doing. They didn't know I was "weighing" it. They didn't know I was putting it on a "scale." They had never heard of kilos and pounds. It didn't take too much imagination to understand what was going through their minds. Look at this *nabuh,* will you? He takes this strange thing and ties it onto a house pole, then he takes the peccary and hangs it up on there, right in the middle of the village. Then he squints at it and makes little designs on paper.

"*Eou, shori,*" they'd say. "What are you doing?"

"I'm *weighing* the animal. I'm seeing how *heavy* it is."

Only I couldn't really say it, of course. All I could say (once I learned the word) was, "Heavy?"—they don't have a term for "weigh." And they would answer (in their own idiom), "So what's the problem, *shori?* Why don't you pick it up, you'll see how heavy it is." Or before I knew the word *heavy,* I'd just laugh and put it up on the scale. And all the while everyone was giggling and pointing and laughing out loud. They had seen some pretty incomprehensible things since I arrived, but this went beyond even what I might be expected to do. Still, as long as I wasn't destroying anything, why not? The *nabuh* wants to hang the peccary on that hook? Okay, it's odd, but hey, what's the difference?

I had to weigh every piece of game that came into the *shapono,* and then I had to try to get *them* to stand on a scale. I wanted to weigh all the villagers so that I could measure energy expenditures and determine protein consumption per kilo of body weight. I had a regular bathroom scale for this, but trying to get them to stand on it was a daunting undertaking. First, this was too ridiculous for words. Hanging the animals was strange, but this was truly bizarre. Second, they simply were not able to stand on it. One foot would go on, the other would slip off. They'd put one foot on top of the scale, the other on the ground, or both feet on top of the scale. "Come over here," I wanted to say. "Stand here, I'll show you how to do it. Just put one foot here like this, then the other here, like that." Except I had to say it in pantomime.

Kenny brought something else to the house one day. It was late in the afternoon, and everyone was resting in the hammocks. He said very loudly, "Heavy?" Then he pointed to everyone in the hammocks. Many people laughed. Older brother laughed more than anyone. But I didn't laugh. I was frightened because I thought Kenny was going to hang me up on the big black hook like a peccary.

The result of all this was that once I really was set up and started getting into my work, I became a big pain in the neck for them, rather than their being a pain in the neck for me. But they were quite tolerant, and most often they just laughed and joked about it. They began to consider me something of a pet, an entertaining diversion.

I didn't mind, at least not while I was in the early stages of developing relationships with them. One of the ways to communicate or break down tension is through laughter and clowning, so I'd laugh and play games. I'd do a little dance for them or an imitation. They'd stare, then go to pieces. They had never seen anything like it in their lives. No Yanomama would ever do such a thing; entertainment wasn't part of their world. There was one man who had recently sprained his ankle and limped. When I imitated his walk the entire *shapono* just exploded in laughter, and the man I was imitating laughed loudest of all. Every day for the next week they wanted to see this imitation—even after his ankle had healed. You might have thought it was the funniest thing they had ever seen. I was like the court jester, the village clown. But it was all right. Instead of staring and thinking God knows what, they all liked me, they wanted me to be around.

And that's what I wanted. I was establishing good rapport, developing relationships, feeling more relaxed. All of which meant it was easier to relate, easier to learn. I knew that, even if it was in a specialized way, they were accepting me. They weren't thinking, Oh, no, here comes this damned guy again.

Making my rounds of the village, I'd stop at each of the hearths and look at what they were doing. I'd see how they prepared the plantains, how they roasted them on the fire. I'd see if there were any other foods there and ask them what they were. *"Weti?"* They would talk to me, which I didn't understand. But whenever they saw me, whatever else they might think, they also thought "trade goods," so I'd hear the words for "pot" or "fishhook" or "machete." There was a certain humor in it. Here I was, beginning to live with them, getting to know them. Here they were, accepting me into their village, getting to know me. And we were both using the relationship. Along with all my myriad questions and thoughts about these strange and interesting individuals, in the back of my mind I was thinking, What is he eating? How much of this is he consuming? How much of that? And they were, no doubt, going through the same process. Strange, interesting, look at that behavior. But what about those trade goods?

As I circled the village each day I began to get to know the families rather well. Slowly I learned their names—not an easy task, since the Yanomama never use their names in public. Instead they call each other by the appropriate kinship term, and the kinship relationships themselves were often confusing at first. Paternal uncles, for example, are called "father" by their nephews and nieces, to whom they are, in anthropological terms, "classificatory" fathers. By the same token, maternal aunts are called "mother," and their nephews and nieces are "sons" and "daughters." But slowly the relationships sorted themselves out, and before long I began to see each of the Hasupuweteri as distinct individuals. To help in the identification I even began giving the adults my own private nicknames: Romeo, Scarface, Two Wives, Droopy, Red, and so on. But it was the children who captivated me. They were a robust group, good-natured, curious, playful, and friendly. They made the forest rock with laughter as they played hide and seek, used a giant fallen tree as a community trampoline, or gave me yet another hysterical lesson in Yanomama vocabulary.

When Kenny came to our hearth I hid behind my mother. Older brother was afraid, too, but he didn't show it. He just smiled when Kenny squatted in front of him. Then older brother touched Kenny's beard and said he wished he could have a thick beard, too. I touched Kenny's beard sometimes when we were all playing with him. I would reach over and touch it when he wasn't looking. But when he looked at me I wanted to look away from his eyes. I was afraid. I thought that if I looked into his eyes, something might happen to me. Older brother held Kenny's wrist where he wore a shiny thing. When Kenny showed it to us it had a little stick going around and around inside it. I asked older brother what it was, and he said it was a sun.

One little girl who lived with her mother and older brother, however, especially won my affection. She was no more than eight or nine years old, and at first she would stand behind her mother, half hiding, whenever I came by. After a little coaxing, though, I'd be able to get a bright smile from her, which always gave me a feeling of satisfaction. Children's names don't have the same restrictions attached to them, and her mother told me that she was called Yarima. She was without a doubt the most charming youngster I had met among the Yanomama. Moreover, Yarima's older brother, a young man of about sixteen, was friendly and talkative, and as time went on I found myself gravitating toward those people who were more amiable and also better able to help me linguistically. Many people would talk to me for fifteen minutes or so, then they'd tire of the effort. Yarima's brother, though, could go on and on as long as I was interested.

Even more helpful was the man I had nicknamed "Red," for the red T-shirt he wore, one of the very few articles of clothing in the village. I had met him a couple of days after I arrived, and from the start it was obvious that something about his personality was a little different. Red was an exceptionally outgoing, animated individual, but what really set him apart was that from the first day we met he seemed to be completely comfortable around me. There was none of the fear mixed with excitement that I saw in the others. Instead of laughing or just being confused by my inability to communicate, he'd try to figure out what I was attempting to say and give me a hand at getting things done.

When I moved from the river up to the village, our relationship grew closer. I started having him come over to my hut to work with me, and he turned out to be very good. He was extremely patient, a rare commodity. And he learned quickly. *"Hen-na-ha-ka-mi-ye-ya-ra-mi-huu,"* he could say—in distinct syllables, instead of "hen-ahakamiyeyaramihuu," which is what it sounded like. No one else could talk like that, or would. So before long Red became my chief informant. We started translating things together, and he got better and better at it. He would do everything to make me understand a word, even acting it out if he had to. He was a good teacher, and he was rapidly becoming a good friend.

In addition to making my measurements in the village, I was also going fishing and hunting with the men. I mapped the areas we walked through, noting the terrain and calculating distances, times, directions, and how many animals were flushed. "We stopped at Point A at 7:23," my notebook would read. "We flushed a curassow. At 8:10 they saw a collared peccary and chased it for 20 minutes but lost the tracks. Then we turned northeast and walked for an hour past the intersection of the two streams." I did time and motion studies. I counted how many shots they made, how many animals were taken, how many were missed. It was strenuous and difficult, nothing at all like sitting back at my desk in State College and writing up my field methodologies and the applicability and validity and the importance of it all. To actually go out to the field and measure all these things was another story altogether.

Just keeping track of everything that happened in the jungle was difficult work, and at first I found it hard to persist physically and mentally. I had never done anything like this before. I had never been one for backpacking or camping out or eating around an open fire with a mess kit and foldout fork and spoon. I was in good shape, and I was athletic. I had always played football and basketball in high school and had stayed in shape in college, but I didn't know the first thing about outdoor life. Nor had I ever been a hunter. I had never fired a gun.

As a result I had to plunge into jungle life, going hunting every chance I got until I had a good feeling for what was going on. In essence, I learned, the Indians had no elaborate hunting techniques or strategies, but they were minute observers and deadly trackers.

I'd try to stay behind because I was so noisy. But they didn't seem to mind, and soon I found that I enjoyed the hunt. It was communal. I'd be out in the woods with a few of the men; we'd go out together, and we'd come back together. Not much talking, but that was okay. I was getting plenty of talk in the *shapono*. In a way hunting was an escape from the village, and I found out later that the Yanomama think of it that way themselves. Being out in the forest is a chance to be away from the group, to have some privacy. Not the kind of privacy we think of, but at least a chance to be apart for a while.

One problem I had on hunts was that the Indians would want me to shoot animals with my shotgun. They'd flush a bird from the brush or spot it in a tree, then point and say to me, "Okay, now shoot it." But I was supposed to be studying hunting. How could I do that if I was the one doing the shooting? Most of the times I wouldn't shoot, and eventually I just stopped taking the gun along. The first time I went out on a five-day hunt with them, I left my shotgun behind. They thought I was absolutely crazy. "Go on a hunt and leave your shotgun behind? You could kill some game with that thing so easily!" I couldn't explain that I was studying their hunting. They would very rightly consider it absurd. You have to hunt to eat. To get food to put in your stomach.

Toward the end of August I had lived by myself, without Bob Carneiro, in Hasupuweteri for almost four full months. But sometime soon I expected Chagnon. When we had seen each other last he had said he was planning to come up to the village to do some genealogical studies and check in on me. On August 20 we heard a motor on the river, and as usual, the Hasupuweteri ran down to the riverbank yelping and hooting. When I got there I saw that it was indeed Chagnon, accompanied by the four mission Indians who had brought him upriver.

Napoleon Chagnon and I had had our problems during the seven months of preparation for this expedition, and the tension hadn't altogether dissipated.

His conflict with Marvin Harris, which I had been thrust into, was not just another inconsequential academic debate, for the Yanomama were not just another exotic people. Many of them were still isolated, unacculturated, cut off from the outside world—as close to a "pristine" people as exists. And because they were, the violence of their society threw a disturbing light on human nature itself. Anyone who read Chagnon's *The Fierce People* was likely to come away with the feeling that mankind was by nature a brutish, homicidal species.

Marvin Harris had mounted his attack on Chagnon's ideas using the methods and principles of cultural ecology—an approach that stressed the interrelatedness of environmental factors and cultural development. Chagnon knew that to refute Harris he would have to use the same methods and principles. It wasn't enough just to *deny* the veracity of Harris's arguments, he would have to *demonstrate* that they were false. But doing this would require an ecological study, and Chagnon himself had little experience in this area. As a graduate student with a background in cultural ecology and a stint of fieldwork already under my belt, I had seemed a likely candidate to gather the data that would finally show that protein capture was not the major factor in Yanomama violence that Harris and his colleagues believed it was.

I had signed on to this project straight from a prolonged stay in Venezuela, and initially I had not been aware that I was inserting myself right into the middle of one of the most heated and vehement controversies the academic world had to offer. But when I did understand what I had gotten myself into, I began to feel very uncomfortable. Here I was, with my Ph.D. sponsor, Napoleon Chagnon, the man who was going to fund my research, saying one thing, while at the same time another eminent professor whose work I respected was saying precisely the opposite. As I began to fully grasp the issues, I started separating myself from the partisan position my situation at Penn State suggested. And when I did, it seemed to me that Chagnon began to suspect he had an ecological fifth columnist on his hands. Then, when he forbade me to go to New York to speak directly to Harris about his theories, I lost my temper (and went anyway). From that point my relationship with Chagnon had gone downhill. And even though we patched things up well enough to go ahead with the project, we never recovered anything like our initial friendship.

But with all of that, after four months among the Hasupuweteri by myself, it was good to see a face from the outside. For the next three days Chagnon stayed in my new house. As always, the man was a bundle of energy. Drinking coffee from a thermos as if it were water and chain-smoking unfiltered Pall Malls, he set up shop and started interviewing nonstop, gobbling up genealogical information from one villager after another. I marveled at the drive, the ambition, that never stopped pushing him from morning till night.

When he was finished we headed down to Tayariteri. With the mission Indians helping, the business of guiding our two dugouts through the rapids was no problem. Chagnon would now be returning to the United States, while I was going to load more supplies and head back upriver. But at Tayariteri I noticed an old aluminum boat that belonged to Chagnon. God, I thought, what a difference it would make if I had that instead of my eighteen-foot dugout. Whenever I traveled I had to get through the rapids alone, and since the dugout was too heavy for one man to guide through with a rope from the bank, I had to shoot them, a dangerous business. The aluminum boat, though, was light as a feather. I'd be able to handle that from the bank with no problem.

"Nap," I said, "you're not doing anything with that boat. It's just going to be sitting here. How about if I take it? I have to shoot the rapids myself, and it would be so much easier with that than with my dugout."

Chagnon shook his head. "I can't, Ken. If I give it to you, I'll have to get an aluminum boat for Ray and Eric. I can't just give something like that to one of you and not the others."

"Look," I said, "Ray and Eric don't have to go through the rapids." (After the first month Ray had moved to a community downriver, and Eric's village was on the peaceful Ocamo.) "If they get sick, they can just get in their boats and drift down to the mission. I've got to get through Guajaribo. And if I can't, I don't get out. What happens if I'm bitten by a snake or if I get malaria?"

"Ken," said Chagnon, "just don't get bitten by a snake."

One day shortly after I returned from Tayariteri, I was in the village gardens measuring the time and energy required for different phases of clearing, planting, and harvesting. Yarima's brother had come along with me as my informant and was answering various questions when suddenly he said, "There are almost no more ripe plantains."

"What will you eat then?" I asked.

"*Kapiromi*," he said—a root that grows wild in the forest.

"Does that mean the village will leave?"

"Probably," came the answer. "Ask the big man. He'll tell you."

I didn't need to ask the big man. I already knew the answer. Plantains made up the bulk of the Yanomama diet while they were living at their gardens. When the plantains were exhausted the village had no alternative but to revert to what was probably their ancestors' way of life before the introduction of the plantain into the Amazon—the nomadic wandering of hunters and gatherers.

The next day I knew for sure that the village would be leaving on a *wayumi,* a trek. They would be gone, they thought, for about one moon. By then the new crop of plantains would be ready. Was I going to go with them? asked the big man. My mind was racing. This would give me the chance to experience and document an aspect of Yanomama life that no one had ever studied. Did I want to go with them? On the other hand, what was I going to do, just leave all my things in the house? And how could I take along everything I needed, food for a month and clothes and medical supplies and notebooks and tapes and my recorder, and I didn't even know what else? Was I prepared to handle this? But if I stayed, what would I do for a month or more of utter solitude—read and go over my note cards?

"Yes," I told him, weighing it all quickly, "I'm coming with you."

4

That day and the next I got myself ready. Obviously I couldn't take everything, but even with a minimal amount I would need carriers. I'd have to make an arrangement with some of the men— a fair one. It would be good; they'd be happy to have the trade goods, and I'd have a chance to keep the idea of reciprocity in their minds. But I couldn't get more than a few of them to carry for me, especially since I was coming along specifically to observe them engaging in their normal activities. Figuring that each of the carriers shouldn't be burdened with more than twenty-five or thirty pounds meant I could only bring what was absolutely necessary.

First of all I'd have to take my food. I wasn't yet able to sustain myself on their diet. Living with the Yanomama is not like going into even a relatively primitive peasant community, where you can eat what they eat, where they have stoves and pots and make soups and other dishes. The Yanomama eat grubworms from palm trees; they eat ants. They pull roots out of the ground. And on a trek there may not even be much of that fare. You can go very hungry, for long periods.

A Westerner does not have the bodily conditioning for a trek. You sweat, you get tired, weak. You can't stop and rest and fortify yourself. You can't put the salt back in your system. The Indians don't appear to need salt; they've never seen it. They hardly sweat at all. A Westerner cannot survive like that, at least not until he has gone through a long period of physical adjustment.

So for starters I'd have to carry bags of food. I'd have to take my camera, my tape recorder and tapes, my notebooks and pens. And my compass. I'd need my sidepack, my shotgun and shells, and my medicines—my antisnakebite kit, my malaria pills, antibiotics, and antiseptics. Then of course I'd need clothing—shirts and pants and socks and an extra pair of shoes. Everything would have to be wrapped up in special plastic bags. Before I knew it I had filled five or six packs with necessities.

And all the while I was gathering my gear I was asking myself, What is this going to be like? Nomadic hunting and gathering, absolutely prehistoric, the way people existed before the domestication of grain. This was not like a hike, or even an expedition, something more or less defined. And the doubts came. Can I really do it? Can I be a nomad? Can I survive in the jungle? The way I looked at it (with my city boy/college student background), living in my little hut on the headwaters of the Orinoco was roughing it. But this would be jumping from the frying pan into the fire. Trekking in the Amazon isn't like walking through a forest in a national park. The dense jungle terrain is marked by rugged hills and crisscrossed by streams, all of which must be traversed along trails that hardly exist. I didn't know about these things. I wasn't good at them, even now, after all the hunting I had been doing.

It took a full day to get my things selected and organized and to secure everything I would be leaving behind in padlocked trunks and aluminum cases, taping shut everything in my hut. But finally there I was, standing in the humid morning air in my Vietnam jungle boots, my shorts and sidepack and shotgun—feeling very heavy and burdened. And standing with me were the Yanomama men, with nothing but a string around their waists and their feather-light bows and arrows and arrow point holders like quivers slung across their backs. Five of them picked up my packs and adjusted the tumplines around their foreheads. Even with the packs, I thought, they are better off than I am with my boots and pants and shirt and knives and gun and sidepack and all the rest. In the soggy air my hundred and eighty pounds felt more like two hundred and eighty.

The men started out first, while the carriers and I brought up the tail. The women and children would come along after a bit. We hadn't been walking long before we hit our first stream, and suddenly I was waterlogged. My boots and socks and pants were sodden, and though I had felt heavy before, now I felt leaden. Somehow sand had gotten into everything, and as I walked I felt it rubbing in my socks and my wet pants, chafing the insides of my thighs. In the humidity, nothing was drying.

After a couple of hours of slogging, the sweat was stinging my eyes and my clothes were wedged up into every bodily nook and cranny they could find. I was more uncomfortable than I had ever been in my life. Watching the lithe, graceful Yanomama flit through the jungle ahead of me, I realized I was mumbling to myself under my breath: "Why don't you people figure out a way to stay home instead of wandering around the jungle? Why didn't you plant more plantains so we wouldn't have to do this kind of thing, which I'm already weary of and can't see how I might do for another day, let alone—how long are we going to be out here, a month? two months?"

The first night it rained, and under the flimsy shelter every item I had with me got soaked. It rained the second night, too, and the third, and almost every night after that. My shoes were never dry. I'd hang them up over a fire until they were brown and stiff with smoke. Then in the morning I'd put them on and a minute later I was in a stream and they'd be wet until I could hang them up over the fire again the coming night.

At the end of the first couple of days I lay in my hammock and thought about the endless hours of playing sports when I was in high school. Then at least when I was through exhausting myself I went home and took a nice shower and ate a good meal and had a refreshing rest in my bed. No mosquito bites and parasites, no low-grade malaria, no lying in a soaking hammock when it's pouring and the rain is dripping in the food and everything is musky and moldy. Pulling my light blanket around me, I laughed about how I used to think that living in my hut was primitive. Now, remembering my hut was like dreaming of heaven. If I ever got back, I'd peel off my wet, rotting socks and shoes and fall into my dry hammock. I'd have a cup of coffee and some crackers and peanut butter. I'd put a cassette in my tape player. I'd be a king in his castle.

What surprised me, though, was that after several days I actually began to feel comfortable out in the forest. Once that happened I was able to watch the Yanomama instead of focusing on my own misery. I noticed that the Indians didn't think the trek was gruesome at all. On the contrary, there was much about it they obviously enjoyed. Out here there were far fewer biting insects than there had been in the *shapono*. The air was cooler. I noticed that individuals and families who might not have had much to do with each other at home were spending time together and building their trek shelters next to each other. Much of the tension and anger that cropped up from time to time in the *shapono* seemed to disappear; people were in a lighter, happier mood.

The entire community was on the move—women and children and old people, too—and that meant that the overall pace of the trek was fairly relaxed. Each morning the men took off down the trail first. They would be there in the encampment and suddenly vanish silently into the forest. An hour or so later they'd stop hunting and gather together, squatting down on the trail to wait, talking about the game and examining each other's arrow points.

Meanwhile the women moved slowly and leisurely, carrying huge baskets on their backs that looked as if they weighed more than the women themselves. Piled inside were hammocks, plantains, pots, gourds, wood ashes (used to make a kind of piquant sauce)—every single thing a family owned. They even carried the roofing leaves that were used each night for the temporary shelter. Many of them also had little children on their hips, and some were thick-bodied and pregnant.

Moving at their slow pace, the women eventually arrived at the spot where the men were waiting. There they eased down their heavy loads and rested, chitchatting about the children and laughing and having a good, sociable time. After twenty minutes or so the men would get up and disappear again in search of game, knowing that the women and children were all right and that they would catch up again in another hour or two.

This pattern went on every day until early afternoon, when the whole group would stop to make camp. First the men cleared the undergrowth and small trees, hacking away with their machetes. You could hear the whacking and clanging for miles. Then each of them would cut six or eight poles that became a structure for one family, with uprights and cross staves for support. The leaves the women carried along were then laid on like shingles for the roof, with branches on top of them so they wouldn't blow away.

All this took about forty-five minutes. The rest of the afternoon was spent hunting the area thoroughly and gathering whatever fruits, berries, and other edibles could be found. The women had brought plantains along, but not many, so the community was dependent on whatever they might get out of the forest—the game, the small crabs and fish from a nearby stream, the roots and berries and fruit the area might furnish. In more or less virgin forest now, the hunting was good. Howler and spider monkey, curassow, armadillo, anteater, it all went into the pots. So despite the lack of plantains people were eating well. It wasn't a bad life all in all, once you got into the rhythm of it.

One day older brother came back from the garden and told us that Kenny was coming with us on wayumi. We were all surprised. He had never gone with us before. He was away, or else he stayed in his house. When we were ready to leave he had many bags for the men to carry. We didn't know what was in the bags or why he wanted to take them along. I thought it must be his food. He always ate in his house so we couldn't see what he was eating.

When we left, Kenny went up ahead with the men. Later, when we came up he would be squatting on the trail with them, waiting for us. His shirt would be wet through with sweat, and he swatted all the time at the mosquitoes and sweat bees. When we stopped to make camp he asked the men to make him a shelter. But his had to be bigger because of his long hammock. He had a beautiful cotton hammock, very big and very long. I always wondered what it would be like to lie in a hammock as beautiful as that one.

On the wayumi my mother would always give Kenny some of the food we found. So would the other women. Now he was living with us, and one must always share food with neighbors. My mother once told me to bring him a roasted crab and a plantain. He took it and smiled at me. Then I ran home.

One day while he was going around to people making designs on paper, he asked my mother if she would betroth me to him. She said no. She didn't want him to take me away. I wasn't afraid then. I knew that he was making a joke. My mother thought he was making a joke, too, but she told him she wouldn't let him take me away to Pensilvaniateri. That was the name of Kenny's village. I thought that Pensilvaniateri must be a very big village. It must be bigger than Hasupuweteri or even Nanimabuweteri.

Toward the end of the first month on trek, I was sitting in my hammock going over the field notes I had been taking on such subjects as distances traversed, speed of movement, and hunting yields when I noticed Yarima, the little girl with the enchanting smile, walking toward me carrying a gourd filled with *pishaassi* sprouts covered with a sharp sauce her mother had prepared. She approached my hammock hesitantly, held out the gourd, and said, *"Pei"*—"Here." Then she turned and ran back to her mother.

Although I was pleasantly surprised by her coming over, I didn't think anything of it. Most of the community shared food with me regularly, especially since we had been trekking. Later that day when I passed her mother's shelter, I said jokingly, "Is your daughter already betrothed? I'd like to marry her someday."

"No, she's not betrothed," came the answer. "But I don't want you to marry her."

"Oh, why not?"

"Because you'd take her far away downriver, and I'd never see her again. I'd miss her too much. No, she's not going to be your wife."

"Oh," I said, teasing her some more, "you know I wouldn't take her anywhere. I'd live right here and do son-in-law service for you. I'd hunt for you and bring you game."

"No"—she laughed—"I doubt you'd do that. You'd take her away."

"Well, maybe you're right," I said, and walked on, highly pleased to find myself bantering in Yanomama. I also knew that the joking had conveyed my appreciation for the food and for the fact that her bright, smiling little daughter had brought it over.

As the *wayumi* wore on week after week, I kept mapping our directions and distances and began to notice that our path was describing a wide arc and that we were now headed back toward the village gardens. But while the Hasupuweteri had thought we would be gone "one moon," it had already been almost two moons—we were, according to my calendar, in our seventh week of trekking. For a while now the game had not been nearly as plentiful as it was earlier, and with the catch getting scarcer every day, I finally decided to go on ahead with my carriers and get back to my hut before the others.

Two days later we were back at the *shapono*. I felt exhilarated. I was home, after not only surviving the ordeal, but actually adapting to it. My hut was overgrown with brush and small trees, inside and out. I marveled at how the seeds had managed to sprout and grow so fast—a dozen or so saplings were busy making a young forest out of my one room. But it was good to be home, where everything I had been dreaming of was at my fingertips, all of it under a good, dry roof.

The day after next, while I was still washing rank clothes and drying out packs and equipment soggy from the damp forest and sudden downpours, the Hasupuweteri arrived. Inside the *shapono* the men stood up their bows and hung their hammocks around the hearths. The women unpacked their baskets and hung up their water containers and gourds, and that was that. In ten minutes they reinstalled themselves, then they went down to check out the gardens to see whether the new crop of plantains had matured. It was as if they had never left.

Not long after we got back I decided to move into the *shapono*. There was no reason I couldn't put my hut to use as a storage shed and as a retreat whenever I needed to get away. But living in the *shapono* would allow me to fully experience this existence I was trying to document. I knew generally what went on, but not the specifics. The trek had made me much more a part of the community. Moving into my hut, even though it was so near, seemed almost a step backward. Inside the *shapono* I could continue to follow the dynamics of the group and the personal interactions that I was now used to seeing close up. Besides, so much of the community's life took place at night. From my hut I would hear the noises and talking and speech making after it got dark and everyone was in their hammocks. Moving from the riverbank to my new house had been an important step. Now I felt I was ready to actually live in the village.

I was roasting corn from older brother's garden when I saw Kenny come into the shapono. *He was carrying two of his boxes. Then he went out and came back with more boxes. Some of them were shiny, like the sun on his wrist. After he had brought many boxes he hung his hammock next to Vulture Belly and Vulture Belly's younger brother. Older brother said that now Kenny was going to sleep in the* shapono.

I could watch him from across the plaza all the time. He had so many things that he had to build racks against the back wall. Many of the boys stood around his hammock all day long, but my sister and I never went there. But Kenny came to visit us and my mother every day. He usually came twice or sometimes more than twice. Now he didn't wear all his clothes anymore, only his small pants. He didn't wear foot coverings, either. He had hair on his chest and on his legs. That looked very nice. The boys used to touch his beard. They wished they could have beards like his. They pulled the black curly hair on his chest. But he had a big forehead that went up toward the top of his head. That looked funny. He was also beginning to talk. He wasn't a Ghost Tongue anymore.

I thought he was very smart to sleep in the shapono. *Kenny could have a fire at night to keep warm. He could be next to people instead of sleeping alone in his house. I wondered why Kenny did not have a wife. He was very big and strong. It was strange that he did not have a wife.*

Once I decided to make the move I just gathered up my hammock and found a free area next to the hearth where Red lived with his older brother, Orawe, and his family. Orawe was another interesting individual. The leader of the lesser of Hasupuweteri's two sublineages and the village's second headman, Orawe seemed to be around fifty years old when I arrived at Hasupuweteri, though that was just a conjecture. With a numeric system that stops at two, the Yanomama do not reckon years or ages; instead they categorize people according to general age groups: infants, children, adolescents, adults, and elders.

Orawe was fairly old for a Yanomama (few seem to live longer than sixty, and one rough estimate of life expectancy is forty-five), but he was still vigorous. His nickname was Watubawemaka— "Vulture Belly." Like the main headman, Orawe was a great shaman. He took drugs each day, powdered *epene* seeds, a powerful hallucinogen that the Indians took turns blowing into each other's noses through a three-foot-long drug-blowing tube. Communing with the spirits, Orawe would heal the sick and help protect the village from malevolent forces sent by enemy shamans. His chanting was loud, dramatic, rhythmic; his imitations of the animals whose spirits he assumed were dynamic and eerily accurate. Orawe also had a highly developed sense of humor that helped him relate to people in an easygoing, friendly way—without losing any of his innate dignity. Like his brother, Red, he seemed better able to accept me than others, relatively free of the confusion and uncertainty that many of the Yanomama felt about *nabuh*. The chemistry between us had been good from the very beginning, and somehow that was translated to his whole sublineage: I seemed to get along with them better generally. It was easier to talk to them, easier to feel comfortable around them.

So it was next to Orawe and Red that I hung my hammock. The first night I dozed off to the friendly buzz of talking and snoring, only to be ripped awake just minutes later by what seemed to be a scream of agony. It was a man's cry, from the other side of the *shapono*. As I listened the voice came again, this time not a scream, but a wail, then another wail that subsided into a series of racking sobs. The rest of the *shapono* was quiet, not a sound. Nobody seemed to have heard, though the wails were loud enough to wake the dead. How could they sleep through it? As I lay there wondering what to do, the sobbing became softer, then stopped. I was wide awake now, listening intently to the silence of the jungle and the peaceful snoring of my housemates.

After a while I heard some movement a couple of hearths down; somebody else was up. In the moonlight I saw a figure pick up an ax and begin to walk toward me. I couldn't make out who it was, and I couldn't imagine that anybody would want to hurt me. But in the back of my mind was Chagnon's story about the Indians coming after him at night with an ax. I tensed as the figure approached my hammock, then watched him pass by and walk toward the *shapono* gate. A moment later the *whang*ing of the ax broke through the night like gunshots, *whang, whang, whang*. Nobody else stirred. I listened, then saw the shadowy figure come back with the ax in one hand and several pieces of firewood curled in the crook of his other arm. As he stooped over his hearth to build up the fire, I realized that he had just run out of wood and had gotten cold. These people were obviously not much for tiptoeing around if someone else was asleep.

Yanomama nights were an event, that first night and every night afterward. It wasn't as if the community just went to sleep, then woke up the next morning. No, a Yanomama night was like another day. All sorts of things went on.

Each family had its own hearth area in the circular dwelling, but there were no walls between them and no privacy of any sort. Adults snored. Babies cried. And everyone heard everything. Some people weren't sleepy, so they talked late. *Huya* laughed over something that happened during the day. A couple of men laid their plans for a hunt the next morning. But not in whispers, as we would do if we were around others who were sleeping. They talked the same way they always talked, at the same volume. They didn't worry about it, and neither did anyone else. People were used to it: so they woke up, then dozed off again, or just slept through it.

Then someone might want to give a speech, one of the *pata*, the big men. Sitting in his hammock, he would address the village: *"Ihirupa, irhirupawe, ware a ta hirii"*—"Children, listen to me." It didn't matter that most of them were asleep; he felt like talking to the community, so he was going to talk. Maybe he would talk about a herd of white-lipped peccaries whose tracks someone saw in the jungle that day; maybe about the fruit of the *eteweshi* trees that had ripened and needed gathering; or maybe about a visit he thought should be made to another village. Most often this happened in the evening, but sometimes a speaker would get started in the early morning. People would stir in their hammocks. Some would awaken and listen. Many would go right on sleeping.

They slept on even when someone yelled out in anger or fright during a nightmare, or when a father awakened from a mournful dream of a child who had died and cried out his anguish, though the death might have happened years ago (which was what I had heard that first night). Meanwhile someone would get up to tend a fire whose warmth was needed by the family sleeping naked in their hammocks; someone else might walk outside to urinate, though not too far outside, because one didn't venture far from the *shapono* at night.

In the middle of the night a shaman might decide he wanted to chant. He'd take his drugs, his conduit to the world of the *hekura*, the spirits. At that hour no one was up to blow them into his nose, so he'd inhale the *epene* powder like snuff from his hand, then stand up and chant for an hour or two, exactly as he would during the daytime.

At the beginning I was constantly cranky. The Yanomama have the ability to wake up and go back to sleep in a minute. I did not. When something got me up, I was up. I'd lie in the hammock for an hour trying to get back to sleep among all the nighttime noises of the *shapono*. Eventually I got used to this, too. Like the Yanomama, I'd spend eleven hours in my hammock at night to get seven or eight hours of actual sleep.

Among the Hasupuweteri night and day were a continuum. Things did not stop for a period of unconscious refreshment; they just went on, as they probably would for any large group of families living openly together in the same house. When I thought of it that way, I was struck by how harmonious Yanomama life actually was. Here you had seventy-five people of all ages, in essence living and sleeping in one room. Although I was having some trouble sleeping myself, these loud Yanomama nights were nothing more than a manifestation of how well these people had learned to accommodate each other.

I also recognized that this was only one dimension of their remarkable ability to live together. With so few individuals in the community the emphasis in Hasupuweteri was on group cohesion. There was no formal leader, no community organization. They didn't have any rules or any enforcement. But they did have ways of conducting themselves that tended to keep the inevitable quarrels and fights under control. There was turbulence and violence all right, Napoleon Chagnon hadn't been wrong about that. But for the most part the Indians expressed their angrier emotions in ways that allowed the community to preserve its essential harmony.

As I began to understand this better, I got increasingly upset about Chagnon's "Fierce People" portrayal. The man had clearly taken one aspect of Yanomama behavior out of context and in so doing had sensationalized it. In the process he had stigmatized these remarkable people as brutish and hateful. I wasn't fooling myself into thinking that the Yanomama were some kind of Shangri-la race, all peace and light. Far, far from it. They were a volatile, emotional people, capable of behavior we would consider barbaric. But even then the forms their aggression took were fascinating, and much of it was ritualized in one way or another.

Public insult and complaint were good examples. Maybe the most striking thing about Yanomama life was its public nature; practically everything was carried on in front of everyone else. So, along with the violence, I was seeing the tenderest examples of love, reconciliation, harmony, warmth, and mutual enjoyment. I was seeing the constant helpfulness, the close friendships, the tenderness with which parents treated their children. At the slightest outcry Yanomama mothers would dash to their children's side to see what was wrong. For all their involvement in food gathering and chores, they never left the children unattended. When fathers returned from a hunt they would recline in their hammocks and let out a bright smile as their children ran to them to be held or thrown up into the air and caught. On the other hand, whenever there was a household argument or a quarrel with a neighbor, or a marital problem, everybody in the *shapono* heard about it. It didn't go on in the privacy of a kitchen or a bedroom. So although there was public harmony, there was also public complaint, public ridicule, public scorn, and public recrimination.

The first aspect of Yanomama anger that hit me turned out to be a false one—the language itself. In a way Yanomama is like German. Spoken German often strikes a foreigner as angry. It's full of harsh gutturals, and the intonations may sound imperious and domineering. When later I spent time in Germany, I would sometimes ask what two people were arguing about, only to be told they weren't arguing at all, they were just having a normal conversation. In this regard Yanomama is more extreme than German. Normal speech seems excited and angry, stresses are powerful, and palatals and stops are exaggerated, giving the language a sharp, emotional edge.

Then there are the public displays of anger, so disquieting to an outsider. Say something has happened in the village and one of the men is screaming at the top of his lungs. If you're not ready for it, it can stand your hair on end. I wasn't used to people exploding like this out in the open. My first tendency was to back off and look around quickly to see if someone was coming for me. When I realized it wasn't me the man was yelling about, I'd breathe a sigh of relief and try to find out what was going on. But after I had been there a while I got blasé about it. I began to feel as if I'd been hearing this kind of thing forever. The man was screaming because he was angry. Somebody probably took some of his tobacco, or maybe he thought his wife was having an affair, or maybe he'd been out hunting all day and she wasn't interested in roasting plantains. I'd find out about it soon enough. Everyone would.

On the other hand, if the incident was about something that had been festering for a while and someone was really offended, an outburst might turn into a red-hot war of insults. Yanomama insults can be creative and raucous. The Indians don't have a profane vocabulary for invective or cursing. Neither do they have vulgar terms for sex or body functions. And since sexual behavior is completely standardized, it isn't possible to insinuate that someone's behavior is deviant. Nor does it make any sense for one Yanomama to question another Yanomama's morality, honesty, masculinity, femininity, or intelligence. What they do instead, with a vengeance, is ridicule some aspect of their antagonist's physical appearance.

You hear this regularly, both in jest and in earnest. Children just learning to talk are taught to say *hitosi* ("fat upper lip"), or *iwa ka mamo kasi* ("big caiman eyelids"), or *teshina potepe* ("black buttocks"). When insults are hurled in fun, everyone laughs, even though a Yanomama finds it deeply humiliating to have some physical defect called to everyone's attention. But sometimes a yelling match can jolt the whole village out of its peaceful activity.

Shortly after I moved into the *shapono,* while I was still cranky from lack of sleep, one of the village women came into the *shapono* screaming and yelling, "You yellow skin, you big red vagina, you scaly ass. You're always having friendly 'chats' with my husband, aren't you?" It was like an explosion, the volume was simply tremendous. I looked around and saw it was Yokami, yelling at her sister, Kraoma. Everyone knew Kraoma was having an affair with Yokami's husband. But though Yokami was screeching at the top of her lungs, after the first surprise most of the people in the *shapono* went back to what they were doing. Only Yokami's sister and mother and husband seemed to be paying any attention. And me. I had made a dive to turn on my tape recorder and was scribbling notes a mile a minute: "Yes, you've been chatting with him, haven't you? All the time while I'm out picking plantains. Chatting, right? He crawled into you, didn't he? He crawled into your enormous red vagina, didn't he? He crawled in so far his fingers came out your mouth! His arm came out your mouth! His penis came out your nostrils!"

By now Kraoma was standing up. "I didn't copulate with him. I didn't, I didn't. We just sat and chatted in the *shapono.*"

"Yes, you did," Yokami screamed back. "He crawled into you, he crawled into you, he crawled into you! He went into your bottom and came out your mouth! You scaly ass, you bucktooth, you protruding fang, you caiman skin!"

"No, he didn't, you black buttocks"—this from Kraoma—"you big black buttocks, you flabby vagina!"

"Listen to that, will you," laughed one of the nearby men from his hammock.

"And you," yelled Yokami, turning on her husband, who had been taking all this in without a word. "You thought to yourself,

She has such a big red vagina, my ass will come right through her. That's what you said to yourself. You said that, you said that. You tumor forehead. You long nose. Your penis is as big as a tapir gut. You heat your big infected penis with embers all the time to relieve the itch."

"*Eou,*" said the neighbor from his hammock, "will you just listen to that."

For Yokami this had obviously been building up for quite some time, and she hurled abuse right and left before she was satisfied that she had demonstrated her contempt and had humiliated the adulteress. She had called Kraoma every name in the book and a few she'd added to the book. Despite the neighbors' amusement, she knew her insults had been taken seriously, and she felt a certain degree of compensation just by having riduculed Kraoma in front of the community.

Sometimes, of course, it did escalate beyond the verbal, and I saw that, too. The men could get very angry if they thought their wives were having affairs. And sometimes a man's anger would erupt into violence. Nobody laughed when that happened. Yanomama men were capable of taking a stick from the fire and burning their wives or cutting at them with a machete. You could see the evidence on some of the women's bodies, scars from burns or machete cuts, even once in a while a ripped earlobe or (rarely) a whole ear missing, courtesy of an enraged husband.

To us such things would be considered utter barbarity. But not in the Venezuelan Amazon. It sounds so awful to say that a husband burned his wife with a stick from the fire, or that he cut her with a machete. And it is, but to understand what has happened the observer has to know that this is a culture where emotionality, the hot feelings of the moment, take precedence, where restraint and thoughts of the future aren't nearly as operative as they are with us. The Yanomama don't seem as conscious of consequences; theirs is not a premeditative psychological universe. Thus a husband is fully capable of attacking his wife, but he will also feel terrible about it afterward. The Yanomama have powerful emotional outbursts, and they do violent things. But they are not cold and indifferent. Outside of warfare, calculated brutality is beyond them.

Nor do they have anything faintly resembling Western sophistication about extramarital affairs. These are not men who would find out that their wives had been unfaithful, then say, "Thanks for telling me, I appreciate your openness. Let's sit down and talk it through. Let's share our feelings." No, if a man's wife has an affair, he burns her or he beats her. He wants to have his own children, which is what he is mainly concerned about. He does not want his nuclear family disrupted. In Yanomama society, as in ours, a woman is not just a companion—she is wife and mother. But there, the economic arrangement between husband and wife is essential to the family's survival. If a man's wife leaves him, he has a grave situation on his hands. So the Yanomama don't "work" on their relationships. They don't have the luxury. They have to eat. And for this a man needs a woman, a woman needs a man, and children need their parents.

The other thing is that in Yanomama land you're dealing with a society that doesn't have any laws and doesn't have any method of enforcement, even if they did have laws. Looking at the occasional domestic violence in the *shapono,* I would try to get a perspective on it. How many men in the West, I thought, would beat their wives if there were no social sanctions and laws about it? How many do anyway? Not that that's an excuse of any sort. But it certainly happens, and even in some so-called civilized societies it happens with disturbing frequency.

The more I thought about Chagnon's emphasis on Yanomama violence, the more I realized how contrived and distorted it was. Raiding, killing, and wife beating all happened; I was seeing it, and no doubt I'd see a lot more of it. But by misrepresenting violence as the central theme of Yanomama life, his *Fierce People* book had blown the subject out of any sane proportion. What he had done was tantamount to saying that New Yorkers are muggers and murderers. If you go out on the streets in New York, they will mug you and knife you and take your money. Of course these things do take place. But that doesn't mean it's an accurate or reasonable generalization to make about New Yorkers. It doesn't mean that someone would be justified in writing a book entitled *New Yorkers: The Mugging and Murdering People.*

Besides the different values and ideals of Yanomama and Western societies, I began to feel that one essential contrast between us and them was not in the frequency of wife abuse and other forms of violence, but in the fact that in their world such behavior was so visible. An American anthropologist can easily observe, record, and even film Yanomama violence—all of which makes for dramatic presentations in textbooks, lecture halls, and classrooms. A Yanomama anthropologist, by contrast, would have a hard time getting into American kitchens and bedrooms to watch angry or drunken husbands battering their wives and children.

I thought too that if the Yanomama knew some of the things that are done in our society, and with what frequency, they would be amazed and horrified. The homelessness and abandonment of people by their family members, the gang killings and drug violence would shock them profoundly. They wouldn't believe that humans could be capable of such brutal, subhuman behavior.

I slowly developed a sense of the context that governed Yanomama violence, and of the emphasis their culture placed on limiting it, rather than maximizing it. Public insult was often a sufficient release for anger and pent-up emotion precisely so that violence would go no farther. When a situation really got heated, the men of two lineages or two villages might get involved in chest-pounding matches, where individuals took turns giving and receiving punches, either open-handed or with closed fists—depending on the level of anger. These were tense, dangerous affairs. But in most cases they resolved the argument without leading to bloodshed. A step up the scale were club fights, where antagonists traded blows to the top of the head with eight-foot-long staves. Often they carried the scars of these duels for life. But this too was ritualized violence, a substitute for deadly bloodshed. And even the killing that did happen in intervillage raids was most often carried out through hit-and-run ambushes. Real battles with large-scale casualties would strike the Yanomama as insane.

But it wasn't only violence that had to be seen in the overall cultural matrix. The better I got to know the Hasupuweteri, the clearer I was about how very integrated their lives were. Every single thing they did had its everyday, normal context—its reason. The purpose of drug taking, for example, was to put them in contact with the spirit world. The shamans took the drug for that specific reason and for that reason only. Other men could also take it, and they did, but only by way of participating in the shamanistic chant. Drugs were not taken just to get high. Without a ritual context and purpose, drug taking would seem a foolish activity.

Sex, too. Sex took place in the forest during the day when men and women were out together. A man decided he wanted to go hunting, and he took his wife along with him; while he was hunting, she'd be gathering. And it was during that time that they would have sex, in the context of a normal daily activity. There was sex at night sometimes, but not between husband and wife. And not in the house. Affairs took place then, but very discreetly. Marital sex took place in the context of an economic activity, which was the essential reason for marriage in the first place.

Of course even while I was learning to appreciate this integrated and purposeful way of life, there were events that seemed to defy explanation. Among them were the Yanomama funeral customs. The second death in the village since I had arrived was that of Henaowe, an old man who had been a great speaker and hunter in his day, but for several years had not been able to get around well. One morning he wasn't able to get out of his hammock. All that day the shamans took drugs and worked on him, urging the evil spirits out of his body. But despite their best efforts, the next morning Henaowe lay motionless.

5

The morning Henaowe died, some of his relatives went out to get firewood, logs big enough to make a fire that would burn the corpse. I knew that at some point they would also prepare the traditional plantain drink into which Henaowe's ashes would be mixed, although the ashes-drinking ceremony might not take place for a week or two yet. Among other things, they would have to kill a lot of game, enough to provide a funeral feast for the entire community, and that would mean a full-scale, five-day hunt. But the cremation would take place right after death.

That afternoon several women unwrapped their packs of *onoto* seed paint and drew serpentine designs on Henaowe's face. Others decorated his hair with white buzzard down, then put arrow cane in his pierced ears and hung brightly colored toucan feathers from his arms. To the sounds of wailing and moaning from the dead man's relatives, men from the community's other lineage built the pyre and lit it. As the fire intensified, the men untied the hammock, in which Henaowe was still lying as if he had merely fallen asleep. Then, with the crying getting louder and more desperate, they carried the hammock and its burden over to the flames and threw it on. Sobs racked Henaowe's old wife as the body began to crackle and burn and as other relatives tossed his bow and arrows and arrowheads into the inferno. Standing around the fire, the family lost itself in grief. Crying uncontrollably, Henaowe's wife threw herself on the ground, rolling in the dust of the open plaza while his elderly sister danced back and forth, moving slowly and heavily in the heat of the afternoon sun. And that was their ceremony, their expression of loss—all simple and straightforward and right from the heart. There were no solemnities, no speeches, just the burning body and the anguish of those gathered around it. In the Yanomama fashion, Henaowe's close friends and relatives from outside the immediate family joined the mourning while at the same time others in the community went about their daily business. From the far side of the *shapono* came the laughter of children playing.

Ten days later they drank his ashes. After the fire had burned itself out on the day of the cremation, the dead man's family had gathered the bits and pieces of unburned bone. Now these skeletal remains were ground to a fine powder in a hollowed-out log, then mixed with a drink made of sweet, ripe plantains. One at a time Henaowe's close relatives took large bowlfuls of the mixture and drank them down. So did a few friends and others in the group who wanted to show their respect. Then the peccary, monkeys, and birds that had been killed in the hunt were divided up and distributed. And when the feast was over, that was it. Henaowe was now done and gone. From this point on his name was never mentioned in the Hasupuweteri community. Nor was the word *henao*—"morning"—from which his name was taken.

But though Henaowe was no longer to be mentioned, he lived on in the hearts of those who loved him, very much so, as he would for years and years. They never forget. Years after a death the night will be broken by the wailing of someone who has awakened from a dream of the loved one. And that will be a delicate moment, even all those years later. The word the Yanomama use is *hushuo*, which means "I'm mourning for my dead" and "I'm angry"—both. And at that time, if the wrong thing is said, it will provoke an emotional storm. The feelings are alive and raw, as if time had never passed.

Exactly why the Yanomama drink their dead relatives' ashes I never did determine to my own satisfaction. They have no rationale for it, and if there ever was some practical purpose served, it is no longer apparent. Nevertheless, they have the strongest feelings about this custom. To them it is the only decent way to dispose of a deceased relative. The Yanomama find it barbaric that we put our dead in a hole in the ground—not just barbaric, subhuman. "Your people know so much," they would say to me, "you have so many things, airplanes and motors and doctors. But when it's all said and done, you're not so smart after all. You don't even drink the ashes of your dead relatives."

As my knowledge of the language improved and as I got to know the people of Hasupuweteri, my protein studies progressed dramatically. I had gotten beyond the initial embarrassment and awkwardness of weighing their food, and they had more or less gotten used to my doing it. So now I was not only weighing every single animal that came into the *shapono,* I weighed and measured all their other food intake as well. I had small diet scales, and I would literally take food out of their hands and weigh it before they put it in their mouths. A plantain, a peach palm fruit, a handful of nuts, I would weigh them before they were shelled and after. I would time how long it took to shell them. I became meticulous about doing the job right, measuring everything, recording it all.

But I wanted to be more than an observer. I wanted to get beyond their tendency to regard me as a pet or a comedian. That was fine at first, even fun. It had been a way of keeping the tension down, of communicating in the absence of language. We had all looked at each other and laughed instead of staring blankly and suspiciously. But that became a problem after a while. They came to expect the laughing and joking, and they treated me as one might a good-natured, funny child. I wanted to be accepted not on those terms, but as a serious person.

They had been conditioned by the early days, and I would still occasionally hear the "tch-tch, here, tch-tch, come here." So I would say, "Come on, don't call me like that. You know I'm not a dog. Let's move on to something else." And that would be a shock to them.

Maybe it's a basic human need, to have companionship and be integrated into a group. Whatever it was, I was feeling it strongly. I wanted nothing more than for them to treat me as an equal. Which was funny in a way. A man from the United States, a Western man, a man from the world of high technology and Judeo-Christian ethics, and there I was, wanting the Yanomama to accept me as one of them. But I did, and that was a strong motivation that kept drawing me more and more into their community.

As I got to know the village situation better, I realized that there was a kind of subtle competition for my friendship between the two sublineages that made up the Hasupuweteri—the winners of course thinking they would have an easier time getting trade goods from me. Red's lineage was headed by Orawe, the great shaman, while Yarima and her family belonged to the other lineage, the larger group, whose headman was the famous Yarimowe, known to all by his nickname, "Longbeard"—from the wispy strands of beard that he never cut.

In his generation Longbeard was the man who personified the Hasupuweteri, by far the most influential of the *pata* and reputedly an even more powerful shaman than Orawe. When he chanted, which he did regularly, he was very loud, very animated. He knew all the chants and was close to all the spirits. Like Orawe, he was an excellent mimic and imitated the various animals as shamans do when they are filled with the animal's spirit. At night he gave long, dramatic speeches to the community. It was obvious that his strength came not just from his numerous kin, but from the force of his personality. Where Orawe was relaxed and amiable, Longbeard was aggressive and dominating. At the beginning he had tried to bully me, demanding goods, not just for himself, but for visiting headmen, as if I were his private resource. He stopped that soon when he saw that I could be just as aggressive as he was. Before long we became friends, though it was a friendship built on respect rather than on good chemistry.

Like everyone else, both Orawe and Longbeard called me *shori*—brother-in-law—but after I had been living with Orawe's lineage for several months he began referring to me as *owasi,* younger brother. From that point on every person in the village started calling me by the appropriate kinship term. Since the Yanomama do not use their names, everyone is ordinarily known by a kinship term. If you don't have one, you have to make one up or establish a kinship. Once I became Orawe's "younger brother," Red and Or-awe's other brothers began calling me "brother," and his children began calling me "father." Meanwhile, Longbeard's lineage, which was related to Orawe's by marriage, continued to call me *shori*, but now it meant something more than "brother-in-law-because-we-don't-know-what-else-to-call-him." It was all fictive, of course, something that happened in the normal course of events to facilitate personal interaction. But still, it was a further sign of acceptance, an indication that their feelings toward me were positive and inclusive.

As I passed my first year with the Yanomama, I found that little by little I was growing to like their normal way of life, the harmony and the cohesion of the group, the interaction and interrelatedness of everything they did. Many of the nuances of their psychology were also attractive, especially when I contrasted them with what went on in our own society. For example, I had always had a big problem with vanity. The amount of time and energy spent on appearance—the exaltation of beauty and youth that we indulge in—I had found upsetting since high school. I could never stand it among my friends and especially among my girlfriends. For better or worse I had a visceral repulsion to it.

But as I got to know the Yanomama women, I saw that they simply did not spend time thinking about how they looked, nor did they watch to see who was looking at them. It didn't seem to be part of their sense of self; nobody was judging their worth according to their looks. From what I could see, a woman in Yanomama land was just a person. She did not care if her hair was fixed right or anything along those lines. And that was a pleasure, at least for me.

By the same token, the men by and large were not macho. They weren't constantly competing with each other. They were not confrontational. They were not interested in establishing pecking orders. Their masculinity didn't depend on it. In the evening men and women both would put flowers or arrow cane in their ears and decorate themselves. So maybe they were not completely devoid of vanity. But it was minimal. It did not play a significant role in their lives. Fat, thin, beautiful, ugly, they were people, and they considered themselves people. They accepted themselves. In fact, it never occurred to them not to accept themselves as just fine the way they were. I found that immensely attractive. Though skills in hunting and shamanism were valued, still every person was on the same level as every other one. There were no traces of superiority, no status consciousness, no class consciousness, no feeling among some that they were important while others weren't. This appealed to something in my own makeup, magnified perhaps by the fact that I was a refugee from the academic world, with its strict hierarchies and many of the people in its upper reaches just brimming over with self-importance. Here, by contrast, human relations were simple and down-to-earth. You talked to men, you talked to women, and there were no walls, no consciousness about how they were projecting themselves, how they were being perceived, and what that might mean for their futures. It took me a while to realize that what I was seeing was equality, a basic egalitarian view of life and other people—equality not as principle or belief, but wholly spontaneous. It was deeply ingrained in them, and it radiated through their culture.

When I first arrived in Hasupuweteri the Indians had seemed bizarre, foreign creatures. The very sight of them was exotic, with their pierced lips, nose sticks, earplugs, and body paint. But the longer I stayed and the better I learned to speak Yanomama, the more normal they became to me. Gradually the language wasn't so grating, and they weren't so strange-looking. As everything became more or less commonplace, I began to think, Well, these people are just like us. They've got different conditions here, different habits, a different culture. But they are just people. I began to perceive aspects of their personalities, aspects of their emotional lives, that I had missed earlier. And I began to know them. They were frightened and apprehensive. They worried and got angry. They laughed and were happy. Maybe different things set us off, maybe we showed our feelings and expressed ourselves differently, but underneath we were the same.

There were no sudden revelations, but it slowly grew on me that I was simply living with others of my kind. And others, moreover, whose way of life may have been basic but also had a profound dignity to it. I liked the way the families interacted, the way they cared for their children and were always together with them, always loving them and nurturing them. I liked their respect for one another. I liked the sentiments and their unashamed ways of showing them.

And I liked the basic, practical nature of their existence and the quality that gave to the way they lived. The first thing that comes to a Yanomama's mind when he or she wakes up, every morning, every day of their lives, is, What am I going to eat today, and how am I going to get it? They hunt and gather each and every day, and it's in the course of these activities that they live their lives. The women go out together in groups. As they go out, they carry the babies and talk and laugh. Out in the forest, some sit down and stay with the babies, having a good social time, while others go off to find fruits and berries; eventually they exchange roles. If it's cool, they'll build a little fire to keep warm and keep the bugs away. It's like a picnic, yet it's their work.

When they return to the *shapono* they stop by the stream to wash off the fruit and clean a frog or snake they might have caught. When they finish that and pack their catch in leaves, they bathe themselves and their babies. They might put flowers in their ears before they go home. There they get the fire going, cook the food, and distribute it to their husbands and children. In the evening they might leave the youngsters with the grandmothers and go out to chop firewood near the gardens. Then they come home with their load of firewood in time for the nighttime activities to begin.

As the community goes to bed there might be a speech from someone, or maybe two or three speeches. People chat while they listen, children laugh, somebody chops wood. Others doze off. It's all part of nighttime in the house. It's the ambience of the *shapono*. Later one of the shamans might wake up and feel like chanting. He'll take his drugs and start a little chant that might go on for an hour or so. The Hasupuweteri enjoy that. It's nice. You wake up to the chant, then fall back asleep to its sound. Or maybe you'll stay up to listen. Then the chanter will go back to sleep. In the morning as people awaken, someone else might want to make a speech, but most often not. People get up, and the day begins. They go about their business again, some go hunting, some fishing, some gathering, some stay home or go to the garden. Yanomama life goes on and on in its daily pattern. They're happy, much happier, I think, than anybody in our society—rich or poor. Despite everything, despite the diseases, the raids, the anger and fights, at bottom they are a happy people living in a harmonious society.

The more I understood the integrated nature of Yanomama life, the more I began to view the food consumption data I was getting as inadequate, or at least incomplete. In another few months my time here would be up, but I began to see that going back and writing up the measurements would just not tell the right story. Measuring the animals and calculating the yields was insufficient. Food gathering and intake had to be placed in the cultural context. There were open questions about the Yanomama's perceptions of hunting, what role it played in their lives, what meat and meat eating meant for them, what the relationship was between their biological need for meat and protein and their cultural need, what significance meat distribution had for the cohesion of the village. I could see that cultural needs could be powerful, even overpowering in terms of what they considered acceptable levels of consumption.

I was flirting with heresy, I knew. Cultural materialists—and I considered myself one—hold the underlying belief that the biological requirements of survival provide the core structure of a people's life and that those needs strongly influence all the other aspects. Their impact radiates into the other areas—out to and including supernatural perceptions. The biological requirements are the causal priorities. The demands of survival: food, shelter, sex, companionship—you must meet those needs, you must do whatever is necessary to meet those needs. Other aspects of culture will be affected by how you go about meeting those needs with the resources the environment makes available. Putting it bluntly, how you make your living—how you survive—is more likely to mold your conceptual world, not vice versa.

Yet when one looked carefully at the Yanomama, monocausal explanations tended not to give a complete picture. Even their trekking was not attributable simply to one cause. Their gardens did run out of plantains, and they did need to go in search of food, but that was not the only reason for a trek. Because if they did not run out of plantains, they would have other problems. They would deplete the wild foods that are an important supplement to the plantains. They would deplete the game, they would deplete the firewood. And other things would happen. If they lived too long in a *shapono*, the environs got dirty. The forest in the immediate vicinity became burdened with excrement. The toilet etiquette was to move off a certain distance from the *shapono*, but it didn't always work that way. People got sick with diarrhea, children didn't go that far, at night nobody went that far. And the house itself got dirty, littered with scraps of wood and other trash.

During the month or several months that the village was on trek, the house got cleaned up. The ants and termites came in and cleaned out the garbage. The dung beetles cleaned out the excrement. Game began to return to the area, and the wild edible plants made a comeback. The *shapono* and its surroundings were restored to a large degree, renewed.

As an observer I did not see these things right away. I only began to understand them after I had lived there long enough to put together a whole series of apparently unrelated observations. So despite the fact that I had already gathered a great deal of data, at the end of fifteen months I came to believe that to do anything meaningful with it I had to understand much more about the cultural context—and that was not a short-term proposition. Also, I had spent an inordinate amount of time learning the language; I was just beginning to achieve a reasonable fluency. In a sense, all I had achieved during my stay was to acquire the background and the tools necessary to study the Yanomama. Now I found it difficult to tear myself away and impossible to consider that my work was finished.

Just as I was trying to decide whether to return or stay, something else happened that decisively tipped the balance. In talking to some of the men about other Yanomama villages, I learned that the Hasupuweteri had old friends and allies among a group of communities deep in the interior that had never been contacted by outsiders. The moment I heard this I started getting excited about the idea of visiting these villages, of being the first to contact them. That prospect would have been enough by itself to get me to stay. But it wasn't just the chance of making the contact that got me excited, it was the opportunity to observe the older Yanomama interfluvial way of life. Traditionally, the Yanomama had lived away from the rivers—that was one reason they had remained so isolated. To do any kind of serious ecological study, it would be necessary to observe them in their natural habitat. My community, the Hasupuweteri, was located on the river, so to that extent they were not living in the traditional manner. But in the past they too had been an interior-dwelling community.

I knew that if I stayed in the Amazon, I would be delaying my Ph.D., and a persistent, annoying voice kept whispering, "Go back. Get the dissertation written. Get a position. Then if you want, you can get a grant and come back for more." But an even more compelling voice was telling me I'd be crazy to leave now. My understanding of the Hasupuweteri was deepening every day, and the chance to see the people of the interior drew me like a magnet. In light of these things, what rational man could care about timing?

6

I stayed. Napoleon Chagnon, of course, did not hear from me. It was almost impossible to get letters in and out—for me each letter meant a trip downriver to Platanal mission. I figured Chagnon would assume I had decided to stay longer to complete my work—eventually I'd be in touch. Anyway, after the last letter I had gotten from him it was pretty clear to me he wasn't overly concerned with my welfare. On a supply run through the rapids I had flipped the dugout and lost, among other things, part of my supply of Parke Davis Camoprim, an especially effective antimalarial that Ray Hames, Eric Fredlund, and I had all brought with us. When I wrote asking for more, Chagnon had replied that the pills were very difficult to obtain and that at present he wasn't able to get any. Even before this our relationship hadn't been a bed of roses, but with the aluminum boat episode and now the malaria pills, it was really frayed. I began to think that Chagnon had simply made up his mind that I was out to prove that Marvin Harris was right and he was wrong. And because of that I wasn't going to get a thing out of him.

Not that I gave much thought to this situation (though I wasn't happy about having run out of Camoprim). What I was focused on now that I had decided to stay was the possiblity of exploring the area between the Orinoco and the Siapa rivers, what the Yanomama called the Shukumini ke U, the River of Parakeets. Near the Brazilian border, the Siapa is a kind of geographical point of reference, an explorer's marker. I knew that Jacques Lizot had flown to the Siapa by helicopter. He had briefly visited one community on the river, then had gone upstream and stopped at a second. But the interior villages were still uncontacted. They couldn't be spotted easily by helicopter, as could those communities situated on the river. And it was not wise to spend time searching for them, for the distances involved meant that copters would have little fuel to spare. Pilots were especially cautious about that region, with good reason: if forced to land, they'd be out of luck. A downed research team would find itself in the middle of a trackless jungle with no way out except to be picked up by a backup copter—if there was money to arrange one, and if the pilot could locate the party, and if he could find a place to land. To visit the interior villages I would have to trek in, through virgin terrain.

The Hasupuweteri had relationships with these villages, known collectively as the Shamatari. They had visited on occasion in the past when they themselves lived in the interior, closer to the Siapa. So I spent time talking with my informants about these communities. Then I started testing out some of the younger, more adventurous souls—to see what their reaction might be to making this kind of journey. I didn't know if they would go so far from the village. My own desire to visit the Shamatari was intense. But they would never think of doing something like this themselves. No one walked from the Orinoco to the Siapa.

A couple of the *huya* got excited about the idea and said yes immediately. And though others were reluctant, before long I had five who were willing, a sufficient number to carry everything we would have to bring along. I would take some food with me, enough for one meal a day, and of course I would need gifts and payments for each village—fishline and hooks, machetes for the headmen, loincloths, cotton thread, and other trade items. The Shamatari consisted of twelve or thirteen communities. It wouldn't be feasible to contact all or even many of these on the first trip. But what I could do was lay out a route all the way to the Siapa. Once I had explored the area it would be easier to go back and visit the rest of them. On this initial trip we'd go to several villages that lay more or less on a direct line southward, stop at each one, rest a night, get stocked up with plantains, and also pick up new guides and information. These were substantial distances that we'd be covering in unfamiliar territory, and the Hasupuweteri would not know the trails.

The first stop would be Mokaritateri, a hard day's walk due south. The morning we were to leave I had the gear ready—all of it adding up to six heavy packs, one for each of the carriers and one for me. We were a little overloaded, but we wouldn't hit the hills until after Mokaritateri, and food consumption and gifts would lighten the packs. As we left, mothers and sisters were crying and saying good-bye, unhappy that their sons and brothers would be out for a prolonged period. But the boys themselves were enthusiastic and eager to get moving.

I started off third in line, but after twenty minutes I was last and falling farther and farther behind. They knew they had to hustle to get to Mokaritateri that same day and avoid having to sleep out in the forest, and they were moving in a steady half walk, half trot that had me breathing hard right from the start. At the rate I was going, there was no question we'd have to sleep overnight. While I was thinking about this and struggling to keep up, the lead carrier came back and took my pack from me. God, was that a relief. Okay, I thought, that pack in addition to his own will slow him down a bit, and the pace will ease up. But the extra weight didn't faze him at all. The jog trot kept up, all day long.

In the late afternoon, after nine hours of hard traveling, we broke out of the jungle into the Mokaritateri gardens, right into the middle of a small group of women who were busy picking plantains. Startled, they looked up, got one glimpse of me, and went into spasms of fear. "Don't, don't don't," they yelled. "Don't kill them! Don't kill them! Don't kill them!" crying and wailing. They were sure I had come to kill their husbands and sons.

Half-breathless from a day of trotting, I panted, "Stop, don't cry, it's okay. I didn't come to hurt you. I'm a friend. *Nohi.* I'm a friend."

At the same time the Hasupuweteri launched into the standard arrival announcement, their sharp whistles cutting through the humid air, bringing a chorus of yelps and hoots from the villagers and howls and barks from their dogs. This was really an unexpected event. As we marched into the *shapono* the Mokaritateri men stood there brandishing their bows and arrows and making an ungodly din.

Of course one look was enough to tell them something special was going on. The young men with me were carrying packs and duffels, which was striking enough by itself. And there I was in addition, in all my white-skinned, black-bearded splendor. Following the standard visitors' etiquette, we stood in the middle of the plaza gazing into the distance to avoid eye contact with any of the excited Mokaritateri men jumping around us and whooping at the top of their lungs. This loud and extremely close examination went on for five minutes or so, while I tried to imitate my traveling companions by standing very still and pretending I was fascinated by something in the trees beyond the *shapono*. But I couldn't keep from glancing around every once in a while. Everyone seemed to be either hooting or staring or doing both at once, giving me an amazing variety of ogles and gazes and gapes and gawks. Even when the noise finally subsided, the stares followed me to the hammock that one of the Mokaritateri men finally invited me to lie down in. The whole village watched spellbound as I accepted the boiled *ohina* root and the gourdful of ripened plantain drink he offered.

At first they just stared, dumbfounded. But after a while they began to come over to squat around my hammock. Once they got beyond the initial shock they wanted to touch and see everything I had with me. What fascinated them most was my tape recorder. Hearing the Venezuelan popular music cassette I had brought along, they became still, listening in awe and wonder. But I made a mistake by recording them on the sly, then letting them hear their own voices. The whole group squatting around me backed off quickly amid frightened exclamations. It's one thing to hear strange voices and music coming out of a little black box. It's something altogether different when suddenly your own voice is inside the box. To a Yanomama who doesn't have the vaguest idea what the little box might be, hearing his own voice come out is a shock, a dramatic shock. The fright of it is enough to kill him. And it might kill him, because the Yanomama are quite capable of dying from fear. They got white and pale and shaky, and more than a little angry. I immediately regretted that I had given in to the temptation to observe their reactions to hearing their own voices.

Over the next few days I studied the Mokaritateri gardens and worked with informants to gather genealogies and other family and historical data. One woman who was especially helpful was named Roobemi. About twenty-five years old, she worked in her father's garden picking cotton while I asked her about the details of the Mokaritateri kinship organization and the relationships between her village and their neighbors. Roobemi had been especially happy to see us, since she had classificatory mothers and brothers (what we would call aunts and cousins) in Hasupuweteri. She seemed completely unafraid, and while she talked her toddler played happily at her feet.

What I wanted most was information about the village of Hawaroweteri, our next destination. Like the Mokaritateri, the Hawaroweteri had never been contacted. And they were farther inland, which meant their knowledge of the outside world was even scantier. They would also be crucial for information about the other Shamatari villages and for guides to lead us toward the Siapa.

But I soon found that our hosts weren't eager to talk about the Hawaroweteri. I had already ascertained that the two villages weren't at war. But the immediate response to my questions was evasive. The Hawaroweteri, said the old women I was talking to, were not at their house. "They're on a trek, way over in that direction. You won't find them, they're not there, don't even waste your time."

I said, "Look, it doesn't matter. If they're over there, we can go in that direction, too. It doesn't matter to us. We can find them there."

I knew the women were lying, that what they were saying had only one purpose: to keep us in their village. The longer we stayed, the more trade goods they could get from us. When I said, "No, we're going to go anyway; we'll find them," they escalated their effort.

"Look," they said, not to me now, but to my carriers, "don't go in that direction. There are *shawara* over there, dangerous spirits, evil spirits living in the forest. Malevolent shamans live there. They'll blow poisonous substances on you. They'll make evil magic on you. You'll get sick and die. Don't go into that part of the forest. It's an evil place. Stay here."

I sat in my hammock and watched. The Hasupuweteri, most of them still in their teens, were squatting and staring at the ground. Their eyes seemed to have glazed over; the treatment the Mokaritateri were giving them was having exactly the desired effect. Searching for a strategy, I jumped in and told them in forceful language that whether there were evil spirits there or not didn't matter. They were traveling with me, and they were under my protection. The spirits—the *hekura*—would not come near us. But my companions kept staring, and I could see the heart just dissolving out of them. Each had made a commitment to go with me all the way, but they hadn't counted on evil spirits and malevolent shamans. They were wavering, they weren't sure they wanted to risk it. And as the Mokaritateri women kept it up, I began to hear mumbles from one about his foot being sore, from another about how he was suffering from stomach pains, from a third about how he missed his relatives. I could see the whole expedition aborting right here unless I did something drastic.

So I began to get angry and told them emphatically, "Don't listen to these women. The spirits are not going to touch you. They're not going to bother you. They're afraid of me, and they can't touch you. The spirits cannot hurt a *nabuh*." That had a healthful effect, because even the Hasupuweteri were unsure of my powers, let alone the Mokaritateri. If I had just suddenly flown straight up into the sky, they would have been surprised, but it wouldn't have come as an utter shock to them. They don't know about *nabuh,* about what they can do. They know *nabuh* have incredible powers. And even though they recognize that it's the technology, still they're unsure of what *nabuh* themselves are capable of.

Even after a year and a half of living with the Hasupuweteri, with all the friendship and understanding we had developed, I was still not clear to what extent they even considered me a human being. They would still ask questions that you wouldn't ask a fellow human.

"Are you going to die sometime?" they would say.

"Yes, sometime."

"Would you die if an arrow hit you?"

That one I had to think about. If I said no, maybe they would think, Okay, let's shoot him, he's not going to die anyway. Or if I said yes and they knew I was as vulnerable as they were, they might at some point get upset with me about something and shoot me. So I said, "Well, maybe, maybe not. It would depend on where it hit me. But I wouldn't die right away under any circumstances. Even if there were two arrows sticking in me, I'd still have time to shoot my gun, boom." Of course I knew that 99 percent of them would never wish me any harm, but there were a couple of wild and aggressive teenagers I wouldn't trust very far. The point was that they just weren't sure about this alien creature who was living with them. They were used to my presence by now, but they still had no idea what the real truth about me might be.

When I told my young carriers that they had promised to make this trip, that I wanted them to do as they promised, that no evil would touch them—all in the strongest, most vehement language I could muster—it made the right impact. Up till now I had made it a point never to interject myself into the Indians' beliefs or even into their personal exchanges and interactions. Within the bounds of my life with them as a participant-observer, to the best of my ability I had remained the detached scientist. But I had spent weeks planning this trip and putting it together, preparing all the equipment and supplies, then hiking through the jungle to meet these totally isolated people. Here I was, smack in the middle of the most exciting experience that could happen to an anthropologist, and right at this point some old women were about to break up my expedition—all because they wanted me to stay in their village to give them fishhooks. Nuts to that, I thought. I wasn't going to allow it to happen. "We are going on this trip," I told the carriers. "Just forget the evil spirits. If they show up, I'll take care of them."

The women, though, were not about to give up, and they redoubled their chorus about the shamans and spirits and magical substances that were sure to sicken us all. With that I turned on them and shouted loudly enough to be heard above the din, putting to use all the excellent lessons in Yanomama invective I had learned in the *shapono, "Weti tehe wamaki shami horemou batayoma ke wani?"* ("What are you talking about, you lying old women? What are you trying to scare these young men for? All you want is our trade goods. So be quiet and stop telling them about evil spirts and shamans. I don't want to hear any more about that. Do you understand what I'm saying? Just don't say these things anymore. The spirits aren't going to hurt anyone!")

And that seemed to put an end to the argument.

Just as we were packing up to continue on, one of my carriers came up and introduced a young man of the village. It turned out that he was originally from Nanimabuweteri, the Siapa River community that was my ultimate destination. In fact, his father was headman of the Nanimabuweteri. He had married a Mokaritateri woman and was living in her village, but he told me he would be happy to come with us and be our guide. Two other Mokaritateri were also eager to come along as guides and carriers. They hadn't been impressed with the malevolent shaman talk either. They knew the Hawaroweteri well and could lead us right there. It would take, they said, two days.

We left the next morning at dawn, walking at the usual breakneck pace. For eight or nine straight hours our little file jog-trotted through the brush, stopping only to drink water and to shoot a curassow for dinner. By now we were in the hills. A little surprised, I realized that I felt good. I had no pack myself, and I finally seemed to have gotten in shape for this kind of thing. I wasn't breathing in those lung-bursting rasps anymore, and even though we were going uphill now, the air was cooler and more comfortable, easier to breathe. The Indians didn't attempt to go around any of the hills. They cut right across them, their tough, spindly legs never stopping or slowing down despite the extra weight they were carrying.

That night we slept in the jungle, stripping the inner bark of some *nari nati* trees to make hammocks. The curassow and manioc were our dinner, along with some rice and bouillon cubes I took out of my foodstuffs. The next day at dawn we were off and running again, still heading uphill.

Early in the afternoon of the second day we came to a small, crystal-clear stream. On the other side a well-beaten trail led up a hillock, the first really defined trail I had seen since we came into the Mokaritateri gardens. "Let's bathe here," said the Nanimabuweteri guide. "This is the last water before the Hawaroweteri *shapono*. We're very close now." Taking off my clothes, I stepped in and let the pure, cool water wash away the dirt and sweat of two days' hard travel, watching as the Indians splashed and swam, obviously enjoying themselves every bit as much as I was.

Twenty minutes later we came to the Hawaroweteri gardens. *Ocumo* roots, avocado trees, and sugar cane grew here in abundance, in addition to the usual plantain and banana trees. It looked beautiful, but the fruit were small and immature. There was no sign of recent activity. When the Indians whistled, no answer came from the *shapono*. As we left the garden and continued on toward the house, I could hear my guides mumbling angrily. I couldn't make out what they were saying from my place in the line, but it was no great mystery. Apparently the Hawaroweteri really weren't at home.

The *shapono* was beautifully made and almost perfectly circular, unlike some of the Yanomama houses. But it was indeed empty, and my carriers weren't happy. Walking around the circumference,

I shared their feelings. Traveling in the Amazon jungle is exhausting. All day you deal with the rough terrain, the undergrowth, the humidity, the insects. You have to drive yourself to do it. And you do drive yourself, because you badly want to get to the next village before night, so you will have food, companionship, somewhere to sleep. All day long you look forward to a good meal and a hammock and the excitement of a visit. To finally reach your destination and find it deserted is a great frustration. To me it was also a severe disappointment, since I was eager to make first contact with these people and to arrange for future visits.

Thinking that the Hawaroweteri might possibly be camped nearby, my lead guide and I went off down the southward trail to see if we could find fresh tracks. In the meantime the others went back to the garden to try to locate anything edible. A little way outside the village we did find prints, but they were several days old, not worth following up. By the time we got back to the *shapono*, the others were also back. There was little to be had, a few plantains and some tubers, hardly enough for nine men who hadn't eaten all day long—the lack of food was not particularly surprising since the reason people go off on treks is that they have nothing left to eat. A few of the boys were so angry that they began slashing at the *shapono* roof and hacking down some of the avocado trees. I knew that could mean trouble once the Hawaroweteri got back, and they could get violent. I would have to compensate them if we ever met up with them.

We spent that night in the empty *shapono* on the top of its high hill. We felt cool, even cold, unlike anything I had experienced down on the Orinoco. It was a beautiful sight from up there. Looking south through the limpid late-afternoon air, I could see the mountain chain that stretched itself out toward the south—the Sierra Unturan, the great Surukuru. From our hill the jungle flowed out in all directions like an ocean, an infinite expanse of green that merged with the far horizon whichever way you looked. That night I fell asleep quickly, hungry but exhausted from the hiking. Sleep overtook me so fast that I forgot to hang my glasses up on the *shapono* and instead left them on the ground under my hammock. When I woke up next morning the glasses were there, but the nylon safety strap was gone, eaten by a swarm of termites.

We left the *shapono* early, without any breakfast. An hour or so out, our Nanimabuweteri guide, who was supposedly taking us to his father's village, led us off the trail and started cutting through the forest. By cutting through, he said, we would hit another trail, the one that we wanted. But we didn't hit it, and after another hour he admitted he was lost. While he ran off to locate the new trail, we waited, squatting in the jungle and slapping at the swarms of sweat bees and mosquitoes that assaulted us. A half hour passed, then an hour, then two hours, but the Nanimabuweteri didn't come back. Finally we doubled back to the empty *shapono*, where we set up camp again. At nightfall he returned with the bad news: he had not been able to find the trail.

That night I used the last of my rice, bouillon cubes, and manioc flour. That and some peach palm fruit the Indians had found made our dinner. Again we went to sleep hungry on the cold hilltop. I had on my T-shirt and was wrapped in a light blanket; the Indians, as always, slept naked. As we dozed off, I heard my lead Hasupuweteri guide lying in the next hammock say to no one in particular, "These Hawaroweteri must use an awful lot of firewood."

The next morning the Nanimabuweteri managed to locate the trail. It was another day through the forest dense with ferns and lianas and cut by pure streams coursing along jumbled formations of smooth rocks. I knew I was walking ground where no one other than the Yanomama had ever set foot. And then we lost the trail again and had to cut through forest, places where not even they had been (it was clear our guide had not been to see his father in quite some time). Watching the Indians cut new trail through the jungle, I marveled at their efficiency. There was none of the energetic hacking and slashing you see in jungle movies (and among amateurs in the real jungle), just quick, deft flicks of their machetes that they could keep up all day.

The expedition turned grueling. We were hungry and tired and lost—we knew how to double back and find our way out, but we didn't know how to get to our destination. My companions didn't seem worried about this, but I became concerned that at some point they would give up and want to go home. In fact, that might have been the rational thing to do, but I didn't want to lose this whole trip and the opportunity to mark out territory for the next one.

We camped in the jungle two more nights, making temporary shelters and dining on whatever fruit we could find. But on the third day we came across an old trail. At least according to my Nanimabuweteri guide it was a trail; to an untrained eye it looked indistinguishable from the rest of the jungle. From the Hawaroweteri village up on that beautiful high rise, the walking had been mostly downhill. The rise was a kind of watershed that we had ascended to from the Orinoco. Now this trail was taking us down into the valley of the River of Parakeets. But going downhill all day proved a lot harder than walking uphill. It meant holding your weight against gravity for long periods of time, and the balance and muscle use was different. My knees began to ache badly.

But a sense of anticipation began to take hold: we were on the right trail at last and heading toward the village of Nanimabuweteri. As we walked the excitement grew. We slept in the forest one more night, and then, on the final day's walk, the rains broke. It rained torrents, an unbelievable quantity of water sheeting out of the sky that soon transformed our downhill trail into a stream that roiled around our ankles. At the beginning it wasn't so bad; we could still keep our balance because the earth underneath was packed and hard. But as time when on the trail bed began to soften, and the ground turned to mud. Even the Indians were sliding down and struggling to get up, although they were barefoot and could keep their grip a lot better than I could with my Vietnam jungle boots. Every few steps I fell and slid around in a river of muck.

Right in the middle of this we ran smack into an old plantain garden, which was among the least pleasant things that could have happened. In the jungle the tall trees ordinarily provide a canopy that prevents sun from coming through and inhibits the growth of vegetation on the forest floor. But in a garden the trees have been cut down. In an old garden that has not been tended and kept clear, a profuse secondary growth takes over—thick, dense, thorny scrub that is impossible to walk through or even cut through. In addition, such places become favorite habitats for poisonous snakes. So now as the rain was beating down we found ourselves on our hands and knees crawling along twisting vegetative tunnels, squirming on our bellies in the tighter places, and wrestling our packs through the viscous mire as the inch-long thorns above us tore welts along our necks and backs.

After what seemed an eternity we finally got through the garden, and by now we knew we were getting closer. I badly wanted those Nanimabuweteri to be home. If they were out on some trek, I didn't know what would happen. I knew I would be extremely disappointed and unhappy; God only knew how my companions would feel. Lost in the jungle, eating almost nothing, hacking our way through for days, caught in this violent downpour, crawling through the overgrown garden . . . I didn't even want to think about it.

By the time we got to the Siapa River the rain had stopped, and we were able to bathe and wash off the muck of our crawl through the gardens. Over the Siapa we found a Yanomama bridge—poles stuck in the river supporting vines that you could walk across, if your balance was good enough. We crossed the bridge and a few minutes later came to the Nanimabuweteri gardens, exhausted and famished. Finding ourselves in the middle of a stand of ripened sugar cane, we dropped our packs and began cutting and gorging on it. Ordinarily we would respect another person's garden. But our diet for the last three days had consisted almost entirely of an occasional fruit and several small birds. A little to my surprise, I suddenly found that when you're starving in the jungle and you see a stand of sugar cane, you don't think about how you'd like to eat some, but perhaps you shouldn't since there's no one around to ask. You do exactly as the Yanomama do. You just take what's there and think about how to pay for it after you've filled your belly.

As we entered Nanimabuweteri the pandemonium was deafening. This was easily the largest village I had ever seen and by far the loudest. By now, though, I was used to the hooting, hollering, and wide-eyed excitement, and the reception seemed familiar, even friendly. The Nanimabuweteri stared and yelled, but I just kept my eyes on the treeline and let it happen.

We stayed in Nanimabuweteri two days, enough time for me to get ID Polaroid photos of everyone and to gather the names and ages of all 155 inhabitants. I was also able to do some rough genealogical charts and to get information about the villages still farther south toward the Brazilian border. Working with several men from the village I learned who was living in that region, who was at war, and who was at peace, all of it with the idea that I would eventually come back and go even farther.

The *wayamou*—the trade chant—started the first night shortly after dark. From his hammock my lead Hasupuweteri guide started a rhythmic, insistent melody. After a moment the night was broken by dozens of sharp, high-pitched whistles—the Yanomama way of announcing that the chant had begun. Then came silence again, then the words of the chant, strange and stylized, although I soon recognized them. "What am I planning, planning to say? Don't ask me why, why have I come here. You should say you will give, give generously to me. Don't tell me no, no, I won't give you." Then from across the *shapono* in the dark came an answering voice, louder and more forceful. "Speak to me now, now make your claims." In the dark I could see a Nanimabuweteri slowly get out of his hammock and walk across the plaza toward his interlocutor, finally squatting in front of him while they both kept up the reciprocal song.

It went on all night, the chant passing from one visitor to another and from one of our hosts to another. Before long most of the community had fallen asleep, but I stayed up to listen as long as I could, recording the back and forth of requests and responses and trying hard to understand the metaphoric language.

"Give me a white woman," said one, though what he meant was a machete.

"No, she's too modest," came the answer, meaning that the machete chose not to show itself.

Among the Yanomama, I knew, a visit is never just a visit, even such a sudden and unusual visit as ours. Regardless of whether the formal reason is a funeral or a feast or just a stopover on a longer trip, trade is always involved. You don't just go to visit, and you never come away without trade items of one sort or another, which will be reciprocated later.

This is the typical pattern, the delayed trade, which underlies the relationships among communities. Commonly, the visitors will be given a pot, a machete, and an ax or some equivalents. In return they will promise a dog that is about to be born in their village— to be given at a later date when the visit is reciprocated. This kind of arrangement leads to repeated visits and an ongoing relationship. But it can also result in trouble, and it often does. When the return visit is made, the puppy may have died or may have been given to someone else. Or even worse, perhaps the owner just doesn't want to let it go. That's when problems develop. The original hosts are angered. They gave the pot, machete, and ax—the others reneged. It can be the occasion for a raid and the beginning of years of hostility.

The trade chant, the *wayamou,* went on through the entire night, from just after dark until just before dawn. Finally, just as the sky began to lighten, the Nanimabuweteri headman got out of his hammock and spoke. "That is enough," he said. "We have spoken long. You have taken this into your ears. That's enough, that's enough, that's all." And with that the whistles broke the air again, as they had when the chant began.

The next day my carriers stayed in their hammocks, sleeping and talking with their hosts. While they kept the low profile expected of visitors, I went out with the headman to examine the Nanima-buweteri gardens. With him I did a rough genealogy of the village, then we talked about the other interior-dwelling Shamatari communities, where they were, and how one might get to them. He wanted me to come back, the headman said, an invitation I had learned to expect once a village realized that I posed no danger. I told him I would. I would definitely come back and visit them on my next trip to the Siapa.

"Good," he said, "and since I am very poor, when you come back, be sure to bring me another machete and a pot."

"Yes," I said, "I certainly will."

7

For the next four months I worked hard to complete my protein studies. Reviewing my field journals, I realized that despite the immense compilation of measurements and observations, I still could not say for sure if there was a causal link between protein capture and intervillage warfare (neither Chagnon nor Harris would be particularly pleased with that result). There was no doubt in my mind that protein was the most critical of a number of limiting factors in Yanomama diet and that it had a direct relationship with village sedentariness and nomadism, with settlement patterns, and even with social instability within the village. But the causal link with warfare was elusive, and that was the burning issue. Once I got back I would do an in-depth analysis of my data; maybe that would turn up something more on the problem. But I strongly suspected I would need substantial additional fieldwork to make a persuasive case one way or the other. Although I was eager to keep up the momentum of my work, I knew it would have to wait. Very soon I would have to leave. I had made several more treks and had contacted more villages. But I had been in the jungle now for more than two straight years, and I was tired. Already I was nine months overdue, nine months in which I had had no contact with the United States. Ray and Eric, my colleagues, were long gone from the Amazon, probably well into their dissertations by now.

I didn't regret my delay for a minute. Now I spoke the language, and I was part of the community, not in the way a Yanomama from another village might have blended in, but in the sense that the Hasupuweteri had come to accept my presence. I had made the transition from being an alien creature to being a fixture in their daily lives.

The Hasupuweteri still had no concept of why I was there, why I had chosen to live with them rather than with my own people. Nor did they have any real curiosity about it. They weren't introspective about their own lives and weren't inclined to question mine on anything more than a surface level. My conduct had been an engrossing novelty for a while, but the reasons for my activities didn't interest them. Even my writing, which I worked at for hours each day, didn't pique their curiosity. They thought only that I was drawing. *"Shertayai!"* they'd exclaim, wondering at my persistence in making little squiggles. "You certainly do like to draw. Let me draw a little." The Yanomama have no idea of letters and words. They didn't think my drawing meant anything, so it never occurred to them to ask about it. They didn't think, That *means* something, what he's doing has a *significance*. They thought, He's making designs; he likes to make designs; we can make designs, too. Then they'd show me. Although they had never held a pen before, they would take mine and draw something—as likely as not right over my page of notes.

They accepted me. That was the only way I could say they had changed in the two years I lived there. My change was more dramatic. As time passed I saw myself becoming less detached, more involved in the community's social and emotional life. I was not exactly a participant, yet I was no longer the detached observer, either. I was developing a stake in the Hasupuweteri, not merely as subjects for observation and analysis, but as fellow beings whose actions and interactions involved me whether I wanted them to or not. The transition was slow, something I hardly noticed until some event would bring me face to face with it.

Several weeks after my return from the Siapa a lone woman

100

walked into the *shapono*. She had obviously walked a long distance and was exhausted. To my surprise and delight I recognized her as Roobemi, the Mokaritateri woman who had been helpful to me during my visit there. It was a stroke of absolute luck that she had come. The genealogy I had collected in Mokaritateri was incomplete, and I had been thinking about making a return visit to fill it in. And now the friendliest, most informative person I had met there had suddenly shown up in Hasupuweteri. According to my friends, Roobemi had *shuwahi kobema*—run away from her husband—and had come to Hasupuweteri because she had relatives here who would feed her and protect her from him.

Later on I was taking a nap in the heat of a drowsy afternoon when the sounds of shouting and scuffling awoke me. They came from outside the *shapono*'s eastern wall. Looking around, I saw that only a few women and children were at home. As hot as it was, most of the people were either in the gardens or out in the forest. One young mother was holding her infant son who had been sick for a long time and looked as though he were near death. Two older women roasted plantains while a third sat on the ground weaving a basket. The children played in the central plaza. None of them paid any attention to the disturbance. Walking across the plaza toward the noise, I asked a young boy what was happening. "Nothing," he said. "The men are only clearing away a big tree."

By the time I got to the other side of the house, the sounds were more grunts than shouts. Crawling through the little opening there, I saw what seemed to be two groups of Indians having a tug-of-war. But instead of pulling on a thick vine, they were pulling on a person, a woman half slouched over between them. One group had hold of her left arm, the other was pulling on her right, and the woman was being yanked first in one direction, then in the other. Coming closer, I saw that the object of this contest was Roobemi. Her assailants on one side were three of the wilder teenagers. Trying to pull her away from them were three elderly women who despite their age were still sinewy and strong and seemed to be holding their own. The grunts were coming from the opposing groups. Roobemi said nothing. Her head rolled on her shoulders, and she moaned as they jerked her back and forth. She was not even trying to pull herself free.

My first thought was that Roobemi's husband had come from Mokaritateri to get her back and that he had had the three young men grab her and bring her to him in the jungle. I knew that in situations like these, confrontations might develop between the husband and the wife's relatives, and that it could end in a clubfight or even a killing. Probably the husband was trying to get her back without a personal encounter.

The tug-of-war went on for ten minutes or so while I watched, my blood rising as instinct told me to put a stop to it. The boys would drag Roobemi a few yards, then the old ladies would get a better purchase and drag her back as she struggled to keep her balance, her head tossing limply this way and that. Then I noticed Yokami, one of the Hasupuweteri women, coming down the trail from the gardens carrying her daughter on her hip.

"Sister-in-law, what are they doing to her?" I asked.

"Oh," she said, smiling at me, "they're taking her out into the forest."

"What for?"

"They're going to rape her," came the answer, as casually as if she had said, "They're going to have a picnic."

Just then another teenager who had been watching this scene from a little way off ran in to help his friends and began yanking Roobemi violently by the arm. Jerked forward, she stumbled, and her right foot wedged itself under a log. She fought to get it out but couldn't, especially since neither side paid any attention to her plight.

By now Roobemi was screaming in pain, her arms stretched out on either side and her right leg extended straight out to where her foot was jammed under the tree. With a concerted heave, the teenagers pulled her free, not just from the log, but from the grasp of the old ladies. Howling in victory, they ran down the trail, yanking her along. As they ran they were joined by more shouting teenagers who suddenly appeared out of nowhere.

I followed behind as the stampede bore her into the jungle. I could see Roobemi turn her head to see who was yelling and screaming behind her, and for a moment our eyes met and held. Her expression was not one of terror or pain, but of resignation, as if she were a victim on her way to the sacrificial altar, condemned but not yet executed. Her eyes seemed to say, "Not you, too." Then, lurching and stumbling, she was pulled into the bushes.

I stood there, my heart pounding. I had no doubt I could scare these kids away. They were half-afraid of me anyway, and if I picked up a stick and gave a good loud, threatening yell, they'd scatter like the wind. On the other hand, I was an anthropologist, not a policeman. I wasn't supposed to take sides and make value judgments and direct their behavior. This kind of thing went on. If a woman left her village and showed up somewhere else unattached, chances were she'd be raped. She knew it, they knew it. It was expected behavior. What was I supposed to do, I thought, try to inject my own standards of morality? I hadn't come down here to change these people or because I thought I'd love everything they did; I'd come to study them.

So why was I standing there shaking with anger? Why was I thinking, Come on, Ken, what's wrong with you? Are you going to stand around with your notebook in your hand and observe a gang rape in the name of anthropological science?

As I stood there the sounds of scuffling in the undergrowth got softer and more distant. At my side a little boy materialized— Amotawe, my classificatory nephew. He seemed to sense my indecision. "Don't go out there, *shoabe,*" he said.

"Why not?" I asked him.

"Because they are 'eating her vagina,' they are copulating with her. Come back and play with us."

I went back. Inside the *shapono,* the older women sat around the young mother who was holding her sick infant; she was moaning softly now. Through the far gate I could see other women coming back from the gardens, their tumpline baskets loaded with a hundred pounds of plantains each. (I had weighed those baskets many times. It was no surprise the three old ladies had held their own so long in a tug-of-war against the teenagers.) As they dropped the baskets, the sounds of their talk and laughter filled the enclosure. "*Fou,*" one of them called to me, "come over here and do a dance for us." More laughter. They were teasing me; I hadn't danced for them in ages. I looked back down the trail, and a hundred yards away I saw the little knot of young men standing in the undergrowth, obviously waiting their turn with Roobemi. Two teenagers were already walking back toward the *shapono.*

"You dirty, filthy ones," a woman shouted at them. It was one of Roobemi's classificatory mothers, really angry. "You and your filthy penises. If I had been there, you never would have gotten away with this."

As I walked back to my hearth I noticed that Yarima's brother had returned from hunting and that Yarima and her mother were also coming back from the forest carrying two baskets full of peach palm fruit. I squatted down next to Red's hammock. "How can they do that?" I said, jerking my thumb toward the teenagers on the trail.

"It's just those *huya, shori*," he answered. "That's the way they behave, they always want sex. Don't worry about it."

Lying in my hammock, I was sorry I hadn't put a stop to it. It was my damn concept of myself as an anthropological observer. How could I live with a group of human beings and not be involved with them as a fellow human being? Was it wrong for me to have struck up a friendly relationship with Roobemi back in Mokari-tateri? Should I have asked my questions as a kind of robot census taker and then been on my way? On the other hand, didn't good cultural and behavioral documentation depend on establishing close relationships, getting to know the people well? And once you were close to them, were you just supposed to turn your back if they needed your help? That's what I had done just now, and I didn't like the feeling at all. What could I expect from Roobemi after this—a deep, informative commentary on the Yanomama woman's cultural experience of rape, which I could then publish in the *American Ethnologist?* And what about my "nephew" Amotawe or the beautiful little Yarima, for whom I felt such affection? How would I treat them if they were in trouble—would I just document that, too?

That afternoon left a deep mark on me; it was a watershed, a turning point in my integration into the community. I knew that for a fact about a month later when Hasupuweteri was the scene of another woman-dragging episode. The woman was Kreosimi, a young wife from Ashitoweteri, a community to the south. She had been stolen from her husband by one of the Hasupuweteri men. One morning the angry husband showed up in our *shapono* just as the women were leaving for the garden. He grabbed Kreosimi and dragged her up the trail, but when Kreosimi's abductor saw what was happening, he grabbed hold of her other arm. Kreosimi had been sick with malaria the past few days and looked half-dead as the men pulled her back and forth. If this had happened somewhere else in the world, the husband might have shot the lover or vice versa, then the survivor would have claimed his prize. But not in Yanomama land. The men were from allied villages, they weren't about to start shooting each other, at least not yet. Instead they fought over Kreosimi, dragging her first one way, then the other.

The two men were more or less the same size and equal in strength, and both were determined. The tug-of-war went on and on. As sick as Kreosimi was, she began to whimper for one of them to take her, just take her. She didn't care which one, as long as the torture stopped.

After half an hour of this scuffling around in the *shapono,* one of the other men got fed up with the noise and got out of his hammock. It was Takawe, a middle-aged man with two wives of his own (unusual, though not unheard of among the mainly monogamous Yanomama). "That's enough," he said, picking up his arrows. "This is really annoying. I'm going to stab her, that will put a stop to it." I watched as he walked up to the three of them with his arrows. He was really going to do it.

When I saw this I yelled, "Ma, *shori, tadiha!*" ("Don't do that!") Takawe stopped and looked around, surprised. Our eyes met, then he walked back to his hammock and put down his arrows. The words had come out of my mouth without any forethought. The instant they did, I knew that I was not the same detached observer I had been before.

On April 5, 1977, the Hasupuweteri left for a trek. They had been thinking about doing this for a while, and they needed to go, the gardens were running out of plantains again. This time I did not go with them. Instead I took six carriers and left for Hawaroweteri and Yehiopateri, another major trek down to the Siapa River, but farther to the southwest. On the return trip I could stop at Mokaritateri to complete the genealogical work I had started.

On the way back my carriers and I met up with the Hasupuweteri on their trek. It was, I knew, possibly the last time I would see them. My studies were as complete as I could make them, at least to the extent that I felt sure I had some knowledge of the cultural context of their food consumption patterns. Beyond that, I had a wealth of notes and tapes on other aspects of Yanomama life. I had been in the jungle for more than two years straight. It was time to get back.

From the Hasupuweteri trek camp I took my carriers and went back to my house by the *shapono.* That night we all slept in the old place, and the next day I distributed the trade goods I had promised them. I knew how badly they wanted to get back to the community, especially after having been out traveling so long. When they left, each one carried a load of gifts on his back—everything I owned that I didn't intend to take downriver with me.

When I thought about how much I was taking with me, and that

I would have to bring it all down to the river, I began to wish I hadn't let them go so quickly. There were a huge number of things up there, the accumulation of two years. Even with carriers it would have taken several hours. As it was, I would have to do all the carrying myself—maybe twenty-five trips a third of a mile up and down the hill to the riverbank.

I started early in the morning, and by five in the evening I had the last of my packs on the riverbank, ready to load into the boat the next day. Exhausted, I sat down on a rock alongside the water. It was getting dark, and in the Amazon night falls quickly. On the river there is some reflection, and you can see a little longer. But the forest is pitch dark, and I was worried about getting back to my house, especially since I didn't have a flashlight with me.

When I stood up, however, my legs suddenly gave way, and I sat down heavily. This is ridiculous, I thought. I mean, I've been tired before, but this is something else. I tried again, and though my legs felt like rubber, I forced myself back up the bank and to my house, barely able to stay on my feet.

That night it hit me. I began to burn with fever and shake violently. Malaria. That night and the next and the next and the next it enveloped me, the scalding fever, the uncontrollable shaking, a constant headache that felt as if it were blowing my eyes out of their sockets. For fifteen or twenty minutes at a time I'd doze off, then I'd wake to the same explosive pain. In moments of lucidity I rummaged through some supplies and found an old liquid painkiller. It worked for a while, giving me a brief but precious respite. I tried to eat some crackers, and when the fever dropped sporadically and the pain lessened, I'd make an attempt at packing some more of my things. But then the exhaustion would strike with a vengeance, and I would collapse again into my hammock. I wondered if I was going to die. I knew that Lizot had been so sick once, his villagers had carried him out of his house and down to the mission. I thought vaguely about the Hasupuweteri, off in the jungle somewhere. There was no one to carry me out. But it hardly seemed important. Most of the time I seemed to be floating in a void.

It took nine days before I felt well enough to think about leaving. Looking at the days crossed off on my calendar, I saw that it was now April 27. That morning, I slowly and gingerly gathered myself up and walked down to the river. As best I could I piled my things into the canoe. I knew that by rights I should be staying in my hammock and resting, but I was desperate to get out. I knew that if I stayed in the hammock and recovered, that would be fine, but if I had a relapse and the malaria got worse, I could be dead. If I was downriver when it came back, at least I'd stand a chance. I had to get out now, while I felt at least a little strength coursing through my veins.

When I got into the canoe and started moving, my mind sharpened. Several hours downriver I would face the Guajaribo rapids. Under ordinary circumstances I would pull the boat over to the bank and portage all my things the two hundred and fifty yards to where the rapids ended. Then I'd guide the dugout through along a side channel with a rope, getting in and motoring where the rock outcroppings forced the boat out into the stronger current. If I had two or three Yanomama along, I would be able to pull it around the outcroppings. But one man couldn't handle a heavy dugout by himself; the weight of it would pull him off the rocks and into the water, even if he were healthy and strong. On the other hand, if I had had that light aluminum boat instead of the log dugout, it would have been easy.

Chagnon was already enjoying a special place in my thoughts for not having sent the additional Camoprim tablets. Now, as I neared the rapids, I thought about him even more—him and that aluminum boat he hadn't let me have. This was going to be murderous. My dugout was so heavy the gunwales rose only four or five inches above the waterline. Even in a calm river I'd be taking water with every bump. But with no strength to portage anything, I'd have to shoot the rapids fully loaded—not just fully loaded, but carrying all the records of my life for the last two years and all the results of my studies: photos, tapes, charts, records, notecards, the whole thing. And then there was my archaeological collection, the extraordinary collection of potsherds I had found on a sandbar in the Orinoco that had been exposed during one exceptionally dry period. They were not Yanomama, though I wasn't sure exactly what they were. Arawakan, possibly, which meant they were from many, many years ago, artifacts of a tribe that had lived on the river generations earlier, the people who might have in an earlier period driven the Yanomama into the interior. I had the sherds, and as a good archaeologist I had also made slides of each one and had drawn each to scale, identifying the temper, thickness, glaze, incisions, and designs. No one had ever gathered ceramics from the Yanomama area, that I knew. Absolutely no one. It was a unique collection.

Just before I reached the rapids I pulled over to the side and managed to get my big Halliburton case full of notebooks and rolls of undeveloped film onto the shore of a long island that extended from the head of the rapids to well below the foot. I walked down the bank alongside the rapids, weak and dizzy, my head aching. I could see the water swirling and foaming where the rocks were, and I located what looked like the passages. I figured I'd go down the middle, then turn to the right, then cut back and over.

I went over and over the whole thing in my mind, imagining exactly how I would handle it. Don't think about what can happen, I told myself. Just do it. But if I don't make it, came the interior response, I'll be stranded. I'll lose everything. I'll lose the boat, the motor. I'll be finished. And no one will ever find me.

Finally, with my heart in my hands, I got into my big, long, heavy canoe. It was piled high with my baggage, and I knew full well I wouldn't have any control over the damn thing. Suddenly there I was, in it, rushing forward as white water foamed over the sides. I laid my course and made the first turn I had planned from the bank. I got through that, then cut back fast away from the rocks. If I lodged the front end on rocks, I wouldn't be able to get it off. The back would swing around, and the canoe would flip. So I cut back toward the major deadfall, the big drop of white water. I was going to hit it square in the middle. The last time I had ridden this deadfall my dugout had been slammed hard to the left, and a big wave had smashed over me and filled the boat with water. But I hadn't flipped. I had stayed with it and managed to get the boat to the embankment at the bottom of the rapids, wallowing but upright. Of course the dugout had been empty then; nobody in his right mind would run the same course loaded. But there was no choice, and besides it was a little late to be thinking this.

In the middle of the deadfall it looked as though I might get through. I was being pounded, but the boat was straight, and I could see the end of the rapids. Then it happened. In the full force of the deadfall, I couldn't tell which way to turn, and I hesitated. It seemed like only a split second, but it was enough. The momentum slowed, and the canoe turned a little to the side and lodged with the front end up on a rock. The instant it lodged I leaped from my seat to get it off. I knew if the front end stuck, the water would pull the canoe around sideways and I'd be finished. With my motor running in neutral, I clambered over the trunks and bags and duffels to the front of the canoe. Pushing off, I turned and raced for the motor before the boat could swing around. I scrambled over the load and grabbed the throttle, ready to bear down and gun it as fast as I could past the rock I had hit. I was going to make this son of a bitch, I was sure of it. I gunned and gunned and gunned—the motor screaming above the roar of the rapids. But the boat didn't move. The impact had broken the shear pin connecting the drive shaft to the propeller. I had motor, but I had no power.

Even as I realized what had happened, the boat was taken by the rapids. Down it went, bam, smashing into a rock, turning sideways, rolling, smashing again, back, then front. And then it stopped, stuck crosswise on its side between two rocks, water pouring over it, the motor still attached to the boat but completely submerged. Hanging on to the side, I watched as my trunks and bags went floating down, down, down the Orinoco, then sinking, one, then two, then another and another and another.

I watched them go without a thought in my head except how to get myself out. My potsherd collection, my tapes, my cameras, who knew what else—it all went, but it went unlamented. I hung on for my life, thinking only that I was in the middle of the biggest deadfall of white water in the most dreaded rapids on this part of the Orinoco. Maybe this was really it, maybe I had had it. I pulled myself up on the side of the boat, then let go and made a grasp for some grassy vegetation that was growing on an outcropping. I got a handful, but it didn't save me. Down I went. The current swept me with it, bounced me off one rock, then another, then ripped me through more weeds, too fast to get a grip.

Gulping for air, I looked up and saw that I was being swept along the far side of a little island that divided the river just below the rapids. Near the end of the island I lunged and managed to swim a few strokes and grab on to some branches extending from the bank. Using them, I pulled myself up onto land and lay there, absolutely still.

Once my pulse stopped racing, I was a little surprised to realize that visions had not flashed through my mind, the way they're supposed to. I hadn't thought about drowning, or about being smashed to pieces against some rock, or about being eaten by a nest of piranhas. I had been scared, but in the vaguest way. I knew I was being carried away by the rapids on the Orinoco River in the Amazon jungle, and that wasn't good. Now that I was lying on this island, it was a little better. But it still wasn't good.

After a few minutes I tried to move and found that I could sit up, even stand up. There didn't seem to be any physical damage. I walked across the island and saw that the only way to get to the long shoreside island that had my Halliburton case on it would be to jump in and swim over through the swift river current. I had just pulled myself out of the torrent, and now I was going to have to dive back in. But there was nothing to be gained from staying, so I jumped in, stretched for the bank, and made it.

There I was. As I stood wondering what might happen next, the sky opened up, heralding the start of a downpour. There was nothing on the island under which I could take shelter, but there was a platform of sorts that had been built some time ago by Inga Goetz, a wealthy German woman who lived in Caracas. Inga and her brother owned Volkswagen of Venezuela, but she was also a physician who had been coming to visit the Yanomama for the last twenty-five years. Unable to sleep in a hammock, she had had a platform built on which she could put an air mattress with a little framework around it for tarps and mosquito nets. She would visit the Yanomama, film them, help them, treat them. She'd fly very sick people out to the hospital in Caracas. She gave a scholarship to one of the Yanomama men to study nursing. She had been a true friend to the Indians.

Anyway, there was Inga's platform and a little of the framework for her tarps. I hung some leaves on what was left of the frame, using part of the fallen structure to try to rig a shelter, but I was so tired, I wasn't able to do much. I had eaten almost nothing for days and had no food with me. I sat there in the rain and wondered how I was going to get out. Nobody ever came up the river. I was weak, I was sick. I didn't know whether or not there was a trail, and if there was, the mission would have been too far for me to walk anyway.

I sat there one day, then a second day. And all that second day I kept thinking I could hear a boat coming upriver. The rapids themselves were loud—a constant roar. But over the roar I thought I could hear the whine of an outboard. Time and again I ran to the river, sure that a boat had come. But nothing was ever there—I was imagining things.

The third day passed in the same way, still no food, marooned. But I couldn't get out of my head the sound of that outboard coming up the river. I thought I must be crazy, running back and forth to the river like this. Maybe I was hearing things because I was starving to death. (But why didn't I feel hungry?) Soon maybe I'd start seeing things.

At about six P.M. on the third day I heard the motor again; the sound was absolutely unmistakable, though I knew nothing was there. To hell with it, I thought. It's getting dark, I'm not going down there again. I lay back down on the platform.

But I could still hear it, and lying there, I thought, Jesus, Ken, you don't have the luxury to disregard the slightest possibility. You've got to go. I went down to the shore again, and there on the island across the way I saw a canoe tied up on the bank. Above the canoe were two men, two acculturated Indians I knew slightly from one of my trips to the mission—malaria workers. I stared at them, and they stared back at me.

Suddenly the two of them jumped into the canoe and headed off downriver. You bastards, I thought, where the hell are you going? I started shouting, "Hey, hey, hey, come back! It's me, come back!" I knew these people and their superstitions. They could easily be thinking that I was some kind of spirit.

But the malaria workers weren't running away. They were just heading downriver so that they could avoid the rocky section between us and come up along the channel. When they did get up to where I was, they weren't all that taken aback by my situation. I was sick and emaciated, I had lost my belongings, but they weren't impressed. Out in the jungle such things happen. And though all I wanted was to get down to the mission, they insisted on spending the time to get my outboard off the swamped dugout so that I could take that back, too.

It wasn't until shortly after midnight that we finally arrived at Platanal.

8

I landed at Kennedy Airport June 1977, twenty-six months after I'd left. By the time I got back to Penn State I had blood in my eye. I was furious with Chagnon. We had had problems before I left, strains during my stay in the jungle, and now this hair-raising finale. I decided I would just show up one day in his office, walk through his door, and confront him. I would let him know point-blank exactly what I thought of him.

My plan was spoiled, though. State College is a small town with one main street, South Allen. And as I was walking down South Allen the afternoon I arrived, who came walking directly toward me but Chagnon's wife. I turned my back quickly and pretended I was looking in a store window. But she saw me right away.

"Ken," she said, "you're back! It's so wonderful! We were so worried about you."

I could barely speak. Carlene Chagnon was a lovely person, but I couldn't even muster the words to talk to her.

"My goodness," she said, "you have to come over and see Nap."

"Well," I mumbled, "I don't know, maybe."

"I understand," she said, looking at me sympathetically. "You probably don't want to see anybody for a while." She knew that sometimes people coming back from the field needed a little time to decompress.

"Yeah, probably," I answered.

"Well, anyway," she said, "you must go up and talk to Nap. He'll be in his office tomorrow morning."

The next morning when I walked into the office, Chagnon was busy typing a letter. He turned, saw me, and said, "Oh, yes, uh, Ken. Listen, let me just finish this letter if you don't mind." Very cool. The last time we had seen each other was almost two years before at Tayariteri when he had refused to give me that aluminum boat. But he had to finish his letter.

"Sure, take your time," I said. "I'll just go to the men's room."

When I came back Chagnon was done typing. "So, Ken," he said, "what are you planning to do now?"

"Well, Nap, the first thing I'm doing is breaking off with you. As far as I'm concerned any continued association with you would be detrimental to my career."

At this Chagnon stood up and moved to the other side of the desk, looking as if he thought I were going to attack him. "C'mon, Ken," he said, "what do you say we go down and have a beer?"

"If you want to talk about it more, that's fine," I told him, "but that basically sums it up for me."

In a bar near State College's bus station we talked with surprising calmness. I told him why I had not come out on schedule and what had happened to me when I tried to come out. Chagnon said that after I hadn't shown up, he sent off several letters to me (which I had never received), then had written to my family to say that if they were in touch with me, they should tell me that he assumed I had abandoned the project. There might even be legal ramifications, he had indicated. I sat there amazed. This man was my field director. If he had really believed I had disappeared, didn't he have a moral and professional responsibility to try to find me? I could have been lost in the jungle or dead. What was he doing telling my family about legal ramifications?

The problems grew more complicated. I was ready to write up my field notes as a doctoral dissertation, but things being what they were, I did not want Chagnon chairing my defense committee (as would have been normal, since he had sponsored my work). "You and I have a lot of problems," I told him bluntly, "and my results may be a little different from yours. You can be on my committee, fine. But I want Bill Sanders as my chair." Chagnon wouldn't accept it.

Eventually the chairman of the anthropology department intervened and decided that my defense committee would have co-chairmen, Chagnon and Sanders—with Chagnon as senior co-chairman. So after all the hot air Chagnon would still be chairman. I dug in my heels and refused to go along with that.

When the department realized the severity of our falling-out, they started to pressure me. One of the senior professors insisted I would have to give a copy of all my field notes to Chagnon.

"You want a copy of my field notes?" I said to Chagnon, incredulous. "I have been working down there for two years with all the difficulties and all the risks, and you want a copy of my field notes? I'm sorry, these are my Ph.D. notes, and they're staying with me."

"No," Chagnon said, "that's not right. Your responsibility was to collect data for the Yanomama project. The fact that you were going to get a Ph.D. out of this was only an ancillary bonus."

This was something new. "I was down there collecting data for the Yanomama project, and my Ph.D. was just an ancillary bonus? I was under the impression for the last two years that I was in there as a Ph.D. candidate doing field research for my dissertation."

"No," said Chagnon, "that's incorrect. It was just an ancillary bonus."

"Well, I'll tell you what," I said. "I'll flush these things down the toilet before I ever give them to you."

The climax of all this was a roundtable meeting with the head of the department, Chagnon, myself, and Bob Carneiro, who was to have been on my committee and had flown in from New York. Carneiro started by saying, "Why don't we let Ken present his points first." So I did.

"First of all," I said, "I don't think it's proper or ethical for the chairman of a student's committee to forbid him to speak to another member of the profession." I had never forgotten or forgiven Chagnon's attempt to keep me from speaking to Marvin Harris. "This is the United States. I think I can talk to whomever I want to talk to."

"Ah, c'mon," said Chagnon, "I never said such a thing."

There seemed to be no point in arguing about this, so I went on to other things. But I was really angry by now. Not only had Chagnon denied it right to my face, he had in essence called me a liar. Inside I was seething. Maybe he thinks I have poor judgment, or that I'm a hothead, I thought. He's welcome to his opinion. But don't call me a liar. Don't ever call me a liar.

Poor Carneiro, who was a friend to both of us, kept talking, trying to find a way to work things out. By the time we finished there was at least an attempt at amicability, with promises that we would exchange letters on the chairman problem, the research notes problem, and any other problems we had between us.

Despite my desire to get on with my Ph.D., I knew I had had it with Napoleon Chagnon. As far as I was concerned, he was responsible for my having almost expired in the jungle—with no malaria pills and no boat. I wasn't going to give him my notes under any circumstances, and I wasn't going to have him chair my committee, either.

"Okay," Chagnon said finally. "This is obviously not going to work out. So let's just drop it. Let's forget it. But, Ken, tell me, what are you going to do with yourself, go to work in your brother's dental lab? Because you're not going to get into any other anthropology department. I'll see to that."

I couldn't believe it. I had just spent two years among the so-called Fierce People, but in terms of ferocity I didn't think they began to match up to this. I itched to respond in kind, but I kept quiet. I knew I wouldn't have any problems getting into another university. Chagnon had at least as many enemies as friends. There were departments that would take me just *because* I was leaving him. But beyond any considerations of that sort, I had two years' worth of significant and unique field data. I turned to Chagnon and said, "Well, who knows. Maybe I will go to work with my brother."

Shortly afterward I called Marvin Harris at Columbia and described the situation to him. "Yes," said Harris after listening to my recital. "It certainly sounds like you have to get out of there. It's unethical. You can't continue working under those conditions. You have to get out."

"What would you think," I said, "if I wanted to come to Columbia?"

"If you want to come to Columbia, you can come," Harris answered. "But don't think that you have to. There are plenty of places you can go. There are departments that have good Amazonian studies people who will welcome you with open arms. The important thing for you now is to get out of Penn State."

I knew that Harris admired Bill Sanders, that he regarded him as one of the finest minds in anthropology, as I did. But with the circumstances that had developed, it was, Harris thought, essential for me to leave rather than simply switch professors. And I agreed.

In the end I applied to Columbia University and was admitted as a Ph.D. candidate. But at about that time I started getting letters from Professor Irenaus Eibl-Eibesfeldt of the Max Planck Institute in Munich. Eibl-Eibesfeldt was the director of the Department of Human Ethology there, the student and now the successor of Konrad Lorenz, who had won the Nobel Prize for his work on animal behavior and had written *On Aggression,* a worldwide best-seller. Eibl-Eibesfeldt had heard about me, he wrote, from Inga Goetz, the German lady in Caracas who had done so much work with the Yanomama. She had told him that I had lived with the Yanomama and done fieldwork there, and that I might be available to do more. Would I be interested, wrote Eibl-Eibesfeldt, in coming to Max Planck and working with him? He was currently conducting cross-cultural studies among various indigenous cultures in the world and was including the Yanomama in his survey.

I was not too familiar with the Max Planck Institute, although I knew it was an extremely prestigious place. Accustomed as I was to American graduate schools' tight-fisted approach to student needs, I wrote Eibl-Eibesfeldt a letter that must have struck him as hilarious. Yes, I would like to know more about what he had in mind, the nature of his project, the nature of the work he wanted me to do, and so on. But if I did end up going into the field with him, I asked, would he be able to buy me such necessary items as a hammock and other field supplies? I had unfortunately lost all of mine in the rapids coming out of the Amazon and could not afford to replace them on my own. Eibl-Eibesfeldt must have been rolling on the floor when he read that, because as I shortly found out, Max Planck had the resources to outfit their expeditions with the finest equipment in the world, which Eibl-Eibesfeldt did as a matter of course.

Eibl-Eibesfeldt wrote back with more details about his work. He added that he would happily buy me a hammock and the rest. Moreover there would most likely be an attractive stipend associated with the position he was offering me.

It was now summer, and as this correspondence proceeded I was busy painting houses in State College, trying to raise money to support myself when I went to New York for the fall semester of 1977. Within days of one another, I received two letters—one saying that an assistantship would be available at Columbia, and another from Eibl-Eibesfeldt informing me that he had arranged a full year's stipend if I would come to Germany.

I found myself attracted to the Max Planck offer. In Germany I would not be a graduate student, but a regular researcher with a decent if modest salary. I would also have the opportunity to get back to the jungle quickly, at least for periodic stays. When I discussed it with Harris, he approved of my taking a year at Max Planck; I could begin my work at Columbia afterward.

I arrived at the Munich airport in late August and was picked up by one of Eibl-Eibesfeldt's students and driven out to the institute through the picture-postcard lake-and-mountain landscape around Starnberg. At the end of a country lane the institute's modern white buildings appeared, set off by the dark Bavarian forest that surrounded them. Irenaus Eibl-Eibesfeldt came out of his second-floor office to greet me in the hallway. He was smiling, and he was wired, this short, stocky man with a thick cap of black hair and a powerful handshake (administered by an unusually broad hand with the stubbiest fingers I had ever seen). He overflowed with energy and enthusiasm as he showed me around and pointed out the dozens of pictures from his expeditions that lined the walls.

I immediately had the feeling I was meeting an important, influential man, but I was a little wary, too. His was a field that was different from anything I had ever studied. Human ethology is the study of human beings, using the same underlying approach that Lorenz used to study animal behavior. It focuses on nonverbal behavior, on communicative gestures and the body language of interaction. Beyond that I was still not clear about Eibl-Eibesfeldt's theories and techniques. What I did know was that he himself had pioneered the study of human ethology, that he had practically invented it, and that this department of the institute had been built around him.

My reception at Max Planck was a new kind of experience for me, especially after my recent ordeal at Penn State. The *Forschungsstelle für Humanethologie* was a very different story. The door Eibl-Eibesfeldt showed me had a name on it: Kenneth Good.

The office behind the door was large, very large, with a big desk, bookcases, and an electric typewriter. When they invited me out for dinner, the contrast to Penn State just about knocked me out.

Then there were the geese. Konrad Lorenz had won his prize in part for identifying imprint behavior in greylag geese. Newly hatched greylags, he found, were instinctively programmed to recognize their mothers by size and sound; they would attach themselves to any maternal object that conformed to their visual and auditory expectations—Lorenz himself, for instance. When Lorenz squatted down and waddled around, quacking with the correct intonation and pattern, the hatchling geese would arrange themselves in file and waddle after him. Once they had locked on to him as their mother, nothing would change their minds, not another greylag goose, not even their real parent.

Lorenz was now long retired to Vienna. But in the pond in back of Eibl-Eibesfeldt's building were his geese, the Nobel Prize-winning geese—the umpteenth generation of greylags, which were still being studied by his institute.

Through close and sophisticated observation, Konrad Lorenz had identified a whole maze of animal behavior patterns. Eibl-Eibesfeldt, his student, had taken many of Lorenz's techniques and applied them to human conduct. Since he was looking for universal behavior patterns, he needed to carry out cross-cultural comparisons. The Yanomama, as isolated as they were, were an ideal group for him to investigate alongside his studies of groups in Ecuador, New Guinea, Africa, and elsewhere.

But the Yanomama, because of who they were, were special. What Eibl-Eibesfeldt proposed at the beginning was that we would go into the field together and observe them. He would work on the nonverbal dimensions of Yanomama interaction; I would look at verbal interaction. He wanted me to record different kinds of verbal behavior: the "big man" speeches to the community, the *wayamou* and *himou* trading chants, public insult and complaint, anything verbal. I was to record, transcribe, translate, and analyze, then publish my findings.

What he also wanted was someone who knew the Amazon region intimately and could manage the task of preparing his expeditions and getting him in and out: someone who could buy the equipment, the food, arrange the transportation, the permits, someone who knew how to handle a boat and who knew the territory and the Yanomama—someone to put the whole thing together for him so that he could give complete attention to his work, which at that point was focused on identifying and recording on film a number of common human behaviors. He declared to me, for example, that the Yanomama kiss each other, that kissing is in the Yanomama repertoire of behavior—not asking me, but telling me, although I was the one who had lived in the jungle for so long.

"They don't," I said.

"Oh, yes, they do," he answered.

"Have you ever seen it?" I asked.

"No," he said, "but I will." And the funny thing was that when we went down there, he did—not exactly the kissing I had in mind, but a kind of kissing, anyway.

That October I made my first trip up the Orinoco with Eibl ("Renki," as his friends called him). To my great disappointment the Hasupuweteri were not at home when we arrived, nor were the Patahamateri, their close kinfolk who lived across the river. As a result we went farther up to the little community at the next rapids, where we stayed for three weeks, filming and recording. The Hasupuweteri, they said, were deep in the jungle on a trek.

Our next visit was a few months later. After flying directly from Caracas to Platanal mission, I again took Eibl through the Guajaribo rapids and up to Hasupuweteri. This time they were not in their *shapono,* but the Patahamateri across the river were at home, and they told me that the Hasupuweteri were at their inland garden, not too far away. They would get them for me.

When the Hasupuweteri heard that we had arrived, they left their inland garden and came down to the river, where we presented them with gifts. Right away, Eibl began carrying out his observations, which unfortunately made them more than a little nervous. They weren't enthusiastic about pictures being taken of them under any circumstances; nevertheless Eibl set up his Arriflex movie camera near the middle of the *shapono* and filmed them nonstop all day long. Parents especially didn't like him filming their children for extended periods. Having this big piece of alien technology trained on them, doing who knew what to them, upset them.

A week or so after they arrived, Longbeard, the Hasupuweteri headman, came over to my hammock and struck up a conversation. The large tobacco roll bulging inside his lower lip seemed to heighten his already serious demeanor. He started slowly, as if this were something he had given a lot of consideration. *"Shori,"* he said, "you come here all the time to visit us and live with us." I waited, wondering what he had in mind. "I've been thinking," he said, stroking the wispy hairs that grew out of his chin, "I've been thinking that you should have a wife. It isn't good for you to live alone."

I couldn't think what in the world had brought this on. I had lived with the Hasupuweteri for two straight years, and no one had ever mentioned the subject. "No, brother-in-law," I said, "I'm doing fine. I don't need a wife. I'm not looking for one."

But that didn't satisfy him. Yes, I should have a wife. Having a wife was important. Having a wife was much better than not having a wife. He had a wife, all the other men had wives, it would be a very good thing for me to have a wife, too. He wanted me to have one.

As he kept at it I tried to fathom what this was all about. Was Longbeard talking about sharing a wife—his wife, maybe? Some of the other men had invited me to share theirs, but I had always declined as gracefully as I could. I had had a girlfriend back in State College, and in Munich there was Greta, a German girl I had been dating since shortly after I arrived at Max Planck; but living in the jungle seemed to do something to an outsider's sex drive, mine, anyway. I found I just wasn't all that interested. Beyond that, sharing somebody's wife would be a big political problem, a really major headache. Her husband and family would have a special claim on trade goods, which might alienate other people and upset interfamily dynamics. On the other hand, this was Longbeard talking (and talking and talking), and as headman he was already getting the lion's share of everything I had anyway.

Finally Longbeard's persistence began to wear on me, and I found myself thinking that maybe being married down here wouldn't be so horrendous after all: certainly it would be in accordance with their customs. In a way the idea even became attractive. After all, what better affirmation could there be of my integration with the Hasupuweteri? But I vacillated. No "marriage" here was going to endure. I wasn't going to stay with the Yanomama forever, and aside from my personal plans, the practical requirements involved simply in mounting an expedition here (not to speak of living here) were immense—none of which meant anything at all to Longbeard. Still, as his monologue went on I thought, What the hell, what would be so wrong in saying yes? I didn't feel that I had to avoid insulting Longbeard. We knew and respected each other. But if he felt so strongly about it, why not? You want me to have a wife, brother-in-law? Sure, okay, I'll have a wife.

"Good," he said, smiling broadly. "Take Yarima. You like her. She's your wife."

Out of the corner of my eye I could see Eibl filming away on the other side of the *shapono*. Fifteen minutes earlier I had been lying in my hammock watching with half an eye and thinking about how best to translate the word *yai*—sibling of the opposite sex—which had come up in one of my transcriptions. The word was so dependent on Yanomama culture that I couldn't find a decently fluent English equivalent. And now, suddenly, out of the clear blue sky, I had a Yanomama "wife"—a wife of sorts, anyway. And not only a wife, but Yarima no less, who couldn't be more than twelve years old.

Yarima herself quite obviously knew nothing at all about this. I looked around the enclosure and didn't see her. She was probably out in the garden with her mother. I was sure she had been "married" before—that is, betrothed. All Yanomama girls her age got betrothed. Many of their marriages were arranged when they were much younger, three or four—not that they had the vaguest idea that they were considered somebody's wife. Of course Yarima had been betrothed before. And she would be betrothed again, maybe four or five times more before she began to menstruate. After that she would become someone's wife for real.

I knew about this. I had been watching it for a long time. Young Yanomama girls have a relationship arranged for them by their parents or older relatives, but nothing changes in their lives. They still live with their parents and carry on exactly as before, except that they are generally acknowledged to be betrothed. During a betrothal, the girl will be sent over to her "husband's" hammock area to give him some food that her mother has prepared. He in turn (the prospective husband is always a productive man, never a child) might send back his own gifts of food. Eventually the girl feels comfortable being around his hearth and being around him. If things work out well, they become friends, in the same way that an uncle is friendly toward a favorite niece—the difference being, of course, that if they are still betrothed when she undergoes her first menses ritual, she will then hang her hammock next to his and they will truly become husband and wife. From an anthropological point of view, the Yanomama custom of child betrothal made a lot of sense. First of all, it created or strengthened ties between families in the community and between different lineages (marriages within a lineage are prohibited as incest). Second, since girls are already spoken for when they reach adolescence, there is no competition for them. A lot of potentially destructive rivalry is precluded this way, as are the problems of out-of-wedlock pregnancies. In Yanomama land every woman is considered sexually available once she has begun to menstruate. And since there are no moral inhibitions against premarital or extramarital sex, having unattached adolescent girls around would create all sorts of difficult and disruptive conflicts.

That was from an anthropological point of view. From a personal point of view, this was not particularly serious. These were an inventive people in some respects, and one of the things they were inventive at was in devising ways to keep a *nabuh* around, with his immense and distributable wealth. The origin of Longbeard's approach may well have been simply to provide me with an additional attachment to the Hasupuweteri. He was the headman, and it was his responsibility to think of the group's well-being. Or it might have been a gesture of friendship, a surge of brotherly feeling—an indication that he and his lineage felt I was really a part of the community. Certainly no one at the beginning ever thought of it as an actual marriage. Who ever heard of marrying a *nabuh?* You might as well marry an alien from outer space. And as for me, in my wildest dreams it had never occurred to me to marry an Indian woman in the Amazon jungle. I was from suburban Philadelphia. I had no intention of going native.

Besides, I was down here with Eibl on a short trip. Maybe I'd be back for another few visits with him, then I'd be off to Columbia University for my doctorate. Who knew what after that. Jacques Lizot, the Frenchman who made his permanent home at the Yanomama village of Tayariteri, was not a model I had any interest in emulating.

But I did say okay, and in this somewhat casual, offhand manner Yarima became betrothed to me. Of course nothing changed, any more than it would with any two Hasupuweteri in the same situation. I stayed in my area of the *shapono,* and Yarima stayed in hers, except when her mother would send her over to me from time to time with a little gourd full of some kind of food.

At the end of four weeks Eibl had everything he needed. But my recording and transcribing weren't finished, so after I took Eibl down to Platanal (from where he would fly out) I came back upriver to Hasupuweteri—to my work, and to this new situation.

Nobody took it seriously at first, just as no one among the Yanomama takes any new betrothal all that seriously. It has to grow. The man has to demonstrate that he is truly interested. The girl has to learn to feel comfortable with him. Beyond that, I was a *nabuh*, and *nabuh* don't stay. They take their pictures, make their observations, then they leave and are never seen again. So I was a *heorope*, a husband, but then again I was also a "brother" and a "brother-in-law," all invented relationships. But gradually, I noticed, perceptions changed—people began to take the betrothal more seriously. Instead of smiling at it, the women started calling me *Yarima heorope*—Yarima's husband. At first it was "*Yarima heorope, hahahaha,*" then just "*Yarima heorope,*" no "hahahaha."

Kenny started living in the shapono again when he came back with Renki, the man from Alemaniateri. Renki had big bags full of beads. He gave them to everyone. Now that Kenny was living with us again, my mother sent me over to him with food. I went many times. When older brother killed a bird he would always cut a piece for Kenny. Then he would tell me to bring it to him. My mother told me not to be afraid. "Bring the food to the nabuh," she said. "He won't hurt you." And I wasn't afraid anymore. Kenny came to our house so often that I was used to him. But he still was very big. Sometimes he would put his big body in older brother's hammock and talk for a long time. When I brought food to his hammock he would always smile at me. Then he would give me some mañoco. He would open his big box and scoop some out in a little container like a gourd. When I went back I would give it to older brother. One day Kenny gave me a beautiful red shirt and told me to put it on. But it didn't feel comfortable. When I got home I gave the shirt to older brother, too. I watched Kenny from my hearth. That was the first time I had a shirt.

Slowly I found myself involved. Yarima would come over to my hearth with food; I'd take it and eat it, then I'd give her something that I knew she liked, some manioc maybe. And she'd eat that. Then after five or ten minutes she'd go home. She was a graceful and charming child. I had always liked her smile; it stood out even among all the smiling and laughing children. Strangely, as time passed, I started feeling almost like another parent to her. In our terms, she might have been a cute little neighbor's kid whom you like a lot and who comes over to your house for milk and cookies. But here I was living in a culture where a young girl like that is considered a wife, or at least a potential wife—a wife in the making. Yarima wasn't the only young girl her age who was betrothed at that time. Others in Hasupuweteri—girls and men—were in the same relationship, and that put a different twist on things. I found myself accepting our betrothal on those terms. In the context of the Yanomama culture it was perfectly normal and appropriate, and I found myself feeling comfortable about it. Not immediately, but slowly and surely.

It takes a long time for a young Yanomama girl to get accustomed to her "husband," whether he's an older man or a teenager. To her he's a stranger. He's from a different family, and he lives in a different part of the house. It may be a communal house, but for her to be in an unfamiliar section takes some getting used to. But whatever it ordinarily took for a young girl to become accustomed to her betrothed, for Yarima the process was of a different magnitude. I was hardly an ordinary person. I wondered what must be going through her mind as she came over and shyly sat on the edge of my hammock or as she prepared a plantain for me. Did it take a special courage? Was it curiosity? Was she aware that she and I were developing a special relationship? What was her mother telling her when she sent her over with a gift of food?

Mainly, however, life just went on. There I was, living in the *shapono* in the section of the other sublineage, those who called me "brother," not "brother-in-law." I did my recording and translating. I continued my protein studies. I was involved in my daily round of work. But sometimes I would look up and see her smiling at me for a moment from across the *shapono*.

After a while I started going out into the forest with Yarima and her brother, who was about eighteen by now. I would never think of going into the forest on my own, even now, and I knew that she would feel more comfortable with her brother along. So the three of us would go. Often we would go fishing at the clear stream that was about an hour from the house. Her brother (*shori* to me) would go out into the water first, she would go in next, and I'd follow along. *Shori* would bring the fishline, hooks, and sinkers that I'd given him. I had my shotgun in case we came across any birds, and I'd bring along a pot and matches and some rice. When we stopped, Yarima would cook the rice and whatever fish we had caught. On the days it didn't rain I enjoyed being out in the jungle hunting and fishing. It was relaxing. I had to be active and alert, but there was no stress about it. Looking back, I remembered how hard Bob Carneiro and I had struggled that first month just to make it through each day (I more than Carneiro, who was an experienced field-worker), how the sweat had poured off us as we lay exhausted in our hammocks from the effort of making our observations. And I thought what a surprising creature this human animal is, so re-markable in its adaptability.

When we walked through murkier streams, Yarima would be afraid that electric eels or stingrays might be lurking on the bottom, and I would swing her up onto my back and carry her. We chatted as we went, about the ripening fruit and the gardens and the fish. In the forest *shori* would look quickly around a tree and point out a roosting curassow or a gray-winged trumpeter, and I would shoot what he had found. We'd come back with birds or small game. Then her brother would invite me over to help cut and distribute the catch. Or he would prepare it and cook it himself, and Yarima would bring me a piece to eat.

As these things happened our relationship changed. Before, she had been the cute little girl with the smile and the hello. Now it was something more than that, and as time passed a good deal more than that. I had done plenty of hunting before, but always with the men. She had been out in the forest all her life, but as a little girl with her mother and the other women and children. Now we were out together, with her brother along, but together, in the way that a prospective husband and a betrothed girl would be. I knew that this, at least in Yanomama terms, was becoming a marriage. Here in the Amazon it was so simple and straightforward—no formali-zation, no ceremony, no exchange of gifts or vows. Marriage just happens. It evolves, it develops, it becomes real. Or else it doesn't.

A month later I motored downriver to Platanal, then flew out to Caracas. From there I cabled Eibl that I was going back to Hasu-puweteri for a few more months. Eibl, I knew, was concerned mainly that I be available to take his expeditions into the jungle. As far as my own work for the institute went—the transcriptions and trans-lations and text analyses—I could do that in Hasupuweteri as well as I could in Germany. And Yarima was not in Germany.

9

*T*he peach palm fruit came and went. We were living then at Wawatoi garden. I was in my hammock holding my little daughter [niece] when Kenny walked into the shapono with three Patahamateri. Everyone jumped up. Everyone was excited and shouting. Kenny went right over to Vulture Belly's place. He was wet from the trip, and he had a funny hat on his head. I watched him hang his big hammock, then sit in it and take off his foot coverings.

All the men were happy to see him and went over to talk. I moved over to my "daughter's" hearth so that I could be closer and see better. When he saw me he gave me a big smile. I could see his white teeth in his black beard. After he unpacked the bags he and the Patahamateri had brought, he called me over. "Bushika," he said. That means "little one." I was happy that he called me, but I did not want to go. Then older brother said, "Go, now!" So I walked over to his hammock. When I got there he reached into one of his packs and pulled out two foot coverings. Then he told me to put them on. I didn't want to do it. Everyone was watching me. When I put them on, my feet felt heavy and I couldn't walk easily. Older brother said they were good, but I didn't like them. I decided to throw them away when nobody was looking. When Kenny took off his shirt I saw that he had gotten even bigger when he was downriver. I thought he must be as heavy as a tapir.

The next morning older brother said, "Let's go. Follow me." When I followed him outside the shapono, Kenny was standing there. Older brother said, "We're going fishing at Rahuawe River." He went first. I followed him, and Kenny followed me. We walked for a while, and when we got to the river Kenny gave us fishhooks and line. Older brother wanted to fish upriver. The Rahuawe River is shallow, and we walked along the bed looking for good fishing places. I was afraid I would step on a stingray, so Kenny lifted me onto his back. I liked being up there. It was fun being on the river with Kenny and older brother.

After that we went out many times. Sometimes we went fishing, and sometimes we found fruits and honey. When Kenny had his shotgun with him, he would shoot manashi birds. The shotgun made a great noise that frightened me so much that I had to cover my ears. Older brother taught Kenny to use tobacco, and every morning my mother would tell me to make Kenny's tobacco for him. "Make the tobacco for your heorope," she said. When I took it to him I would sit in his hammock for a little while. His big cotton hammock.

Four months later I was still not ready to leave. I didn't know if I'd ever be ready. Yarima had become exceedingly dear to me, almost like a daughter, yet not like a daughter. It wasn't something I understood completely. Nothing in my life had prepared me to understand it. Yet there it was, a feeling as deep as anything I had ever experienced, a feeling, I knew, that was very, very Yanomama.

Still, I had to go. The time was long past that I should have been back at Max Planck. When the day came, the whole village escorted me down to the river, gathering around my canoe to see me off. Yarima was standing on the bank as I loaded my things and got in. Then, just before the dugout was pushed off, I took a little aluminum pot out of one of my packs, leaned over to the bank, and reached up to her. She took it and smiled, then turned and ran for home.

Back in Munich I worked on my transcriptions and text analyses, preparing them for publication. I had recorded over a hundred speeches by big men at Hasupuweteri and other communities I had visited, then transcribed and translated some of them, working with informants. I had, I felt, a good grasp of the subjects speakers tended to address, their distinctive use of language, and the function such speeches served in the life of the village. I had also recorded scores of insult and complaint tirades, with their inventive and intensely colorful locutions, and dozens of ritualized trade chants couched in exotic stylizations and symbolic terminology. At the beginning of my work with the Yanomama, I had regarded their language as little more than a tool that would enable me to conduct my field-work. I had quickly seen, though, that the quantitative measurements I was making could only be understood properly against the cultural background, and to do that I needed real fluency. Now the language had become a fascination in and of itself—a medium whose patterns, variations, and ambiguities pointed toward the underlying structure of thought and feeling. I also started the immense task of cataloguing and organizing my notes on Yanomama hunting patterns, gardening activities, and trekking and their relation to the availability of game. I was looking forward to making a doctoral dissertation out of them.

In many ways it was an interesting time. The Max Planck Institute was highly regarded, and there was a lot of curiosity about the Yanomama in Germany. I was interviewed on television, and I went with Eibl to high-level conferences, giving reports on my studies. The exposure was new to me. At Penn State I had been a graduate student in a department where the physical anthropologists dominated the scene and even seasoned cultural anthropologists were looked down on—"soft science" people as they were.

Living in Germany wasn't bad either. I had friends there, including my girlfriend, Greta, who by now had started talking about moving in with me. I traveled to France and Italy, rode my bike in the Alps, did all the things an American in Europe might do, but despite it all I missed Yarima. I felt attached to her, as if some bond had knotted itself around my heart. In an album I had slides of the village and slides of her. In some of them she was wearing the red shirt, pants, and sneakers I had given to her, the first clothing she had ever worn in her life, the first clothing any Hasupuweteri girl had ever worn. At night I would take out the pictures and look at them and itch for Eibl to start planning another Amazon trip.

But Eibl was looking at a number of cultures, not just the Yanomama, and for the moment, at least, there was nothing firm in the works. When months passed and Eibl was still not gearing up for the Amazon, I went to him and told him I wanted to go back in. I had finished the current text analysis project, and in essence I had nothing to do except wait for his next trip. If he wasn't planning to organize something, I didn't see that my staying any longer in Germany made much sense. I might as well return to Columbia and get to work seriously on my Ph.D. Eibl thought about it briefly, but I was fairly sure he would send me back in. In short order he did.

By the time I got back to Venezuela it was April, almost nine months since I had left. In Caracas I ran into Carlos Carvallo, a Venezuelan friend who had been after me for a number of years to take him into the interior. He would be happy, he said, to take pictures for me if I let him come along. That would be fine. It never hurt to have companionship on the Orinoco.

By now I knew that the Hasupuweteri probably wouldn't be on the river, that they had more or less moved permanently to their inland garden. Consequently, when we got up to the area I stopped at Patahamateri first. But the Patahamateri *shapono* was strangely quiet, and when we walked in it was obvious that the entire community had been hit by a malaria epidemic. Many of them were lying in their hammocks, extremely ill. Others were doing chores, but slowly. All seemed thin, wasted with disease.

As Carlos and I were hanging our hammocks in an unused section of the *shapono,* a young man came crawling on all fours toward us across the central plaza. Behind him walked an older woman, obviously his mother, crying. Fifteen or twenty feet away, he stopped. When I went over to him and squatted down, he collapsed on his stomach in the dust, unable to say a word. His mother looked at me, her eyes imploring. Between sobs she managed to get out, "*Wedicina, koamini; wedicina, koamini.*" Medicine, she wanted the bitter medicine for him. I gave him three 500 mg. tablets of chloroquine, putting them on his tongue, then bringing him some water to get them down with. But it was clearly too late. He had used the last of his strength to crawl across the *shapono* to me. His mother said the shamans had been chanting over him for many days.

The young man died at six P.M., two hours after we arrived. All night long his family and friends wailed and cried around the body as it lay in his hammock. At dawn, with the mourning still going at full intensity, they painted him with red *onoto* dye and decorated his arms and legs with parrot feathers in a splash of yellows, blacks, whites, reds, and blues. Then they carried his corpse into the forest, along with that of an older woman who had also just succumbed to the disease.

I knew what they were doing; I had seen it once before, in Hiom-isiteri, on one of my trips to the interior. When a person dies of a disease that the Yanomama think is contagious, they don't immediately burn the corpse. They believe the smoke will harm them. Instead they wrap up the body in mats woven of long saplings and secure it to a tree out in the jungle. Only after the corpse has putrefied sufficiently do they cut it down. By that time it's thought that the evil spirits have fled and that it will be safe to cremate the remains.

By the time they had the young man and the woman rolled up in the mats and covered the mats with leaves, everyone in the village who could walk had congregated around and was wailing at top volume. As sick and decrepit as they were, the noise filled the air and seemed to ring through the forest. Carlos and I followed the crowd a little way and watched as several men shinned up trees, then secured the corpses so that no wild animals could get at them. I wondered how long they'd be left up there and if somehow I'd be able to be there when they brought them down.

Among the healthy Patahamateri I found two guides to take us to the Hasupuweteri inland *shapono*. But here too we were greeted by silence. No answer came to our whistles, and as we walked toward the building there wasn't a sound. I wondered if they were off somewhere. But no, they were there all right, sprawled in their hammocks with malaria. Almost the entire community was lying motionless, much sicker than the Patahamateri. With a sinking heart, I saw that many of them seemed near death, that I was looking at the decimation of the village.

One of the farthest gone was Orawe, my "older brother." As soon as I came in and started hanging my hammock in the usual place, Orawe's wife dragged herself out of her own hammock and came over to ask me to cure him, to get the evil spirits out of him, "as a shaman does," she said. To my eye he seemed at death's door. I had no idea if I could do anything and it certainly would never have occurred to me to treat him as a shaman would. But knowing how strongly the Yanomama believe in spirits, I decided that I might as well try. God knows, I thought, I have been watching their exorcisms long enough to imitate them. Bending over Orawe, I started to chant in a slow but strong rhythm. Then I ran my hands over him and began pulling the spirits out of his body, physically exorcising them and expelling them into the air. Orawe's eyes were glazed, but he could still see, and he watched me with a trustful, resigned stare. Then, still staring, he took on his tongue and swallowed the three 500 mg. tablets of chloroquine I held out to him.

When I finished with Orawe I made the rounds of the other hammocks, distributing the rest of my chloroquine to those who seemed worst off. I also gave out my supply of sugar to those who had enough energy to ask for it. At least, I thought, it might give them a little lift.

Over the next few days many of the Hasupuweteri seemed to improve, and I realized we must have gotten there at the lowest point in the malaria cycle. No doubt the chloroquine had helped, too. Most amazing to me was Orawe, who made a remarkably fast recovery, coming back from what really had seemed to be his last moments.

When Kenny left I was very sad. Older brother was also very sad. We watched until his boat disappeared around the bend in the river. Then older brother said, "Come," and we went home. At dawn and at dusk I thought about Kenny. That was when I used to bring him things. Now I had no one to make tobacco for. I had no one to bring food to.

During the day I took care of my "daughters" and "sons." I went gathering with my sisters and cousins. When we walked through the stream it reminded me of when older brother and I went fishing with Kenny. I remembered how he would carry me on his back. I saw the place where we bathed when we came home from gathering eteweshi fruits. I didn't know if I was still Kenny's wife. I didn't know if he would come back. They said that nabuh go back to their villages and stay there. I thought that Kenny had gone back to his village. I wondered what nabuh women were like. I thought they must be very beautiful. They must have very white skin and beautiful black hair.

I threw away the foot coverings Kenny gave me. My fishhooks were all gone. My mother's pot was old and dented. I was sure that Kenny would come back now because he knew we needed more fishhooks and another pot. I was sure he would come back. I was sure. But he didn't come. We went on a long wayumi, and when we came back to Wawatoi garden he was still not there. Many moons went by.

When the prisi-prisi *came many people got sick. Older brother became very thin. He was hot, and he shook for many days. My mother, my sisters, and I sat around his hammock and cried. Long-beard came to chant and drive away the evil spirits. So many people were getting sick. No one hunted. People did not eat. They grew thin. Vulture Belly, the great shaman, looked like he would die soon. We were sad and afraid when we thought about him dying. The shamans chanted all the time. They chanted all day and all night. We were too weak to flee from the evil spirits.*

One morning when it was raining, a Patahamateri came into the shapono. *He said the Patahamateri were sick, too. Two had died, and others were dying. He said that Kenny had come on the river with another nabuh from Caracasteri. Kenny and the Caracasteri had stayed in Patahamateri the night before, and now they were on the trail.*

Kenny and the other one arrived when the sun was already going down. People were in their hammocks when they came in. Kenny walked to Vulture Belly's hammock and looked at him. Vulture Belly's wife had been crying all day long. She asked Kenny to chant over Vulture Belly to drive the spirits away. Kenny chanted loudly. Then he gave medicine to the sick people. The Caracasteri called me Kenny-yoma. That made me laugh.

Yarima was not sick. Her family had had it a little earlier, and they were now almost fully recovered. She and I saw one another the moment I came into the *shapono,* but in Yanomama fashion we did not greet each other or talk. I did what I had to, hung my hammock, unpacked my clothes, treated the headman and others who were ill. It wasn't until that evening that I sat down with her and her family. It was so Yanomama—to show up after not having been there for eight months and then just be there as if nothing had happened. There were no demonstrations or exclamations of re-union, none of the social niceties. I simply had the sense that I had arrived after a long journey and now was with friends. And I liked that.

In the following days Yarima began to come over to my hammock, little by little reestablishing the relationship we had had before. Again we started going out into the jungle together—Yarima, Yarima's brother, myself, and Carlos Carvallo, Carlos taking roll after roll of film with his Nikon. Aware of the Yanomama name taboos, Carlos called Yarima Kenny-*yoma,* Kenny's woman.

Two weeks later I took Carlos down to the rapids, where we had arranged in advance to meet two mission Yanomama who would take him to Platanal. Going downriver I felt tired, and when I started back up it seemed as if I were operating in slow motion. Every movement became an effort, and I realized that my own bout of malaria was coming on.

By the time I hiked in to the *shapono* I was as sick as I had ever been. Aching in every joint and muscle, I collapsed in my hammock and fell asleep. My last thoughts as I did were that I had given away all my chloroquine. There was nothing left to take.

By the next day I wasn't even aware of my surroundings. In and out of sleep, I woke up enough at one point to know that I was lying on the ground beneath my hammock. I didn't remember falling, but there I was. Around me the air was full of noises, chants, and yells. I could feel someone massaging my chest, then bringing his hands up along my arms and shoulders and on either side of my head. The words rang in my ear, exploding inside my head: *"Aaaah krashiii, aaaah krashiii, aaaah krashiii!"* With a gigantic effort I opened my eyes and made out two shamans working on me—Orawe, fully recovered now, and a younger shaman named Hudowe. They danced, and strutted back and forth as they drew the spirits up out of my chest and into the air, prying them loose from their malignant hold on my throat and liver.

I also heard softer words in my ear, and I was aware that Red was bending over me whispering something that I could just make out through the din: "Don't worry, older brother. Don't worry at all. We will drink your ashes."

I was too weak to open my mouth. But I wanted to speak. I wanted to say, "Don't bother about it, it's all right, old friend. It's all right, younger brother. Don't drink my ashes, just put me in a boat and float me down to the padre." If only I could open my mouth, I thought, struggling to make the muscles of my jaw obey. I'm slipping into a coma, and once they think I'm dead they can pop me on the fire pretty fast. So no, Red, please don't drink my ashes. Just float me down the river.

Two days later I knew that this time I had falciparum plasmodia, the killer strain of malaria. I could tell from the cycle. With falciparum one day you feel like you're on the verge of death, the next you've made a dramatic recovery. You wake up, and you feel you can function. Your body seems better, and your head is blessedly free of pain. But then comes another knockout blow, and once again your fever shoots up and the top of your skull dances with an agony that is simply not human. In lucid moments you worry about blackwater fever, a complication of falciparum that turns your urine red, then black, then dries it up altogether, just before it kills you.

On the mornings I felt good I started construction on a hut just outside the *shapono* to use for storage and for work with informants. I also set up a remote mike so that I could record conversations for transcription and begin another stage of the project I had been doing with Eibl. If I lasted more than a couple of hours, I'd work with an informant until my hands started to shake and the weakness began washing over me. By nighttime I would be plunging toward the abyss again. I didn't seem able to shake it.

Journal, April 28, Wawatoi: Tomorrow I should get out to Platanal. I must tell Red that if anything happens to me, he should carry me out in a hammock and get me to the padre in Platanal. I worry that the Hasupuweteri wouldn't get through the rapids, that they will be afraid to go. Floating just by the current might be too slow to get me there in time. Six P.M. Headache is unbearable. Scared. I took three Fansidar [a new antimalarial drug that was supposed to have dangerously severe side effects]. Chloroquine is gone. All given out.

Journal, April 29, Wawatoi: After taking Fansidar the headache began to abate. But I was sweating profusely. Nauseous and dizzy. Near panic. Hudowe, the young shaman, came over and took his *epene* [the hallucinogen]. Then he began to work on me. Then Orawe came over and chanted for a long time. When he stopped the headache and fever were both gone. They were ecstatic that my forehead had cooled. Last night I slept right through to dawn. Am still very weak, but much improved. Decided not to return to Platanal.

I was still sick when a messenger from Patahamateri arrived to ask the Hasupuweteri to come for a funeral. Apparently enough time had passed since they had tied the dead man and the woman up in the tree, and, as was the custom, they were asking their Hasupuweteri kinsmen to take them down and prepare them for cremation.

Sick or not, there was no way I could miss this. I not only had to see it, I had to photograph it. But I also knew the six-hour hike to Patahamateri would be murderous, and I decided to carry nothing with me except my cameras, not even my shotgun. But even unencumbered I found the going really rough. The jungle seemed to quiver and reel, and my mouth and throat were unbearably parched. Three-quarters of the way there I collapsed on the trail, groaning for water. Red got some for me in a gourd, digging a hole in a dry riverbed. Then I got to my feet and staggered on.

When we arrived at the place, the Patahamateri came out to meet us. Amid the clamor of screaming and wailing, climbers shinned up the trees and cut down the bodies. On the ground several of the Hasupuweteri unwrapped the rolled matting of sticks and palm leaves that encased the young man. I could see the denuded skull still attached to what looked like a mummified body, except that the flesh was falling off the bones. The stench was overwhelming, so bad that many of the mourners stuffed rolled-up leaves into their nostrils. Working quickly, the Hasupuweteri helpers gathered together the bones and rotting flesh, then rewrapped everything in new leaves. As soon as they had finished with him, they got to work on the woman. But when they opened her windings a thrill of horror raced through the crowd. Like her companion in death, the woman's body had putrefied, but for some reason the process had not advanced to the same stage. The flesh still clung to her bones, and her face was intact, its eyeballs popping like a scene out of a horror movie. For a moment the onlookers stood there in shocked silence, then the helpers shrugged it off and got down to business. They took the head off, then the arms and the legs, and wrapped them again in leaves, as they had done to the young man. Then, mourning at the top of their lungs, the whole group moved into the village to give the corpses to the fire that was already roaring in the central plaza. I followed them in, sweating profusely and snapping away as fast as I could with both cameras. That night we stayed in Patahamateri. When we finally got back the next day, I fell into my hammock, exhausted by the excursion and prepared for the relapse I could already feel coming on.

Once the plasmodia took hold again, they would not release their grip. Week followed week as I worked halfheartedly in the mornings, then collapsed, shivering and feverish. There was no improvement. The anemia had become chronic, and I suffered from what seemed to be a new variety of headache every day. I estimated that I had probably lost thirty pounds. Every day Yarima came over to my hammock with water and a little food. But I couldn't eat. At night she sat with me, looking worried and often crying. There was nothing she or anyone else could do.

Eventually I lost all hope of getting over the illness and realized I'd better get out. I had arrived at the beginning of April. Already it was June; I had been sick for almost two straight months. Rest and treatment in Germany would probably do the trick, but if I left now, I would have to wait until Eibl was ready for another trip before I could get back, and who knew when that might be. Still, there seemed no alternative.

The Hasupuweteri, many of them still sick themselves, took me to their old river clearing, where I rested a week, trying to gather enough strength for the trip down. When I felt well enough they came with me to my canoe, tied up just below the remnants of my first house. Just as we reached the bank the surprising noise of a motor broke the air, and as we stood there a large dugout rounded the bend and made for the landing spot. In it were Padre Bórteli, Padre Santos, and two nuns from the mission. They had heard about the epidemic and had come to distribute medicine. My last sight as I motored off was the missionaries moving among the Hasupuweteri and handing out malaria pills.

On the way back to Germany I stopped off to see my parents in Havertown and to rest a bit. Then, when I felt up to it, I visited Marvin Harris, who had now moved from Columbia to the University of Florida in Gainesville. Almost as soon as I got to the States my health began to improve, and when I returned to Germany at the beginning of July I knew it would be only a matter of time until I was a hundred percent.

My mental state, though, wasn't good. The last three months in the Amazon had not been happy, either for me or for Yarima. I was acutely aware that every moment I had there was precious, and because I'd been so sick, this time it was almost worse than not having been there at all.

Back in Germany I found myself irritable and depressed, and also a little disoriented. One thing that bothered me was that I had been living in so many cultures that instead of locking into the niche of whatever culture I was in, I had the sensation of just sliding across from one to the other without getting my bearings too well. When I was with the Yanomama I had to behave a certain way. People there expected a certain pattern of interaction and response—very simple and straightforward. When I left the jungle for Caracas it was altogether different. I had to use a completely different repertoire of manners and even emotions. "Would you be so kind . . ." "It would give me great pleasure if . . ." "I am most delighted that . . ." Smiles and thank-yous and shaking hands and courtesies. You couldn't do otherwise without being considered wildly boorish. Whether you knew a person or didn't, liked him or disliked him—it didn't matter, you went through the same social rituals.

The Yanomama did none of that. They didn't share the state of mind these graces derived from (or the hypocrisy they often reflected). Forcing myself back into the Venezuelan mode was an effort. But what bothered me more was that everyone I met seemed to believe the whole world was more or less the same as they were. And I'd think, These people talk about the isolation and lack of perspective of the Indians, but they themselves are just as ethnocentric as the Yanomama. Even more, because they have less right to be so.

Then of course in the United States there was yet a different set of social expectations; you had to rein in the Latin directness and emotionality. But compared with Germany the United States was so relaxed and informal, it seemed almost anarchic. I found myself jumping back and forth from one language to another and trying to adjust my behavior to the different cultures, and it was disorienting. In the United States I would go to talk to Professor So-and-so, and somehow I might not show the proper respect, which he wouldn't like. I'd just sit down and say, "How are you?" and sometimes I'd get a strange look. ("Who are you to come in here and talk to me like that?") But in Germany it was far, far worse, Germans being the kind of formal people they are. To treat a Herr Doktor Professor there in an egalitarian fashion was unheard of. The Germans by and large considered even standard American manners reprehensible. But Yanomama manners? The contrast was so extreme, they sometimes thought I must be putting on some kind of play.

At the Institute for Human Ethology, every morning the researchers and students would gather for Eibl's ten o'clock roundtable discussion, all of them looking as though they had entered a church. I had a hard time with this kind of excessive gravity even under ordinary circumstances, but in my current state of mind I wasn't tolerating it well at all. Eibl would sit up front, talking in a very formal way, most often about nothing at all or about trivialities. It was, after all, only a little morning get-together. But to look at the researchers and students, you'd think they were undergoing an experience of profound enlightenment. They seemed absolutely frozen with reverence. Inevitably Eibl would say something about the Yanomama that to me seemed trivial in the extreme—the Yanomama frown in a certain way when they're angry, or they smile in a certain way when they greet a friend—and I wouldn't be able to hold back.

"*So,*" I'd say, "*das ist eine Überraschung?*" ("This is a surprise?") And the place would go into shocked silence. You just don't say something like that after the Herr Doktor Professor makes a pronouncement. But then, after a nervous moment, the group would break out in laughter, and Eibl would, too—though a trifle uncomfortably. I didn't exactly mean to upset him, but this was the kind of situation that would have struck any American as a bit preposterous. And for someone who had been living with the plainspoken and blunt Yanomama, the German respect for persons seemed almost like a farce. Or could it be, as I sometimes thought, that I was harboring some exotic parasite that had just reduced my tolerance level to zero?

By the time Eibl and I got out to the field again it was December of 1980, almost six years after I'd made my first contact with the Yanomama. I hadn't seen Yarima for almost two years. Once again we flew into Platanal, then headed upriver. But when we got into Hasupuweteri I found that the village's two sublineages had had a serious falling-out and had decided to separate, though not really to split up completely. As a result Yarima's sublineage had built a house for themselves a few minutes down the trail. They still shared the same garden and visited constantly—but they no longer considered themselves one community.

As usual I hung my hammock next to Orawe. Then, as Eibl started filming, I made arrangements for Yarima to come and live with her relatives who were in Orawe's *shapono* so that we could be closer together. She had still not reached puberty, and she was not ready to hang her hammock at my hearth. We were not husband and wife in any sexual way, but in all other respects we were, at least in Yanomama terms. With her near me, I felt very much as if I were home.

Renki the Alemaniateri came with Kenny. He had a big thing for taking pictures that had three long legs. He stood behind this thing in the middle of the village. He went to stand there in the morning and stayed there until the sun was directly overhead. Then he would go to his hammock to eat and sleep. After that he would stand behind it in the afternoon. Kenny always told the boys not to touch Renki's things. They could not touch anything. Especially they could not touch the clothes that he put on when he went to sleep.

After Renki stood in the middle of the village for a few days, people didn't want him there anymore. They went up to him and said, "Enough. Go away now." But he just smiled at them and stayed there with his big thing for taking pictures. Then some of the men said to him, "You have to stop. We will drive you away." But he still only smiled. Orawe's wife was very unhappy because he was pointing his thing at her baby all the time. She was crying, and she asked Kenny to drive him away. But Kenny didn't. I wondered why Kenny did not make him stop. I wondered why he did not drive him out of the shapono.

During my last period in Germany my relationship with Eibl had been strained. The personal chemistry between us, so good at first, had broken down, due partly to my own difficulties, I knew, and to the tensions I was feeling in my own life. For some reason, on this trip the friction seemed to blossom. I found myself getting angry with him, and I recognized that he was short with me, too. Little things irked me, and when it was something substantial I didn't hold myself in. One day something happened to the special side-angle lens Eibl used for most of his filming. This lens enabled him to aim the Arriflex on one thing or on nothing and actually film whatever was to the side of him, which allowed for more or less candid shooting. But without the mirror lens, he had to aim straight on.

Normally the Yanomama don't like to have their pictures taken. In common with some other primitive cultures, their word for "image" is the same as that for "soul" or "essence." In some ways, taking pictures smacks of capturing a person's soul, his *noreshi*. Of course if you snap a quick picture or even a series of pictures, that's one thing. But if you're standing there pointing a camera at them for hours on end, they don't like it at all. I had had trouble before with Eibl on this score and had talked to him about it. But the mirror lens allowed him to avoid really disturbing people. Now, though, it was different. Following his regular daily routine, Eibl would set up his camera at eight in the morning and film till noon. He'd take a two-hour lunch break, then shoot till five or six—right in the middle of the village.

After a while people started getting unnerved, particularly since he was shooting right at them. They were especially upset about their babies, whom Eibl was concentrating on in an effort to record mother-child interaction. They were sure that what he was doing was detrimental and harmful. Some of the women were crying about it, and finally two of the men came up and asked me to drive Eibl out of the village.

I had been watching all this develop from my hammock, wondering how he could continue when he saw how nervous he was making people. But when the men talked to me about it, upset and angry, I really blew a fuse. "Renki," I said, interrupting his shooting, "you can't keep doing this. Don't you have any consideration for these people? You're making them cry. They're already asking me to drive you out of the village."

Eibl wasn't at all happy about this. He didn't say anything. But he was not used to hearing himself addressed in this manner, and at that moment his feelings toward me weren't benign. My whole purpose in being there, in his view, was to facilitate his work and help him keep to his schedule; now I was interrupting his work. Eibl invariably kept to a strict routine, even in the jungle. He had breakfast, he filmed, he had lunch, he took a short siesta, he filmed, then he had dinner. And disruptions like this did not fit into the schedule.

So he wasn't happy about this, and it especially aggravated him coming from me because in principle he did not like the way I worked (my irritation with him was balanced by his with me). I never did things in the formalized, regular way that he was used to and that he expected. And what I did do didn't seem to him like real work. From what he could see, most of my daily activity consisted of sitting around in my hammock, or in someone else's hammock, gabbing with the Indians. It didn't make any difference when I explained that you cannot take a Yanomama and say, Look, I want to know about your incest taboos or your funeral customs. They will not tell you. They can't work in that fashion. So what you do is you sit around and talk and work your way into it, so they don't even realize that you're after something specific. You just blend it into the conversation.

But it was not just the small annoyances and differences in style that bothered me, it was Eibl's overall work with the Yanomama. Eibl had been Konrad Lorenz's protégé, and in the field of ethology—the study of animal behavior—he was good, really good, a smart man and a first-rate scholar. But then he had invented human ethology, which was basically the application of animal study techniques to human activity. I didn't dismiss human ethology in its entirety. But I did feel that it focused on the superficial. I'd look at Eibl's conclusions about human demonstrations of affection or hostility, and my only reaction would be, Okay, fine, so what? Eibl was studying universal nonverbal behavior patterns in human beings. He noticed, for example, that all people in certain situations raise their eyebrows. He wrote articles on it—eyebrow raising. He scrutinized mother-child interactions and wrote articles on comforting and rejection behaviors. And he had unbelievable equipment for his observations: two huge Moviolas for editing film, first-class commercial studio editing equipment. He'd look at frames and say, "There it is! Do you see that woman? Her child is bothering her, and she's pushing him back like that. That's universal. I've seen that exact gesture with the Bushmen. I've seen it in New Guinea. And now I've seen it here."

My reaction was, "Renki, really. Her kid's making a nuisance of himself, so she's pushing him away. So what? You're trying to prove it? We already know it." This really got on his nerves.

The result was that while in some ways Eibl and I continued to appreciate each other, our working relationship was heading quickly for a breakdown. On the other hand, the strains between Eibl and me had no effect on my life with the Hasupuweteri and with Yarima. Although Yarima had hung her hammock at her relatives' hearth, we were together all the time. We went fishing and gathering together, sometimes with her brother, sometimes just the two of us. In the evening she would roast plantains for our dinner and prepare whatever meat might have been brought in from a hunt and distributed. During the night I would see her get up to tend her fire, adding wood to keep the sleepers warm. I felt I wanted to squeeze each day, to keep it from ending. But the time slipped by like magic, and as hard as I tried to put our return out of my mind, it loomed closer and closer.

For the first time I had anxieties about leaving. Always before when I went away I had left a young girl behind. And although a special relationship had grown between us, Yarima, I knew, would in due course make her way into adulthood and assume the life of a Yanomama woman. I would have had an unusual experience with her, a unique experience—who else had been as enmeshed as I in this lost world? But if I was unable to come back for some reason, we would both keep it in our memories, and we would live through the parting.

But this time it was different. Yarima was older, thirteen or so now, more mature and obviously nearing puberty, in Yanomama terms nearing womanhood. The situation with Eibl being what it was, I had pretty much decided not to stay at Max Planck. And without Max Planck I wasn't sure how I'd get back. Mounting a trip into the Amazon is an immensely expensive affair. Even if I did stay with Eibl somehow, we still wouldn't be returning for another six or eight months, maybe more. So the chances were good that Yarima would have her first menses while I was gone. And that put a whole different light on things.

The day before we left and far into that night I discussed the situation with Red. What could I do? I had to go. I couldn't take Yarima with me. But I wanted to come back, I was going to come back—to her. That's what I wanted to tell the Hasupuweteri, that I would be coming back. I was coming back, and I was going to live with my wife. I wanted them to know that—and I wanted them to respect it. I had heard the *pata*—the big men—speak a thousand times. If you wanted to tell the people something, you addressed the community. That's what I was going to have to do. Because if I didn't say anything, if I just said good-bye and left, I could forget the whole thing.

All that night Red coached me on the speech, telling me what to say and how to say it, what points would be most effective, and what terminology would have the most impact. The next morning at seven I took Yarima back to her lineage's new *shapono,* on the outskirts of the garden. I had in mind clearly what I was going to say. I knew what I felt, and Red had prepared me well. With everyone still in their hammocks I went up and stood in the headman's area, thinking to myself that this was just what the Yanomama did—they expressed what they felt, immediately, without necessarily judging all the consequences. They were an emotional, immediate people. And that's how I felt, exactly, emotional and immediate.

Pacing the area, I began to speak. "Today I am going away," I said. I could see they were listening. Most often people just went about their business during a speech, but this was an event. Everyone was looking. "But I am coming back. I am coming back. I am coming back. No one here is to break into my storage house. If you do, when I come back I will be very angry. Very angry." Pause. "And her . . ." I pointed to Yarima. "No one is to touch her. No one is to touch her! No one!" I could feel the anger coming over me. Pacing up and down, I threw my arms around, slamming myself hard on the sides and back with my open palm, punctuating the words. "She has been given to me! She is my wife!" Slam! "I have never touched any of your wives." Slam! "You do not touch my wife! You do not touch my wife! You do not touch my wife!" Slam! "If I come back and find out that someone has touched her, I will know!" Slam! "I myself have never touched her! And no one else is going to! No one!" I turned around and swung a roundhouse at the *kanekanini* wood house pole, smashing it with my fist so hard that the roof shook. Wham! I looked around at all the people in their hammocks, staring into their eyes. They were all staring back. They looked pretty impressed.

10

Back in Caracas Eibl and I had a formal parting of the ways. He had, I think, expected an apology from me for the rough way I had handled him at the *shapono*. When it wasn't forthcoming, he became distant and angry. In a way I couldn't blame him, but I also knew that our relationship had about had it anyway. He may have had some regrets about our parting; I know I did. Whatever my criticism of Eibl and his methods, the man was no Napoleon Chagnon, and even if our working relationship had reached a point of no return, I still wasn't altogether happy about the breakup.

The obvious course now was to go back to Gainesville and get my doctorate. But after my second year in Germany and now with this breakup with Eibl, I felt sick to death of the academic world, sick to death of institutes and universities. I didn't even want to see one, let alone spend more time studying in one. When I thought about my experiences with Chagnon and Eibl and with some of the others I had dealt with over the years, I realized I was deeply disillusioned with anthropology. As it was, I had only stayed in it for so long because of people like Bill Sanders and Marvin Harris, who had the expanse of mind and personal integrity to commit themselves to the pursuit of ideas without giving a great deal of thought to their own status and importance. But such people weren't all that common. I had just about given up anthropology once before, seven years earlier when I'd left my teaching job in Venezuela. Now maybe it was time to really do it. Examining myself, I knew that I couldn't face any more studies. Neither did I want to teach, at least not now. So then just what was I going to do?

You are thirty-six years old, I told myself. You're not a kid. It's laughable, a thirty-six-year-old graduate student. True, I loved the fieldwork. But what could I look forward to at this age, finishing up and getting some assistant professorship, where I'd be locked to a desk with no funds and few chances at grants that would get me back into the Amazon? Maybe if I really believed in myself as a dedicated anthropologist, I could do it. Good anthropologists are subsumed in their work. They have a field, and they are focused on it, and that makes up for the subsistence salaries and harsh contentiousness of their profession. But I wasn't that way. I didn't see myself as a born teacher. I didn't feel driven to scholarship. I had never really been able to stand the pettiness of much of the academic world.

Down deep, all I really did want was to find some way to make a living and to get back into the jungle. Not only to study the Indians—I already had enough data for three books—but to live with them. More especially, to live with Yarima. That was what I had come to, after all these years of struggling to fit into the Yanomama world, to speak their language fluently, to grasp their way of life from the inside. My original purpose—to observe and analyze this people as an anthropological researcher—had slowly merged with something far more personal.

Oddly, it began to seem that maybe the idea of finding some way to live with the Yanomama wasn't completely impossible. Five years earlier, during my first year in the field, I had met a German in Puerto Ayacucho by the name of Martin Stummer. I had come out for supplies, and, short of funds, I was trying to hitch a boat ride up to the mission. Stummer was going in that direction and offered to take me along. He was, he told me, in the adventure tour business. He took wealthy tourists into some of the world's most interesting and forbidding places: New Guinea, the Ecuadorean and Colombian jungles, the Kalahari, the Philippine rain forests. Now he was down here investigating the possibility of laying out a route up the Orinoco, talking to local officials and checking the availability of accommodations and supplies. Stummer was an interesting character, energetic and feisty, and we had exchanged addresses. His tour company was based in Munich.

Three years later when I arrived at Max Planck I had looked him up. He immediately invited me over for dinner and showed me around the city. His business was going well; he had even opened up a shop in downtown Munich that dealt in exotic artifacts, native crafts from the areas he visited: elaborate ceremonial masks, shell jewelry, tooth necklaces, even shrunken heads—real ones. He had five or six of them there from the headhunting Jívaro of Ecuador.

Martin Stummer was not a sophisticated, jet-set kind of person, yet he was a real cosmopolitan. He had seen many things and many peoples and had enjoyed his travels immensely. He was an adventurer, an explorer, a guide. He had led expeditions, he had captured wild animals for zoos. The German anthropological community knew him, but they looked down on him. He was a little too off color for them. The idea of taking people to see primitive tribes was not something the anthropologists thought highly of. The rich Germans he brought in would take pictures and try to talk to the tribespeople. And in their view that was bad. Only anthropologists should be able to go in and take pictures and talk to them. Only professionals had the right to have contact with them.

That was conventional anthropological thinking, but it wasn't necessarily my thinking. And back in Munich Stummer and I started talking about the possibility of opening up an American office of the adventure tour business. Stummer argued—and I agreed—that I had had a tremendous opportunity to know the Yanomama. But why should it be restricted to me and other "professionals"? Why shouldn't laypeople who had the interest and the means have the right to see them, too? And of course it was already happening. Wealthy Venezuelans would fly to the mission and just go in. Wouldn't it be better if they were accompanied by someone knowledgeable who could explain so that they could better understand and so that there would be some kind of control?

The basic idea was that I would go into partnership with Stummer and set up an American base. I would also be the "jungle man"; I would lead expeditions in Venezuela, Colombia, Ecuador, and other

146

places. And in between organizing and leading tours, I'd be able to go back to the Yanomama. I was quite optimistic about it.

Returning to the States, I went to live with my brother in Havertown. From there I began exploring what it would take to set up an office for the adventure tour business, what publicity would cost, what kinds of permits and insurance might be needed. As I dug in I began to feel that this just might be the thing. I'd be able to use my skills, and for the first time in my life I'd earn a decent living. I would be able to get back and forth into Yanomama land without being at the beck and call of someone else. I knew how hard it would be to parlay the kind of experience and knowledge I had into some productive avenue, especially outside the academic world. This was a rare chance, a golden opportunity; also, I could be with Yarima. I was ready to work till I dropped to make it happen.

In January of 1981 the whole thing came tumbling down. Stummer called with the bad news that despite assurances he had had, he was not able to get the financing necessary to make an operation in the States feasible. It was too bad it had turned out this way, but those were the chances of business. He was sorry, really sorry. He knew how much it had meant to me.

When this happened it came crashing home to me that I was at a dead end. I had left Yarima down there, and suddenly there seemed no hope of getting back. I couldn't believe the way things had gone. First Chagnon. Then Eibl. Now this. I felt as if the whole world had come to a halt. I sat in my brother's house and vegetated, my mood growing blacker and more pessimistic each day. To make matters worse, the malaria, dormant for many months, came back to life with a vengeance. Once again the plasmodia started wreaking havoc in my bloodstream. Fatigue and lethargy added their weight to problems that already seemed almost too heavy to bear. I knew I was sitting in the middle of a personal disaster area.

January passed, then February, as my depression deepened. At the beginning of March Marvin Harris called from Florida. He had heard I was sick and at loose ends, and he said, "Look, why don't you come down here?" He said I didn't have to come to Florida, that I was still officially accepted at Columbia, and if I felt like going back to school, I could always go there. But I could also move down to the University of Florida and study with him, if I did decide to go back to school at some point. He didn't want to pressure me at all, he just wanted me to know that the opportunity was available.

At that moment Harris's voice sounded like an angel's. I would never myself have considered going back to school. But somehow the idea that this man cared enough to call and offer his help meant a lot, especially given the state I was in. I didn't like the idea of going back, but I had enough sense left to realize that I was at the end of my rope. At least I could go down to Florida and look around. It would give me something to do other than sit and brood.

On March 18, 1981, I went down to Gainesville. There I took a seminar in anthropological theory with Harris, which turned out to be a good, intellectually stimulating experience. Despite my general cynicism about professors, I found that studying with him was a pleasure. Then, after I had been there several weeks, Harris asked me to give a number of seminars on the Yanomama, more or less turning the class over to me. To my surprise I found that I actually enjoyed myself. It took an immense effort to start digging into the boxes full of tape recordings and field notes I had brought along, and I didn't see how I might be able to muster enough determination to begin writing a dissertation. But who knew, maybe that could happen, too. The significant thing was that I seemed to be coming out of the blackness that had swallowed me.

By June my emotions had calmed down enough so that I was beginning to look at things more rationally. It had now been six months since I had left the Amazon, six months since I had seen Yarima. I tried not to think about her, knowing that nothing good could come of it. But my mind carried me back anyway. I remembered every word of the speech I had given to the Hasupuweteri. But what significance could that speech have had? I was sure it had made an impact, but how long might it have affected them? A week? A month? Two months? I knew how things worked in the jungle. And by now Yarima was fourteen years old, a mature Yanomama woman. I did not want to think about what was happening with her. Better to think about something else—my notes on protein capture, for example. Maybe I could start work on my dissertation after all.

I had just started to do that when I was hit by another bout of malaria. When it was over I got back to work, cataloguing my notes and beginning the daunting task of arranging and analyzing my data. In the fall I took another course with Harris and one with Charles Wagley, one of the great experts on Amazonian Indian cultures.

But early in the new year I was sick again and this time when the chills and fever faded, they left behind an ugly cough, which soon turned explosive. Racked by violent paroxysms, I couldn't write or read or even think. Sleeping was almost impossible, as was eating. The X rays showed something on my left lung, some shadow, though nobody was sure what it was. Possibly some parasite, the doctors said, possibly cancer, possibly something else. Whatever it was, they were going to have to open me up and take care of it.

The operation was performed at Shands Medical Center in Gainesville, where the doctors removed a benign growth from my left lung. When I was up and around again, a Venezuelan friend of mine by the name of Mauricio Eggenschwiller invited me out to recuperate at his place in Colorado. The clear air and quiet he was offering seemed like just the thing. I'd have a chance to jog, swim, and rest and think through what I ought to be doing with myself.

One day at Mauricio's house I received a letter from the Venezuelan government that had been forwarded to me from the University of Florida. It was from the office of the president. "Dear Professor Good," it began. "As part of our national census project, we are inviting you to participate in carrying out the Indian census for sector six in the Yanomama region." On the maps that accompanied the letter I found sector six—the region between the Orinoco and the Siapa, exactly where I had spent so much time exploring and contacting the isolated villages of the Shamatari Yanomama.

The project was going to be carried out by helicopter. I would go in with an air force crew, locate the villages, and count the inhabitants, keeping statistics on sex and age. Several other foreign anthropologists had also been called in to conduct this part of the national census, people who had lived and worked in the different regions of the Venezuelan Amazon: Lizot, Chiappino (another Frenchman), and Colchester from England. The pay would be ten thousand dollars, with all expenses covered.

At first I didn't want to do it. I was just recovering from the jungle as it was and I didn't want to open up my relationship with Yarima again. I knew that I had blown it, that it was gone. I had been away from her far too long, and I was doing my best to accept the reality. How could anything like that have worked anyway? I asked myself. What would you have done, lived your whole life with an Indian girl in the jungle? What would you have lived on? What kind of life would you have had? What kind of life would *she* have had, married to a *nabuh*?

The problem was that now I knew without a doubt that I had

been happiest when I was there. Had I stayed with Eibl, perhaps I would have been able to sustain the relationship. But I hadn't, and that had closed the door on my ability to get in and out. Considered rationally, the dissolution of what might have turned into a real marriage was really for the best, for both Yarima and myself. Why should I subject us to the immense trials that would inevitably be our lot if we were husband and wife? No. I did not want to open up this relationship again, no matter how much she was still in my mind. And if I went down there, wasn't that exactly what would happen?

But the Venezuelan census people were persistent. The fact was that I was the only person who had been through the sector six territory and knew the villages and the people—and even I didn't know all of them. The census would be a difficult and delicate job. It would require not only finding the Shamatari villages, it would mean being able to talk to the people without frightening them off or creating confrontations. So despite my initial rejection, they kept writing and calling, sending me maps of the area, and describing the pay and the resources I would have available. As hard-pressed as I was, eventually I decided to do it. Okay, I thought, this will be easy—I'll just go in by helicopter, do it, then come out—with enough money for graduate school. I let the Venezuelan authorities know that I agreed to their terms, then I began to work like mad to get back into shape. I jogged, swam, and rode my bike every day. And I quickly began to recover full function of the damaged lung.

But in getting ready to go back, I found my thoughts drawn to Yarima. Certainly she would have had her first menses by now, and a young, unattached girl would just not be left alone, not in the Amazon. Only two things could happen there. One was that she would be considered fair game by every man in the jungle, all the time. She wouldn't have any choice about it; they'd be after her constantly. But more likely she would be married. Yanomama girls at age fourteen are women, fully prepared to shoulder the responsibilities of adult life. Surely someone had taken her as a wife. By now she might even have a child. Whatever was happening, I told myself, you stay out of it. It's finished.

When I arrived in Caracas and checked in at the census office, they handed me the paperwork for sector six. But there was more. Now the government wanted to expand my contract to include sector seven, from the Siapa River all the way to the Brazilian border. I wasn't eager to do it since I was scheduled to deliver a paper at an anthropological conference in Washington in December and there wouldn't be time. The census directors were insistent, though, and they offered to pay my way back and forth to Washington. They wanted me to sign a contract for the two sectors right then because they needed to have it wrapped up. I signed.

Over the next few days I got my supplies and equipment together. Then I flew into Platanal mission and caught a lift upriver with a national guard colonel who was in charge of helicopter arrangements for the Amazon census. He was planning, he said, to clear the island at the Guajaribo rapids where I had been stranded. That would be the perfect place for a landing pad and supply depot, where the helicopters we would be using for exploration and contact could refuel and resupply.

From Caracas to Puerto Ayacucho to Platanal, then upriver with the colonel, I talked to myself about Yarima. It's over, my inner voice said. Don't get involved again. Forget it. Motoring by myself up from the rapids, this interior monologue intensified. Don't dare let it grab hold of you again. You've been through enough. You are going to get yourself going now. You're going to finish your doctorate and be more independent. She's made another life for herself by now. So just forget it.

Kenny gave his loud speech in front of Longbeard's place. He told the men not to touch me. He was very angry, and he hit the house pole. Later we looked at it, and there were marks in the wood where he had hit it. It was very hard wood. My mother told him she would not let anyone touch me. But she knew that my older sister's husband had wanted to take me as a second wife for a long time. He didn't like it when Longbeard told Kenny to take me for his wife. I didn't want to be Abami's husband's second wife. He was an old man and was often angry.

When Kenny left I cried and my mother cried. Older brother said that he would come back, but only after many moons passed. We went on wayumi, and after we returned the Patanoweteri came to our shapono to visit. They told us that Kenny was not going to come back. Older brother said that the Patanoweteri lived near the padres, so they must know. Already the peach palm fruit had come and gone again. Sometimes I hung my hammock at older sister's house now. Her husband told me to do it. I liked to be near older sister's baby. I liked taking care of him.

One day while I was carrying my sister's baby I noticed that I had blood on my thigh. I knew that the yiipimou *had come. When I told my mother, she made me sit in the back of the house while she and older sister went into the forest to gather leaves from the* yiipi *tree. Then they made a little house for me out of the leaves, and I sat inside for many days. I only ate and drank what they brought me. If a mosquito bit me, I had to scratch myself with a little stick. When they let me come out they took me into the forest and decorated me with cotton armbands. They put a skirt around my waist and beautiful white down in my hair. When I entered the* shapono *I walked across the plaza with my armbands and my skirt. Everyone was looking at me as I walked slowly across to my mother's hearth.*

I hit Patahamateri first. They were the first group on the river in my sector, and I stayed there for two days censusing them. When I finished I headed inland to the Hasupuweteri with three Patahamateri guides. But when we got there, Yarima's entire lineage was gone. The only people there were Orawe and Red's lineage. But they seemed wary, distant, frightened. They watched me closely as I came in and hung up my hammock in the usual place, next to Orawe's hearth.

I wasn't expecting a rousing welcome—that wasn't the Yanomama way. But I wasn't expecting this, either. I could feel tension in the air. Even Orawe and Red, my closest friends, were looking at me strangely. Of course I hadn't been there in a year and a half, but why this strangeness? Had I done something I wasn't aware of? Had something terrible happened in my absence?

By night the atmosphere was a little more relaxed. I could feel the apprehension easing up, though people were still keeping an eye on me and tended to keep their distance. But as I settled in, things seemed to return to normal. The next evening Red sat down with me and told me why everyone had been so cautious. The day before I arrived, one of the Patahamateri had run in with word that I was at their village. I was enraged, he said. According to this Patahamateri, I had vowed to raid the Hasupuweteri. I had sworn to cut off my wife's head and kill all the men of her sublineage. That's why they had gotten scared and run off.

When I heard this I was upset, but not particularly surprised. I knew well enough that among the Yanomama lying is pervasive. Rumors and tall tales are the region's lifeblood. Who could tell what this Patahamateri's motive might have been, or if he had had any motive at all? Lying is often a political strategy, but it can just as well be done for entertainment or for no reason at all. What disappointed me was that Yarima's sublineage had believed the story. On the other hand, I thought, who in their right mind would stick around to find out if such a story were true? If somebody tells you that your mailman has a gun and says he is going to shoot you, you would think, The mailman? Why would the mailman shoot me? Then again, you probably wouldn't go outside to the mailbox to test the rumor, either. People do go insane, abberant things do happen. The chances are that you would watch the mailman from the window and let him move on.

From the Yanomama's point of view, that meant getting out before I arrived. Of course *shori* wouldn't kill us—but who's going to stay and find out? As far as the census went, their absence didn't make a lot of difference. I knew how many Hasupuweteri there were anyway, and Red could fill me in on births and deaths. But it would make for an odd report: I was hired to do the census in this area because I knew the jungle and knew the people. Then the first thing that happens is that I arrive and they take off into the forest.

I was sad and disappointed not to see Yarima, but not terribly— or so I told myself. After all, it had been a year and a half since I'd last seen her. She was out of my life, period.

I got to work, but not with any great rush. I had no stringent deadlines, and as I settled in I felt more and more comfortable, more and more at home. My old friends came around to talk; some of them had new babies. They told me about their lives since I had left. They were obviously happy to see me again, as I was happy to see them.

Through it all I tried to seem casual and relaxed, but underneath I was tense, angry that Yarima's people had run off. Didn't they know better after all this time? We had been through so much together—the treks, hunts, friendships, hardships, the laughter and jokes. Why had they packed up and run? And why hadn't they come back by now?

By the third day I finished censusing Orawe's lineage and was catching up on some informant work with Red. I hadn't mentioned anything to him about Yarima, yet I wished he knew what I was thinking. If anyone could understand, he would. But I didn't want to talk about it; I still wanted to convince myself that these feelings were over, not once again coming to a boil inside me.

Red sat in the extra hammock I had slung next to mine and talked. I was sure he sensed something was wrong. I had sat with this man in earlier times hour after hour, day after day, and discussed Yarima and Yanomama marriage. He was the one who had told me what to do. He had told me how I should talk to the people before I left. He had been my close companion and friend. Now here I was back after so long, and I hadn't mentioned Yarima, and neither had he. I hadn't asked whether she was married, whether she was well. I hadn't mentioned her at all. But he had to know.

The next morning Red told me that some of the men had seen peccary tracks the previous night. "I think they're still close," he said. "We're really meat hungry. We're going to try to shoot some of them. I'll be back later today." Then he took his bow and arrows and left.

I was a little irritated that he had gone. He knew me, this Red, this Oporawe. I'm not saying anything, I thought, and he's not saying anything, but he knows my feelings about Yarima. He knows what I'm going through, even though nobody's said a word. How can he just go off and hunt peccary?

Late that afternoon I was lying in my hammock with Tanashina's baby on my lap, the women sitting around me on the ground talking. The conversation was going on, chitchat about this and that. I glanced at my watch; it was five o'clock. A cool, sunny afternoon, blessedly free of insects.

Suddenly there was silence. The women seemed to freeze. Then they stood up and scattered to their hammocks. I jumped up too and handed the baby to her mother, wondering what was happening. Had visitors come? Were we being raided? I whirled around toward the *shapono* entrance, and through the opening I saw Red and Longbeard marching into the village. Behind them was Yarima. She was clutching a bunch of roots in her hand and sobbing.

11

*I*t was early morning when the Patahamateri named Shidowe came running into our house. He was very excited. He told Long-beard that Yarima's husband was back. He told Longbeard that Yarima's husband was in Patahamateri and that he was furious. He said Yarima's husband was going to come to our shapono and kill all the men. He said he was going to cut my head off. When we heard this we all jumped up and started packing our things. We were very frightened, and we wanted to go deep into the jungle to get away. Now I was staying with older sister and her husband all the time. At first my mother had told me not to stay with them. But then she stopped telling me that. No one thought that Kenny would ever come back. All the nabuh leave and never come back, even Kenny. But now he had come, and the Patahamateri said he had vowed to kill us.

I carried older sister's baby, and older sister carried the plantains in her big basket. The men ran up ahead, and we followed. We *walked one day, then we camped. We walked the next day, then the next day. We were already far away from the shapono when Vulture Belly and his younger brother caught up to us. They said that they had come to get me. They said that Kenny wanted me to come back. He was not angry, and he was not going to harm anyone. Longbeard told me to pack my hammock. Older sister's husband also told me to go.*

Longbeard came with us, and we walked very fast all day long. Before darkness came we arrived back in Wawatoi garden. When we entered the shapono I was frightened. I was trembling. What if the Patahamateri had been right all along? He said that all nabuh are very fierce when they are angry. I could see that there were many women sitting around Kenny's hammock. But when they saw us they ran off. Kenny jumped up from the hammock and looked at us. I began to cry. Longbeard squatted down in front of Kenny and listened while Kenny told him that he was very angry at him. But he did not look angry, and he did not speak loudly. Kenny told him he was disappointed that Longbeard had run away from him. He was disappointed that Longbeard had believed lies about him. Why did he believe the Patahamateri's lies? When Kenny looked at me I knew he was not angry. He smiled at me, and I felt happy. I stopped crying. Then I hung my hammock next to his and got in so I could rest. My legs were very tired from walking so fast.

Longbeard came in and squatted in front of me, extremely nervous. The speech I gave before I left had obviously made a lasting impact. Red walked up and said, "I knew you wanted to see her, and I was planning to go and get her. But I didn't know whether I could find her, or whether I could get her back. That's why I didn't want to say anything."

I was in a state of absolute shock seeing Yarima; for a moment I couldn't talk, she looked so different. Then I tore my eyes away from her and looked at Longbeard. "How could you believe lies like that?" I said. "After all the time we lived together?" While I spoke Yarima was undoing her hammock and hanging it next to mine.

And there we were. It was astonishing to see her, to see the difference between what she had been when I left her and what she was now. A year and a half had passed, the crucial period in her life. The transformation was dramatic, striking. She had blossomed into a stunningly beautiful young woman. Her childish contours were gone, and now she had a womanly curve of breasts and hips; her lovely face was fuller, darker, her eyes black against the dusky bronze of her skin. I hadn't asked Red to bring her back. I hadn't expected it. But suddenly it was done: Yarima was there, her hammock was next to my hammock.

The next day her brother arrived. Word had gotten around that I wasn't angry, that I wasn't harming anybody, and all of them, he said, were on their way home. When the group arrived they settled in as if nothing had ever happened. In the Yanomama fashion, it took them about five minutes to reinstall themselves in their *shapono* on the other side of the garden, to where they had moved after they'd split off from Orawe's lineage almost two years earlier. I visited with them, renewing my friendship with Longbeard, Yarima's mother and older brother, and the others in the group with whom I had been close in the past. None of them spoke about the incident or about why they had run away. The whole thing blew over like a summer breeze; it might never have happened.

Over the next couple of days I censused the new arrivals, then mustered the young men from both Hasupuweteri lineages to clear a landing area for the air force helicopters I was expecting would soon show up to take me into the interior. They would come in from Platanal, where they had set up a refueling site, and land on the Guajaribo island, then move on to Hasupuweteri. Together we would fly in toward the Siapa River and the Brazilian border. All the helicopter routes had been carefully laid out. Now we'd see if they were really up to the job of locating the tiny villages hidden in the vast green sea of jungle.

As the days passed, Yarima and I went about reestablishing our relationship. It was a delicate situation, as it would have been under any circumstances, but complicated now by my having been away so long and by the traumatic events of my return. I saw it in her, the reserve that had never been there before, the uncertainty in her eyes, even a hint of fear. Before, she had been a young preadolescent girl still part of her family, and the ties between the two of us had been different, easily broken. Now, at about fifteen, she was an adult by Yanomama standards, and she understood that this was a different situation, that we were now truly husband and wife, that her hammock was next to mine, at my hearth. For anyone it would have been an unsettled time, full of anxiety as well as happiness. For Yarima it was that and more. She had to get to know me again, and she had to cope with the rumors and threats that had put the fear of death into her.

For me too it was a time of adjustment. I had come back to a previous life that in many ways was the same, yet in others was dramatically changed. This beautiful little girl, Yarima—whom I had know for so long and in a way had helped raise—had become a woman, the wife that she was supposed to become. But now that it had happened, I wasn't prepared for it. Despite the betrothal and the examples of those around me and the Yanomama cultural expectations that I had become so at home with, I had to get used to the idea. I had to put it on and feel comfortable with it.

I didn't want to rush anything. I didn't want to push Yarima, nor did I want to push myself. I'd lived in the jungle for a long time without any sexual relationships, so that could definitely wait. The happiness of being in Hasupuweteri again seemed enough for me at the moment, the rest could come later. I had thought it was all gone—and now, magically, it had been given back to me. There would be time for everything.

Shortly after we began living together, Yarima had her period, so I knew that at least she wasn't pregnant. But I still wasn't sure what had happened in my absence. I knew Yanomama men, however. They will grab a woman while she is out gathering and rape her. They don't consider it a crime or a horrendously antisocial thing to do. It is simply what happens. It's standard behavior. In such a small, enclosed community this (together with affairs) is the only way unmarried men have of getting sex. But still, I thought, maybe not, maybe living with her sister and brother-in-law she had had some protection.

I also thought a lot about *nohi harupo*, literally "jealousy," or "suspicion," though among the Yanomama the term has a power the English doesn't convey. One night when Orawe was visiting my hearth, he turned the discussion to wives. Sitting in my hammock, his intelligent face illuminated by the fire, he said, "Younger brother, do you know what *nohi harupo* is? If you do not already know, you will know it now. You will really know it. You will never live in peace. You will always have to watch her." He nodded toward Yarima, who was chatting with his wife a few yards away at their hearth. "When she goes to gather you will have to watch her. When she goes to chop firewood you will have to watch her. When she goes to bathe you will watch her. You will never rest from watching her. Not even when she becomes pregnant will you cease to watch. Not until she bears your first child."

I already knew what he was talking about. There was no way not to know. Yarima was supremely attractive, at the absolute peak of her beauty. In all my years with the Yanomama I had only seen one other woman whose beauty compared with hers. That had been on my initial trip in, with Chagnon and Carneiro and Bill Sanders and my fellow grad students Eric and Ray. As we had pulled up to Jacques Lizot's village, all the Indians had gathered on the shore. And there among them was one young woman so magnificent that we had all lost ourselves for a moment gazing at her. Beauty like that is rare in the jungle, where the Indian women by and large don't conform to Western stereotypes of attractiveness. But that woman's beauty was so extraordinary, she had distracted us all. Seeing this, the man next to her—her husband, I guessed—had begun waving his arms and shouting at us, *"Iba, iba, iba,"* which I later found out meant "Mine, mine, mine." That man must have died a thousand deaths from *nohi harupo*.

Yarima was certainly at the most desirable moment in her life, her prime, for all the Yanomama men. The truth was that I wouldn't let her go get firewood herself or go gathering by herself. I could feel the sexual tension in the air, the smoldering desire, at least among the young men who were related to her as potential "husbands," not as "brothers" (who would have been inhibited by the incest taboo). As Orawe said, a man with a young wife is never at peace. He never stops *nohi harupo*. Even when she's pregnant the Yanomama feel a young wife must be watched, because they believe that sex during pregnancy contributes to the growth of the fetus.

I felt the tension, and I tried to deal with it. I wanted to think that Yarima would be faithful to me. But I knew the limits of any woman's faithfulness here. Fidelity in Yanomama land is not considered a standard of any sort, let alone a moral principle. Here it is every man for himself. Stealing, rape, even killing—these acts aren't measured by some moral standard. They aren't thought of in terms of proper or improper social behavior. Here everyone does what he can, and everyone defends his own rights. A man gets up and screams and berates someone for stealing plantains from his section of the garden, then he'll go and do exactly the same thing. I protect myself, you protect yourself. You try something and I catch you, I'll stop you. In general, life is carried on in an orderly way, in part because of people's reluctance to get into fights and also because of the unspoken weight of the community's interest. By and large they do not commit antisocial acts because they want to preserve the group's essential harmony. So most often one person will respect another's garden or property.

But sex is a different story. The sex drive demands an outlet, especially with the young men. It cannot be stopped. Thus the personal and social constraints have less force, they're more readily disregarded. As a result, a woman often has no choice. And if a woman is raped, she will not tell her husband, because she knows that her husband will beat her, or worse. In most cases the husband will become extremely angry, at both his wife and at the man who has raped her. But his anger will most likely not have the intensity or duration to provoke a village-shattering conflict, unless perhaps his wife is young and has not had a child yet. In that case the husband might find he cannot tolerate it; he might lose control utterly and embark on violent action. He badly wants to at least get his family started himself, rather than have someone else make her pregnant. It's then that *nohi harupo* can set in in earnest.

At this point I wanted nothing more than to be with Yarima. By now her brother had moved in with us, hanging his hammock on the other side of the hearth. Early in the morning the two of us would go hunting together while Yarima went out to the gardens with the other women to harvest plantains. But neither Yarima nor I ever went far. Each day I expected to hear the air force helicopters coming in to land, so there were no leisurely day-long gathering walks in the forest; even two-hour walks made me nervous that I might miss them. As a result, we weren't exactly living the normal Yanomama life. We spent most of our time in the *shapono*. I would write (even now I never stopped recording observations and dietary data) and listen to music, watching as Yarima strung the beads I had given her, or took care of her sister's children while she was off in the forest or the gardens, or helped her mother get firewood. I marveled at her cheerfulness and at her golden-skinned beauty, which seemed to grow more radiant with each passing day.

I often wondered if the Yanomama saw beauty the way I did. Some things made me question it. Hudowe was one example, a strong young hunter who had pursued Yarakawe's wife for years. He insulted Yarakawe—and fought him with clubs. He knocked Yarakawe out and made him spit blood. He broke his head open. He did everything except shoot him, but Yarakawe stood up to it all, refusing to give in or to give up his wife. This went on for years. It was a constant irritant to the entire village. And all this over a woman who was considerably older than Hudowe, fat, unusually ugly (to my eyes, anyway), and aromatic in the extreme—one of the few women who didn't like to bathe.

For a week I waited for the helicopters. Then I waited for a second week. One day I heard them off in the distance, circling, searching; finally the beating of the engines grew fainter and disappeared. They hadn't been able to find me. Eventually I decided to get started myself, on foot. I'd go overland into the interior.

Packing the necessities, I chose a few guides and carriers and set off with Yarima and her brother for Mokaritateri, the nearest of the inland villages, the community I had made first contact with six years earlier. About two hours after we left we heard the sound of helicopters back in the direction of the village. We heard them circling and circling, but we were too far out to turn back. We would only have missed them again, and who knew when they might be back. So we continued on, arriving in Mokaritateri late that afternoon. The next day I censused them, and the following day we returned. It was an enjoyable trip—made easier by the contacts I had developed there in earlier years.

When we got back I found that the helicopter had actually located our landing pad the second time around, and though I wasn't there, it had dropped off supplies for me. Inside my little house were an entire boxful of machetes the team had brought me to use as gifts for the different headmen. They had pushed them one at a time through the high, horizontal window of my hut, taking out the screen to do it. They had also given boxes full of aluminum pots to Orawe, who had kept them for me. To my great surprise and disappointment, Orawe also had a note for me from Roberto Lizarralde, the prominent Venezuelan anthropologist who was in charge of the Yanomama census. He had unexpectedly accompanied the helicopter team in and had wanted to visit me. Lizarralde was an old friend, going back to my days at the Central University, and it was a shame to have missed him.

Armed with new supplies of gifts, I took off again after a few days, this time bound for Hawaroweteri, a trek of four days to the southwest. At the Hawaroweteri *shapono,* Yarima and I hung our hammocks together, as we had at Mokaritateri. And as at Mokaritateri, the Hawaroweteri accepted her completely as my wife. The whole situation was strange to me still, and I was on the lookout for the gesture or the remark that would have conveyed that it seemed strange to them. Here I was, a white man in the jungle, with a Yanomama wife. This was a first in the history of this tribe. It may have been a first in the history of similar tribes. And I wondered sometimes, Is this true? Will this actually take? But as I went on I saw indications that our relationship was regarded seriously. Everyone all referred to Yarima as my wife, no smirks, just plain, normal talk—my wife.

Several weeks had passed since Red had brought Yarima back to the *shapono*. Although we were living together, trekking together, getting used to each other again, sex had not yet entered the picture. I wanted things to take their natural course. When Yarima felt completely comfortable with the situation, then it would happen. Besides, first the landing zone had to be cleared—an immense job; then we made the visit to Mokaritateri and the long trip to Hawaroweteri. And Yanomama do not have sex on trips. Sex between married people almost always happens in the daytime, in the forest or around the gardens. A couple might have a favorite trysting place, or maybe several of them. And when they are alone, away from the community, that's the time for it. When wives want to complain about being neglected sexually, they'll say, "He doesn't take me gathering anymore," or, "He doesn't take me along when he goes fishing." And everyone knows what it means.

Several weeks had gone by, and there had been no opportunity for Yarima and me to be alone, or at least I hadn't pressed to make the opportunity. It was Red who finally brought up the subject, telling me that it was time I had sexual relations with Yarima. He did it with a certain amount of sensitivity—understanding, I think, that while on the one hand I did not want to rush Yarima, on the other this was still hard for me to accept fully myself, that I was going through my own period of adjustment to the fact that Yarima and I were really husband and wife now. We were no longer betrothed. She was no longer a girl. It was time.

"She's your wife," he said one day while we were out fishing, "you have to have sex with her. When you go bathing," he said, "that's the best time." And he started giving me instructions about how to prepare the scene. In the middle of the jungle there are beautiful streams, pure clear water under a dense canopy of trees. You can drink the water. The rays of sunlight penetrate here and there and illuminate the shadows under the canopy with shafts of radiance. You don't have to worry about anything. Nobody lives nearby, and nobody will disturb you. "Come down by the stream," Red told me, "but first clear away a little patch of brush so that the ground is nice and soft. Then come down here with her."

I followed his advice and cleared it away, thinking, Okay, tomorrow will be the day.

The next day I asked Yarima to take a walk with me down to the stream. It had rained all night, and as we started walking a soft mist was still in the air. I was sure she knew what I had planned. Walking down, we didn't talk. I could practically feel the heat of her body as she walked close behind me on the narrow trail. But when we got there the little clearing that I had so carefully prepared was all covered with water. The stream had overflowed its banks and had filled the nooks and bowers along the shores. It was a different scene, wet, muddy, almost unrecognizable. Damn, I thought, and wondered what Yarima was thinking.

But that broke the ice. By this time we both knew we were ready, and late that night in my big matrimonial hammock, we consummated our marriage, keeping as quiet as we could so as not to disturb the nearby sleepers.

Yarima and I quickly got used to sleeping together in the same hammock, an experience the Yanomama don't have. The traditional Yanomama hammock is small. There's barely enough room for one person, and the occupant's feet have to rest on the supporting cord. At first I thought it odd they'd make their hammocks so short, and early on in my stay I even suggested that if they extended the length a foot or so, they'd be much more comfortable. "Why don't you make it longer?" I asked one of the men while he was making a new hammock. "Relax a little, enjoy yourself. You won't have to have your feet up on the line."

The individual I mentioned this to didn't know what to make of my saying such a thing. He didn't know why they made them so short, but what was the sense in such a question or suggestion? Hammocks always had been made like this, they always would be made like this. I later came up with my own theory after I had moved into the *shapono*. Everyone in a family sleeps naked around the same hearth, their hammocks slung in a triangle more or less equidistant from the fire and as close as they can get them. Longer hammocks would force everyone to move back another couple of feet to where they couldn't get any warmth. Or so I guessed. But whatever the reason, Yanomama husbands and wives never slept together, so the big Colombian "matrimonial" that Yarima and I occupied was a strange and rather shocking innovation.

But Yarima shrugged off the embarrassment. She liked it very much. She liked sleeping with her arms and legs twined around me, the warmth of our bodies making the cool nights comfortable. It amazed me how she adapted to it so readily, how she seemed to flow into it as if it were the most natural thing in the world, though she had never seen or imagined such behavior before. I loved it, too. Sleeping with her like this, her body making a nest of mine, made me feel that we were now truly a couple, truly married.

I had arrived at Wawatoi gardens in October 1982. In January 1983 I had to leave, to give the paper I had promised at the American Anthropological Association's annual meeting in Washington. While I was gone Yarima would live at her family hearth, with her mother and brother.

"Don't let her go out gathering alone," I told *shori*. "And don't let anybody bother her. Can you do that?"

"Yes," he said. "Of course." But it was hardly enough to quiet my fears.

In the plane from Caracas I had planned to put the finishing touches on the paper, but instead I found myself reading my journal entries for the past months and writing new ones.

Journal 1:00 P.M. Over the Caribbean: "Ever since I left the jungle my mind is fixed on Yarima. My love for her is so great. I knew her as a little girl. Then I left and she became a woman. So I was not the first. I'm almost sure it was Shatakewe [Yarima's sister's husband] but can't be positive. Now that I have really decided to stay there, I am concerned that she might become pregnant by someone else. I must find a way to an income. At least I earned enough money from the census for six months.

3:30 P.M.:   Thinking again about how I missed her most important year down there. But there were so many things. The break-off with Eibl, the Martin Stummer business, the Ph.D., sickness, money, depression. So many things. When I went down for the census I had really gotten her out of my mind. Or so I thought. But once I got down there it started right back up. I couldn't let it go, couldn't.

And then, when I saw her, that was the end. Like a thunderbolt. Red brought her back, and I just fell head over heels into the whole thing again. She was tired, dirty from the trip. I told her to get into the hammock and rest. And that was it. She was scared stiff, clutching some *kapiromi* roots in her hand.

Longbeard squatted in front of me, and I reprimanded him for allowing himself to be deceived. I guess I will hear the whole story one day, though I haven't yet. But it always comes out eventually. The Patahamateri guy will of course claim he never said such a thing. He'll say Longbeard is a liar.

So here I am hoping I will be the first one to make her pregnant. Not the first to make love to her, just the first to make her pregnant. Unbelievable. I raised her. I'm sure it was that bastard Shatakewe. But at least now I have Yarima again. Granted, full of anxieties. But the important thing is that we are together.

The entire plane ride I was thinking about her. She was my wife now, but if I didn't return in a reasonable time, I would lose her again. And what about the future, when I had finished the census? I would have no job, no way of supporting myself. I had to find a way to do it, find a way to stay there with her.

Journal, 11:05, Washington, D.C., the Sheraton: Time to go and give my paper, but all I can think of is Yarima. I guess it's an obsession. I open my attaché case, and I smell the smoke on my camera strap. Which reminds me of her. I look at myself in the mirror and wonder what she thinks of my balding head. I awake at three in the morning wondering how she is. In the day I think about what she might be doing. Has she left for the garden? Is she gathering today? Are they bothering her? Are they? Incessant worry.

Dying to get back, I gave the paper—on hunting and meat consumption as a limiting factor in Yanomama life. "You'll have to bear with me," I told the audience. "I've just come out of the jungle, and my voice is still a little shaky from a bout of malaria." Afterward there were questions, not so much about the details of my presentation, but about Yanomama life more generally. One anthropologist, though, did ask about the division of game, sharply questioning to what extent women were involved in the gathering process and wondering about their share in the distribution. I answered that women were instrumental in motivating hunts and that though the distribution was made through male heads of family, women and children generally received equitable shares. For a few moments it seemed that the question might generate some heat over the issue of male and female roles among the Indians. But I was happy when the subject faded out. My mind wasn't in the lecture hall at all, it was with Yarima, at her hearth in Hasupuweteri.

12

A week later I was back at Wawatoi. When I walked in Yarima was sitting in her hammock at her mother's hearth. But when she saw me she jumped up and ran to me, laughing her beautiful laugh and throwing her arms around me. It was an astonishing display, surprising and wonderful, like nothing she had ever done before, like nothing any Yanomama had ever done. I held her tight, crushing her against me, not caring that every pair of eyes in the village was staring at us in wonder.

The census proceeded, but slowly. Even going in by helicopter was slow and uncertain, prone to delays and mishaps. By helicopter, the best I could do was census one community at a time. Then we would have to go back to our base at Platanal or Guajaribo and get resupplied. The helicopter teams were on loan from the air force for only two weeks at a time, and the pilots were tentative and unsure of themselves and more than a little frightened of the jungle.

In addition, finding the Yanomama villages from the air turned out to be an almost impossible task. The only way to locate them was to scan; you could not see them easily. You had this vast green world under you, and a *shapono* would show up only as a tiny hole in the forest. Unless you were directly over it you couldn't see it at all. If you were off just a bit, or looking at it from the wrong angle, you'd miss it for sure. Even if you did see it, you'd be lucky to find a place to land.

On my first trip inland by helicopter, we got lucky. Circling over an area where I knew one of the villages was, we saw nothing but forest. But then our attention was attracted by smoke, and when we flew over we saw that the villagers were burning the undergrowth of a garden site in preparation for a new planting. And suddenly, there below us, was the *shapono* itself, with people scattering into the jungle. Hovering down, we saw a cleared spot off to the side of the garden that looked like a potential landing zone. But when we were only a few feet off the ground we made out a log lying diagonally across the area, and the pilot started yelling, "No, we can't land, we've got to get out of here. We'll wreck the copter!"

What is wrong with these guys? I thought. God only knew what was really going through their minds, probably that the Indians would cook them or something. They didn't want to take any chances, even though there was a backup helicopter hovering above us if something went wrong. Fortunately, as we circled around again we saw another spot, a second, abandoned *shapono* no more than a quarter mile away. We landed right in the middle of the central plaza. The people of Prararaiteri had never seen a non-Yanomama, let alone a helicopter. They had never seen a motorboat or anything else from the outside world other than a few trade goods. These were really dwellers of the remote interior. As soon as these unearthly flying monsters began circling around their village, swooping in, then rising and hovering, then swooping again with the roar of the engines and flap-flap-flap of the blades, they bolted into the jungle, as any reasonable person would.

Our first copter landed, lights blinking, while the other settled in behind it. For the Indians it must have been like a visitation from another universe, truly a scene out of *Close Encounters of the Third Kind*. The doors opened, and out popped three air force crewmen from each copter, all of them dressed in jungle uniforms with white gloves on and mosquito nets over their heads. And then me, with my beard and glasses. If there were still any villagers around when this happened, they must have taken off for the deepest recesses.

"*No hay nadie aquí,*" yelled the crew chief above the roar. "*¿Dónde están?*" ("No one's here. Where are they?")

"Where do you think they are?" I shouted back. "They're in the jungle. They're all gone. Look at you guys—I'd be scared of you, too."

I waited alongside the helicopters for about twenty minutes. Then I saw a young man over in the bushes, keeping hidden but watching us, overpowered by curiosity despite the extraterrestrial peril. I caught his eye. "*Shori, eou, shori.* Come on over here. I want to talk to you. We're friends, come on over here."

"No, no, no." he said.

"Yes, come on, come on out. We've got gifts and everything. Come on out. Bring everybody."

"No, I'm staying here. You're going to trick me"—edging closer—"I think you're tricking me. You're a tricker. No, no, no."

"No, *shori,* no tricks. I won't trick you. Come on, don't be stubborn. Come on. We came to visit you. We want to see your house. We want to give you fishhooks. Come on, show us the way."

And finally he came, but not too close, talking all the time. "*Eou,* you're not tricking me, are you? You're not going to do anything, are you?"

"No, of course not. Come on." And I started joking with him, in the most casual, relaxed way I could, until finally his fears were sufficiently alleviated. A few minutes later we were in their *shapono,* which was just beautiful, the most magnificently constructed place, large and perfectly circular. Very clean and brand new. And empty, of course, since all of the inhabitants were still hiding out in the jungle. In the living areas were an array of the most beautiful baskets I had ever seen.

I had hardly had time to look around when the other men started to come in, squatting down about fifteen feet from where I was. "Are you a friend? Friend?"

"Yes, I'm a friend."

I could see the headman all the way in back urging the young ones up: "Go ahead up there, be friends with him." And they kept edging closer, little by little, for a half an hour. "*Nohi? Nohi? Nohi? Nohi?*"

Finally one young man reached out, an act of great daring, and touched my arm. Then he pulled his hand back and said, "He's warm!" I couldn't imagine what he was thinking. But they had never seen anybody like this, white skin, hairy arms, a big, dense beard, glasses, and the size—a gigantic size.

The women and children never did come back. I had to count the hammocks and hearths to estimate the population. I also gathered as much information on nearby villages as I could—how far, how many people? How long does it take to walk there? How many nights do you have to sleep on the way? Where's the sun in the sky when you get there? More people than this village? Fewer people? I was rushing for the information, because the sky was now beginning to darken with storm clouds, and the pilot was acting nervous, nudging me that we had to get moving. "Let's go, we have to go. It's clouding up, we might be getting a storm in here."

"Look," I said, "hang on, there's still a little information I need," and I kept talking. Finally the crews just got up and walked back to the helicopters in the abandoned village, while I kept pressing to get everything I could. Then I heard one of the engines revving up, which gave me a little start. I hadn't even given gifts to these people yet. If the pilots left me, it would take two weeks to get out by myself. I ran back to the helicopters, followed by the young men. One was up in the sky already. The other had its engine running and was waiting for me. The door opened, and I hopped in, almost on top of a beautiful big woven basket that one of the crewmen had taken. As I watched, the pilot leaned out of the window toward the man who'd given him the basket and handed him a packet of coconut crackers and a pencil. The poor guy just stood there looking at these things. He had never seen a cracker, didn't know if it was food or what. And he certainly didn't know what a pencil was.

I yelled, "Don't worry, I'll pay you for it." The helicopter was taking off, and I was tossing spools of fishline and boxes of hooks out the door as we veered up into the sky, thinking to myself, Can you imagine—a coconut cracker and a pencil.

Over the next three months I censused the villages in sectors six and seven, mostly by foot, but a few by air. On one excursion two helicopters landed in Hasupuweteri to pick me up, the usual lead and backup. But when the dust cleared from the pad in front of the *shapono*, it turned out that the backup copter had sprung a small fuel leak. The pilots decided to return to Platanal to fix it, then start off from there.

At Platanal mission, the helicopters swooped in right in front of

the door, and who should be standing there but Irenaus Eibl-Eibesfeldt and the fellow who had taken my place, Harald Herzog,
whom I had heard about, a linguist who had no field experience.
Eibl's eyes widened. Here come these two air force helicopters,
landing right in front of him, and who should come bounding out
but me. Not actually bounding out, but running crouched over, the
way you do from a helicopter even though the blades may be twenty
feet above you. It must have looked like an invasion.

But Eibl recovered quickly and smiled, holding out his hand. *"Ach
so, Ken, Wie gehtes dir, mit deine grosse Nase?"* ("How are you,
with your big nose?") An inside joke, since I used to say to him,
"Renki, Was machst du denn, du mit deine grosse Nase?" Which
was pretty funny coming from me since I was the one with the
grosse Nase. "Yes, Ken," said Eibl, "I knew you were down here.
Let's take a little stroll, shall we?" And taking me by the arm, he
walked me up toward the landing strip, leaving Harald standing
there in front of the mission. "I was talking with Elka [Inga Goetz's
daughter] about you just a few days ago," Eibl said. "She thinks
maybe we ought to get together again. It occurred to me that I can
probably use Harald in another situation, and you and I might start
collaborating again. What do you think?"

For a moment my eyes lit up. All I really wanted to do was stay
with Yarima, and suddenly here was this godsend—from Eibl, no
less. But at the same time, there was poor Harald Herzog, standing
back in the mission doorway, and I could imagine what he was
going through watching Eibl and me strolling together. Instead of
taking Eibl up on his proposal immediately, I said, "Renki, it
wouldn't be a bad idea. I'd like to very much. But I'm sure Harald's
been preparing for this for the last year. Maybe the two of us could
work together—he's a linguist, I'm an anthropologist. There must
be some way we could cooperate. What do you think?"

And Eibl thought it might be a good idea; he'd give it some
consideration, he said, try to figure out exactly how to do it. In the
meantime he was going to take Herzog up to a village near the Río
Bocon and do some filming there, then he'd be coming out. Could
we meet at the mission when he got back? With these plans made,
I flew off to do another census with visions in my head of arranging
something with Eibl that would give me the means to exist.

I got back from the helicopter census just in time to leave for a
trek with the Hasupuweteri. Despite the scarcity of food, I probably
should have stayed at Wawatoi garden, working on the census

material and preparing for my next expedition. But Yarima was intent on going with the group, and I wasn't about to be separated from her more than was absolutely necessary. So we went.

A week later Yarima and I left the trek encampment with her brother, on our way to the river so that I could get down to see Eibl, who would be coming out himself right about now. On the bank of a little stream a short way from the Orinoco, we stopped to eat some fruit and rest. It was an unusual place. Just down from where we were sitting the stream widened, and on either side open sandy banks stretched out along the watercourse for thirty or forty yards. While *shori* sat and ate, Yarima and I went exploring. In the stream's widening the water flowed over a sandy, shallow bed that inclined very gradually to form the beach. The entire area was almost flat, a feature one rarely encountered in the rugged and hilly jungle. Without a word to each other, Yarima and I started to race, then quickly the race turned into a chase. We ran after each other, laughing and dodging and flying through the ankle-deep water, then onto the beach and back through the stream.

I knew that stream. It has a nice deep bend. When the water is deep you can go swimming there. You can swing from vines and jump off into it. It's also a good place to bathe. When the water is low you can have fun running up and down the beach. That's what Kenny and I were doing when he hurt his ankle. Kenny didn't play like we played. When the huya *play with girls they wrestle and hold them down. The girls fight back and try to escape. Sometimes a girl gets hurt and begins to cry. Sometimes while you are fighting you get scared because you don't know if the boy is playing or if he really wants to hurt you. But Kenny didn't play rough games. At the stream he was chasing me, and I was screaming and laughing. No one could run as fast as he could. He could not walk fast in the jungle, but on the beach he could run as fast as a jaguar.*

Running at full speed with Yarima just in front of me, I didn't see the little depression in the sand. I hit it in full stride, and my entire weight came down on my right foot, which turned over completely on itself. I could hear the ankle pop just before I sat down heavily. It didn't feel broken, but it didn't feel good, either. When I stood up I realized I couldn't put any weight on it. Already the ankle was beginning to swell.

Fortunately the river wasn't far, and once I was in my canoe, I thought, if I was very lucky, I might just be able to make it down to Platanal. Unfortunately it was March, the end of the dry season, a time when you often have to drag a canoe over sandbars only inches below the surface, even on the Orinoco.

Getting to the river was painful. I had to support myself with a branch that *shori* had cut and that I pressed into service as a make-shift crutch. One look at the river was enough; it was as dry as I had ever seen it. My ankle was badly swollen, but by the time we got to the dugout it didn't seem as tender as it had at first, and I thought that maybe I'd be able to do it. As Yarima and *shori* stood on the bank and watched, I headed the canoe downriver, but before I had gone fifty yards I was already hitting sand, and in another fifty I was lodged on the bottom. I climbed out and started to push, but with the first real pressure my ankle collapsed. There was no way I was going to get the boat through the sand. Turning around, I waved at *shori*. *"Eou,"* I shouted, "Wait, I'm coming back."

As painful as it was, the ankle was only half the reason I was turning back. I had had injuries before and had never let them get in my way. The other half was that I just found it too hard to leave Yarima. Had it been a matter of life and death, I would have found a way to get out. But it wasn't, and consequently I did not get to see Eibl.

It was a week before the ankle healed so that I could walk comfortably. Once it did I got to work on the census again, trekking into the villages now, since the helicopter situation was not working out too well. That was fine, as far as I was concerned. Yarima went with me everywhere. I loved being alone with her and with the Yanomama, immersed completely in their universe.

Journal, April 4, 1982, Irokai: If I weren't keeping my notebooks in English, I think I would really be disengaged completely. Anthropologists talk about missing things. But I don't miss anything. I don't miss a shower in the morning or cigarettes or hamburgers. I can't think of anything I do miss. Maybe that's the main reason I've been able to stay here. Other people can't imagine how you could go without fresh clothes and good food or a drink or a nice bed. I thought that myself seven years ago. How am I going to sleep? I sleep on my stomach, and you can't sleep on your stomach in a hammock. But I got used to a hammock. Now I'd have trouble with a bed.

But there's a lot more. I'm in love. Unbelievable, intense emotion, almost all the time. In the morning when she gets up to start the day, when I see her come in from the gardens with a basket of plantains, especially when we make love. Sure it's universal, except that being in love in Yanomama culture with a Yanomama girl is different, a different game, different rules. But the feelings, they're universal. I would have other things to deal with if I had been in love with a girl from Germany or Italy or Venezuela. Problems would have arisen there, with jealousies and so on, and I would have had to deal with them in those cultures.

The thing is that often I think my personality is more compatible with the Yanomama. Maybe that's the closest I can get to being myself or allowing myself to be myself, without all the constraints of our culture. Down here it never occurs to me that I better talk this way or act that way. Of course there have been occasions where I've thought, Now I have to stand up and assert myself, show my discontent or my anger. Otherwise whatever it is will just go on and get worse. But most of the time you don't think too much down here, you mainly react, total emotions coming out, just as the Yanomama do. No cultural restraints saying, If you act emotionally in this situation, you are going to leave a very bad impression, your image will suffer, you'll burn your bridges. In Yanomama you simply do not think like that. In that sense maybe I am more adaptable to this situation. Maybe somebody else wouldn't be.

My behavior here—in many ways it's typical Yanomama behavior. Just what a Yanomama would do. What people, even some anthropologists, do not understand is how truly different it is to live with people whose conception of morality, laws, restrictions, controls differs so radically from ours. If you don't protect yourself, if you don't defend yourself, if you don't demand respect—you don't survive. It's as simple as that. If you act down here as you would up there, you'll be so intimidated, so worked over, you'll be running out of here. And lots of guys have been.

But those things don't bother me, and there's so much else I am at home with. I like the absence of vanity, really like it. And the question of level, status, scale. Who are you? I'm this or that. None of it. You don't have it. I'm a better hunter than you, or I've got more arrow points than you. Or I come from a very good family of gatherers. You don't have it.

This is by and large a very harmonious society, obviously so. They couldn't live together otherwise. The whole crux of describing the Yanomama is here. In Chagnon's first book there were no outright lies. It was just the proportions that were distorted, the way it was presented, the context, the perspective that was wrong. I could write a book about Yanomama society—all the women are having affairs, the men are raping the women, everyone is stealing plantains—and make them come out like the Ik, those terrible, distasteful creatures from the Uganda escarpment who were supposedly capable of starving their nearest relatives to death. But then someone would come down here and say, Wait, that's not what I see at all. They're nice, they're smiling, they love their children tenderly, they care for each other. I don't see any fights going on. There's complexity here, emotions, behaviors, the whole gamut.

The point is that it's what you want to see, it's what you are drawn to write about. And that's supposedly anthropology. Chagnon made them out to be warring, fighting, belligerent people, confrontations, showdowns, stealing women, raping them, cutting off their ears. That may be his image of the Yanomama; it's certainly not mine.

Then there is their concept of beauty. The Yanomama love body hair, facial hair. They have none themselves. The men still all like to touch my beard, wish they had one. Pubic hair on women would drive them wild. Even the thought drives them wild. I heard some of the *huya* talking about our last visit: Boy, did you see the pubic hair on those girls up there? What could they have seen, a few wisps? They like light skin as opposed to dark. A dark-skinned person they call *ete*—skin of an anteater. They know that *nabuh* women have pubic hair, and that excites them. They ask me to tell them about my girlfriends' pubic hair. Describe it. The more detail the better. And what about sex? Do the *nabuh* women like it, do they move? Many Yanomama women just lie there, I guess. So the idea that a woman would enjoy sex, that she would *waikou*— hump—fascinates them, titillates them. When I tell them, Yes, sure they like it, sure they move, they go crazy. They believe the sex organs are dirty, penises and vaginas—*shami, shami*. The idea of oral sex would be inconceivable to them. But though the *huya* are really interested in sex, I never see the kind of obsession you get among adolescents in the States, where so much in your life at a certain age seems to revolve around sex, to be focused on it.

On our way back from censusing Hawaroweteri, we joined the Hasupuweteri, who were on trek yet again. When we got to their *wayumi* encampment there was news: the Patahamateri had invited us to Boriana gardens, where they had their *shapono*. It was peach palm season, and they were expecting an abundant harvest. From the *wayumi* camp it took almost a week to get to Boriana, but the trip was lightened by anticipation of the peach palm feast we'd be enjoying and the chance to trade and visit with relatives.

When we finally arrived at Boriana gardens, we stopped to decorate ourselves before going on to the *shapono*. All the Hasupuweteri painted themselves and each other with red and black dyes, making circle and line designs and adorning their hair with puffs of snow white down. When Red wanted to put some face paint on me I didn't say no, as I usually did, and he drew the lines thick with the *onoto* seed paste. While the women were finding flowers to insert in their ears, one of the men went into the *shapono* for the ritual exchange. The hosts presented him with a basket of meat and plantains, an indication that the feast was on and we were welcome, that indeed there was food.

But despite the basket of meat and plantains, the Patahamateri feast turned out to be a disappointment; in fact, there wasn't that much peach palm fruit. Longbeard was really upset about this. It had taken a week to walk to Boriana, and now not only was there no feast, there was hardly enough to go around. People can get into real fights about such things. We had been on the move. We were hungry and tired. We hadn't had that much to eat along the way. People tolerated it because they had an expectation of a great feast in front of them, and then all of a sudden there wasn't. In some circumstances this could be enough reason to kill. The Hasupuweteri were angry. We ate what there was that night, then the next day turned around and went home. There were no explosions of hostility, but nobody was in a good mood, either.

By now it was the end of April. With my census data all gathered, I was going to have to go out to Caracas to write it up and turn it in. As the Hasupuweteri moved steadily northeast, toward the Orinoco, I made my own emotional preparations for the leavetaking. We talked about my leaving. Yarima showed no outward concern; she never did. But I sensed her unhappiness about it. Afterward she and I built a separate little encampment for ourselves as we traveled, where we would have some privacy, at least for a few days. By the time we got to the river, I had steeled myself, suppressing the anxieties that were never far below the surface. I hated leaving her; I was worried about her already. And the last several weeks had put a new light on things: Yarima had missed her period; I was pretty sure she was pregnant.

We were on our way back from the feast at Boriana gardens when Kenny told me he had to go downriver. Even though he always goes downriver I was sad. I was sure that I was pregnant. I had not said anything to him about it, but I was sure he knew. He always knew when my squatting time should come. He told me that he could tell because he wrote it on his paper leaves. He explained to me that even if he forgets something, the designs he makes on the leaves never forget. He could look at the leaves and remember the names of all the people in all the villages we had visited. Sometimes if he didn't know a word, he looked at the leaves, and the designs told him.

I said that he should go downriver quickly and come back in a few days. I held up all the fingers on one hand. But he said he couldn't come back that fast. He said he had to go far away downriver to Caracasteri. He said it was so far that he had to go by avión and that the avión didn't come right away when he wanted it to. But he had to wait for the avión anyway because it could carry him to Caracasteri. If he walked to Caracasteri, he said, it would take many moons. The avión would take him in half a day. I wondered if the avión could really be that fast. I also wondered if Caracasteri could really be so far away. If you walk very fast, you can get all the way to the River of Parakeets in five days.

In Caracas I got all my census material in, and I started working on an article. The census money was not going to last too long, and I knew I'd better start some writing. I would need a source, some magazines or journals that would be interested in having pieces from me. I also wrote to Eibl; we had missed our connection, but an arrangement of some sort might still be possible. Even more worrisome was my permit situation. While I was doing the census I had been working under a special permit from the president's office, which had now expired. I would have to apply for another from the Indian Affairs Bureau office in Caracas, then get it countersigned by the governor in Puerto Ayacucho. I had been around long enough to know that this kind of thing could turn into a problem.

Journal, Caracas, May 16, 1983: I have been thinking more and more and missing Yarima. I can tell that in another week I will be getting desperate to see her again. Already the first twinges of desperation. I hope she doesn't forget about me. It's hard to tell how the Yanomama mind works, if it's any different from ours. Even after all these years. In most cases anthropologists tend to generalize and believe that all Yanomama think more or less the same way, that their thinking is a product of their culture, more or less undiversified. Only with really long-term, close relationships will I find out. My inclination is to look for individual differences. But all my training has been to focus on general characteristics rather than individual traits.

While I was in Caracas I talked by phone with Madeline Harris, Marvin's wife. She told me that *Science* magazine had reconsidered an article of mine they had originally rejected, the paper I had given at the anthropological conference. I was to call one of the editors. When I finally got through, the editor told me that she didn't think the article had been reconsidered. But when I pushed her on it, she checked the file. Eventually she came back on and said that indeed it had been reconsidered. One of the chief readers had recommended publication, but people on the staff had not agreed with his conclusions. So the probability was that it would not be published.

It was a bad phone call, an unpleasant discussion. My hopes had shot up for a moment, then crashed just as quickly. And I was really eager to get something in *Science,* especially after my last experience with them. Several years earlier Jacques Lizot and I had written a joint letter to *Science* condemning an article Chagnon and Ray Hames had coauthored. That Lizot and I had collaborated on a letter of this sort was a phenomenon by itself. Lizot had been Claude Levi-Strauss's student, while I was Marvin Harris's, and Harris categorically rejected Levi-Strauss's approach to anthropology and attacked it at every opportunity. Levi-Strauss (one of the founding fathers of French structuralism) was, so Harris liked to demonstrate, an idealist in whose thought myths and other mental phenomena played a wildly exaggerated role in understanding human culture, while actual human behavior that could be observed and recorded was considered essentially irrelevant. At the same time Harris, of course, was held in equal disdain by the French structuralists, for whom he was (when they were in a magnanimous mood) "a vulgar materialist."

So, as far as our anthropological orientation went, Lizot and I were 180 degrees apart. But both of us were astonished and shocked by a Chagnon/Hames article in *Science* entitled "Protein Deficiency and Tribal Warfare in Amazonia," which purported to show that the Yanomama diet contained plenty of protein. According to Chagnon and Hames, if Harris's theory about the impact of protein scarcity on warfare was correct, there should be more warfare where protein consumption was lower, less where it was higher. But obviously warfare was common where protein intake was high; therefore Harris was refuted.

It was a crude, simplistic correlation that demonstrated an astounding ignorance of Harris's leading thesis—that warfare functioned to keep groups dispersed precisely so that hunting territories would not be subject to competition and consequently would indeed provide adequate protein. But it wasn't the ignorance that shocked Lizot and me. What shocked us was that the Chagnon/Hames data had not come from a legitimate Yanomama village at all, but from a small group of Yanomama refugees who had attached themselves to a village of Ye'kwana Indians, a completely different culture, much more advanced technologically and far more acculturated than the Yanomama. The Ye'kwana village where this small group of Yanomama lived and worked was especially advanced, a riverine fishing community with four or five outboard motors and several docking points for their dugouts. They had a little store where they could buy canned meats and other foods, and they owned a big boat to take their garden crops down to Puerto Ayacucho and sell them, bringing back the things they needed, gasoline, shotgun shells, and so on. They even had a political co-op that the local political party had put in. In effect, the Ye'kwana with whom these Yanomama were living constituted a small peasant community.

But Chagnon and Hames had neglected to mention any of this, leaving the impression that the Yanomama from whom they derived their data were an integral group living a traditional Yanomama life. Lizot and I had responded that this was not the case and that in our opinion Chagnon and Hames had had an obligation to explain to readers what kind of data they were presenting, and they hadn't done it. To my disbelief, *Science* had rejected our letter. I had even gotten on the phone and pleaded with them to publish it. For the sake of anthropology, I had said, the readers have to know about this. That's what I said. What the editor said was no, the case was closed, they weren't publishing it.

So this was a bad phone call, and it got me to thinking again about the academic world, about the jealousies and politics that I hated so much.

Journal, Caracas, May 17:   I am so fucking sick of it. The Yanomama would never dream of this kind of behavior, the struggle for acceptance, the infighting and backbiting. What do I want to come out for, a life with these people? I hate them. Madeline told me that one of the Florida anthropologists had called another one a "female Ken Good." Can you imagine! I will stay down here with the Yanomama. They are so uncivilized—and that makes them tolerable. No insomnia, no bad dreams, no anxieties. No feeling that people are driven by envy and spite. I realize that someday I will have to come out for lack of funds or bad health. But for now I have an adorable Yanomama wife. She sleeps with me in my hammock every night. We keep each other warm. We hold each other and play and laugh. I hold her close. I smell the *onoto* paint still on her skin. It stains my hammock, but I don't care. Her bronze skin is so warm, although I am almost shivering from the cool Amazon night. It feels so good. We build the fire up, then go back to sleep. She finds a comfortable position, entwined in my legs and arms. As dawn approaches the frogs begin to croak, and slowly the village comes to life. Yarima gets out of the hammock and begins peeling plantains and reviving the dying coals of the night. Her fingers are covered with the resin of the green skins. When they are cooked, she gives me three or four and says, *"Pei"* ("Here, for you"). Later she'll say, *"Ya naiki"* ("I'm meat hungry"). "Let's go hunting downstream, and you'll shoot a *manashi* bird."

She walks behind me on the trail when we leave the village. I can feel her there. Sometimes the happiness I feel overwhelms me, so much that one time tears came to my eyes. She spoke softly so no one would hear her. "Don't cry," she said. "If you do, the evil spirits will come upon you." I fill my notebooks with descriptions and data—fifty-six of them this far. She wonders why I have such an incessant desire to make designs on paper—"leaves," they call it. It seems strange to her, but she accepts it, as she has so many other strange things of her husband. I ask her so many times, Does she really like me? Does she want to be my wife? "Yes," she says. "If I didn't, I would have run away to my mother's sisters' village at night long ago. I'm not afraid. Don't worry," she says. "We will have a child, and you will play with it in your hammock. You and only you will make our child. I have told you now," she says. "So don't *nohi harupo*."

I pray to God she doesn't get hurt while I'm downriver, and that I don't get sick. Malaria and hepatitis will finish you down here. Why would I want to go home? To ambition, greed, jealousy, crass competition? To racial hatred, fear, and danger in the streets, to endless debates on the meaning of man's existence? Why do I need it? This will end someday, I know. But my whole purpose now is to make it last as long as it can. If I wrote a successful ethnography, I know what it would be like in the anthropology community. But I don't want that phony attention. What I want is Yarima's warm smile. Her black, sparkling eyes, her smooth skin.

Journal, Caracas, May 25:   I spent two weeks on the census wind-up. Have now done most of my shopping for supplies. I miss Yarima terribly. I wonder if she is really pregnant. My heart jumps each time I think she might be. I also have anxieties about whether I am going to get this permit, if I can get funds, how it all will end up. Journal articles would get me a good job, though not the kind that would let me be with her. But I am preoccupied. I know it. I am obsessed. I have changed my whole life for my love of Yarima. I can't believe that if I have a child, I might not be allowed to see it. That if my child needed care, I wouldn't be allowed to provide it. I can't think like that. Must be optimistic. They can say, No, you can't have another permit. What am I going to say, I have a wife and a child upriver? "What, you are a foreign scientist who comes to this country. We gave you a permit to do research in a restricted area. Not for any wife or kid." I'm playing that Julio Iglesias tape in Italian, missing Yarima. I must know, Is she pregnant? She missed her period just before I left. If she is, I should be giving her vitamins and proteins.

Journal, Caracas, June 13, 6:05 A.M.:   It's been six weeks. I'm getting desperate. They are moving like molasses on my permit. They keep saying it's almost ready, then when I come back it's not. I've been awake since three-thirty. Yesterday I only slept two and a half hours. It's been so long since I sat in the village and filled out the census forms while Yarima sat on a barrel next to me and sucked on a piece of sugar cane. It seems ages since I came back and she was frightened and my biggest challenge in life was to get her to relax around me, to like me. I wonder how I can muster the resources to stay there. At least I've got all my supplies now. I spoke with Eibl today. He is very enthusiastic. Says he wants to work together but is in the red for this year. Will try for next year. Is sure he will be able to arrange it.

On July 8 the Indian Affairs Bureau notified me that my permit was ready. I had been waiting two and a half months. Even under ordinary circumstances the bureaucracy here could be maddening, but my circumstances weren't ordinary. Each day of the last few weeks had been torture. On July 9 I flew to Puerto Ayacucho, hoping I'd now be able to get the governor's countersignature without any trouble.

When I gave the permit to the governor's secretary, he seemed to think there wouldn't be any problem, though it might take a day or two to get it processed. Could I check back, he said, tomorrow or the next day? It was difficult not to get my hopes up, though I knew so well that even the friendliest reception could easily be the prelude to some mindless bureaucratic atrocity. How many times had I seen that happen?

Walking down the main street, I ran into Yorusiwe, the man I called the toll taker. I wasn't happy to see him. I didn't like him, and I didn't know anyone who felt differently. Yorusiwe lived in the Yanomama village outside Platanal mission and specialized in intimidating travelers who wanted to go upriver. Usually he was able to either threaten or cajole trade goods out of them. Then he'd come down to Puerto Ayacucho, where it was rare to see a Yanomama, and beg, passing himself off as a poor starving Indian. We hadn't had an exactly sparkling relationship since he found he couldn't pull his usual routine on me. But at least we'd been civil. He told me I am thin this time. According to him, the last time I came from Caracas I was really big. The reason I'm thin now, he said, is probably because my wife is pregnant. A pregnant wife makes a husband get thin.

Journal, Puerto Ayacucho, July 15, Gran Hotel Amazonas: The most devastating problem yet. The governor does not want to give me a permit! I found this out from Dr. Rumbos, the governor's assistant. He tells me that too many foreigners have been going into the area. I am in such a state of shock. If the governor doesn't reconsider, I'm afraid it will take the president to get it done. I must think of Lizot and what he went through. At first he wasn't allowed to go back in, but he just stuck it out and lined up his allies. I'm going to have to do the same thing. The fact that I had come from the U.S. to work for the president's office on the census makes no difference to these people. No, he says, it's a restricted area. For Christ's sake, I know it's a restricted area. I've been up there since 1975.

Hanging around Puerto Ayacucho while the governor made up his mind was like a season in hell. I was haunted by anxiety. Not that it was such an unusual thing to have permit problems. It happened, though normally it was no more than a bad annoyance. You had to go back to Caracas to start the whole process all over again, instead of going upriver to do your work. It might take you another month or two months to get it resolved. Or at the very worst, if you couldn't get it resolved, you'd go back to the States, write a paper, write a book, then come back when there was a new governor, six months or a year later.

But I didn't have that kind of luxury. I had to get upriver. I had to get to Yarima. I couldn't wait six months or a year. I'd already been out far too long.

Journal, Puerto Ayacucho, July 16: Unbelievable, just unbelievable. Some of my friends here have now talked to the governor, including Gonzalez Herrera, the former governor, former health minister. And suddenly my permit is approved. As sudden as the shocks are in this place, they vanish just as quickly. Now you see it, now you don't, now you do again. Life in the Amazon can get very heavy at times, but oh, can one become addicted. Hope this governor is gone when I need to deal with the governor's office again.

Journal, Wawatoi garden, July 20: Guajaribo rapids up to the river camp. Stopped upriver at Shuimuiteri, told them I was going in to Wawatoi, asked them to find Red, tell him I'd be in Wawatoi. A torrential downpour. *Shapono* all muddy. Nobody here. They're not home. No one here, no Orawe, no Longbeard. Feel a little desperate, but under control. No way to get to Yarima unless Red shows up.

Three P.M.: Still no Red.

Twelve midnight: Red never showed. Must see Yarima, I admit, in part because I am *nohi harupo*. And how the mind can go wild in that respect. Not that this is anything new for me. I can always think of a dozen new reasons why this time may be it, why this time I may be at a dead end. Maybe they're afraid of me again, maybe they've stolen things from me and won't show. Listened to the Armed Forces Radio talking baseball. A different world. I can't wait another day. If Red comes tomorrow, I will push to reach the group.

Journal, Wawatoi, July 23: Still alone. *Nohi-iyopo,* I miss her. *Nohi-iyopo,* I need to be with her. My gear is still down at the river. Two Shuimuiteri came by. They say the Hasupuweteri are at Irokai, a day's walk. Good. They also say that Lizot is looking for me. They say he is out to kill me, and he has gone to my father's village to look for me. These people are amazing. They will say anything, believe anything. Rumors, lying, the lifeblood of the Amazon. Of course in Yanomama terms it sounds perfectly logical. If Lizot were actually angry at me, where would he go to find me except my father's village? They think Pennsylvania is a *shapono.* I wonder what they've been telling Lizot about my intentions toward him?

Journal, Wawatoi, July 25: Red came at last. Took me to Irokai. Hard to believe; they're on trek again. We were on trek four months before I left for Caracas. I get back and they're out again. All they do is trek. Absolute hunter-gatherer nomads. Who ever called them horticulturalists?

When I arrived at Irokai the whole group was there. I dropped my packs and walked over to Yarima, who stood up and waited for me to come to her. Amid all the noise of the *shapono* she stood there quietly, looking more radiant than she ever had. And most amazing, most wonderful, her belly seemed rounder, slightly swollen. There was no doubt about it.

She was pregnant, she told me. Two moons and two moons. My calculations were the same; it had to be four months. Which meant the baby would be born in January. She seemed very happy about it. I could hardly express my own feelings, not to her, not even to myself. I was flooded by happiness.

When the Hasupuweteri left Irokai to continue their trek, I wanted to stay behind. But Yarima didn't; she insisted on going. She was determined to stay with her family, especially her sister and her sister's children, whom she calls her children also. I felt I had to settle down and write, something I couldn't begin to do on a trek. But much more important, I was concerned about her condition, making a hard trek while she was carrying the baby, even though I knew that she and the other women would consider that completely normal and my fear nonsensical. On the other hand, staying behind would have created its own problems. Yarima was already crying when I brought the subject up. Her brother was visibly dejected, as were her mother and some others when they heard we might not be coming along. It's remarkable, the love and affection they have for each other. Besides, what would she have eaten, what would she have done while I was trying to write?

This trek will be toward the Siapa—"over there," Red told me, pointing generally toward the south, at least his arm pointing generally southward, his extended index finger jutting off toward the right. When daylight ran out I used my flashlight so I could keep writing. Yarima crawled into the hammock and snuggled next to me, almost asleep in the warmth of the fire. While I wrote I talked to Rookoowe's little boy, who had also climbed in and was half sitting, half lying, in the crook of my arm. He must be about six, open, curious, relaxed, a happy kid. It seemed to me almost like a family scene. A picture of the future? I often wondered and worried (characteristic of me) about where this would lead, with Yarima and a baby. I felt so comfortable here, and so uncomfortable in civilization. But then, weren't the Hasupuweteri hungry now? Didn't they have wars and fight and kill and hate? Weren't they constantly in search of goods from each other, begging, complaining? And weren't they sick and dying? Didn't they steal and deceive and live in fear of evil spirits? Didn't they raid each other's gardens and quarrel and ridicule each other in public and get furiously angry? And where did I fit in to all this? *"Wa maharishi?"* said Yarima, her eyes lidded with sleep. ("Aren't you sleepy? You are drawing so much.") She looked at me for a minute, then drifted off, content. I watched her sleep, her eyes closed, the trace of a smile on her lips, her breasts rising and falling gently, almost imperceptibly. What more, I thought, can I ask?

After almost a month of trekking, the Hasupuweteri headed back toward Wawatoi. As we neared the gardens Yarima and I decided to go on ahead. We both wanted to get back, and we were impatient with the leisurely trek pace, stopping so often, building a shelter every afternoon, waiting around. The *wayumi* could come behind us.

Taking *shori* and three *huya* to carry packs, we set off. Yarima was in her fifth month now, her belly larger, obviously pregnant to anybody who looked. But despite the pregnancy she insisted on carrying her basket full of gourds, pots, and hammocks, all our household possessions. Personally, I was eager to get organized and get some work done, to piece together some articles and to get out a transcription or two to Eibl. Ever-present in my mind, though not of course in Yarima's, was the fact that I had to start writing. If I didn't produce, it wouldn't be long before I'd be completely out of money. I could have kicked myself that I hadn't taped the two women who got into a fight at the last encampment. That had really been unusual. They were actually hitting each other with sticks. I had never seen such behavior before; a transcription and analysis of it might have been publishable.

That morning we stopped at the Rahuawe River to fish, but they weren't biting so we continued on. I followed Yarima, watching her basket jiggle slightly as she walked. Early in the afternoon we met the Mokaritateri community on their way to a feast at Yehio-pateri. They had just left their house that morning, which was where we were planning to spend the night. We squatted on the trail, talking with them for an hour or so, then kept going. By now a light rain had started to fall, and as we walked through the hilly terrain I could feel my legs getting tired. A moment after the thought passed through my mind, Yarima turned around and said, "I'm tired, I don't feel like going on."

"I don't either," I answered, "but I think we're near the *shapono*. We should try to get there before dark."

As *shori* and the others forged a little way ahead of us, Yarima and I slowed down. In a hollow at the base of a hill we crossed a small stream, and Yarima motioned me to go on as she stepped off to the right into some bushes to relieve herself. "I'll catch up to you," she said, then disappeared into the undergrowth. A moment later I heard her call out, and breaking through the brush, I saw her squatting down in a sandy area next to the stream. "Eou, eou," she said, "my stomach hurts," and she pointed between her legs. Something white was there, hanging out of her. As I came closer I could see a loop of umbilical cord dangling almost to the ground.

Oh, shit! I thought, Damn! Damn! I pounded the sand. I didn't know what to do. I tried to calm her, but she was frightened and shivering. "It's okay," I said, knowing nothing was okay. "It's okay, it's okay, the fetus is just trying to come out."

Shaking, she told me that her stomach had hurt her all last night, but she hadn't said anything. Then she began to cry for her mother. I squatted next to her, putting my arm around her, wanting to keep her warm, wanting to keep her calm. Trying to keep myself calm.

"Are you crying because the baby's being lost?" I asked.

"No," she said, choking down her tears, "I'm not. Tell the boys to keep going. Don't let them come down here."

Just then *shori*'s voice came through the jungle from the hill up ahead. "Where are you? Brother-in-law, younger sister, where are you? You can't stay down in there. Evil shamans can come to that place. What's wrong? Come up, come up!"

"Don't tell him what's happening," Yarima whispered, getting control of herself a little. "He'll get too scared."

Walking up the stream a few yards toward *shori*'s voice, I called out to him. But he wouldn't come down any farther. Through the jungle I yelled for him to take the others and go on to the Mokaritateri *shapono*.

This was so awful. Yarima had had severe pains the night before. Had I known I would never have gone ahead or allowed her to go ahead. Especially not the way we were traveling, up and down hills at the rate of men when they are visiting another village. And on top of that her brother and the other boys wanted to get to the Mokaritateri *shapono* before dark, because this was supposedly an area of evil shamans and they wanted to get through it as fast as they could. And I was too goddamn stupid to tell them to slow down.

Shori's voice came through the trees, calling me like some kind of disembodied spirit. What had happened to us? Had something happened? Were we all right? Was there anybody else down there with us?

"Go up to the house," I yelled. "Just take the others and go up to the house. Don't worry. We'll be right there." In back of me I could hear Yarima crying. I walked back and forth between her and her brother, trying to comfort her, shouting at him through the trees to go on, to go on to the *shapono*. Finally, after what seemed hours, I heard him yell, "*Shori*, we're going to the house now," and I went back to Yarima, who was still squatting on the sandy bank, weeping softly.

At five-thirty I told Yarima we couldn't stay there any longer. It would be getting dark soon; she'd have to try to walk up to the house. Wrestling with the tumpline, I finally got the basket settled on my back and led her up the hill, my anxiety rising as I listened to her crying. The *shapono* wasn't more than a quarter mile away, but when we reached it Yarima would not go inside, not with the men there. I carried the basket into the house while *shori* and the other three watched me. There was dead silence. Ordinarily the sight of a man carrying a woman's basket would have brought gales of laughter from them. But now there were only grim stares. They knew something was terribly wrong.

As quickly as I could I gathered some wood and got a fire going, then hung our hammocks. When I got outside again I didn't see her at first. Then I found her hidden in a patch of dense brush just off the trail, worried about the evil spirits. She wanted me to send the *huya* for water, but she didn't want them to pass by her on the trail. That's why she had gone into the brush. Back in the *shapono* I asked them to bring some water, and though I could see they were very reluctant to leave, eventually they did. But Yarima would not go into the house while she was having the miscarriage. A woman doesn't go through something like that in front of other people. They don't expect any comfort or help, at least not from men. A man is never near a woman in a situation like this. A man never sees a birth. It's not exactly that he can't. A man wouldn't want to see it, and a woman wouldn't want him to.

Back in the bush Yarima was squatting again, crying to herself. The mosquitoes were swarming around her naked back, and when I asked if they were bothering her, she said yes. Although I was sure she wasn't overly concerned with mosquitoes at this point, I crawled out of the undergrowth and into the *shapono* to dig a can of repellent out of one of the packs. When I got back I sprayed her back and arms, then sat down next to her. I felt so bad for her, alone here with just a bunch of young men, away from her mother and her family, going through this with the umbilical cord hanging out. It was almost too much to bear. I wanted to do something, to save her, to help her. But I could think of nothing to do.

After dark Yarima looked up and said, "Let's go home." To the *shapono*, she meant. Since it was night the *huya* wouldn't be able to see her. With the cord dangling she took down her hammock from where I had hung it next to mine, then restrung it in the back of the house. Squatting next to her, I timed the contractions, which had now started coming regularly. When they were down to three minutes apart, she said, "I think it's near." Three or four hard contractions followed, then she squatted and grabbed the low roof supports above her. At eight P.M. exactly she said, "I had it." I shined the flashlight, and there under her was a seven- or eight-inch-long fetus. Pulling a large leaf from the roof, Yarima picked it up, wrapped it, then walked over to the opening and put it down in the bush. I could feel the tears welling in my eyes and running down my cheeks. *"Shami,"* she said as she sat down on the ground next to the hammock, *"shami."* As I draped a clean shirt over her shoulders, I could see the ground under her turning dark with her blood.

13

The next morning I made soup and coffee and packed our bags. Yarima had slept well; after the miscarriage she'd dropped off like a stone, utterly exhausted. I packed her basket as she sat in the back of the *shapono;* still bleeding a bit, she was ashamed to stand up in front of the young men. Thank God she's not hemorrhaging, I thought as I took all the heavy items out of her basket—I'd carry those. It would-be a long eight-hour trip home, over the hills from Mokaritateri.

We left at eight A.M., twelve hours after she aborted. As we trudged along, the pain of losing the child began to seep in. I had been so happy about the pregnancy, and the loss preoccupied me, that and continuing worries about Yarima's condition. We followed the *huya* some way behind, and although I told Yarima to go very slowly, she didn't listen and walked at the usual pace. Then, about a third of the way home she asked me to carry her basket, in a playful way, laughing about it—just as she had when two or three days earlier she had told me her stomach ached because she had eaten caiman meat. I had thought it was a joke or one of their superstitious beliefs. "Eat caiman meat, your stomach will hurt." Was this a sign that something was wrong again? Maybe if I had taken it seriously the first time, the child would have been saved.

As I took Yarima's basket from her, she laughed; men don't carry baskets. Then she took the shotgun from me, and I laughed; women don't carry weapons. Although the basket weighed no more than ten or fifteen pounds, the tumpline put an unaccustomed strain on my neck, and I marveled how the women were able to carry loads four or five times as heavy all day long. About an hour and a half from home we stopped, and I put up the plastic covering to shelter us from the light rain while we rested and ate *kareshi* fruit before taking off again.

As we got near the *shapono* Yarima and the others picked up the pace until they were going so fast, I began falling behind. "You're not walking well," she said, looking back. "You're not keeping up. Let me have the basket, I'll carry it." Her toughness was unbelievable. Once she hoisted it onto her shoulders and adjusted the line, she hurried to catch up, walking effortlessly and quickly, this woman who had had a miscarriage the night before. Even without the basket I had trouble keeping up.

All through the day she seemed much more concerned about hiding her bleeding (there was still a trickle of blood) than about her physical state. But I was sure she was frightened, particularly since she had neither her mother nor any other women around, only these four young men and me. *Shori* and the *huya* wouldn't go near her, they wouldn't look at her. A Yanomama man—even her husband—would never have had anything to do with her in this situation. Their feelings were so unlike mine, so unlike those almost any Westerner would have. You help, you hold, you comfort. You do what you can. But not the Yanomama. I could see that it was a struggle for Yarima to accept my behavior. At times she seemed relieved that I was lending a hand. But she was definitely not thinking how wonderful it was that I was taking care of her and how awful Yanomama men were by comparison. On the contrary, sometimes she would get angry if she thought I was acting too solicitous or too fond. That she didn't like at all.

After my baby came out dead I wanted to get home as fast as I could. Kenny seemed so sad, but I told him not to be because we would make another baby. I wanted him to be the way he was before when we would play and laugh together and I would tease him. That's why I told him to carry my basket. That would be funny, and I thought he would laugh and feel better. I thought if he saw that I was laughing, he would laugh, too. The *huya* smiled when they saw Kenny carrying the basket, but they didn't laugh. Kenny's forehead had no hair to protect it from the strap, so he had to hold each side with his hands.

I felt strange carrying Kenny's shotgun. I had never carried it before. He showed me the thing I was not allowed to touch. He said that if I did, it might shoot by accident. Kenny couldn't walk well with the basket, even though it was not heavy. He didn't know how to carry it. I thought it was very funny to watch him struggling to walk up the hills, like an old woman. It was especially funny because Kenny was so big and powerful, and he still couldn't go up the hills. But I knew he was doing it because he felt sorry for me. No other man would carry a woman's basket.

I spent most of the day unpacking things and drying them, dealing with a big invasion of *shukumi* ants, washing clothes. The milk was dripping from Yarima's breasts, which sent a pang through me. "Don't be upset," she said. "We'll make another baby." Her fortitude was amazing; it's youth, I thought, youth conquers everything. While I was lying in the hammock trying to take a nap, she came over and laughed as she squirted milk in my face. Her breasts had gotten huge; she looked as if she could feed three babies.

That night we listened to my tapes. We both like that Julio Iglesias song in Italian, "Dove Sará." The others do, too; they asked me to play it loudly. The *huya* also like Soledad Bravo, the Venezuelan singer, and Al Jarreau—they really like Al Jarreau.

The next day the rest of the village returned. It had taken two days for us to get home, four for the rest of the village at the normal *wayumi* rate. I was depressed that I had ever agreed to go on that long, arduous trip. The only reason I had gone was because Yarima's mother and *shori* had been so sad at the prospect of being separated from us. And Yarima had insisted on going. She does have a stubborn streak; it's part of her strength. But I could have kicked myself for having given in.

I wondered how long the Hasupuweteri were going to stay now. They seemed to be trekking all the time. Anyway, I was not going to go on *wayumi* with them again soon, that was that. I had to get work done: produce at least two or three articles before I went out again for another permit. If not, I'd have no way to stay here, no means to buy supplies for myself. I wanted to hole up in the house for a while, just Yarima and I. I felt that I needed time off. I knew that Lizot got away from his villagers when he needed to. I was sure Harald Herzog did, too. Sometimes the atmosphere seemed to close in on me. I don't know, I thought, maybe I'm still suffering the aftereffects of losing the child. For Yarima, for the Yanomama, a miscarriage is a normal event. You consider yourself lucky if your wife doesn't die, then you get on to the next thing. You don't have the luxury to bitch and moan or indulge your sorrow. Have people comfort you? Not here. I had to tell myself that these feelings of mine were normal.

All day long I kept telling Yarima to get in the hammock, to rest. But she told me that she couldn't, she'd get bad skin sores. Yano-mama wisdom has it that menstruating women will get skin sores if they lie in a hammock during the daytime; women bleeding from miscarriages will, too. Finally, after Yarima went to sleep I listened to the shortwave and heard the news about U.S involvement in Lebanon against Syria. Reagan was asking Congress for an eighteen-month extension of the marines' presence. That's American wisdom, I mused. The Russians had downed a South Korean airliner. Russian wisdom. Riots in Manila. Preparation for the Olympics in Los Angeles next summer. The Olympics! It was a different universe.

The next morning Yarima had just about stopped bleeding. We went down to the river, to that little crystalline pool we liked so much, and I scrubbed her down with soap. She was filthy from the blood and the milk and the dirt of the trek. As I shampooed her hair, she told me she was feeling weak and nauseated. She's anemic for sure, I thought, even though I had started giving her iron tablets, vitamin/mineral supplements, and time-release vitamin C. She was probably getting better care in terms of vitamin and mineral intake than any other Yanomama in history.

Journal, Wawatoi, September 23: Evening. I'm listening to Bach on the shortwave with Makawe, one of Yarima's classificatory brothers. I can't believe it, they're playing the Cantata 30, my favorite. *Gelobet sei Got, Ge-elo-o-bet sien name—nahahahahaha-ahahahame.* Imagine, sitting here eating peccary and plantains and listening to Bach. Nothing like old Johann Sebastian to go with a meal of peccary and plantains. This loss has been a tremendous blow for me. Yarima not so much. She's young, in no hurry to have kids. But for me? What happens when I go out for my next permit? What happens if there's a new governor? For all the problems, at least Sanchez finally let me in. Twinges of desperation and depression. To see her big stomach, to know that it's empty. To see her swollen breasts, the milk still dripping. Of course I could stay here even after the permit's expired. Nobody's going to come in this far and haul me out. But if you do that, you're in deep trouble when you do come out. You'll never get back in again.

Journal, Wawatoi, October 1: At night they told me a *bore,* a ghost, was outside the village. They always say they hear a *bore* out there. They're afraid, because an angry *bore* can come into the village and get very aggressive, clobber them over the head. Being Yanomama ghosts, they stick to the trails, just as they did in life. At night the villagers block off all the trails around the *shapono* with brush and branches to keep them out. No ghost, they think, would go off into the forest to get around the barricade. They were sure there was a ghost out there tonight. They know they heard it. Please shoot the shotgun, they tell me, please drive the ghost away. Don't know why they were so edgy tonight. Finally, when Yarima asked me to do it, I gave in. They didn't have any luck with me, so they went to her. They know I'll do anything she asks. Went outside the *shapono* and fired the shotgun. A resounding crash. That was good enough. I guess I frightened the *bore* away.

Journal, Wawatoi, October 6: The Hasupuweteri left yesterday. They were going to Irokai, their new garden. I needed to stay behind to get work done, and I asked Yarima to stay with me. I don't know, maybe it's the miscarriage thing, but I feel closer to her than ever. My jealousy is also rising. Last night it came out. I knew she had had sex with other guys. I strongly suspected it. But whenever I've brought the subject up she has said no. She wasn't going to talk about it. But I wanted to know. I had to know. I asked if she would tell me if she had. She said yes, she would. But of course she wouldn't really. No Yanomama would. At night when she got in the hammock with me, I got out, angry at her for not talking to me about this. I left her there and moved to the blue nylon hammock and listened to the radio with the earphones on, really angry. I'm sure she has something to say and is not saying it.

. . .

The next morning Yarima was in a terrible mood, sensing my suspicions and getting angry herself. She wanted to join the others, and I told her, Fine, go, I'll stay here alone. Irrational or not, I wanted to get this out on the table now. "Okay, look," I finally told her, "the baby's gone. We don't have a baby anymore. Now you can tell me whether it was mine. I must know. Now you can tell me if anyone else has had sex with you. It doesn't matter now."

For some reason that did it. Suddenly it all came out in a flood. "Yes," she said. "Yes. It happened when you were downriver, when you went out to Caracasteri. But I was already pregnant with your baby. It was your baby."

I felt as if a cement truck had hit me, even though I had half expected to hear there had been someone else. "Who?" I asked. "Who was it?" I could taste the bile in my mouth. "Tell me who it was!"

"Yes," she said, "him, my sister's husband."

Shatakewe! I just knew that bastard had been watching and waiting for me to leave, waiting for his chance. Yarima had grown up in my sight as my betrothed wife; I had been such a part of her life, invested so much of myself in her. As her husband I had been through so much with her—grief as well as happiness. The possessiveness began to roll over me like a wave, and it took me a minute to catch my breath. Then I started. "You didn't tell me. Why didn't you tell me? Why did you lie to me?" I couldn't sit still. I got up and paced back and forth, feeling an emotional fury building up. Before I knew what was happening I was stamping and storming around the plaza, scolding and shouting at her. I shouted at the top of my lungs, waving my arms around. "I'm angry because you deceived me, more than because you had sex. You deceived me! Why have you deceived me?"

"*Ta diha,*" she said. "Don't be so angry. Don't be angry with me. Don't." She huddled up in the hammock, sobbing, with that fearful look in her eye.

I had seen that look before. I had seen it in the eyes of other Yanomama women whose husbands were on the edge of violence. It froze me for a moment, though inside my stomach was still doing flips. I stepped back, feeling a sick black anger still roiling inside me. I moved away from Yarima into the shadows, getting control, bringing it down. Come on, Ken, I told myself, take it slow, calm down, go easy. What the hell are you doing? Yarima was crying, but quietly now, watching me warily, her eyes shifting with my movements. "Okay," I said to her, "it's okay, *bushika*. Don't worry, it's okay. Don't worry about anything." I wanted to hold her, to press her to me. She was so vulnerable, so beautiful.

"Come on," I said, "let's take a walk around the *shapono*."

Yarima got out of the hammock and came over to me. We started walking, slowly. "*Bushika,* do you like me?" I asked. "Do you still want to be married to me?"

She didn't answer, but I could see she was a little calmer. She wasn't crying anymore, and she didn't have that terrible frightened look. I began to imagine her fear. If she had been alone with a Yanomama husband and had told him what she had just told me, she wouldn't have known what to expect. A Yanomama husband might have picked up a stick and beat her and told her to get out or burned her with a piece of firewood. Women used to come up to me with bruises and burns and ask me to put ointment on or an antiseptic.

"Look at what he did, my husband," they'd say, giggling nervously.

"Jesus," I'd mumble to myself, staring at a third-degree burn. "What did he do that for?"

"I don't know, he's jealous, *nohi harupo.*"

But instead of a Yanomama husband she's got me. And I explode and roar at her, but I don't touch her (I could never touch her in anger). I ask her if she likes me, if she'd like to go for a walk around the *shapono*. Could you just imagine a Yanomama husband asking his wife to go for a walk so they can talk things out? Maybe hold hands? That was the ritual back in the States. You go out for a cup of coffee and talk it out. You share your feelings, resolve your problems, you make up. What must be going through her head?

"Do you like me?" I ask her. "Do you want to be married to me?" These are not questions Yanomama ask of each other. Marriage is marriage. No one asks if the other person likes them or wants to be married. They were ludicrous questions.

I tried to make light talk, but it was hard. My heart was dead. But what she was going through had to be worse. So many things had happened to her—the miscarriage, her family off to their new garden without her, the two of us alone (a thing that rarely happens in her culture). And she's not even with a Yanomama, I thought, she's with me, the foreigner. And now I subject her to an outburst like this.

We walked around the *shapono,* and I chatted mindlessly about when I carried the pack for her, about going out hunting and gathering together. Small talk, jokes, attempts at humor. "Okay," she said, stopping suddenly and looking me straight in the eye, "now you go home. Now it's time for you to go back to your village. Go back to Pensilvaniateri."

My heart leapt, as if jolted by electricity. But when I looked at her lips she was smiling, and when she saw the expression on my face, she started to giggle. Some joke. A Yanomama joke. She picked up some sticks, put them in her nose and lips, and turned to me. "Do I look good?" she asked.

"Yes," I said, "you look good."

"Let's go to join my family, then. I'll tell my mother we came because we missed her. We won't tell her you were angry."

I asked her never to deceive me again. No, she said, she never would again.

It only took a day to catch up with the Hasupuweteri on their way to Irokai at the leisurely trek rate. The first person we saw was Horeima, who was bringing up the rear of the women's group. *"Shoabemi,"* she shouted when she saw me (I was her classificatory "father-in-law").

An elderly Patahamateri man who was traveling with them yelled, *"Shori,"* all smiles. The greetings gave me a lift, reducing some of the remaining tension between Yarima and me. Little indications that I was accepted, that I was one of them. Somehow I felt I needed that, still.

When we arrived at the *wayumi* encampment Yarima's classificatory brother Koobewe came to talk to me, said he really missed me. We talked for a bit, laughing and joking in the usual way. "Do you really mean that?" I asked. "You probably didn't miss me at all. You probably said, 'Oh, I'm happy that brother-in-law of mine stayed behind.' " Yarima and Koobewe laughed; everyone standing around did. Even Orawe lying in his hammock burst out laughing.

While I talked with Koobewe, Yarima went over and lay down in her mother's hammock. But after a while she got up and came over to me. "Hang your hammock over here," she said. "Let's roast some plantains." I think she saw I was wounded, and this was her way of making up, of showing tenderness. She had never said such a thing before: "Hang your hammock here." It's not the kind of thing a woman would say to a man.

But that evening the depression set in again. I stayed in the hammock most of the time, talking to Koobewe. I told him that I was sad, and he said, "Yes, I know you are sad, *shori*. I can see it in your face." It was important for me to hear that. I was always trying to figure out how the Yanomama feel, what they think. Were they indifferent if their wives had miscarriages, if they lost a child? Did that kind of thing grieve them? Were they sympathetic? Empathetic? Did they respond to Yarima's feelings, or to mine? We tend to think that if people don't express themselves the way we do, maybe they don't experience the same feelings. So it was good to hear Koobewe say, "Yes, I know," and to see that he was trying to console me, to commiserate with me.

It wasn't only the loss of our child that upset me; I could feel myself catching fire with anger, too, a slow burn deep inside about Shatakewe. The crisis with Yarima at Wawatoi hadn't resolved anything; it had just cut off my outburst, forcing me to keep the emotions bottled up. That night as I was going to sleep Yarima stirred next to me instead of dropping off quickly as she usually did. She could feel my agitation. Her fingers found the swirls of my chest hair, her nails caressed me lightly. "Don't be angry at me," she whispered.

I lay there without speaking. I knew that the reason she had never told me before was that Shatakewe was her sister's husband. He provided for her nephew (her "son"), whom she loved so much. I shifted my position in the hammock, rolling on my side a little so I could look at her. Our faces were almost touching, I could feel her warm, sweet breath on my cheek. In the darkness I could barely make out the whites of her eyes. "On my face I'm laughing," I said, "but in my stomach I'm burning."

Lying there in the dark with our arms around each other, she told me how it had happened. She had been out gathering with her mother in the forest. Shatakewe must have followed them, because shortly after she and her mother split up to cover different areas, all of a sudden there he was. He grabbed her arm, but she pulled away and ran. After a few steps he caught her and threw her to the ground. As he lowered himself over her, she fought, spitting at him that when I came back I would beat him. "No," he said, "the *nabuh* won't beat me. The *nabuh* won't beat anyone." Then he grabbed her hands and raped her while she screamed at him. As he finished and was getting up, her mother came running; she had heard the screaming. Hurling insults, her mother managed to get Yarima away before anything else happened. That night her mother complained in the village about him. But that was the end of it. Nobody joined in the complaint, and nobody did anything else.

And where was I—her husband who was supposed to protect her—while this was happening? Out in Caracas screwing around with the census reports, then beating a path to the government to get a damned permit.

After a sleepless night I got up the next morning steaming—steaming and disillusioned, not only at Shatakewe, but at all the men in the village. It wasn't only that none of them had stood up for her—you didn't quite expect that. But nobody had ever said a word to me about any of this, not Red, not Orawe, not *shori*, none of them. I was happy that the next day we would be at Irokai, where Shatakewe had arrived several days earlier. I already knew what I was going to do to that son of a bitch. I'd just let him have it, punch him, break his arrows, some damned thing.

In the afternoon I went with Shiroi and Buusiwe to hunt on the trail. I got two *manashi* birds. The hunt released the tension a little, but not much. I was still furious, but not showing it, I hoped, planning exactly what I would do. I asked Shiroi if he liked Shatakewe. No, he said, no, I don't. I asked if he knew that when I was downriver Shatakewe had raped Yarima. Jesus, when I thought about it in English—"he raped her"—the words really did it to me. In Yanomama it wasn't quite as bad, you got it in their context. But in English? He raped her, he raped my poor, beautiful wife.

Journal, trek camp, October 8:   What am I really going to do to this Shatakewe? It's a problem, living in a place like this. You live communally, and there you are. Someone has an affair with your wife, or rapes your wife, or does something awful to some other member of your family, or steals your plantains or whatever, and that guy may be living two hearths down from you. And you've got to watch him lying in his hammock, cooking his food, eating, laughing, joking—you've got to just watch him. It's tough. It's not like at home where if you have problems with somebody, at least you don't also have to live with him.

But this guy is going to get his. I know there isn't a Yanomama woman who hasn't been raped. There isn't one who hasn't had two or three affairs. But I am not going to accept it. I accept a lot of things down here, but I am not going to accept this. I draw the line here. I don't have it built into my makeup that I can put up with this kind of thing. And it's not that I'm some strange bird who can't bring himself to adapt. The Yanomama don't like it, either. They'll club each other over the head and break their skulls open over it.

At Irokai it turned out that word had preceded us. Shatakewe had heard I was coming, and he knew that whatever happened wasn't going to be pleasant. As a result he had broken off from the main group and had moved with some of his relatives to a temporary encampment in the forest beyond the garden, about fifteen minutes away.

By the time we arrived I was really geared up. I still didn't know what I was going to do—chest pounding, a clubfight. I didn't care; my anger was going to come out, and he had better look out for himself. Shiroi trailed after me as I marched down the path to Shatakewe's camp, maybe just curious about what would happen or maybe because he thought someone would have to drag me back if I got shot or something. Not that I was thinking about getting shot. I was absolutely seeing red by now, just dying to get my hands on him. But on the trail we ran into Shatakewe's nephew. He took one look at me and zipped off to warn him. As a result, when I got to the cluster of four or five temporary shelters, Shatakewe was gone. He had run off into the forest.

"Where's Shatakewe's hearth?" I asked one of the women.

"Over there," she answered, then watched as I walked over, cut down Shatakewe's hammock, took his arrow points, and smashed his arrow holder. Then I cut up his one shirt—a shirt that I had given him. In a way I was happy he wasn't there; I was in such a state of grim fury that I didn't know what I might have done had he been right in front of me.

On my way out I motioned to Shiroi, who was sitting on the trail outside the encampment. When he looked at me questioningly, I said, "I raided him. Tonight I'm going to let him have it in front of the village."

That night when the Hasupuweteri were in their hammocks, I made a public insult against Shatakewe. "Listen, everybody," I said, pacing around in front of my hearth. "If I ever see that man again, I will throw him to the ground. If I ever see that snake-eyes, I will beat him. I will beat him. I will beat him. That is what I say. That is what I say. He has the eyes of a snake. He squints like a snake. He squints like a blind man. I ridicule him in public. I show my contempt for him. I am not afraid to show my anger. I will wait until I see him again. He is a coward. He is afraid to see me. He is a damn ugly coward. He is the one I will beat. He is the one."

Journal, Irokai, October 10:   When I came back from Shatakewe's, Yarima's anger at my anger seemed to be completely gone. She may have been worried something would happen to me when I went after him, but when I told her I had missed him, she wanted to go back with me to his encampment. She was really angry herself now. I think that my reaction was giving her the opportunity to let her own feelings come out. She had taken it like a Yanomama woman. What could you do when someone abused you? Move away? Not talk to individuals you had to coexist with and survive with? The woman had to accept it, she couldn't do anything about it. Just as the man had to sit across the village and look at the guy who raped his wife.

Yarima wasn't kidding about getting Shatakewe. The next day she insisted on going back there with me. I think she wanted to see me do something to him, pay him back. Not that it took much insistence. I wasn't about to let this thing go. I was still burning about it. I also knew that if I didn't do something severe here, I was just asking for trouble in the future. If they thought they could rape Yarima with impunity as long as I wasn't around, she would face it whenever I went anywhere. And it wasn't only Shatakewe; I was angry at the rest of them. Not only hadn't they stopped it, they hadn't even said anything to me when I came back, so that I could do something about it. They had accepted it. And, if that was true, as far as I was concerned they could all go to hell.

Together, Yarima and I took the trail to Shatakewe's camp, walking softly. Even before the leaf and vine shelters came into view, we heard his voice inside. *"Ei,"* said Yarima quietly, "that's him."

But just at that moment Shatakewe's sister looked out down the trail, saw us, and started screeching, "He's come back! He's come back!" By the time we got inside nobody was there.

"Shatakewe!" I yelled. *"Haimo haimo!* Shatakewe, *haimo."* ("Come on, come on! Shatakewe, come on.") But there was only silence.

Walking back toward our *shapono,* I felt leery, watched. I knew that if Shatakewe had the guts, he could kill me at any moment. Their arrows are not play arrows. They're light, but they're six feet long, and the bows have a sixty-pound pull. They can stop a peccary or a five-hundred-pound tapir in its tracks. Even though I knew that the Yanomama don't go in much for personal confrontation—it isn't their style—I walked down the trail carefully, scanning the jungle, whirling around every ten yards or so, looking for the ambush. Yarima was being extremely watchful, too, but she must have thought I had lost my mind.

When we got back, Yarima squatted by the fire to roast some plantains. I could sense her tension. The next morning the tension was still in the air, so we decided to go for a day-long hunt, hoping to give ourselves a little respite. *Shori* decided to come along with us, and he got a *yapi* bird early on. By the end of the day I had four *manashi*—five birds all together. We had a good time and a good meal when we got back.

Journal, Irokai, October 12:   My blood pressure is still up there. I am pissed off at all the people who call me brother-in-law because they didn't tell me what was going on. And at her brother, too. Maybe her brother especially. His basic attitude toward this is, So what? What do you care? It's just a *naka,* just a vagina. What's the big deal? It's not that he doesn't have feelings for Yarima and for me. He does. But he also has a relationship with Shatakewe. He'd rather protect his brother-in-law and have this thing blow over than level with me. And I'm burned up at her mother for the same reason. The fact that they didn't tell me means that they are willing to let it happen again the next time I go downriver.

Yarima is sleeping a lot during the day, sick, possibly malaria. I gave her two chloroquine. She also has headaches all the time. At first I thought it might just be from tension of the last week. But lasting headaches like these tend to come from parasites, and they can make you feel as if your head is coming off. Last night she couldn't take part in the big song dance. The women carried on all night long for the success of the hunters, who are again away on a five-day hunt. When I fell asleep they were still singing.

This *nohi harupo*—sexual jealousy—is torturous, really rough. Orawe sat down with me today. Why, he asked, had I been so stupid as to let Yarima go on that trek? I should have known not to go on the long trip with her. His wife had also miscarried, he said. It was her first pregnancy, and she had aborted on a trek, just like Yarima. He had been very foolish that time, like me. He also said he understood my feelings about Shatakewe. He himself would be enraged. He knew how to deal with it, he said, he had been in clubfights before.

That night I awoke with the sense that something was wrong. Groping around to find my flashlight, I felt a wet area in the hammock. Still half-asleep I wondered what it was: could Yarima have peed in her sleep? Could it have somehow rained on us? When I finally found the flashlight and switched it on, the lower part of our white hammock seemed dark. It took a moment before I realized that the hammock was soaked with blood. Oh, no, I thought, Yarima's bleeding again, she's hemorrhaging. On the ground under us were several small pools of blood, some of it partially congealed. Quickly I shined the light on Yarima, waking her up. But though her legs had some blood on them, I saw that it wasn't from her, it was from me. Both my big toes had chunks taken out of them, and blood was trickling from the wounds. I was so shocked that I jumped up and started bellowing, waking up the entire community. By then I knew that the vampires had gotten me, an extremely unpleasant surprise and the first time it had happened since 1975. Swearing under my breath, I got Yarima up to find our water gourd so we could wash ourselves off. Then we had to take down the matrimonial hammock and string two small hammocks, while I cursed the whole time: "Goddamn lousy vampire, bastard really gives me a pain in the ass."

Journal, Irokai, October 13:   I just came back from the bath, my toes hurt. That thing took some real pieces out of me. Yarima seems fine today, no headache, no fatigue. Whatever it was, she seems to have gotten over it. She asked to hear tapes. Julio Iglesias, "Dove Sará," again. Such a feeling of joy came over me to hear him singing. A touch of civilization. My people. Can you imagine, Julio Iglesias, a Spaniard, singing in Italian, and I'm saying "my people"? I can't understand all the words, but the music is Western, the melody, the orchestra. I realize how you can never eradicate your roots, your original culture. I thought of how it would be, living back in civilization, enjoying all the things I used to enjoy. How good it would be to document this life I have been living here, to write not just the typical anthropologist's ethnographic record, but a personal history. But how can I do that here? Hasupuweteri is always going on *wayumi,* and I'm always having to go in and out for permits.

I'm always worried about Yarima. What makes me love like this? What makes me love?

Journal, Irokai, October 14: I've made up my mind. Mulling it over for days now. I am just too angry at these people, and it isn't dissipating. I am determined to get away. They have demonstrated that they don't care that much about Yarima; no one spoke out about Shatakewe raping her, no one protected her, and no one told me.

I'm beginning to formulate a plan. I'd like to leave, at least for a while—get a house built for myself on the Orinoco, next to the Patahamateri. I wouldn't have to look at Shatakewe and his family, and that would be a major plus. I'd be able to get things up and down the river with the malaria people or anyone else who might come along. I'd be able to set up my desk and typewriter and work for a change.

The Patahamateri don't trek so much, and they would love to have us living there, if only for the trade goods. More important, they're related to Yarima through her father's side—her father lives there. Not that she has much to do with him, since he has not lived with her mother, at least not since I've been down here. Most of the Patahamateri are classificatory brothers to her, and so, with the incest taboos being what they are, chances are she'll be a lot safer. I'd have to learn another group, but that wouldn't be so bad. Maybe some good would come of it.

We are going to meet the Patahamateri at Boriana garden, when everybody comes together for the manioc harvest. There's a ton of manioc at Boriana, and it will be a huge gathering: more than two hundred people in the same *shapono*. I'll have a chance to talk it over with the Patahamateri headman. After that I'll make a final decision.

14

The gathering at Boriana was like nothing I had ever seen. When we arrived with the Hasupuweteri, Red's group and the Patahamateri were already encamped, filling almost two-thirds of the giant *shapono*. The house was buzzing with children running all around, hunting groups and harvesting groups going and coming, women cooking at the hearths, babies crying—all the normal activities, except that three times the number of people gave the usual quiet flow of life a busy feeling.

Walking over to the Patahamateri section, I picked out Yarima's father, who invited me to sit in the hammock next to his. When we talked he was reserved and polite, even a little deferential. The Patahamateri, he said, had heard about my encounters with Shatakewe, and about my *waiteri*, my fierceness. They had heard that I was angry with the Hasupuweteri. His tone put me at ease. I didn't know the man, but fathers-in-law often take a dominant stance toward their daughters' husbands, and if we were going to be living with him, I was just as happy that he was respectful and a bit distant.

As we discussed my plans to move in, the irony of the situation wasn't lost on either of us. Yarima's father himself had moved to Patahamateri three or four years before I arrived in the Amazon because of a fight he had had in Hasupuweteri. His antagonist had shot him in the shoulder with an arrow, and Yarima's father had become so frightened and angry that he had moved out and never returned. He had been living with the Patahamateri ever since. As I went over the Patahamateri genealogies in my mind, I realized that six or seven other people had moved in with the group for the same reason. Conversely, Hasupuweteri had several people who had left Patahamateri because of unresolvable disputes. So it wasn't strange that Yarima and I would want to move. On the contrary, it was typical Yanomama behavior. And now I knew why.

That night I made a public complaint. With all three groups listening I faced the Hasupuweteri. I could see them sitting in their hammocks by the glow of the hearths. "I will not live with you," I told them. "I will not live with you anymore. Not a single one of you complained when my wife was raped. No one complained when my young wife was raped. Why was that? Why? You complain plenty when someone steals your plantains. Your complaints echo to the sky if someone takes your sugar cane. But when my wife is raped you do nothing. You say nothing. No, I will not live with you anymore. I will go somewhere else and live with other people."

The next day, after talking briefly with Touwe, the young Patahamateri headman, Yarima and I hung our hammocks in the Patahamateri section next to Yarima's father. That night we slept well in the matrimonial, our arms and legs intertwined, even though Yarima said she was *kiri*, embarrassed. The Hasupuweteri were used to us sleeping in the same hammock, but the Patahamateri had never seen such behavior. It seemed like the first time in ages that I had had a solid night's sleep. Maybe it was a sign of things to come. The next morning my old friend Red came over, bringing some *kapiromi* root as a gift and asking for some cotton in return.

"When you move down to the river," he said, "I will come to visit you often."

Yarima seemed happy to be with her father and her younger half sister. I could see that she would have at least one close friend here. She was also getting along well with the other Patahamateri young women. She seemed to fit right in, laughing and talking with them as if they were old friends. However, over the next few days she hardly spoke to any of the Hasupuweteri, even her mother. It was obvious that her anger hadn't cooled in the least. That was fine with me. I was eager to leave Boriana and start building my new house next to the Patahamateri's main *shapono* down by the Orinoco.

On November 7 I asked several *huya* to go with me to Wawatoi and carry my things from there to the river. It took a day to march in, then a day to pack everything up, then another to bring it down. But by the time we arrived the Patahamateri had already put up a temporary shelter for Yarima and me.

Journal, Patahamateri, November 24: It took almost a month to build the new house, but I'm very happy with it. We finally finished the mud, put up the screens and door, got my papers unpacked and my typewriter set up—so I'm ready to start working.

The house is just outside the *shapono*. It's easy to close myself off and concentrate yet be part of whatever's going on. And from here I can still keep one eye on Yarima. The river is only a quarter mile away, which means I won't miss whoever comes up. For a change I'll be able to keep in touch with the outside. That's one of the principal reasons for coming down here.

It's so good to be alone, to be able to lock out the rest of the world and just think. It's funny. I'm down on the river, where I started out, in almost the very same spot I inhabited nine years ago, except that now I'm here with a Yanomama wife.

The bugs are a plague on the river—bloodsucking gnats. There are clouds of them; sometimes a black mist hangs over the river. I wonder what it will be like nine years from now. Can I endure down here? I haven't had any contact with the outside world for three-quarters of a year. I'm eager to see the malaria team, get some mail out, start attending to my responsibilities, my writing.

Kenny worked all the time in his house. He was not with me so much during the day. He spent all his time making designs and using his maquina [machine]. *At night some of the Patahamateri would talk to me. They would ask me why I was married to the* nabuh. *He is old, they said. All he does is make designs. Why are you married to him? They said that Shiriwe really liked me. Shiriwe was very kind to me. Every time he came by he smiled at me.*

Journal, December 25, Patahamateri: I woke up this morning at about five. Red is here visiting, and we're getting a lot done together, mainly on my transcription and translation of public complaint speeches. Life at Patahamateri has been so different. It shows how varied existence can be even down among the Yanomama. The Hasupuweteri are nomadic, on *wayumi* much of the time. With them you live a nomad's life. Here it's somewhat more sedentary, there's more food. It's easier to do other things—work, for example. I'm working well, turning out transcriptions of verbal behavior, working on my dissertation. Funny thing, it wasn't until Yarima and I had had our breakfast of plantains that I remembered it was Christmas.

Journal, Patahamateri, December 31:   I wrote the census article and the complaint transcription while Red visited me, working every day for three weeks. So ends 1983. Where did the year go? I spent most of it trekking with Hasupuweteri. Now I'm just lying in my hammock waiting out the last of the year. In Yanomama land, of course, New Year's Day is just another day. I wonder how things will be this coming year. I can see how much I've changed this year: in love and in worry. Capitani, the headman's little boy, just came home. He's been out for several hours, and his father was getting worried. Very happy to see him back. The *Voice of America* is playing the great hits of the past year. Lionel Richie's "All Night Long" was number one. Michael Jackson's "Say, Say, Say."

By the spring of 1984 I had been working hard for several months, spending most of each day at my worktable with my notes and typewriter. I was still worried about what the future would bring. There seemed so much to sustain, so many problems: Yarima, funds, the permit, my friends in Caracas, and my family at home whom I hadn't been in touch with for so long. In addition, I now had to worry about a raid. Word had come that the Konoporepiweteri believed that they had been shortchanged by the Patahamateri in a trade and were vowing revenge. I started taking my shotgun with me everywhere, even when I went into the forest to relieve myself.

Life was different on the river. Kenny worked in his house all the time. He built it right in back of my father's section of the shapono, so we were always close, even when I stayed at my father's hearth. Many days I spent with Kenny inside the house. I liked being inside

because there were no insects and I could take naps without being
bothered. All day long Kenny made his designs, and now he used
his maquina, *too. He said it was a* maquina *that made* libros [*books*],
but I did not understand that. He had many libros *with him, but*
they did not look like the leaves he was making. Often I sat on the
floor and strung beads. Kenny also showed me how to use his
grabador, *the* maquina *that makes voices. I put the pieces in my*
ears and listened to the shamans chanting and the women singing.
I liked being there. I liked being his wife—the only woman with a
nabuh *husband.*

The radio was my lifeline to the outside; it kept me connected, and
the incongruity between what I was hearing and what I was living
often made me laugh out loud. A new medical study, the radio
would announce, indicates that homogenized milk may be carci-
nogenic. I should be sure to limit my egg consumption, the same
serious voice told me, to two a week. My worst anxiety was the
permit I would need at the end of the year, that and money. I would
need the permit to get back in. The funds I'd need for essentials
like gasoline. How would I be able to work these things out?
Thoughts occurred to me about an anthropology job. I could go
back, I thought, finish the dissertation, and get a teaching position.
On the other hand, how could I take Yarima out of the jungle? And
how could I leave without her?

My moments of greatest anxiety and greatest creativity seemed
to come in the morning while I was still nine-tenths asleep, just on
the verge of wakefulness. Sometimes in this twilight state I would
imagine that I had left the Amazon, and I would feel such pity for
Yarima. I was sure she loved me deeply and would be profoundly
affected by my leaving. Other times I felt that after the initial period
of separation she would adapt nicely without me. She would probably not suffer any great trauma, though I, of course, would. As
often as not, these waking dreams and contemplations would come
riding on the melodic waves of Touwe's chants. Unlike the other
shamans I knew, the Patahamateri headman habitually awoke to
chant in the early hours of the morning, and his song had a way
of blending itself into the sleep and dreams of those around him.

It amazed me how even when I was fully awake the remnants of
my dreams would stay with me. Even when the dream had passed,
the mental effect was still there. At those times I seemed to drift
into a soul-searching calm in which everything seemed so clear,

when analysis of even the most complicated situation was simplicity itself.

Half an hour later my state of grace would have dissipated entirely. The day's work and the day's demands would take over, and I would feel my pulse begin to throb. As if by magic I'd suddenly become aware of the beating wings of anxiety that always seemed to hover over the thin membrane of my consciousness. So many of my problems had been caused by my abundance of nervous energy, or maybe it was just my nervousness. I knew that people had been attracted to me because of that nervous energy—I was always wired. But so much had suffered because of it, too. I knew that I had to focus on the good things that had happened, that were happening; otherwise my anxieties about the future would eat me up. I sometimes thought that if I had three lives, I might choose to spend one among the Yanomama, but I had only one. . . . Then I'd look at Yarima. Her beauty overwhelmed me, her skin a deep bronze that caught the shifting patterns of sun and shadow, her mouth with its subtle, expressive changes of form and shape. When she would say to me, *"Buhi"* ("I like you"), all my grief faded.

Journal, Patahamateri, May 3: A very ominous happening today. This morning at 8:30 the malaria team came by, but they didn't stop—though of course they're supposed to, and in addition they saw my canoe at the bank. At 3:30 they came back down but again didn't stop. I heard them, grabbed the packet of mail I had ready, and ran to the river along with Yarima and Shiriwe. We jumped into my canoe and went after them, wondering what was going on. At the sharp turn downriver we caught up to them. We came on them so suddenly that we almost raced right by them. They were just sitting there off to the side, fishing. The DDT—four malaria workers and one Yanomama: Yorusiwe, the toll taker.

When we got over to them I said in Yanomama, "What's wrong with you guys? You drove right by!"

I knew one of them, one of the men who had gotten me out of Guajaribo all those years before. But no one made a sound, except for Yorusiwe. He looked me straight in the eye and said, "Why are you taking a Yanomama wife when there are so many women back in your own village?" He said he was going to get the *policía* to have me locked up. While he was saying this the rest of the malaria team didn't look at me. I can't understand either their behavior or his, though I must say, there's never been any love lost between the two of us.

The malaria team not stopping was bad news. Number one, they were supposed to stop—albeit irregularly—at all the villages. Number two, this is a region where no one ever goes, and these people are like lifeblood for whoever is up there. But they hadn't stopped, and that was a strange thing, strange and ominous. I hadn't had any contact with the outside for months, and I was eager to get my mail out. But it wasn't just that. I had the feeling that something funny was going on. I didn't like the way the four malaria workers hadn't looked at me and hadn't talked to me. And I didn't understand the threat from Yorusiwe. What business was it of his if I had a Yanomama wife? And why should he care about it, anyway?

Thinking over this incident, it seemed to me that Yorusiwe must have somehow kept the malaria team from stopping, either by threatening them or by telling them some crazy lie about me or about the Patahamateri.

Although I had not had that much to do with him, I knew that Yorusiwe was a bad character. Over the years I had seen him regularly in Platanal. He lived at a Yanomama village near there, and he made it his business to find out whenever there was a visitor at Platanal who planned to go upriver. Invariably he would show up and demand money or trade goods, as if someone had given him the right to tax any traveler in the territory. Half wheedling, half demanding, he projected an air of menace. The toll taker, I called him. I would also see him on occasion in Puerto Ayacucho, where it was rare to find a Yanomama. There he seemed to have a regular route, going around to homes and begging handouts, coming across as a poor, needy Indian. But I had also seen him pass himself off as the *comisario* of the Yanomama and demand gifts "for his people." When he went upriver he liked to present himself to the unacculturated Indians as a man of knowledge and influence among the *nabuh,* an experienced, traveled person. He got a kick out of impressing them, and intimidating them.

The first year or so, every time I went by his village he'd stop me and ask me to give him things, just as he did to everybody else. But I had rebuffed him. On principle I'd never give anything to anybody because of intimidation. As a result, he had been angry at me for years. When he began his diatribe to me in front of the malaria people on the river, I ignored him. I wasn't going to give him or the others the impression that I gave a damn for what someone like him might say or think.

As 1984 began to wind down I was a little encouraged by news I'd received. Mail had come up with a malaria team. Eibl had written, saying he would pay twenty thousand bolivars for the transcription I was working on. One of my anthropologist friends from the States had also written, saying that he thought I would have a good chance for an NIH grant. I was making good progress on my writing. The articles on village movement and acculturation were coming along well. All the ideas were there, the only problem was putting them into final form. Checking references and pulling together a bibliography were impossible tasks in the jungle.

Almost every day Kenny stayed in his house. He came out only in the morning and afternoon to ask questions. He asked what animals everyone had killed and where they had gone and other questions. Since the mosquitoes had come he even slept in his house. I told him I did not like to sleep in the house. I wanted to sleep by the fire, but there was no fire in the house, and the dampness made my head hurt. So I slept at my father's hearth.

All day long we could hear Kenny's maquina *making its noise. Many days I asked him if he would come with us to gather in the forest or to fish. But he always said that I should go with the women or with my father and his wife. He said that he had to work. He said that the* nabuh *downriver liked the designs he made on leaves and that he could trade his designs for money. Then he could trade the money for axes and pots and beads and bring them to us. Kenny told me that Shaki [Chagnon] had made a libro and Lizot had made a libro, and Renki [Eibl-Eibesfeldt] had made a libro. But he had not made a libro yet because when we lived with Hasupuweteri we were on trek for a long time and he could not work. Now he just wanted to make designs.*

When I was not gathering fruit or catching crabs, I would stay with him in the house. But it was not as it was before. I missed his company. I remembered how Kenny and older brother and I would catch fish and crabs. Then when we came home we would stop to bathe in the stream. I missed those days when we lived with Hasupuweteri.

By now I was not going into the *shapono* all that much; instead I stayed mainly in my house, writing. But I kept an eye on what was going on, maintaining my relationships and watching. Toward Yarima I still had the most intensely protective feelings. But she seemed to have integrated herself very nicely here. One young man I knew I had to watch out for was Shiriwe. He hung around on every occasion. Once when Yarima was out gathering with her half sister, he had appeared and said, "Come."

"No," she answered. "I have an earache."

Before anything further developed, the friend's mother appeared and told Shiriwe to go away. "The *nabuh* will get you," she said.

That night Yarima got very sick. She believed that he had blown magical substances on her. That's a common form of retaliation and, of course, one more way to scare a woman into submission.

On November 5 the shortwave was all preelection news from the United States. It looked as though Ronald Reagan was going to win a second term by a landslide. I remembered the 1976 elections—I had been in the jungle for a year and a half straight and hadn't even been aware of what was going on. When I came out on a run to Platanal, Padre Bórteli had greeted me with, "Congratulations, you have a new president."

"Oh, really?" I had said. "Who is it?"

"Jimmy Carter," came the answer.

"Who?" I asked. I had never heard of the governor of Georgia.

Journal, Patahamateri, Thanksgiving: I could really use a good American dinner, but I would rather be here with Yarima and beans than back in the States with pie and turkey. I heard on the radio that for American Indians, Thanksgiving is a day of mourning. Apparently the western Indians blame the northeastern Indians for letting the Pilgrims land at Plymouth rock. There was also a report on hunger in Ethiopia, tens of thousands of people starving to death. Here we have *agouti* and peccary for Thanksgiving. By world standards the Yanomama are not that bad off.

Journal, Patahamateri, November 28: Yorusiwe came up again, an extremely unpleasant surprise. This time he was in his own boat with a couple of young men from his village. They were up at Shuimuiteri, then on their way back down they stopped here. No announcements; they just came in—not the Yanomama way at all.

Very aggressive. Yorusiwe was wearing store clothes, some kind of old chino pants, a pair of torn sneakers, and a T-shirt. All for display purposes. Look at me, he was telling them, I wear these *nabuh* clothes—I don't need to wear your poor penis strings and loincloths. Even more impressive, he had a shotgun over his shoulder and four shells in his hand, which he jiggled constantly as he talked to the headman. Touwe was squatting down in front of him, very intimidated. He had never seen a Yanomama with a shotgun. They're not afraid of mine, but here was this Yorusiwe, from Carlitos's village, traditional enemies of the Hasupuweteri, from whom the Patahamateri had split off. Then Yorusiwe began to make demands, for arrowheads and feathers. Not at all a typical Yanomama scene, where no matter how intense the trading gets, it's never carried out by intimidation.

I was observing all of this from my hammock, just a few feet away. Touwe looked really scared, frightened by Yorusiwe's arrogance and implicit threats, his eyes watching the shotgun shells jiggling around in Yorusiwe's cupped hand. So I said to Touwe, "Look, just because he has a shotgun and shells, don't worry about it. You don't have to give him things. If you want to, fine. But don't think that you have to because of the shotgun. He's not going to hurt you."

At this Yorusiwe turned chartreuse. Here he was, going through a big display in front of his own friends and in front of the village, intimidating the headman. And now, before everybody I had told them not to be afraid. He was enraged, actually turning colors, all the while attempting to smile at me. Touwe's little boy, Capitani, whispered, "Go and get your gun, father-in-law."

"No," I whispered back, "don't worry." My gun was at my house. "This guy isn't going to shoot anybody."

But now Yorusiwe had turned his attention to me. Followed by the two men with him, he walked slowly over to where I was lying, smiling and trying mightily to appear innocent, but with a deceitful look in his eyes that you would just never trust. *"Hola,"* he said, standing over me, his missing front tooth and ruined mouth catching my eye (almost all the Yanomama have perfect teeth). "Let's go to your house, and you can give me some shotgun shells."

"No," I answered, "I don't have any extras."

"Well, you can give me empties, then." Brazening it out, people still watching him. Speaking to me in terrible broken Spanish instead of Yanomama, conveying the message of his power and knowledge.

But when the answer to that too was no, he left, coolly enough, but angry. He and his friends went down to the river, followed by many of the village's teenagers and young men.

That evening Pakewe came over to our hearth. When I invited him to sit in my hammock he began to talk. He was one of Yarima's classificatory brothers and had been quite friendly to her and me ever since we had come to live with the Patahamateri. *"Shori,"* he said, "this afternoon I went down to the river with Yorusiwe and the other *huya*. Yorusiwe was very angry and said many things."

"Oh, what did he say?"

"He said that he was not afraid of you. He said that no one should be afraid to steal your things. He said that no one should be afraid to shoot you. He said we should just take anything we want because you cannot hurt us. He said he knew this because he has been to Ayacuchoteri. He said he knows the *nabuh*. He knows the big men downriver. He has talked with the governor in Aya-cuchoteri. He said that if you hurt anyone, even if you defend yourself, the *policía* will come and take you away. They will put you in jail, and you will never come back. He said that then anyone who wants can take your wife away. He said that if we want to shoot you, we should do it with a barbed monkey-bone arrow point so that it will stick in and not come out."

As Pakewe spoke I started to feel queasy. Because Yorusiwe was absolutely right. For years I had lived in Yanomama land on a bluff. I had refused to allow anyone to intimidate me, and I had made a point of standing up for myself aggressively whenever a situation called for it. It had all had a beneficial effect—it had allowed me to live here. The Indians did not know what might happen to them if they stole from me or abused me. So they didn't. And that was essential to our getting along. It was just the same way they got along with each other. You don't make a habit of abusing other people, first because family and village ties work against it, but also, and more especially, because you may find yourself on the wrong end of the confrontation. And now this toll taker, this intimidator, was telling them that I was harmless.

He knew, even if he couldn't explain it, that if I ever did hurt any of the Indians and word got downriver, that would be the end of my permit, forever, Yarima or no Yarima. On the other hand, any of the Indians could shoot me, and that's as far as it would ever go. There would be no repercussions. White man dies in the jungle, that's all. So what Yorusiwe was telling them was true—in point of fact they could do anything they wanted to me, while I would find it quite difficult to retaliate. And the idea of the *policía* taking me away and putting me in jail was enough to fill these people with amazement. Upriver Indians like the Patahamateri don't know anything at all about the police. They believe the police are a village of particularly ferocious people who live downriver. Whenever I leave they tell me to be sure not to go near the police village. Many of them believe the police eat Yanomama. Jail is just a word— they don't know what it means, but it conjures up horrors too terrifying to be described.

Shortly after Yorusiwe's troubling visit I began preparing myself mentally for another trip downriver. My permit this time had been a long one, but it was up again, and I would have to get it renewed. That meant leaving Yarima behind for a minimum of several weeks. As always, I felt apprehensive about what might happen in my absence, even though I was sure she'd be safer here with her father than she had been in Hasupuweteri. The permit itself was another problem. Nothing about it was ever sure, and it was still appalling to think about what had happened last time, when I had had to wait for almost three months. The thought of having to go through that kind of experience again sent a wave of apprehension through me. I was so consumed by this worry that, strangely, I didn't feel as upset and heartsick about leaving Yarima as I had in the past. It wasn't until the last moment, when I saw her standing on the riverbank, crying, that I felt a rush of emotion and realized that my own eyes were filled with tears.

15

*K*enny said that he would not be gone long. Not like the last time. He said he would be back before the new moon, but I knew he always stayed longer than he said he would. I worried about him every time he went because the downriver Yanomama always said that he was dead or that the policía had captured him. My father told him not to stay too long downriver. He also told him not to go too close to the policía village.

The huya carried his bags down to the DDT canoe. When we were there Kenny called me to come to him, and put his arms around me like he often did. I put my arms around him, too. I liked him very much.

It was sad to see the canoe drift toward the bend in the river. When the DDT man started the motor, Kenny looked back at me and waved. It was then I began to cry.

The malaria team I hitched a ride with took me to Platanal, then I caught a lift with another crew on its way down to Mavaca mission. At Mavaca Padre Bórteli came out to greet me as usual, holding a cigarette in his outstretched hand. I never smoked upriver, but the moment I came out the craving would hit me. A smoker himself, Bórteli understood and always greeted me with a cigarette. He wouldn't even say hello until I had taken my first long draw. When we sat down in the mission to talk, he looked troubled.

"Ken," he said, "I want you to be prepared. Last week people from Puerto Ayacucho were up here. The new director of the governor's Indian office met with representatives from some of the mission Yanomama. Yorusiwe was there, too. They hadn't invited him, but he barged in anyway. He said things about Lizot and you, Ken, very bad things, *malas noticias, muy malas noticias*. You should expect trouble when you get to Puerto Ayacucho. Be prepared for it."

The next day, December 6, still with the malaria people, I went by boat to Ocamo, then to La Esmeralda, right along the line of missions, on my way to civilization. And the closer I got, the more I heard about what was waiting for me. In La Esmeralda I had a long talk with two Ye'kwana Indians I knew who lived at Toki, the village where Ray Hames had been. They had heard the stories, too. Yorusiwe had been at La Esmeralda. He had told people that I was terrorizing the upriver Yanomama, that I had stolen a woman from them and forced them to work for me without pay. I had several children, he said, but he, Yorusiwe, had told the national guard all about me, and now they were planning to go in and arrest me.

On the flight to Puerto Ayacucho I had time to think. The notion that Yorusiwe might have the slightest interest in the welfare of the Hasupuweteri or the Patahamateri, or any Yanomama outside his own village, was laughable, but nobody downriver would know that. The stories he was telling would make it appear that he was attempting to protect the upriver Yanomama against a foreign exploiter. And just the idea of a white man going into this primitive culture and using the people for his own ends would strike a chord. After all, what were the Venezuelan Amazon authorities there for if not to protect the indigenous tribes against exploitation by outsiders?

It was really clever; this man understood, at least to some degree, the mentality of the *nabuh* in Puerto Ayacucho. He knew what the *nabuh*'s values were. He knew what *nabuh* would condone and what he would condemn. He knew, for example, that any word of my having sexual relations with a Yanomama woman would get me in trouble with the authorities. It was ironic: no Yanomama would ever imagine there might be something bad about having sex. It would never occur to them that someone might be condemned for it. But Yorusiwe knew. He was savvy enough to grasp that this was a sensitive issue. A white man taking an Indian woman (especially stealing an Indian woman), a white man fathering Indian children—these were things the *nabuh* officials, the *gobernador,* the *policía,* the *guardia nacional,* wouldn't like at all. Yorusiwe might not have understood why such tales would be interesting to politicians and others, especially those with an anti-American bent to begin with, but he was perceptive enough to know that there was indeed an audience for stories like these. I knew what this man's capabilities were, I knew he could be a convincing liar, especially in Puerto Ayacucho, because nobody down there would ever know what did or did not happen upriver. Even when you lived upriver you hardly knew from one day to the next what was true and what wasn't. All you knew was that time would almost always clarify what was fact and what was rumor. I wasn't afraid of the accusations he was making. In one way or another the truth would eventually come out, I wasn't worried about that. But God knew how long it might take to happen. And any long delay in getting my permit was bound to cause dire problems.

When I got to Puerto Ayacucho a festival was going on celebrating the frontier town's fiftieth anniversary. Paraders marched down the main street, and caravans of jeeps rolled by filled with teenagers cheering and waving Venezuelan flags. Almost immediately I ran into my old friend Gonzalez Herrera, the former minister of health who had also served a turn as governor of Amazonas. Outside the town auditorium where the official anniversary speeches were going on, he introduced me to the new governor, General Muller-Rojas. I was extremely happy to meet him, especially since the introduction was through somebody like Gonzalez Herrera. That would carry weight when it came time for the governor to countersign my new permit. Muller-Rojas seemed pleased by the introduction as well. "I'm happy to meet you," he said. "Why don't you come around tomorrow to my office so we can talk a little."

The next day I met Muller-Rojas at his office in the *Gobernación,* the big mildew-stained government building that dominated the main street. He was extremely polite, coming into the outer office to invite me in, then having espresso served at the coffee table in his large inner office, where we sat to talk. Speaking in Spanish, I began telling him something about myself and my work. Before I had gone too far he interrupted me, telling me that if I preferred, he would just as soon use English. As it turned out, he had a near perfect command of the language, and this too was a good development, another sign of courtesy. But as I was in the middle of describing my situation with the Patahamateri, he suddenly broke in. "You know," he said, "there are some people up there who want to get you out of the region."

"I know," I said. "And I know who it is, too."

I tried to explain the situation to him. I told him about Yorusiwe, about how he had come to our *shapono*, threatening people with a shotgun. I told him about the difficulties this man had created for visitors for years and about the wild stories he told among the Indians about the authorities. I described my past experiences with Yorusiwe and what had happened more recently. And I told him I was aware of some of the rumors he was spreading about me.

"I hope you can help me get this matter straightened out," I said. "Of course it's all lies, nothing but vicious lies."

But when I finished there was no reaction from the smiling face sitting opposite me, not that I necessarily expected one. Reaction would have been commitment. Reaction would have been a demonstration of his understanding or an expression of his point of view. So as a good politician it was unlikely that Muller-Rojas would react. Instead, what I got was a smile and a handshake. "It was good of you to come by, Señor Good. Perhaps you should take the matter up with Señor Chavero. I'm sure he will be able to handle it."

Manuel Chavero was head of the Puerto Ayacucho branch of the Venezuelan Bureau of Indian Affairs. It was this department that would have to issue my permit in Caracas before I could ask Governor Muller-Rojas to countersign it. When I was shown into his office, Chavero was signing checks.

"Just a minute," he said as I came in. I stood there looking at him as he went on with what he was doing, taking his time. When he was finished he looked up. There was no smile on this man's face. "I have heard," he said, "certain things about you. I have heard that you are frightening the Yanomama. I have heard that you stole a wife from someone. They tell me that you stole someone's wife and that he had to steal her back. They tell me also that you have many Yanomama women. I have heard that you have children with native women."

"Look," I answered, "this is very bothersome, very upsetting. These are malicious lies. Absolutely malicious. All of it is false. You cannot possibly believe that any of it is actually true."

Thinking about it later, I realized that my reaction to Chavero was a grave mistake. I should never have shown my distress. The last thing you want to do in this kind of situation is show any sign of weakness. Later, I knew exactly what I should have done. I should have gotten angry and taken immediate, deep offense. I should have said coldly and bluntly that the stories he had just mentioned were outright, libelous lies and that if anyone tried to pursue them— anyone—I would take legal action instantly. The right approach would have been to scare him, because neither Chavero nor anyone else wanted trouble. And my getting a good political lawyer to look closely at his administrative activities would have been exactly the kind of trouble he least needed.

But I didn't do that. Instead I betrayed how upset and worried I really was. "Well," said Chavero, looking at me, "however that may be, I have a report I've prepared on this for the governor, and I will be sending it to him immediately."

"Could I see it?" I asked.

He started shuffling through the mess of papers spread all over his desk. "No," he said, "I don't seem to find it here; it's probably in my file." While all the paper shuffling was going on, it struck me that the man was waiting for me to take the initiative, to put my hand in my pocket and deposit something appropriate on his desk. But I didn't do that, either. I wasn't sure, and I hesitated. Besides, I had so little money left that I was guarding every bolivar.

"Look," I said as the paper shuffling continued, "you must clear this up. If you are writing a report, don't you think you should do an investigation? If you go upriver and talk to people in the village, you'll find these are nothing more than lies."

"Yes," came the answer. "I think that is exactly what we are going to have to do in this case. In fact, I have been planning to do that already. There are extremely serious charges being brought against you, and they must be investigated. I will soon be going to look into them. If they are lies, as you say, then you will be fully exonerated."

I explained to Chavero how to find Patahamateri, how he would have to go up the river, past Guajaribo, past several islands, until he came to a concentration of large rocks on a bend where he would see my aluminum boat tied up. It seemed a little odd that he would actually do this. In all my years I had never seen a government official go up there. But that apparently was what he had in mind. "This is the only way to clear this situation," he said. "In the meantime you should go to Caracas and wait. By the end of the month we will have this thing cleared. We will inform you when to come back here."

Before I left for Caracas I stopped by to see Cuto Magnilia. Cuto was in his fifties, a man whose family had originally moved to Venezuela from Italy and had done well in the Amazon. He was acquainted with everyone in Puerto Ayacucho, and he and I had gotten to know each other fairly well. I told Cuto what had happened. "I'm going to Caracas," I said. "Could you keep an eye on things for me and let me know when they come back from the investigation? I've got to get back up as soon as possible."

By December 15 I was in Caracas, staying with Manuel de Pedro, a filmmaker friend of mine who was in the middle of a feature-length documentary on Venezuelan folk music. I started the permit application process as soon as I arrived, but there was no telling how long even this part of it might take. If Chavero had informed his superiors in Caracas that an investigation was going on, I knew I could be in real trouble. It was already a week and a half since I had left Patahamateri.

As the application process made its usual glacial progress from one administrative office to the next, my state of mind became darker and more agitated. After a few weeks of cooling my heels in a succession of government waiting rooms, I started calling Cuto Magnilia to find out what progress was being made in Puerto Ayacucho. But he could tell me little. He wasn't even sure whether anyone had left for upriver yet.

As January turned into February I tried to keep myself busy writing. I had started an article on the trekking patterns of Yanomama villages, and I was revising the piece on protein as a limiting factor that had originally been turned down by *Science*. *The American Anthropologist* had now accepted the article, but the editor was asking for some revisions and a statistical analysis of the data. I was also working on the text for a photographic essay on the Amazon that was being done by a Caracas photographer, and I was

My first hut among the Hasupuweteri tribe of the Yanomama. The villagers were drawn to the river by the sound of my dugout's motor during one of my many goings and comings.

My hut and one of the Yanomama who helped build it.

The *shapono,* communal home of anywhere from 80 to 100 villagers.

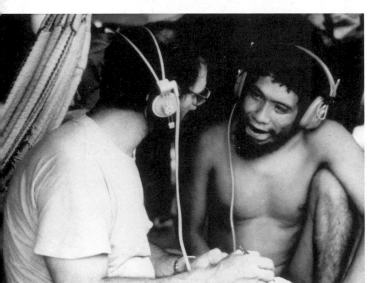

Inside the *shapono* the villagers crowd around a newly arrived visitor to hear the news of his village.

Listening to an account of the names and genealogies of a deceased villager.

Taking notes as the children watch me make curious designs on "paper leaves."

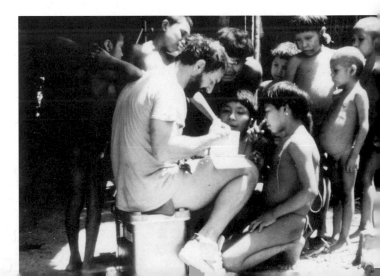

I weigh a peccary for my nutrition studies of the Yanomama, while the tribesmen look on in total bewilderment.

Yarima, in 1979, on her first fishing trip in my canoe. She and her brothers helped me find the good fishing spots.

Writing in my notebook as Yarima and her cousin look on.

(ABOVE) Nanimabu-weteri man crossing on a pole-and-vine bridge over the Siapa River, which the Yanomama call the River of the Parakeets.

(ABOVE) At night, the young girls dance so that their husbands and brothers will have a successful hunt.

A young girl celebrates her *yiipimou*, or first menses, rite.

A woman roasts an afternoon meal of plantains after a day of gathering.

Huya (young men) painting each other in preparation for a feast.

The *huya* engage in a tug of war with a long vine.

One of my companions on a trip to visit the Nanimabuweteri waits to be escorted to a hammock.

Patahamateri warriors rest before joining the Hasupuweteri in a revenge raid on another village.

(BELOW) Raiders line up before an attack on another village.

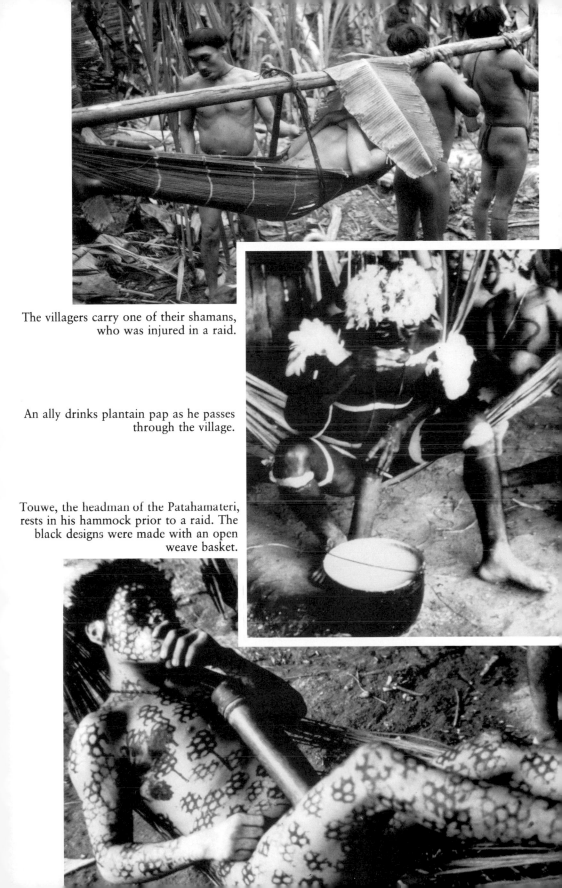

The villagers carry one of their shamans, who was injured in a raid.

An ally drinks plantain pap as he passes through the village.

Touwe, the headman of the Patahamateri, rests in his hammock prior to a raid. The black designs were made with an open weave basket.

(RIGHT) The Yanomama catch fish by drugging them first. The tree bark in which the potent drug is found is left to soak in the river until the fish become "stupefied." The women gather the fish up in baskets and bring them home to be smoked.

(BELOW) I share a laugh and a drink of plantain with Yarima. This was at about the time she was "betrothed" to me by the village elder.

(LEFT) A grandfather weaves a basket for tobacco—a task reserved for men—as he relaxes in his hammock.

Yarima helps a burdened woman as the group leaves on a trek.

(ABOVE) A chest-pounding duel between rival villages. The man on the right takes a return blow from the suitor of his father's young wife.

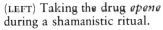

(LEFT) Taking the drug *epene* during a shamanistic ritual.

(BELOW) The Yanomamö believed I had great powers. Here, I lay my hands on Orawe, the great shaman, whose wife believed I could cure him of malaria.

(LEFT) Orawe, in turn, tries to cure me during my severe bout with malaria.

(ABOVE) Repairing my propeller as I motor up the shallow Orinoco during the dry season.

(RIGHT) Yarima sits in the forest near my hut.

(BELOW) Preparing peach palm fruit for cooking prior to a feast with the Patahamateri.

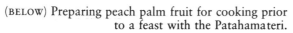

(ABOVE) A bedecked guest at a feast awaiting a gift of plantains and meat to take back to his fellow villagers.

Having put on the final touches of her adornments, Yarima awaits her entry into the *shapono* for the Patahamateri feast.

Boys against girls roughhousing during a feast.

Yarima and I in our matrimonial hammock.

A young *huya* in the throes of celebration.

(ABOVE) Yarima decorates herself for a dance.

(LEFT) An Ashitoweteri man enjoys a large wad of tobacco as he awaits entry to the *shapono* at Wawatoi to begin a feast.

(ABOVE) The Hasupu-
weteri offering trade
goods to their Shama-
tari visitors on the
morning of their depar-
ture. At a later date the
Hasupuweteri will visit
the Shamatari and re-
ceive trade goods in re-
turn.

(ABOVE) Orawe initiating Touwe
into the shaman's fold. This is the
final moment of six days of drug-
taking, during which time the spirits are to have entered the new
shaman's body.

(LEFT) Drinking the ashes of the
dead. The Yanomama think our
method of burial abhorrent. To
drink down the ashes of a loved
one is to make that person live on

(LEFT) Showing Yarima the helicopter that eventually would take her out of the jungle.

(BELOW) Yarima showing photographs of our Caracas friends on one of our trips upriver.

Pulling my dugout through the Guajaribo rapids.

(LEFT) Yarima and our children, David and Vanessa, on our return visit to Wawatoi. David was born in Pennsylvania. Vanessa had just been born in the jungle.

(BELOW) Yarima and our son eating *mokohe* seeds at our hearth in Wawatoi.

(BELOW) Yarima with the children in our home in Gainesville, Florida.

putting together a piece for *Geomundo* magazine, whose editor I had met the first week I was in the capital. There was no lack of work to keep me occupied, but as the weeks went by I found it less and less possible to concentrate.

It wasn't until the end of February that I received notification from the Bureau of Indian Affairs in Caracas: they had granted me a one-year permit. But from Puerto Ayacucho there was still no word. By now I had stopped writing; I couldn't focus long enough to put one sentence in back of the next. Nothing stayed in my mind except Chavero and his damned investigation. I tried not to allow my waking nightmares about what might be happening to Yarima to run away with me. I didn't have to worry about real nightmares; I seemed to have stopped sleeping altogether.

At last I decided I could not wait any longer. On March 5 I bought a plane ticket for Puerto Ayacucho. At the governor's office I was told curtly by his secretary that since I was back in town the governor's Indian commission would make a decision about my permit. They would set up a meeting for ten o'clock the following morning.

The commission was new, put together by Muller-Rojas to make decisions for him on subjects like permits. It was headed by the governor's appointee, a bureaucrat from Caracas, and included five *comisionados*, the governor's appointed representatives for each of the Amazonian Indian tribes (though the Yanomama representative in Puerto Ayacucho was half Ye'kwana; a second upriver tribal representative who lived at Ocamo was a full-blooded Yanomama). I had no idea what to expect from it.

The next day we met in the Indian commission's office, a single decrepit room in one of Puerto Ayacucho's oldest buildings. The room looked as if it might have been painted a washed-out green sometime in the distant past, though now the color was indecipherable and the last remnants of paint hung off the wall in scabrous patches. Several broken chairs, a dilapidated wooden table, and a rust-eaten file cabinet made up the furnishings, along with an antique typewriter with a secretary behind it and a rattling air conditioner that may have given some psychological comfort but barely stirred the hot, fetid air. The place had the musty stink of never having been cleaned.

Sitting behind the table were the five Indian *comisionados*, but not the governor's appointee, who supposedly was the head of this group. And in a chair off to the side sat Yorusiwe himself, dressed in a clean pair of pants, a colorful sport shirt, and a brand-new pair of sneakers, a far cry from what he was wearing when I last saw him in Patahamateri. But his beady eyes had that same deceitful leer, and his thin lips stretched into something he must have thought was an ingratiating smile. For a moment I hardly believed he'd have the guts to be there in the same room with me. I stared at him, my head swimming, but he looked quickly over at the *comisionados* and refused to return my gaze.

After I sat down on one of the rickety chairs and collected myself for a moment, I asked the Ye'kwana-Yanomama representative (who seemed to be in charge) about Chavero. "What is the status of the investigation?" I said. "I want to have these matters cleared up."

Looking at me with vacant black eyes, he said very matter-of-factly, as if he were relating some trivial detail, "There has been no investigation." I sat there, stunned. "This is the investigation," he went on. "Yorusiwe has accused you of stealing his wife."

I caught my breath. Three soul-wrenching months in Caracas waiting for their goddamned investigation to come back, and there had never even been an investigation? I couldn't say a word. For a second I felt as if I were losing my hold on reality.

"*Señor*, do you hear me? You are accused of stealing this man's wife. What do you have to say?"

I looked at Yorusiwe, then back at the tribal representative. "What? Are you crazy? What would I have to do with his wife? Yorusiwe's not even from my village. He doesn't even live in the same area."

"No?" said the half Yanomama, surprised. "He's not?"

"No, he doesn't live with us. For the ten years I have been living there he never even visited our village until just a few months ago. That was the first time. They don't know him."

"I see," said the half-Yanomama. "I guess that straightens that item out. However, he also says that you stole a woman from another man in Hasupuweteri."

"No, I didn't steal anybody from anyone. The woman was offered to me as a wife by her older brother, the headman of the village. This business of stealing her is another blatant lie. Besides, how could I possibly steal a woman from a Yanomama?"

"Well, he says you have children up there."

"No, I have no children, that's more ridiculousness."

"And you have other women in the village?"

"No, I have no other women. Don't you see that these are complete fabrications?"

By the time the hearing was over I felt certain that not a single tribal representative believed Yorusiwe. His answers were so devious, his stories so wild, that it didn't seem possible that anyone could treat his accusations seriously. But even though the half Yanomama had said they would make a decision about my permit soon, I couldn't get anything out of them the next day, or the next, or the next. For an entire week (the twelfth since I left Yarima) I kept going back to that suffocating office to talk to whoever was there, to lobby them, to try to get them on my side, but I could not get an answer. I went to see the governor but couldn't get admitted. "I'm sorry," said the secretary, "he won't see you." I went back the next day, and again he wouldn't see me. I sat in his outer office waiting, thinking he was bound to come out and then I could collar him. But he didn't come out, either.

When I couldn't get an audience with the governor, I went back to the half-Yanomama to point out again how patently false Yorusiwe's stories were and to press him for a decision. By now I had learned that in addition to being the governor's *comisionado,* this man was also an evangelical minister—converted and ordained by the American New Tribes Mission, which for many years had been in competition with the Catholic Indian missions.

When I kept pressing him he said it was plain that Yorusiwe was lying. "But still," he said, "there is one thing wrong here."

"What's that?" I asked, wondering what new bureaucratic sinkhole might open up in front of me.

"What's wrong," said the half-Yanomama minister, "is that a white man and an Indian should not get married, they should not cross their blood." That was his firm conviction. "It is not right," he said. "It should not happen."

"I was taught to believe," I told him, "that we are all the same, that we are all God's children." To this there was no response, just that vacant, expressionless stare.

I was still shocked that Chavero had never even attempted to send someone up to the Patahamateri or Hasupuweteri. He had never even written a report. I had been twisting in the wind in Caracas for three months, and he had never even bothered. (What I didn't know was that while I was in Caracas, Yorusiwe had been up to Patahamateri and told them that I was in jail, that I was never coming back.)

What Chavero did tell the governor was that he had spoken with Luis Urdeneta, the Yanomama *comisionado* who lived upriver, and that Urdeneta had said that he didn't want me up there and that he would personally shoot me if I ever showed up again. This was a tremendous surprise, since Luis and I had been on friendly terms for years. I didn't believe he could have said such a thing, but on the other hand, the lies and deceit had become like a black cloud of bloodsucking gnats hovering over the river and obscuring the sky. There was no avoiding them, no way of breaking free. At every step one was buffeted by impossible, gratuitous malice, staggering bureaucratic inertia, stupefying lethargy. Even under ordinary circumstances it was enough to make you weep or drive you insane. But under ordinary circumstances at least you could say, Who needs this? Under ordinary circumstances you send them all to hell and be on your way, leaving them to wallow in their own slough of tedium and caprice.

At the end of that awful week I was walking toward the Indian commission office for yet another fruitless day of talk and argument when I ran into Luis Urdeneta himself. He greeted me as amiably as ever, as if nothing out of the ordinary were happening at all. Then we sat down in a cafe to talk. Over soft drinks I told him what Chavero had said to the governor, that Luis disliked me so much that he would shoot me if I ever came up there again.

"What?" he exclaimed. "He said what?"

"That you'd shoot me."

"That's the most ridiculous thing I've ever heard. I never even talked to him. I never said any such thing. How could he say that? Don't worry, *shori,*" he told me, finishing up his soda, "I'll let the governor know that the whole thing is complete nonsense."

And he did, which helped me quite a bit (as I understood later) but still didn't resolve the situation. It seemed to me that a political decision must have been made. I was the subject of controversy, and the easiest way to make the problem disappear was to get rid of me. I was only in the Amazon on sufferance anyway, by permit to do scientific work. If I had problems with the Yanomama, it wasn't important who was right and who wrong. There was, too, a vague but general prejudice against anthropologists, especially American anthropologists. So the obvious answer was just to get the gringo out of there. False accusations or not, what's the difference? That's what they must be thinking, I said to myself. As it turned out, I wasn't far from right.

My pleas to the governor, which I made through his secretary (I still wasn't allowed to see him), didn't seem to have any effect, even when I protested that my boat, my motor, my gasoline—everything I owned—was upriver, a whole houseful of supplies and equipment. How could they not let me go back up? I had been working there for ten years. Maybe if I emphasized the scientific aspect, I thought, and played down the personal, they'd look at this more objectively. But it was only when my old friend Dr. Gonzalez Herrera, the former minister and governor, made the same argument on my behalf that Muller-Rojas relented.

"Yes, *señor*," said his secretary when I arrived to make yet another plea, "the governor has made a decision. He will allow you a permit to go upriver, but only in order to retrieve your belongings and come back out. No more. A permit has been granted to you for twelve days."

In a state of despair, I went back to Gonzalez Herrera. I wasn't going to go back up there only long enough to say good-bye to Yarima, I told him. How could they make me do that? Did they think I was just going to quietly leave, with her up there? Jesus!

Finally Gonzalez Herrera went back and said to the governor, "Look, twelve days," he said, "that's barely enough time for him to get up there. Give him something reasonable, at least give him a few months." The next day I was walking along the main street, my stomach turning flips with the tension, when I looked up and saw the governor himself walking down the other side of the street very fast with his entourage following him. Puerto Ayacucho is like that. If you're there for a few days, you're bound to see everyone in town strolling down the main street. For the past four weeks I had been trying every day to get in to see the governor without success. Maybe what I should have been doing was keeping an eye out for him on the street.

I crossed over and quickened my pace to keep up with him. "*Señor Gobernador,* I'm happy to see you," I said, walking faster. "I'd like to talk to you about my case."

"No, *señor,* there's no reason to talk," he said without breaking stride. "The case has come out in your favor. Instead of twelve days we have decided to give you a permit for three months." I felt like a condemned man who had just been given a stay of execution.

Still in a state of disarray, I quickly got my things together and with my next to last bolivar chartered a plane to La Esmeralda. At the mission I looked all over for a ride upriver, but nobody was going. I couldn't even convince any of the boat drivers to take me. One had a broken motor, another couldn't do it now, a third told me he had had trouble with the Yanomama and was afraid to go up so far.

While I was looking I stayed in the little one-room house of Juan Eduardo Noguera, whom I had met during my first trip. Juan Eduardo was an old man now and a fixture in the Venezuelan Amazon. A full-blooded Indian himself, he served as the government-appointed *comisario* for the entire region from La Esmeralda to the headwaters of the Orinoco. In earlier days he had been the motor driver and expedition organizer for Inga Goetz. He was also the man who had found Helena Valero, the white woman who had been kidnapped by the Yanomama and spent twenty years with them. (It was a horrible irony that a year later one of Juan Eduardo's sons was accused of killing one of Helena Valero's sons in a drunken brawl.) Finally, when it seemed as if none of the motor drivers were willing to make the trip, Juan Eduardo and his son Carlos, who lived with him, offered to take me up. I hadn't asked him, thinking he was too old for a journey like this. But he must have seen how desperate I was. "Pack your gear," he said one night. "We'll push off at dawn."

Juan Eduardo's canoe sliced through the olive green waters of the Orinoco. It was the end of March 1985, and like last year at this time the river was at its low ebb—sometimes no more than knee deep, and often that was only through a narrow canal along the extreme edge. It was a time when even the best motor drivers had terrible problems. But despite the difficulties, there wasn't much for me to do. Juan Eduardo was a master boatman, maybe the best on the river, and his son was an expert navigator.

Traveling from break of day till nightfall, I had plenty of time to daydream. I could see Yarima so clearly that sometimes I would snap back from a reverie thinking that I had actually been with her. Her smile always seemed to be there in front of me. I saw us splashing in the water together. I could feel her pressing against me in the matrimonial, the heat of her skin spreading its warmth through my body. As each day passed and we lopped off another stretch of the seemingly endless river, my emotions began to race. The harrowing desperation I had felt in Caracas, then in Puerto Ayacucho, took ever-livelier, more concrete form. The peach palm fruit season had come and gone since I was away. The Patahamateri had no doubt made at least one or two treks to visit relatives for feasts and trading sessions. Those are the times women can easily be abducted, grabbed by young men from the host community. If they had visited the Hasupuweteri, even Shatakewe might have told himself that here was another opportunity. Or perhaps he had decided to avenge himself on me by killing her. Four months was more than enough time for the Patahamateri themselves to start thinking that I wouldn't be back. What about Shiriwe and the others whom I had seen looking at her? And they weren't the only devils ready to pounce—she might have been bitten by a snake. Maybe raiders had come, or disease. At every bend of the river I could feel myself becoming more impatient and more apprehensive. I watched the rocks and the trees, feeling as if I knew every one of them.

After we shot the Guajaribo I stared constantly, hoping and praying to see a Yanomama out fishing or standing on the bank looking for the *motoro* that was making the noise. If they were in the vicinity, they'd come down. But there was a good chance they'd be gone— at the other garden, out on a trek, who could tell. If they were at their other garden, it would be a day's hike to get to them. If they weren't, I'd have to find somebody to help me track them. But whom was I going to find? A thousand hopes and fears chased each other through my head.

As the canoe plowed its way around the last bend, I made out my docking point on the shore. Nobody was there, no Indians, as there would have been if they had been at home. And my aluminum boat; that was gone, too. As we pulled up I saw that the tree to which I had chained and padlocked my boat had been chopped down. "Wait here," I called to Juan Eduardo as I jumped out of the canoe. "I'm going up to the *shapono*. I want to check how long since there were hearth fires."

Carlos followed me as I walked quickly along the trail, my heart pounding. It was obvious that no one had been here for a while; the trail was all overgrown. They're on trek, I thought, wondering what had happened to my boat. Judging from the overgrowth on the trail, the Patahamateri hadn't been here for a month.

Not that there was anything particularly strange about this. Realistically I knew there was a good chance no one would be at home. But a wave of anxiety began to wash over me. After all that wrenching frustration in Puerto Ayacucho, the expectations and fears and hopes, what was I going to do if she was gone, if I couldn't find her? My step faltered, and I stopped to catch my breath. Behind me Carlos was talking, asking questions about the Yanomama. But the words didn't register. God, please no more, I thought. I've had enough. What was this doomsday cloud hanging over me? I had walked this jungle for ten years, strong and confident, aggressive when I had to be. The Indians had called me *waiteri,* fierce. But now my heart was racing. Fifty yards up the trail I could see the opening in the foliage that led to the *shapono* and to my house. I felt some horrible premonition of disaster.

A minute later I reached the clearing and stared at the *shapono,* or at what was left of it. Blackened, charred remains with half-burned rafters and support poles were strewn around a fire-ravaged clearing. In an instant my eyes sought out my house, just a few yards to the right of the *shapono.* The shock almost knocked me to the ground. Where the house had stood there was nothing, only cinders. Not even the mud walls were standing. The ground was black with ashes and soot. Here and there I could see what was left of my notebooks, their maroon covers drawing attention to themselves amid the mounds of debris. There had been more than a hundred of them, meticulously indexed and coded. Food cans were there, too, burst, scorched tins, and my cameras and recording equipment, black-and-silver balls of melted plastic. A little to the side was the twisted skeleton of my Olympia portable typewriter. My broken aluminum cases had spilled out their wealth of notes and cassette tapes in little lava flows of charcoal. Medicine, tools, clothing, food—everything I had in the world was gone.

16

I walked back down the trail in a state of shock, Carlos following behind me, completely silent now. "I'm wiped out," I said to Juan Eduardo as I approached the canoe. "Everything's burned, the *shapono,* my house, everything. It's all gone. Please come up," I said, "I want you to be a witness."

"*¡Coño!*" rasped Juan Eduardo when we got back up the trail. We easily could see what had happened: the *shapono* had caught fire somehow, an accident at a hearth, or more likely raiders who had showed up while the Patahamateri were away. Then the fire had leaped the twenty feet to my hut. It was the dry season, and the whole forest was like tinder. The blaze must have been immense, an inferno, especially when it hit the kerosene jerries I had locked inside. I knew that nobody would have burned the hut on purpose, at least not without taking the trade goods and food first. And there it all was, dozens of blackened machete blades, the wooden handles burned off, kilos and kilos of ceramic beads melted into globs, fishhooks, carving knives scattered all over. Juan Eduardo bent down and picked up one of my maroon Papelería Amazonas field journals—water- and heat-resistant. "Look," he said, "some of these can be saved. They're only burned around the edges and a little down the middle."

"I don't care," I answered. "I don't give a damn. Yarima's gone."

We stood there a minute in silence. "Ken," he finally said, "let's go back to the boat. There's nothing you can do here. You have nothing, no equipment, no food. You don't have any medicine or antivenom. Your boat is gone. Your village is gone. The Indians aren't coming back here. Your wife isn't coming back either. Forget her. You've got to come out with me. You have nothing left here."

"No," I shot back, "I'm going to find my wife!"

Juan Eduardo looked at me as if I were insane. "You're going to do what?" he said, his eyes widening. "Ken, how the hell do you think you're going to find your wife? They've been gone a month at least, maybe two. You're not going to find her. She's probably with another man, anyway. You'll either get lost or get an arrow in you, maybe both. She's not worth it. Don't be crazy, you've got no choice. You have to come out with me."

But I knew I wasn't going back downriver. To what, I thought, Puerto Ayacucho? Caracas? Home? When the only thing I had left in my life after the past ten years was here, out in the jungle someplace? The only thing that really meant something to me. "No," I said, "I'm going to find her. Please, what you can do for me now is take me up to the next rapids, up to the Shuimuiteri. They'll know where the Patahamateri are."

But Juan Eduardo wasn't happy about that idea. "The river's dry," he said, shaking his head. "I've worn the propeller down just getting this far. Upriver it'll be nothing but rocks and sand."

"Goddammit, Juan Eduardo, she's my wife! I'm not going to lose her. If we get stuck, I'll drag the damned canoe through. Just take me up, will you?"

"Ken, please, how are you ever going to get out? Carlos and I can't wait for you while you're trying to find her. The malaria control hardly comes up here anymore. They can never find the Indians. They're never around."

"I'll worry about that later. All I want you to do now is take me up. I'm not asking you to wait for me or anything. Let's just go, okay?"

As I talked I unloaded the things I had brought, thinking all the while that one of the Shuimuiteri would take me in to find Yarima and the village. I'd need my shotgun, but that was it. I'd have to live off the land, but what had I been doing out here for the last ten years if it wasn't learning to hunt and gather and eat whatever there was to be eaten? Maybe I couldn't deal too well with the petty officials and bureaucrats in Puerto Ayacucho who wanted to keep me out. But up here it was a different story. Here I'd find my way.

Still shaking his head, Juan Eduardo told Carlos to shove off, and we started upstream. With the river so dry, our progress was slow and painful. Sandbars blocked the passages and diverted the channels of water that were all there was of the mighty Orinoco. We scraped along, Carlos and I pulling the canoe over the obstacles. At one point we had to stop for half an hour while I chopped through a tree that had fallen across our channel. Juan Eduardo's forty-horsepower motor was much too big for these conditions, and the propeller drove through the sand at the bottom of the foot-and-a-half-deep water.

When we finally got to the Peñascal rapids where the Shuimuiteri lived, no one was on the bank to greet us. When I went to their *shapono,* that too was empty. Looking at it, I felt a surge of anguish and desperation. How could I possibly track Yarima and the Patahamateri myself? Even a Yanomama would have problems. For all my familiarity with the jungle, I had always taken guides and carriers with me wherever I went. But I knew I had to do it.

Heading downriver, I realized that my mind was racing. I'd have Juan Eduardo drop me off at Patahamateri. There I'd salvage whatever I could from the burnout and get it under plastic, along with the few supplies I had just brought upriver with me. Then maybe I'd find my way to Wawatoi, the Hasupuweteri garden. Or somewhere else. Somehow I'd find somebody to hook up with.

Not ten minutes downstream from Shuimuiteri is a marsh area where the Orinoquito tributary flows into the Orinoco. As we passed by the marsh I saw two Yanomama crouching in the short grass, trying to hide but unable to get completely out of sight. I stared in disbelief. Juan Eduardo stopped the motor, and I yelled at them to come out so we could talk. "Don't run away," I shouted. "Don't be afraid. Nobody's going to hurt you. I want to talk to you."

After taking a moment to think about this, the two young men stood up and began to walk cautiously toward the river. "Who are you?" I asked. "Where are you from?"

They were Tokonaweteri, they said, they were trekking. Their camp was just a little way off.

"Do you know where the Shuimuiteri are, or the Patahamateri?"

No, they didn't, but probably some of the older people in their village did. I could come into their camp and ask.

Juan Eduardo drove up the tributary to where they were. "Wait for me," I said. "I'll just ask these people, then I'll be right back."

"Hurry up," came the reply. "I'm not going to wait around here forever. I want to get back to the mission before dark."

In the Tokonaweteri encampment were a number of people I recognized, including a few who had relatives among the Patahamateri. When I asked them about the Patahamateri, and about Yarima, one of the men said that they were off on a long trek toward the Siapa. He had heard that my wife wasn't with them, that she had gone back to her mother and the Hasupuweteri. Another said that she had indeed gone back to her mother, but then she had returned to the Patahamateri and now was living with her father again. Someone else said that the Patahamateri had started toward the Siapa but had been invited to visit the Hawaroweteri. "Wait a minute," I told them, "just stop. Don't send me off in different directions. Don't lie to me. I miss my wife, and I want to see her. Do you understand that?"

At this, two old women who were sitting there listening began to cry. The men had stopped talking, but one old man hobbled over from his hammock. "I know where the Patahamateri are," he said. "My nephew visited with them a few days ago in their camp. They're off near Eshemowe. Your wife is there with them."

"Yes," said one of the women, "she's there. Go quickly to her and take her back."

"Good," I said. "That's good. Now is there somebody who can take me in there?"

"I know where it is," called one of the men from his hammock. "I'll take you in." It was Pusiwe, a man I recognized. He had visited Patahamateri a number of times, a relative of Shiriwe, if I remembered correctly.

"Okay," I said, "that's great. Let's get started."

"Here," said one of the old women, handing me several manioc cakes, "take these with you. You can eat them on the trip."

At the boat I said good-bye to Juan Eduardo and asked him to throw a plastic tarp over the supplies I had left on the riverbank at my old dock. "Don't worry about it," I said, "I'll come back and get them later, after I find Yarima." With that, Pusiwe led me onto a trail going into the jungle, and we were on our way.

After a few minutes at the usual Yanomama men's pace I was gasping for air. I couldn't believe how out of shape I had gotten in the last four months. With all the stress I had been chain-smoking and sleeping very little. I hadn't realized what a toll it was taking.

When it started to get dark we had to stop since I had no flashlight. While Pusiwe stripped bark off several *narinati* trees to make emergency hammocks, I shot a spider monkey, then watched while Pusiwe gutted it, burned off the hair, and roasted it over our campfire. We went to sleep that night to the chittering of vampires and the otherworldly croaking of frogs. In the distance we heard the low, unsettling rumble of a jaguar.

The next morning we ate the manioc cakes the old woman had given me, then moved off toward the south. We traveled all that day, stopping only to drink and to eat some Brazil nuts we gathered. Near nightfall of the second day Pusiwe called a halt. But it seemed to me that if what the old man had said about the Patahamateri's location was right, then we should almost be there. "No," I told him, "I want to push on. The old man said their camp was on top of a high hill, and I think that's got to be the one he was talking about right over there. Let's keep going."

Pusiwe wasn't happy about this. Dark comes in a snap, and the Yanomama don't travel at night. They're especially afraid of the poisonous nocturnal snakes. I was terrified of them myself, but the thought of being so near Yarima made me determined to forge ahead.

We began to move up the hill in front of us, more cautiously now in the rapidly dimming light. I was almost ready to pack it in for the night myself when Pusiwe said, *"Hai"* ("Shhh"). I stopped and listened intently, straining to make out whatever had caught his attention. In a moment I heard the faint sound of what seemed to be children's voices.

"It's them," I whispered. "It's got to be them. There's no one else out here."

We walked quickly, almost running. Against the gray of the sky in front of us, I thought I could make out smoke curling up from campfires. The voices grew louder. We were about two or three hundred yards away when suddenly Pusiwe stopped and turned to me. "Wait," he said, taking my arm. "Wait, *shori,* maybe we shouldn't just go running in there. There's something you don't

235

know. You were downriver a long time, many moons. While you were there, Yorusiwe came up in his boat and told all the Pata-hamateri that you were dead. I know because I was visiting them when he came. He said the police had put you in jail and that you died there. He said that now everyone could take your things. They had already taken some of your machetes before the fire came. Your wife cried many days for you. But now she is living with someone else. She mourned for you, but now she is with someone else."

"Well, we'll straighten that out right now," I said. That son of a bitch Yorusiwe, I thought. I wasn't able to get out of Puerto Ayacucho, but he was free to come and go as he pleased and say anything he liked.

"No," said Pusiwe. "I don't think you should go in there. I think they will be frightened and run off into the forest. I think they will be afraid that you are a ghost who has come to kill them. They took your things, and your house burned down. Then someone took your wife. I think they will be very afraid to see you. I think they will run and hide in the dark. By tomorrow they will be far away, and you will never find them."

That could happen, I knew. I wasn't sure how much of what Pusiwe was telling me was true. There was no particular reason to trust him. But it could be. And I knew for sure that the Patahamateri were capable of spooking and taking off if I surprised them, espe-cially at night when the *bore* roam the trails and attack people. *"Shori,"* said Pusiwe, "I think it would be better if I go in first. You stay out here and I will walk in. They will think I am just visiting. I have kinsmen here. I will go in and tell them that you are not dead and that you are coming. I will tell them that you are not angry. I will tell them that you will not kill or hurt anybody. I will find your wife and tell her that you are not angry with her. I will calm her down so she will not run away. Then, after I have said these things, you can come in. Then you will have your wife."

The plan sounded reasonable enough, so I whispered, "Okay, you go in first and calm her down. I'll come right in behind you." Then I motioned him to go ahead while I followed through the forest, stopping when I caught glimpses of the campfires flickering through the trees.

Standing there in the foliage fifty yards from the encampment, I watched Pusiwe's shadow disappear. I couldn't hear if he was ad-dressing people inside, but I thought I'd give him about five minutes, then I'd come in. In the darkness I heard voices. They sounded excited, but as much as I strained I couldn't make out what was being said.

After a couple of minutes had passed I started to walk up the last little stretch of hill, when all of a sudden I heard what sounded like a herd of peccary stampeding through the undergrowth. As soon as I heard it I started sprinting as fast as I could, but when I broke into the encampment, out of breath and gasping for air, it was already deserted. Nobody was there except three ancient women who were either too sick or too weak to run.

I stared around at the vacant hearths and empty hammocks. "Where did they go?" I asked. "Why did they run away?"

"He came in here," said one old lady, a woman I had once saved from a bout of hepatitis by giving her a course of injections. "He came in here," she said, obviously shaken and afraid. "He said you were coming. He said you were going to kill everyone. He said to get out or you would kill us all." She was quaking, trying to be friendly, but quaking.

"Calm down, mother-in-law," I told her, "don't be afraid, I'm not going to hurt you. I'm not going to hurt anyone. I just want my wife. Where is she? Do you know where she is?"

"Oh," said the old woman, doing her best to smile at me, "I'm sure she must be very nearby out in the forest. Don't worry. She'll come back soon. I'm sure she'll come back soon."

I waited, trying to breathe slowly and regularly. My heart seemed to be racing out of control. I wondered if they could hear it pounding. I had no flashlight with me. There was no way I could go out looking for her. But I couldn't just wait here for something to happen.

"*Bushika*," I called into the blackness, cupping my hands around my mouth. "*Bushika*. Come back, *bushika*. Come home! He's lying, *bushika*, come home!"

There was no sound from the forest. Even the usual nocturnal noises seemed to have gone dead. "*Bushika!* Come back. I am not angry with you. I would never hurt you. I miss you. I want you to come back to me." I listened, but all I could hear was the silence of the monstrous jungle. That and the sobbing of the three old women. They had seen plenty in their lives, men dragging women and raping them, abducting them, even shooting them. But they had never heard anything like this, a man calling out for his wife to come back to him.

At nightfall I was roasting plantains at my father's hearth when Shiriwe's cousin ran into the encampment. He told everyone the nabuh was coming. He said the nabuh was furious and would kill everyone. The whole village jumped up at once and ran into the forest. I ran, too, but I was confused. Before we went on trek Yorusiwe had come upriver to trade. He had given many beads in return for feathers and baskets. Yorusiwe said that the policía had captured Kenny. He said that they were going to keep Kenny until he was an old man, and that the pata in Ayacuchoteri said the Patahamateri could take all of Kenny's things.

I thought this was a lie. But when Kenny did not come for many moons I thought maybe it was true. Or maybe Kenny had gone to his own village to marry a nabuh woman. Yorusiwe came a second time to trade. That time he said that Kenny was dead. He said the policía had killed Kenny in jail.

I ran because I was frightened. I did not know what to think, and I hid in the forest. Then I heard Kenny calling out to me, calling, "Bushika, bushika, come back." I listened to him. It was Kenny, calling for me to come back to him, to come home. I stood up to walk toward him, but Shiriwe's cousin saw me.

"Don't be foolish," he said. "Run away. He will kill you." When he said that, I did not know what to do. I thought maybe I could sleep in the forest, then go to my mother in Hasupuweteri. But then Shiriwe caught me and told me to go with him. I said no, and he became very angry. He said if I did not come with him, he would shoot me. He took my arm, and we walked away from the encampment. I could still hear Kenny's voice calling to me.

Every ten minutes or so I got up from the hammock I was sitting in and shouted into the blackness. After a while two figures materialized from the forest, two young men, Kayuriwe and Kasiwe. "Why did you get that man to bring you here?" asked Kasiwe, walking right up to me. "Why did you get someone who would cause us such trouble? We have been out there in the dark because of him. He's nothing but a troublemaker. I almost shot him when I saw him come in. If I ever see him again, I am going to shoot him. Why did you bring him with you?"

"He is the only one who would guide me here," I said. "Everyone on the river is gone. You were gone, the Shuimuiteri were gone. Everyone was gone. I thought I wouldn't find anybody. He said he would bring me to you. Where is my wife? Did you see her out in the forest?"

"She ran out when we all did. That one you brought along told us you would kill everyone. She was hiding near me. When you started calling I thought she was going to come back in. But Shiriwe told her not to. He said he'd shoot her with an arrow if she did. He pointed an arrow at her while she was squatting on the trail. Then she went off with him. Who knows where they are now? Didn't you know that the one who brought you here is Shiriwe's cousin?"

At about midnight I collapsed into an exhausted sleep. Several more young men had come in by then, and when I woke up the next morning it looked as if the entire group had come back—except for Shiriwe and Yarima.

I got up the next morning determined to get her back. I longed for her. I had not endured all the pain only to come this close, then fail. The previous night had been filled with nothing but desperation and anguish. Now I knew that I was going to find her if it was the last thing I did.

I sent a couple of the *huya* back to the river to get my things, then I sat down with those I was closest to, to ask them to help me find Yarima. It wasn't difficult; I knew that almost all the Patahamateri were eager to have me living with them again. Eventually I organized them into five groups; each would search out toward likely areas where Shiriwe might try to hide. With two of the men, I set out for Warokoaweteri up beyond the Orinoco's headwaters, a place where Shiriwe had a number of relatives and where he might think he could take refuge. I felt driven. Despite the bad condition I was in, I kept to the pace the hunters set, even urging them to move faster. We kept on until dark, then made ourselves hammocks and slept till morning. At around noon the next day we reached the Warokoaweteri *shapono*. It was empty, abandoned. "They left on trek," said Poawe, one of my companions, as he examined the ground. "The tracks are old; the hearths have been out a long time."

Disappointed, we headed back to the Patahamateri encampment. All the way I prayed that one of the other groups had located her, but when we got back I found that they had all returned empty-handed. No one had so much as picked up their trail. "It's dry," said Poawe, "it isn't easy to see tracks. Besides, he's probably staying off the trail. He might even be carrying her on his back to fool us."

The next day I sent runners out to all villages in the vicinity to see if there was any sign of them. Four days had passed since my arrival. There was very little food in the forest. I knew Shiriwe had to start getting hungry soon. They'd have to show up at some village for food, and when they did, I'd hear about it.

For the next week the searchers went out, even as the Pataha-materi resumed their own *wayumi*. But Yarima and Shiriwe seemed to have disappeared from the jungle. "*Shori,*" said Poawe one day after a long, fruitless search, "we have looked for her and looked for her. But I do not think we are going to find her. The forest is very big."

By this time I was scarcely sleeping at all. The thought of the two of them out in that jungle was driving me to a nervous edge. But I knew that they couldn't stay out forever. I knew Shiriwe's plan had to be to stick it out until I gave up and left. And that gave me my advantage. Because what he didn't know was that I wasn't leaving the jungle until either I had her back or they carried me out.

On April 3 I was returning with Poawe and two others from a search that had taken us far to the south. We had been out for three days and hadn't seen a sign or heard anything about them from the two trekking groups we had run into. We were about half a day from where we assumed the Patahamateri trek camp would now be when we saw three Patahamateri hunters coming toward us on the trail. They were looking for us, they said. Two days ago Shiriwe's brother had told Touwe, the headman, that he was afraid I would take revenge on him if I couldn't find Yarima. Shiriwe, he said, was hiding with Yarima on the far side of a large rock outcropping a day's walk off to the southwest. Yarima's father and some of his kinsmen had gone out to find her. This morning they had brought her into camp.

I was overcome with joy. I wanted to race back and enfold Yarima in my arms. But at almost the same instant I felt a warning tremor. I checked my shotgun to make sure it was loaded, then fingered my pocketful of spare shells. Maybe it wasn't true, maybe this was another story they were making up. Maybe Shiriwe had decided that if he couldn't wait me out, he'd have to kill me. He was a tough, aggressive character and such a plan would by no means be beyond him. He could be using Yarima as bait to draw me into an ambush. Get the *nabuh* to throw caution to the wind, then shoot him down on the trail.

On the way in I watched carefully, but I couldn't control my excitement or the flood of relief and happiness I was feeling. When we got near the encampment I quickened my pace. A gaggle of children playing on a fallen tree pointed toward one of the trek shelters where a group of women were sitting around a hammock. When the women saw me they scattered like a herd of frightened deer. And there in the hammock was Yarima. I walked toward her slowly, and our eyes met, for the first time in four months. Hers seemed luminous, larger than I remembered, set deeply against more prominent cheekbones. She had lost weight; it was especially evident in her face. She had an older, harder look about her. I was appalled at how thin and worn she seemed, and how frightened. As I drew near she shrank back in the hammock. Turning her face to the left, she cupped her right ear and held it toward me. Her earlobe was torn in two, and the two folds dangled unnaturally. I squatted down next to her and stroked her hair. I could see that someone had attempted to sew up the torn ear. Thread looped out of the coarse stitching. I put my arms around her and held her.

"*Bushika,* why did you run away from me?" I asked softly. "I missed you so. I tried so hard to get back to you. Why did you run away?"

"He made me go with him," she whispered. "He said he would shoot me if I didn't go. Why didn't you come back? You don't know what they did to me while you were gone."

17

Yarima hung her hammock next to the trail hammock I was using, but she was withdrawn and distant. Neither of us slept much, but we didn't talk either. She seemed almost unable to speak, as if she were too traumatized by what had happened. In the silence I thought about the last four months, about what I had been through in Caracas and in Puerto Ayacucho. I pictured the burned-out *shapono,* and my own house, the blackened ruins of ten years' worth of work. But for all the horror of it, I suspected that whatever had happened to her had been far, far worse.

The next morning we went down to a nearby stream to bathe. She still had said little, and I wanted to lead into this as gently as I could. As we squatted next to each other in the cool, clear water, I thought about how to start. But before I had a chance she began to talk, her tone quiet and serious.

"I have been thinking," she said, "maybe we should not be married to each other any longer." The words hit me like a sledgehammer. "You are *nabuh*. It would be better if you were married to a *nabuh*. I am Yanomama. It would be better if I were married to a Yanomama."

"I don't understand," I said. "Why can't I be married to a Yanomama if I love her? Why can't you be married to a *nabuh* if you love him? Why are you saying this? We are happy with each other. Why should we not be married after all we have suffered for each other?" I felt suddenly drained, so tired I could hardly move. I sat down heavily on the bank and stared at her as she came to sit next to me.

The only noise was from the stream as it rushed past us. I didn't know what to say. After seeing the devastation at Patahamateri I had been driven by only one desire: to find her. In a way, the fact that she was missing had made it possible for me to avoid being consumed by the disaster. My single-minded obsession had given me the strength to organize the search parties and drive myself back and forth across the jungle. And now I had her back—it was an unbelievable feat, a miraculous feat. But I had never anticipated such words. Suddenly I was aware that every muscle in my body was aching with fatigue.

For a long time neither of us spoke. If I could tell her how I feel, I thought. If I could tell her what I had gone through just to be sitting here next to her. Then Yarima turned toward me and said a single word. "Why?" I looked at her; our eyes met and held. "Why did you stay downriver so long?"

"I tried to come," I answered. "I tried to come as fast as I could." What could I tell her? I thought. About my permit? A meaningless concept to her. About the so-called investigation? About dying in Manuel de Pedro's place waiting for a phone call? I couldn't even explain a telephone. About the politics of the Indian Affairs Bureau and the governor's Indian commission?

"I tried to come back," I said. "I did everything I could to come back quickly. But for a long time there was no way for me to get here. There was no plane that could take me. There was no boat."

"Then you should have walked." Her voice was low but determined. "You were gone many moons. You should have walked here. You had time."

"*Bushika*, I couldn't. It is too far to walk."

She didn't seem to hear me. "After you were gone a long time they said you were in jail. They said you died in jail. The Yanomama from downriver with the shotgun came up and said that you were dead. He told the Patahamateri that they could take your things. Afterward they took your boat and your gasoline. I cried for you. I cried because you were dead."

Yarima's words were like fire; each one seemed to burn my heart. "After everyone thought you were dead, they started to come for me." She was speaking slowly and deliberately now. "When I went out to the forest to gather, they came for me. When I went out to bathe they came. They never left me alone. My father could not help me. He tried to stop them, but there were too many. Sometimes one would take me. Sometimes two at the same time. Sometimes three. They were always there. Shiriwe and Didikiwe, Hukokawe and Batawe, and Dokunawe and Mamokawe. Even the filthy, ugly ones. One time one of them took off his loincloth and choked me with it so I could not breathe. The world turned black, and I thought I was dying.

"At night they dragged me out of my hammock. During the day they dragged me into the forest. They never let me alone. One day Shiriwe found me in the forest. He said that you were dead and that now I was his wife. He said that he would protect me, that we should run away together. Then he became angry with me, and I was afraid of him. We went together into the forest. I thought that you must be dead, as the one from downriver told us. I knew that if you were alive, you would not let this happen to me.

"When Shiriwe and I ran away, Touwe and his brothers came to find us. Touwe wanted me to marry his younger brother. They caught us on the big hill beyond the Rahuawe U. Touwe wanted me to come back to the *shapono*. But I did not want to go back there anymore. I wanted to stay with Shiriwe because he could protect me from the other men. Shiriwe and Touwe argued and threatened each other. They pulled me by my arms. When Shiriwe let go, Touwe and his brothers pulled me through the forest. I shouted at him that I did not want to go, that I wanted to stay with Shiriwe. I tried to get away from Touwe. Then Touwe became angry. He put his finger in my earlobe and ripped my ear.

"When I got home the women tried to sew my ear together. But the thread came out and did not hold. Now I will never put flowers in my ears again. I will be like an old woman. Soon I will cut off the piece of skin that is hanging down. It is ugly.

"Now you will say you will not leave. But I know that another day you will go downriver again. You always do. You will leave me here, and no one will protect me against the men. You should go and marry a woman from your own village."

As Yarima spoke I began to feel light-headed, adrift on a moment of terrible stillness. A flood of tenderness for her rushed over me—for this warm, lovely girl whom I had treasured in all her beautiful, laughing innocence. But at the same time my mind's eye held another picture. Of Shiriwe, and Didikiwe, of Hukokawe and Batawe and Mamokawe and Dokunawe. I could see each of their faces as they crowded around her. I could see one of them drawing his loincloth around her neck and pulling and pulling. Suddenly it became the most crucial thing in this world to keep control, to calm the blood, to sit in the absolute stillness and breathe in and out as if it were utterly normal.

And breathing like that, the dangerous moment passed. Yarima had not looked at me. She hadn't seen the panic in my face. Did she mean what she said? Now, maybe. I knew that her anger could go as fast as it came. Now she had to vent those feelings; it all had to come out. But later, I was convinced, so would her warmth and affection—her love. As for the rest, for Shiriwe and the others, leave them alone, I heard the interior voice say. Just leave them alone!

When Kenny came I was frightened of him. I was sure that when he saw my ear he would be angry. I remembered when Maniwe's wife ran away from him. She had run off with Shatiwe into the forest, and they had camped near Irokai. Maniwe and his father found them there, and Maniwe told her to go home with him. When she refused he became furious and struck her in the stomach with a piece of burning firewood. Afterward she had big scars on her stomach. Maniwe had said she was ugly and he was going to get a new wife.

I was afraid that Kenny would be angry and beat me. But I was angry, too. I hated the men for what they did to me. Even my father turned against me and told me to find another husband. All this had happened because Kenny stayed away so long. I did not want these things to happen again, and I knew they would because he would go downriver again and I would have no one to protect me. Shiriwe told me that when the nabuh goes the next time, he would borrow me again. So I told Kenny that I did not want to live like this anymore. He should marry a nabuh, and I should marry a

Yanomama. I didn't like to say this to him. I knew it would make him feel very bad. But I didn't know what else to do.

Journal, trek camp, March 28:   Shiriwe has not come back to the village, and I don't think he will, at least not until he feels sure I won't hurt him. He forced Yarima to flee with him, but that was more or less standard conduct. Men will threaten, and they'll carry out their threats, too. They'll shoot a woman for not going with them. I know of more than one woman who has been killed for rejecting advances made under threat. What usually happens is that she goes along with it. There isn't any choice. You go and make the best of it. You learn to live with him. That's all. If the man continues to treat you brutally, you run away. But he's not going to abuse the woman any more than ordinarily; he only wants to compel her to go with him and get used to him. You go with me, you're my wife now, you live with me. So she does it.

As the days passed Yarima began to regain some of the weight she had lost; she became friendlier, more affectionate. To my great relief she didn't refer again to breaking our marriage. I could see she was going through a healing process. From what I could learn, almost everything that happened to her had taken place in the last month or so. Everything had held together until the Patahamateri were convinced I was dead, or at least that I was not coming back. Then the furies had broken loose.

The *shapono* fire, I was told, had happened while the Patahamateri were visiting Boriana garden three months after I had left. Akiwe, an unmarried young man, had been in love with the wife of Irokawe for more than a year. Throughout that time he had been trying to take her from him (I had watched this happening along with the rest of the village). He had challenged Irokawe time and again. Three times he had run away with her, and each time Irokawe and his allies had found them and brought her back. When the village went to Boriana gardens almost three months after I had left, Akiwe argued with Touwe, the headman, over the affair. When Touwe ridiculed him before the community, Akiwe's anger reached the breaking point. Secretly he returned to Patahamateri and set fire to Touwe's section of the *shapono*. Of course the entire structure went up in flames, then the fire leapt across to my house. The Patahamateri were shocked when they found out what had happened. But for Yarima it had been worse; now it seemed that every trace of me had disappeared. In the ruins of my hut she had read the end of my life with her people.

Journal, trek camp, April 1: Yarima's emotional toughness matches her physical toughness. She has been through a terrible ordeal, but she is rapidly getting back to normal. She's laughing again, joking with me again. Long Feet, she calls me, Big Forehead . . . her old pet names. She's still more distant than she was before, she seems somehow wary. But not damaged permanently. By our standards she should be in a mental institution. A girl from New York who had been raped, strangled, and mutilated like that might not be the same for the rest of her life. But here there's no stigma, no community scandal, and, as far as I can see, no lasting psychological repercussions. What was truly terrible for Yarima was that she had no protection, no stability, she was fair game all the time. That's why she's watching me like she is. She still can't understand why I was away so long, and she doesn't know if I might not leave her to the same fate again.

Journal, trek camp, April 5: Today I brought up the subject again of taking her downriver to get her ear fixed. She was talking about cutting off the lobe. She can't stand it dangling down like that. I had told her before that we could get it fixed, but she was too frightened to even talk about it. I think she's almost as frightened by the thought of the downriver Yanomama as she is by the *nabuh* in Puerto Ayacucho, of whom she has only the vaguest notions. If we go downriver, she knows that first we will have to pass the Konoporepuweteri, with whom the Hasupuweteri have been at war for years, one revenge raid after another. Then Platanal, where Yorusiwe lives in Carlitos's village, more enemies of her older brothers. And then Mavaca, an even greater unknown. She might be abducted to strange lands from which she would never return. The young men there might throw *heri* on her, magical substances that could make her deformed or sterile, or even cause her death.

But today when I mentioned again that the doctors in Puerto Ayacucho could heal her ear, she said she didn't believe me. How could they heal it when it happened a long time ago and the torn edges are already closed over? I told her they can open the wound again and sew it so that it will be completely healed. Talking about it is a clear sign she's considering the possibility.

Journal, trek camp, April 12:   *Shori* showed up today to visit us. This was the first time I've seen anybody from the old village since Red came to work with me on the transcriptions back in November. Yarima is overjoyed to see him. So am I. It's a little like the old days. I'm happy it's having such a good effect on her. *Shori* had heard all about Yarima and said it would never have happened if he had been living with us. But he was far away so he couldn't help. He said we should come back. "You shouldn't think of living with anybody else," he said. No one in his village would have forced Yarima to run away with him, as Shiriwe had.

Even though I felt better with Kenny, I was sad and angry because my ear was broken. I taped the two pieces together with Kenny's brown tape, but it was still ugly. I thought, This is the way it will be for the rest of my life. I will never be able to wear flowers or be pretty.

One day older brother came walking into camp. He stood his arrows at our hearth and got into my hammock. I was very surprised and happy to see him. We had grown up at the same hearth, and I always missed him and my mother. Kenny and older brother talked a lot, which made me feel good. When we lived with Hasupuweteri they were good friends, and when they talked it reminded me of those times. Kenny told older brother that he was tired of the Patahamateri and that he wanted to move back with the Hasupuweteri. He told older brother that the doctors in Ayacuchoteri could fix my ear. After that we would come back and live with Hasupuweteri. Older brother said that he was angry at Patahamateri. He said that he had never liked them. When he told me that he would leave in the morning, I roasted some plantains for him. He said he did not like these people and would never come to visit them if we were not here.

Before *shori* left he helped convince Yarima to go downriver with me to have her ear treated. When we return, he said, we should leave the Patahamateri and come to live with him and their mother. Her mother misses Yarima terribly. Longbeard, Koobewe, Shiroi, and many of the others would be very happy to have us back. I could tell by the way Yarima was listening to him that she was ready to go to Puerto Ayacucho. She had been thinking about it herself, and her brother's words meant a lot to her. But she was terrified at the thought of flying. She thought that to fly on an *avión* she would have to sit on top, and the wind would sweep her off into the sky. Finally I said that we would go all the way to Puerto Ayacucho by boat, a prospect I dreaded and wasn't even sure was possible, since we would have to catch a ride with someone who was going down.

The day after *shori* left, the Patahamateri trek crossed a trail that led to the Orinoco. There Yarima and I split off from the group and continued northwest toward the river. In her basket were some plantains and bananas in addition to our hammocks. I carried the last of my equipment that Juan Eduardo had covered up at my old docking point. I knew this was a chancy situation. We'd have to camp by the river and hope for a boat to come by, and Juan Eduardo had told me that the malaria teams weren't coming up much anymore. But we had no choice. If no one came, we would have to try to make it to the American evangelical missionaries up on the Orinoquito tributary, a four- or five-day walk.

Two days later we were at the river setting up camp and fishing for piranha, using small catfish for bait. If we had to stay here long, feeding ourselves was going to be a problem. As we were waiting for someone to pass, we wouldn't be able to leave the river to hunt and gather, and we only had a few plantains with us. The piranha were biting, and their soft white meat wasn't bad, though it was full of tiny, sharp bones. But piranha by itself makes a tasteless, meager diet.

For four days we ate piranha. Finally we decided we had to visit an abandoned garden that was just an hour away to scavenge whatever food might be available there, even if it meant taking a chance. In a little clearing on the riverbank I set up a long pole with a piece of red cloth tied around it and a note to make sure no one would pass us by: "Please stop. We need emergency help."

We were about ten minutes up the trail when we heard the motor, a distant humming noise that broke in above the screams and twitters of the toucans and parakeets. By the time we raced back to camp three malaria workers had pulled up and were looking around. Our red flag had caught their attention.

The malaria leader was happy enough to take us down to Mavaca mission, where he had his base, even though he was already heavily loaded. He had heard about my house burning down, he said, and had been wondering what had happened to me. From Mavaca he thought there would probably be someone leaving for La Esmeralda fairly soon.

While I got our things together, Yarima put on a T-shirt and stepped into the brown skirt I had once brought her from Caracas; I had told her that the *nabuh* downriver would stare at her if she had no clothes on. As we moved quickly down the center channel, Yarima watched the passing shoreline apprehensively. When the boat accelerated to full speed, her apprehension turned to real fear. The only boat she had been in before was my dugout, puttering slowly along the river's narrow stretches. But now we were racing; the wind blew her hair, and the speedboat's wake threw up white-topped waves that she stared at with frightened eyes. I tried to calm her, telling her that she was safe, that nothing could hurt her in such a powerful boat. But my own thoughts were already running ahead to Mavaca, where we were going to have to stay overnight. The mission there was the main Salesian center in Yanomama territory. Close to the mission lived over five hundred Indians in several *shaponos,* the largest concentration of Yanomama anywhere. I knew that a Yanomama girl from far upriver coming in with a foreigner would arouse intense curiosity. From the moment they saw us they would be crowding around; there would be no way of shielding Yarima from their attention or from whatever they might choose to tell her about the *nabuh* in Puerto Ayacucho or what might be waiting for her there. Yarima had never in her life seen a stranger—except for the malaria teams and the rare visitor from the outside world. She had never met a Yanomama whose lineage and garden history she didn't know.

It was the biggest boat I had ever seen. The motor was much louder than Kenny's motor. The DDT who drove the boat sat in front instead of in back like Kenny did. When he started, the boat went so fast the front raised out of the water. I grabbed the seat and screamed. When we went around the curves in the river the boat tilted, and I thought I would fall out. When I looked behind I saw big white waves, the kind the water monsters make when they are angry. The wind went by my face so fast it made me sick. I was sure that if I fell out, I would die. I thought that an avión must be like this except it takes you through the sky instead of the water. I thought how strong the wind in the sky must be, and I decided I would never go up there.

*As we went down the river I became sadder and sadder because
I thought that my mother and brother and sister were farther and
farther behind me. I was also afraid of the Yanomama at Konoporepiweteri and Yorusiwe's village. Older brother had told me not
to go near them. But the boat went by their villages very fast. We
also passed by Platanal, which Kenny had told me about. That was
where the padre and the hermanas lived. At Platanal they had planted large gardens right on the shore. I had never seen the river so
wide.*

We arrived at Mavaca late in the afternoon after about a five-hour
trip. Stepping out of the speedboat, Yarima looked around. Her
eyes stopped on the mission building, a long one-story palmwood
structure with a tin roof, like nothing she had ever seen before. (It
was directly across the river from here that Chagnon had lived with
a New Tribes mission while he carried out the research for his *Fierce
People*.) Just down from the main building were a number of small
concrete houses, also topped by tin roofs. All the buildings were
surrounded by trimmed grass, a minor but conspicuous sign that a
different mentality held sway here. For a long minute Yarima stood
rooted to the spot, staring at this primitive Amazon settlement as
if she had stepped out of the boat directly into downtown Manhattan.

As fast as I could, I got her into one of the little houses that the
malaria control people used. But I knew there was no chance I'd
be able to hide her. By this time she was so frightened that she had
retreated into silence. Inside the house she huddled in one of the
hammocks, covering her face with her hands.

*After a long time we came around a bend, and I saw many gardens
on one side of the river. There were also a few nabuh houses, then
a shapono, then another shapono. This is Mavaca, Kenny told me,
where the Bishaashiteri live. On the other side of the river it looked
like they had cut down all the trees. Suddenly we came to the shore
and stopped. A great wave came in from behind us and picked the
boat up, then put it down. I was very happy to be on the ground
again.*

*We climbed to the top of the steep bank, and I saw many houses.
There was a row of yellow ones, and in the other direction there
was the biggest house I had ever seen. Actually, the only nabuh
houses I had seen before this were Kenny's mud houses. I wondered*

*who lived here, and Kenny said it was only Padre Bórteli and the
DDT. There must have been many DDT, I thought.*

*When we walked into the big house, Padre Bórteli came out. He
was very friendly, as he was when he came to visit us upriver. The
ground inside was strange—smooth and hard. It was a color I had
never seen. Kenny said it was cemento. Walking on it felt unusual,
but pleasant. It was cool on my feet. Inside there was a Yanomama
who worked with the padre, and he seemed nice, too. He laughed
and joked with Kenny, but he didn't say anything to me. He only
smiled.*

*But when we went outside again there were some huya standing
there. I hung my head down so I did not have to look at them. The
Patahamateri had told me that the Yanomama here would shoot
Kenny and take me away.*

We hadn't been in Mavaca for fifteen minutes when the local Yanomama started coming across the river in their canoes. They
crowded around the house, sticking their heads in at the window
and pushing on the door, which I quickly latched. They all seemed
to be talking at once—not to me, but to Yarima, asking her a million
questions, telling her a million things at the same time, while she
huddled in the hammock, her arms over her head as if she were
trying to fend off the noise. From the babble of voices, phrases leapt
out: *"Weti bei urihiteri ke wa?"* ("Who are you?") *"Weti hami
waheki huu?"* (Where is he taking you, the *nabuh?*") "Why are you
going with him? Stay here with us." "He will take you away to his
land." "You will never see your people again." "Who are you? Who
are you?" She was overwhelmed by the sound, by the strange faces
and voices, by what they were asking and saying. Opening the door,
I ran outside, waving my arms and shouting at them to get away.
They backed off but watched the house from a little distance. That
night I put blankets up over the windows and locked the door. I
knew they'd be back the next morning, but I was hoping to leave
early enough to avoid them. A motor driver I talked to said a team
was supposed to be pushing off shortly after dawn. We'd be welcome to come along.

Early the next morning Yarima and I clambered into the dugout
along with two malaria workers. No Yanomama canoes were on
the river yet, though I was sure that in another half hour they'd be
making a beeline for our little house. I silently thanked the malaria
team and congratulated myself on our luck. I was sure we wouldn't

face the same problems in La Esmeralda; it was far beyond Yanomama territory. The real difficulty would be finding a ride from La Esmeralda to Puerto Ayacucho.

Six hours later we landed in La Esmeralda. I was planning to take Yarima straight to Juan Eduardo's house, but as our canoe pulled up to the river edge Juan Eduardo and his son Carlos were watching us from the front of a little hut a dozen yards from our landing point. The last time I had seen him was when I had walked into the jungle a month earlier carrying only my shotgun and looking for my wife. But in his typical way Juan Eduardo didn't say a word. I had obviously found my wife, now I was here, that was that.

As we talked Yarima stood behind me silently. Then we went into the little hut, where Juan Eduardo had a gas-powered grinder and a big pile of manioc roots. When he started the grinder Yarima grabbed my shirt. Then she watched in fascination as Carlos fed fifty or sixty kilos of roots into the machine, which ground them into a coarse flour. The whole operation took ten or twelve minutes. I could just see what was going through her head. At home, grinding that amount of roots would have taken a week of hard work, grating them by hand on a piece of thorny bark.

When the grinding was done, Juan Eduardo and Carlos covered the flour trough with a sheet of plastic, and we all walked the quarter mile to their thatched-roof hut, where we were received with open arms by Juan Eduardo's warm-hearted wife. For the first time since we had set up camp on the river, Yarima's face was wreathed in smiles. She was even happier when we strung our hammocks in an abandoned hut next door. It was half falling down, but it was ours, and it was obvious that nobody was going to molest us here. I had to convince her to use the primitive shower Juan Eduardo had rigged out back, but when she finally stood under it with me, we both luxuriated in the cascade of cool, clear water. Our last bath had been in the muddy Orinoco, where it had been a race to see if we could get clean before the clouds of bloodsucking gnats devoured us.

La Esmeralda was flat, and there were no trees. I could see for a great distance. After Juan Eduardo and his son ground all the manioc roots there was a pile of flour as big as a termite hill. We could have made enough manioc bread with it to feed all of the Hasupuweteri for many days.

Then we all walked to Juan Eduardo's house. Carrying the packs in the hot sun made me tired and thirsty. I had never been in a place like this, with no trees to give their shade. At the house Juan Eduardo's wife and daughters greeted us. It was nice to see friendly nabuh *women, and I felt very comfortable. Inside, one of the daughters was making a skirt using a* maquina. *She held the cloth in one hand and turned the wheel with the other. While she turned the wheel the needle went up and down very fast. This was the most interesting thing I had seen. Kenny had told me before that* maquina *had made his clothes, shoes, and packs. I thought this must be the* maquina.

I gave Juan Eduardo's daughter a piece of cloth Kenny had given me upriver and asked if she would make a skirt for me. I only had the one I was wearing, and it was dirty with onoto *paint and tobacco stains. She was very kind and smiled at me. Then she made me a beautiful skirt with a tight band around the waist.*

While Juan Eduardo's daughter was making the skirt, a monstrous animal with a man sitting on it came up to the door of the house. I jumped back and crawled under the table, I was so frightened of it. Juan Eduardo's wife and daughter laughed loudly when they saw my fright. They talked to me, but I couldn't understand. Kenny said they were telling me not to be frightened, that the animal was a caballo *and would not hurt me. Kenny had told me about* caballo, *but I never imagined it was so big. They wanted me to go outside and pet it, but I wouldn't. I felt relieved when it left. The man was still sitting on top of it.*

That afternoon I took Yarima to look around La Esmeralda. The mission there was large, at least five times as big as Mavaca. It even housed a boarding school for Indian children. Yarima was as amazed at its size as she was by the expanse of grass and rolling hills. La Esmeralda was, in fact, a kind of natural phenomenon, a rolling plain in the middle of the forest. An early explorer had been so taken by it that he'd called the area "the emerald of the Amazon"—La Esmeralda.

As we walked around I asked among the merchants and boatmen if anyone would be going toward Puerto Ayacucho soon. But none of the motor drivers was planning a trip; besides, there was a temporary shortage of gasoline. A river merchant was expected before too long, though. When he arrived he might be able to take us down with him, they told me, though no one seemed quite sure when he would be coming.

The next morning Yarima and I were strolling by the mission when the sound of an airplane engine broke through our talk. Looking up, we saw a twin-engine Cessna low in the sky making an approach run at the mission's landing strip. As Yarima stared in amazement, the plane swooped by us, settled onto the grass runway, and coasted to a stop. Painted on its fuselage was the name "La Pajarita"—the Little Bird. I was almost as surprised as Yarima when a moment later the doors opened and, instead of one of the usual bush pilots, two white-haired ladies climbed out of the cockpit.

Walking over to the Cessna, I was even more amazed to find that the two were Americans. While I talked with them, Yarima didn't take her eyes off the plane; she seemed mesmerized by it. She had seen planes before on occasion, but only as distant objects in the sky. And here was one just a few feet away. As the two pilots watched, I pointed out the basics to Yarima: the engine, the seats for the pilots and the passengers, the straps that kept everybody firmly in their places, emphasizing all the while how impossible it was to be blown away into the sky.

The two women watched all of this with interest, as surprised to find another American down here as I was, and especially one with an upriver Yanomama. One of them, it turned out, was a retired teacher with a pilot's license. Her friend, the schoolteacher said, was also retired, but she had been one of the first women to train as an astronaut. She had never gone up, but she had been part of the initial group that included women. Both pilots were devout Catholics, and they had been volunteering their plane and services to make flights for the mission fathers, mainly bringing in supplies and medicines from Caracas and Puerto Ayacucho. When I told them briefly about my own situation, and that Yarima and I were waiting for a boat to take us to Puerto Ayacucho, they couldn't have been kinder. "We're taking off for there this afternoon," the former astronaut said, smiling at Yarima. "If you'd like to come with us, we'll be happy to take you, as long as it's okay with the padre. Why don't you go ask him?"

"I don't know," I told her. "I'd love to, but I'm not sure she'd be able to take it. She's never even seen a plane close up, and I can't imagine what it would be like for her. I've already told her she won't have to fly."

"Well," said the first one. "I don't think it would be so bad. We've flown Indians before in Colombia and Ecuador. At first they're scared, but they end up loving it. I don't think she'd have a problem. I know that a couple of Yanomama women have been flown out from Mavaca for medical treatment. I haven't heard that there were any problems with them, either."

I explained this as well as I could to Yarima. I told her that the two women would take us if she wanted to fly to Puerto Ayacucho. If we did, we would be there before dark. Or we could take a boat. I was sure one would come along at some point, though I did not know exactly when. If we went by boat, the trip would take a long time, five or six days (I held up six fingers). If we did take the boat, we would not have much food, and the trip would be long and tiring. But if she did not want to fly, that was all right, either way would be all right. We would do what she wanted.

By now others had started gathering around the plane. The mission carried on all sorts of educational activities as well as its religious proselytizing, and an airplane's arrival was an event that drew people like a magnet. As a group began to gather I could feel my apprehension rising. At Mavaca Yarima had been terrorized by the Yanomama strangers crowding around. Here she had had a chance to get used to others because she hadn't had to deal with any crowds. I watched her as a number of nuns and brothers came up to talk to the pilots and as a group of schoolchildren clustered around with their teacher. She seemed calm, not a bit flustered. From the intent look on her face I could see she was trying to decide whether to take a chance on this thing, this *avión* that could take her soaring through the sky like a bird.

As she stared at the plane, a Ye'kwana friend of mine, Juan Gonzalez, walked up and joined us. Juan Gonzalez had grown up in the Ye'kwana village of Toki, where a group of Yanomama also lived. Like all Ye'kwana, he had taken a Spanish name, and he spoke Yanomama as well as Spanish. He even used to surprise me at times with a few words of English.

Juan had recently gotten work as a nurse in La Esmeralda, a job he had held at Platanal for many years. I had stayed at his house there often, and he had come upriver a number of times to visit me and to hunt. While I talked to the pilots, Juan talked to Yarima, whom he knew from his stays in Patahamateri. Listening with one ear, I heard him tell her that the plane was good; there was nothing to be afraid of. Other Yanomama women had flown, and there was no reason she couldn't also. No harm would come to her.

Whether that tipped the scales I didn't know, but a moment later Yarima turned to me and with a grave look on her face said, "Yes, this is better than the boat. This will take us to Ayacucho." I was so proud of her I almost burst; I knew the courage it had taken for her to say that. And I knew she'd need a lot more of the same when she encountered the unimaginable world of Puerto Ayacucho.

An hour later the plane was ready to take off, and I had gotten the padre's okay for us to take off with it. The two pilots climbed in, then three other passengers, a nun and two mission directors from Caracas, then Yarima and me. We sat all the way back in the tail, where the last two seats were crowded in by extra packs and baggage. I strapped Yarima in, then myself, and held her hand while the pilots went through their checkout and turned the engines over.

As the engines started their roar, Yarima looked up at me and let out a scream. When the plane began to taxi, she grabbed my arm and leg, her fingers digging deep into flesh. I put my arm around her trembling body, trying to reassure her. As we picked up speed and lifted off, she glanced out the window, then threw her head down into my lap and clamped a death grip around my knees. I tried to imagine what she was going through but couldn't think of any reasonable analogy. A ride through space for us would be a simple affair; we've seen it a thousand times in movies, and the idea is at home in our imaginations. Maybe time travel, I thought, some kind of unimaginable, life-threatening time travel. Then she began to scream again. Even with her head buried in my lap, Yarima's screams pierced the roar of the engines. The other passengers looked around, wondering. I could read the annoyance on their faces, then concern as the screaming grew louder. Looking back, the nun tried to get Yarima's attention. "No afraid," she said in broken Yano-mama. "No afraid, *avión* good. *Avión* good."

After a bit the screams subsided into sobs, but Yarima was still shaking, pressing against me, and moaning in terror. Her grip around my legs felt like a steel vise. I kept talking to her softly, telling her over and over, "It's all right, it's all right, *bushika*, don't be afraid, please don't be afraid, we'll be in Ayacucho soon, *bushika*, don't be afraid."

The two and a half hours to Puerto Ayacucho were nerve-racking. Although Yarima stopped crying after a while, she never looked up and never relaxed her grip. I prayed that we wouldn't run into any bad weather. I couldn't imagine how she might react if the plane got into some turbulence and started dipping and falling.

Fortunately the weather held, and although I was beginning to wonder if the flight would ever end, after about two and a half hours we lost altitude and made a final swooping turn into the Puerto Ayacucho airport, about five miles outside of town. As the plane settled onto the runway, Yarima raised her head for the first time. When we climbed out she was calm, relieved beyond measure to be on the ground again—but no more relieved than I was to have her there.

As I unloaded our packs and walked across to the little cinderblock terminal, my protective instincts were aroused, especially when I noticed the group of customs people and national police waiting for us in front of the building. With all the tension of the plane ride I hadn't thought this through in advance. We were clearly in for the usual scrutiny—identity paper check, questioning, maybe a search. Gold and diamond smuggling was rampant down here. Besides, the Amazon was a closed region with a bookful of restrictions. You weren't allowed to bring out vegetation or live animals; even photographs and undeveloped film were subject to special regulations. Anthropologists were always suspect. What might they not think about one who had an undocumented Indian girl with him? You have to be cool, I told myself, taking a deep breath, this whole thing could blow sky high right here.

Meanwhile Yarima was blissfully unaware of any of this. She seemed totally absorbed in taking in everything around her. The airport itself, the vast flat open space, was like nothing she had ever seen. Even La Esmeralda hadn't prepared her for this. She had never been able to see so far, she'd hardly ever set foot on a flat surface. In her entire life she had never been out of the familiar, enclosed feeling of the rain forest. And here it was all different, the earth, the vegetation, the smell of the air, let alone the buildings and strange-looking people.

In front of the terminal one of the policemen stopped us; his hooded eyes and high cheekbones were those of an Indian, maybe a Baré, I thought. His military-style uniform with the hat and epaulets gave him a dictatorial look. "Let me see her papers," he said in a flat voice, his face immobile, his eyes on Yarima.

"She doesn't have any," I told him. "This is her first time out. I'm bringing her in for medical attention."

He stared at her for a moment without saying anything. But it wasn't all that unusual for Indians to come in for treatment, and he finally dismissed us with a wave of his hand. As we walked into the building I noticed the nun from the airplane talking to one of the other police. She seemed to be looking in our direction. I hustled

Yarima inside, then stopped for a minute to adjust the packs. Stooping down, I unbuckled one of the straps, trying to rearrange the load a little, and when I looked up she wasn't beside me. I had an instant of panic before I saw that she had wandered over to the dirty little cafeteria area. There she was, standing next to four men at a table littered with Coke cans, dirty napkins, and remnants of whatever it was they had been eating. She just stood there motionless, right at the table edge, staring at them—standing much closer than a person ordinarily would. They seemed to be trying to start up a conversation with her, and one of the men was offering her a Coke.

Yarima had never had a Coke. Other than rice or the occasional taste of one of my crackers, she had never eaten anything that wasn't part of the Yanomama diet. At this point I wasn't interested in observing her reaction to Coke or getting involved in a casual conversation. I just wanted to get out of there and into town, into a hotel room where she wouldn't be the center of attention. "No, thanks," I said, coming up and moving Yarima toward the door. "She doesn't drink Coke."

We went through the door and out onto the sidewalk where the taxis pulled up. Dusk had come quickly; a couple of old cars were standing by the curb, but nobody was around. "Here, *bushika*," I said. "You stay right here while I get the rest of our packs. Don't move, I'll be right back."

Ducking inside, I picked up our things and pushed open the door to the outside—only to find that she wasn't there. I couldn't have been inside for more than a minute, but she had disappeared again. Frantically I twirled around, trying to look everywhere at once. Then I saw her, crouched behind some bushes at the end of the sidewalk. It took a moment before I realized that one of the old cars sitting at the curb had just started up. I hadn't even noticed it at first—internal combustion noise is such a commonplace thing that we hardly even hear it. But it had startled her, especially when the headlights suddenly flashed on.

"What is it?" she said when I ran over to the bushes and crouched down next to her. "Is it an animal? Is it going to attack?"

"No, it's okay. It's not an animal, it's a . . ." For a second I was at a loss. "It's like an *avión*, except that it goes on the ground. It doesn't fly."

"But look at its eyes." She pointed, her own eyes wide open.

"Those aren't eyes, they're lights . . . like big flashlights. They're so the people inside can see the trail at night. The *nabuh* get into it, see?" I pointed to the man behind the wheel. One of our fellow airplane passengers was just opening the door at the curb. "It runs on the ground and carries them where they want to go. We'll get into one soon ourselves, and it will carry us. It's nothing to be afraid of."

Just then a big flatbed truck pulled up, and a young driver got out to take the bags from the nun and the two pilots who had just come through the door. I took Yarima by the hand and drew her along onto the sidewalk. She came—tentatively, but she came. She was more interested now than afraid. The driver was a friendly young cleric from the mission office who had come to take some of the church people into Puerto Ayacucho. We were welcome to come along, he said. We could sit up on the flatbed with the two lady pilots; the sister would sit inside the cab with him.

The truck drove slowly down the straight two-lane road into town. Yarima sat next to me, as relaxed as if she had been riding in the backs of trucks all her life. After that plane ride, this must have been a lark. The astronaut and the schoolteacher smiled at her, relieved no doubt when they saw they weren't going to be subjected to another fit of terror. A cool, steady breeze washed over us. Yarima held her head high, looking down the road in back of us, still visible in the waning light. She had never been able to see so far into the distance. Slowly she extended her arm and pointed. *"Huuwaaa!"* she said. Wow!

In Puerto Ayacucho, the driver let us off at the Hotel Gran Amazonas, whose owner, Irene Riberol, had been a friend for many years. Irene had heard about Yarima for a long time; I knew she would have a room for us. The Gran Amazonas is a big old colonial-style hotel, the only real hotel in Puerto Ayacucho. It's there that anyone traveling into the Amazon from the outside stays. Scientists, anthropologists, photographers, filmmakers, visiting officials, they all end up meeting each other in the hotel's cafeteria and eating and drinking together in the restaurant/bar.

When we walked up to the counter Irene gave us a broad smile, happy to see us, as I knew she would be. "So this is that wife of yours," she said, coming out from behind the counter and enfolding Yarima in a big hug, beaming. To my surprise Yarima returned the embrace, smiling shyly at this obvious bearer of goodwill. As quickly as politeness allowed, I took Yarima to the room Irene gave us, anxious to get her away from the eyes and questions of the hotel guests. My last encounter with the political bureaucracy down here had left me more than a little gun-shy, and I knew I had to take time to think out exactly how to manage our stay here.

As we walked down the hall I was thinking about whom I could ask for help to ease the way. I didn't even know if the doctors in Puerto Ayacucho would be able to take care of Yarima's ear properly. And if we had to travel to Caracas for it, she'd need identity papers—which might really be a problem. Given my less than cordial relationship with the governor and the Indian Affairs Bureau, just my presence here with Yarima might really be a problem.

All these troubles vanished like smoke in a wind the instant we walked into our room and closed the door. Even before the door clicked shut Yarima had dropped her skirt and ripped the T-shirt over her head. She had been wearing these—what she considered nonsensical impedimenta—for an entire day, and she could not bear it another moment. Free at last, she scanned the room quickly. The double bed caught her attention first. "That's where we sleep," I said. "It's what *nabuh* sleep on." After considering this a moment, she stepped over the footboard and onto the mattress, where she stood, bouncing a little, feeling it out and trying to keep her balance on the strangely resilient surface. "It's nice," I said, "comfortable. You can lie down on it."

"No, I don't think so," she answered. "I don't feel like sleeping."

Suddenly she stopped dead, then almost fell off the bed backward. On the wall facing the bed was a dresser with a large mirror over it, and while she was standing on the bed she glanced over and for the first time in her life saw her full image. I had brought little three-by-five-inch mirrors upriver with me, so she had seen her face before and was familiar with the idea of a mirror. But seeing her entire self was something different. She stared at it, her body rigid. She thought something malevolent was about to happen. I understood: I had seen Yanomama react this way to pictures of themselves, even to their facial reflections. They believe the captured image will generate some kind of evil force that will attack their throats. I grabbed a couple of towels from the bathroom and, covering the mirror with it, told her that the image wouldn't hurt her. With the towel covering the mirror there wouldn't be any image. It was definitely nothing to worry about.

The room light had been on when we came in; now I showed her how pushing the switch up and down turned the light on and off. That fascinated her, but she wouldn't touch it, as it was clearly magical. Another magical item, or at least wondrous if not magical, was the toilet. By this time I was feeling the need for a cigarette and thought that I might just go across the street where there was a little grocery store and pick up a couple of packs and some food for us. I'd only be gone a minute, but I wanted to show her how the bathroom functioned so she could use it if she wanted. I explained the toilet, what you did and how it worked. Yarima was amazed by the water that was released in a flood when I pushed the handle. Mustering her courage, she decided to try to sit down on the seat, as I had demonstrated. Slowly she lowered herself, ready at any moment to respond to danger, but just before she made contact she jumped up. "No, it will bite me if I sit down," she said nervously. I was sure she could come to terms with it soon enough. With the toilet, yes, but definitely not with the mirror, maybe never with the mirror. "Where does the water go when it runs down the hole?" she wanted to know.

"To a bigger hole in the ground," I said. But when I showed her the sink and the faucet, she refused to touch the water that came out, thinking that it must come from the same source that the toilet water ran into.

When I asked her if she wanted to come with me to the store across the street, Yarima looked out the window to where I was pointing. But the scene below, especially all the cars passing by with their headlights on, unnerved her. "No, I'll stay here," she said, stepping up onto the bed again. "Maybe I will be sleeping when you come back."

"Good," I said. "Try to sleep. I will come back very fast."

18

I was crossing the hotel parking lot when I saw a jeep pull in. Out of the jeep stepped Manuel Chavero, the head of the Puerto Ayacucho branch of the Indian Affairs Bureau, the very individual who had kept me waiting in Caracas for three months without ever intending to investigate my case. I was sure this was no coincidence; we hadn't been here more than forty-five minutes. Someone had informed him we were in town, very likely the nun who had flown in with us.

While Chavero was walking over, I decided to take the initiative. The last thing I wanted to do was be on the defensive, answering his questions and insinuations. The best way, I thought, would be to let him know exactly what was what and to be very strong about it. That way he'd have no grounds to accuse me of doing anything behind the government's back or of trying to conceal anything.

"If you've come to see me," I started off, "I suppose you know I'm here with my wife. The story's very simple. I brought her down to get surgical treatment for an injured ear." Chavero looked at me with hostile eyes. There were no smiles or handshakes. "I'm planning to take care of that here," I went on, "once I see what the hospital can do for her. If I have to take her to Caracas, I'll be in to get ID papers." (In Venezuela everyone has a national identity card; it's impossible to travel without one. As an Indian, Yarima could go anywhere she wanted in the Amazon territory, but to leave it she'd need ID.

Chavero digested this information. "Look," he said. "I want to talk to you later. I have some questions I want to ask you. And her." Then he turned and left.

Across the street I bought a pack of Marlboros and an armful of plantains, which Irene had said she could cook up with some fish for Yarima. When I got back to the room Yarima was lying in bed, not sleeping (even though it had been such an incredible and exhausting day for her), just lying there quietly and smiling. She had tried it out and apparently found that it was comfortable.

A half hour later we were in Irene's office eating the dinner she had prepared, Yarima again wearing the skirt and T-shirt. When I had told her it was time to go see Irene, she had opened the door and was halfway down the hall, completley naked, before I caught up and brought her back to the room. I gave her a little discourse on keeping her clothes on when she went outside. It wasn't easy. An upriver Yanomama who has a shirt or a pair of pants will wear it for an hour or so if the insects are particularly bad. But the notion of body shame is totally foreign. "Don't go without clothes here," I said. "The *nabuh* don't like it. They think that walking around without covering yourself is very strange and embarrassing."

Just as we were finishing dinner with Irene, a knock came at the door. It was Chavero, this time with an Indian who spoke Yanomama. "We want to talk to you outside," the Indian said directly to Yarima. "We want you to come with us and answer our questions."

Yarima looked at me in surprise, then broke into tears. She didn't say anything, but she didn't have to. She had heard all sorts of incredible talk upriver about what the *nabuh* do to Indians. "Wait a minute," I said. "You can't just take her away." What was racing through my head was that Yanomama never go off anywhere with strangers; a woman especially would never go off alone with someone. What could it seem like to her—an abduction, the beginning of a rape? Or something even worse, something like what she had heard about *nabuh* at home.

I was on the verge of shouting at the interpreter; the words were already in my mouth. (What do you think you're doing, telling her something like that? What's wrong with you? Can't you see how frightened she is?) But then again, Chavero was standing right there, and although I was ready to stand up to him, he had the power to revoke even the permit I was carrying. So though I was damned if I'd show any weakness with him, I wasn't eager to antagonize him, either. I choked back my words and caught my breath. But Irene spoke right out. Yarima's frightened reaction had been enough for her.

"No," she said. "Yarima is my guest. She's with me, and she's staying right here. She doesn't have to go anyplace."

Momentarily flustered, Chavero turned to face me. "Would you be willing to bring her to my office tomorrow? I want to talk to her in private, without you there. Do you understand? If you're present, she probably won't answer, or she'll be inhibited about answering."

"I don't know,"I said. "Maybe it would be better if you talked to her here."

"Okay," came the answer. "We can do that, too. We'll be back tomorrow."

The next morning while we were eating breakfast in the hotel restaurant, the Yanomama interpreter arrived with another official from Chavero's office, who asked if I would mind waiting at another table while they talked to Yarima. While they sat down with her I went outside for a bit and walked around. When I came back into the restaurant to check on what was going on, Yarima was crying. "All right," I said, walking up to the table, "that's enough for today, we've got an appointment at the hospital." They broke it off and left, but not very graciously.

Actually, the hospital appointment wasn't until later on. In the meantime I left Yarima in the hotel room and went to try to get her an ID card. "It's for a Yanomama Indian woman," I told the two clerks at the Indian Affairs office.

"No problem," they answered, "all you have to do is bring her in along with two witnesses who can attest to her identity. It's only a formality, any two Indians will do. Then we'll give her a card."

Right after lunchtime I was back at the ID office with Yarima and two local Indians who had agreed to act as witnesses. But this time the two friendly women clerks weren't so friendly. "No," said one when I introduced the witnesses. "In order to issue an identity card we'll need to see both her parents."

That pulled me up short. "Her parents? This morning you told me any two Indians. Why all of a sudden her parents?"

"I'm sorry," the clerk said. "The regulation is that we need the parents as witnesses."

Something had obviously happened in the three or four hours since I had been there. Somebody had given these people instructions. "Look," I said, "that's impossible. She lives all the way upriver. I can't just go back there and bring out her parents. Besides, her mother and father live in different villages."

"If the parents can't appear as witnesses," the clerk said, "then testimony from the grandparents will be acceptable."

"Are you serious?" My voice was beginning to rise. "Do you know where she comes from? The headwaters of the Orinoco."

"I'm sorry," said the clerk, "those are the regulations. If she doesn't have the proper witnesses, we can't issue a card."

Before I got too overheated about this, I thought it would make sense to check out the hospital, where we were going later that afternoon. If there was no need to fly to Caracas, Yarima wouldn't have any need for an identity card. As it turned out, the hospital could treat Yarima's ear rather easily; earlobe injuries weren't all that uncommon among the Yanomama. There was even, said the doctor, a nurse at one of the missions who could have handled the repairs (had I only known). We set up an appointment for the surgery and went back to the hotel. Yarima had managed the hospital experience without any problem, though she had a tendency to wander around, inspecting things closely and touching them as a child might. The nurses, who watched her curiously, thought it was cute. But she had been unnerved by the interrogation that morning and was eager to get back to the familiarity of our room.

I told Kenny what the man who spoke Yanomama had said to me. He had asked me if I liked Kenny. When I said yes, I like him, he asked if I truly liked him or was I just afraid of him. I said no, I am not afraid of him. He doesn't beat me. Why should I be afraid of him? Then he asked me if I wanted to remain as Kenny's wife. When I told him yes, he said I was lying. He said that if I didn't tell him the truth, they might put me in jail and never let me see

my parents again. That's why I was crying, I told Kenny. But I was
not afraid. As long as he was there I was not afraid.

She might not have been afraid, but I was. I knew what these people
were capable of doing, and I knew exactly how defenseless I was
here. As I thought about it, I could feel myself breaking into a cold
sweat. The interpreter wouldn't have told Yarima anything like that
on his own initiative. What it meant was that Chavero had decided
to cause as much trouble as he could, which was plenty. The chances
were that the governor also knew we were here, and he wouldn't
be friendly, either. No doubt Chavero had already talked it over
with him.

Deeply worried, I went over what resources I had here. Irene was
a friend and had a certain stature in Puerto Ayacucho, but she
carried no political weight. Unfortunately, Gonzalez Herrera, who
had helped me out of my earlier difficulties, was in Caracas and
was not expected back. The only person I could think of who would
be sympathetic and who might know what to do was Colonel Borrell. Borrell was a tough, steely-eyed, retired army officer who had
previously headed the Venezuelan antiguerrilla forces. When he left
the army he had settled on a ranch near Puerto Ayacucho, but since
then he had been locked in conflicts of one kind or another with
the regional administration. He was embittered and angry at what
he was going through, and by this time he had had a lot of experience
at butting heads with the governor. Borrell was a political heavy
himself, with friends and influence in Caracas. I decided to talk to
him about my situation.

Over the next few days I met with Borell several times, telling
him my entire story and asking his advice on how to handle things.
"You know," he said, "they don't like outsiders here. They want
to keep tight control over everything, and that means keeping outsiders away." (I knew that Borrell's own ranch had burned to the
ground under suspicious circumstances.) "You know that this will
go on forever with you. They don't want you here. You're an in-
convenience. They're uncomfortable with people like you who go
in there and stay. And now you have an Indian wife on top of it."

While Borrell was telling me these things, the harassment from
Chavero's office went on. Each day two or three interrogators would
return to the hotel, questioning Yarima and frightening her. They
tried to pressure her to say that she did not want to be my wife.
They told her I was planning to take her away forever to a place

far beyond the ocean (a body of water she couldn't imagine). They threatened her with jail, though jail was something else she couldn't imagine—even the word filled her with terror.

As the days passed I sensed Yarima changing toward me. At first she asked me to drive the men away, as she knew I would have done in Hasupuweteri or Patahamateri. Bad things had happened to her there, but only when I went downriver. While I was in the village no one ever dared to touch her or treat her with anything but respect. To her I was strong and protective, the person who loved her and kept her from harm, who had fought with all his might to get her back from Shiriwe.

But what she saw now, day after day, was only my impotence. Instead of driving these people away, I could only sit and watch as they brutalized her psychologically. She couldn't understand it. Could it be that I didn't like her anymore? Or that I didn't care about her enough to protect her? Maybe they were right when they told her she shouldn't trust me. If Chavero was trying to undermine our relationship, he was doing a beautiful job. For the Yanomama, a husband who can't protect his wife doesn't keep her very long.

"The only possible thing you can do about it," Borrell said one day, "is make it public. You don't have any other way to protect yourself. Right now you're helpless, and they can do whatever they want with you, but if you make a statement in the newspapers, people will know about it and you'll get support. Take the offensive. If you do, I think you'll see them back off."

That night in the double bed I thought about it. Every material thing I had was gone: my boat, my motor, my supplies and equipment. My notes, the intellectual work of over ten years, were burned and scattered over the ground at what used to be Patahamateri. And now my wife, the one thing I had left in this world, was slipping away, too. As soon as her ear was operated on she would want to go home. She was frightened and confused by this crazy place I had brought her to. And meanwhile I had less than a month left on my permit.

I began to give up hope. Maybe I could eventually find a way to fight it, I thought. If I borrowed some money and found the right friends, I might be able to wangle a new permit somehow. The more I mulled it over, the surer I was that I could find a way. I was not going to let these bastards beat me. But nothing was going to happen instantly, and in the meantime I would have to get Yarima out of here and back upriver. Her appointment to get her ear repaired was for the next day. After that I'd take her back, then come down myself to see what I could do. Borrell was right. I needed allies, and a newspaper piece in Caracas would bring my case to the attention of whatever political enemies this governor had. Intervention from the outside was my one hope, and I was damned if I wasn't going to fight for Yarima tooth and nail. The newspaper idea carried risks; an article might infuriate the governor without stirring up any meaningful support for me. But I couldn't be in a worse position than I was in now. What could I lose?

The next day we went to the hospital, where the doctor performed the ear surgery in his office. Initially he wanted to put Yarima under general anesthesia, but I wouldn't let him. He had told me it could be done with a local, and I didn't want to take any unnecessary chances. Yarima underwent the procedure calmly; she didn't bat an eyelash while the doctor opened the old tear, then sutured it carefully. When it was over we went back to the hotel room, where Irene could watch over Yarima while I went to talk to Borrell.

When I told Borrell what I had decided, he gave me the phone number of a friend and political ally of his in Caracas by the name of Alvaro De Armas. De Armas was from a wealthy and influential Venezuelan family that ran, among other things, a political consulting office. He had good access to the press. On the phone I described the situation to De Armas, and his response was swift and unequivocal. "I think we should put something in the papers for sure," he said. "You need to bring this out and clarify it. You have to defend yourself, and once you go public you won't be at the mercy of these people."

"Okay," I told him, "let's do it. But you have to promise me one thing. If you're going to write an article, it can't come out until I get Yarima back to her village. When I return to Puerto Ayacucho I'll be ready to face the consequences and make a fight of it. I'll do whatever I have to do. But it can't come out until I've gotten her away from here."

"Absolutely," said De Armas. "*Seguro.*"

That Sunday morning, three days later, Yarima and I were sitting in the hotel restaurant talking with the two lady pilots who had flown us from La Esmeralda. They had been staying at the Amazonas, and each morning as we had breakfast together they'd listen wide-eyed while I unfolded the latest episode in our ongoing story.

Our chat this morning was interrupted when Irene rushed up to the table with a Caracas newspaper in her hands. She was breathless and stuttering.

"Kenneth, Kenneth, Kenneth—what is this, Kenneth? What is this? My God, Kenneth, what have you done to yourself?"

The headline she was waving in front of me read, THE AMAZON: NEW CONFLICT EXPLODES. GOVERNOR PROHIBITS ACCESS TO NORTH AMERICAN SCIENTIST. Grabbing the paper, I ran my eyes over the article. "The North American anthropologist Kenneth Good, who has been in the country ten years, accused local authorities in Puerto Ayacucho of prohibiting his relationship with a Yanomama Indian woman with whom he has been living for seven years. He has charged that pressure groups have influenced the attitude taken by Governor Muller-Rojas."

By the time I got this far my eyes were practically bulging out of their sockets. "The North American anthropologist affirmed that sociologists from the group FundAmazonas, who espouse the thesis that the Indians should remain isolated from contact with persons alien to their culture (with the exception of FundAmazonas members), are the ones who have instigated the governor to take measures against him."

My head was whirling. "Kenneth, you cannot say these things. Don't you know you cannot say these things?" It was Irene, but I could hardly hear her. How could that guy have done it? The FundAmazonas, for God's sake! I had never said a word about the FundAmazonas—an alliance of left-leaning intellectual and political groups. I had never even met them! And he had released the article now? While Yarima was still in these people's clutches?

I jumped up. "I'm going to get a lawyer," I told Irene, then stopped. Jesus Christ, I thought, Jesus Christ. Where was I going to get a lawyer on Sunday? Besides, who was going to defend me in this place where the governor was the next thing to an absolute monarch and was about to come down on me boots first? What had this De Armas done to me?

"My God," said the former astronaut to her partner, "who needs to watch television? We've got the most incredible soap opera in the world going on right in front of us."

I spent the rest of the day in a panic. If I were in Caracas, it would be one thing, but I was in this Amazon town with Yarima. Even if the article did arouse support from powerful people in the capital, it would take time before any of that got translated into practical help. In the meantime we were absolutely at the governor's mercy, and mercy was not a quality he exuded. That night I packed our things and told Yarima we were going home the next morning. She was delighted.

On Monday at 8:00 A.M. Yarima and I were in Irene's office calling the charter airline company. I knew in a pinch Irene would lend me the money. "I need a plane immediately," I told the agent. "I have to go upriver right away.

"I'm sorry, sir," came the answer. "I can't do anything for you until one o'clock. All our planes are out until then."

"What?" I said. You must have one. Please, it's an emergency. It's urgent that I leave right away."

"I'm sorry, sir," the voice said again, but I didn't hear the rest of the sentence because Irene had knocked on the door and stuck her head in the office.

"The police are here, Ken," she said. "They want to see you."

In the lobby two plainclothes police were waiting for me, not even regular police, but PTJ agents, the Technical Judicial Police, who handled the serious crimes. "Señor Good," the first one said, "we have warrants to detain you and your wife for questioning. You will be so good as to get her now and come with us."

Yarima was in the office with Irene. Speaking in Yanomama, I told her that the men outside wanted us to go with them. I didn't tell her they were police because I didn't know what her reaction might be. Among the upriver villages it was commonly understood that the police ate Yanomama. "They want us to go with them," I told her, "but I want you to refuse to go." If they had to interrogate us, I wanted them to do it in the hotel, as the Indian Affairs people had done. Being taken to the police station was something I had to avoid at all costs. I had visions of them separating us or locking us up. And if that happened, what would Yarima do? How would she survive it?

When the police came in Yarima refused to go. She was frightened and crying, and when the two agents saw her they seemed to relent a little, or at least they lost some of their harshness. They tried to explain that no one was going to hurt her, there was no reason to be afraid. They just wanted to ask her some questions—a line she had heard already from the people who had been browbeating her every day.

When I finally realized that they were not going to agree to talk to us at the hotel, I said, "Look, she's afraid to go with you. She's never even been out of the jungle before. Maybe if you brought a female agent over, that would calm her down and she'd come." That seemed reasonable to them, but they insisted that I come with them; so I did, riding in their jeep to the police station. We found a female officer and brought her back to the hotel, where Irene was doing her best to keep Yarima calm.

A minute later we were being escorted to the jeep for the return ride to the station. Before we left I quickly jotted down the numbers of the American embassy and a friend of mine in Caracas, then gave them to Irene. "If we don't come back," I said, making sure the PTJ agents heard, "call these numbers and tell them what happened."

The Technical Judicial Police headquarters was an old colonial building right on the town's central plaza. We walked down a long tiled hallway, then stopped in front of the big reception desk. To the right was a metal stairway leading to the second floor. Just beyond the reception area I could see the cells. A rank, unwashed odor pervaded the place. Yarima and I were told to sit down on a gray wooden bench facing the desk, but other than that no one said anything. We waited in silence, watching the cop behind the desk ostentatiously clean his pistol, spinning the barrel and peering into each chamber with one eye closed. Yarima said nothing, but she moved close to me so that we were pressing against each other despite the sticky humidity.

A half hour later I was called into a side room where a clerk was sitting in front of a typewriter ready to take my statement. I wasn't told whether there was a problem or whether I was being accused of anything, only to make a statement, my *declaración*. Standing there in front of the clerk, I proceeded to relate the entire story, beginning with the moment Yarima had been offered to me as a wife by the village headman. I said that we were married according to Yanomama custom and with the total support of her village, that we had been living as husband and wife for several years. I described what had happened when my permit was delayed for four months— how when I had finally been able to go back upriver I had found my house and equipment burned. I had brought my wife into Puerto Ayacucho for the sole purpose of having her ear treated.

By the time I was finished, more than an hour had gone by. Outside, Yarima was still sitting motionlessly; it didn't look as if she had moved a muscle since I left. They took her in, along with an interpreter, a Yanomama Indian who lived at Ocamo mission and worked for the government. I asked if I could accompany her, but my request was denied. I was to sit on the bench and keep quiet.

From inside the room came a mumble of voices, though I couldn't make out anything that was being said. A half hour passed, then another. At one point I heard Yarima start to cry, and I jumped up and went toward the door. But the cop at the front desk yelled at me to sit down. I asked him what his name was, but he just shouted, "Sit down there and don't move." I was ready to go in anyway; I couldn't stand it. But I was afraid they'd lock me up. I could see the malevolent bastard glaring at me, just itching to do something like that. I could imagine Yarima coming out of that room and finding me gone, her only link to anything she knew. I walked slowly back to the bench and sat down.

Yarima didn't come out for two hours. By then it was noon, time for the police to break off and go out for their usual three-hour lunch, but not before telling us to stay exactly where we were. Even the agent at the front desk left, his place taken by two young officers. Yarima was crying again, not any longer from what they were saying to her, but from hunger. Neither of us had eaten since the previous evening. She wanted to leave, but I told her that we had to stay, that the man wanted to talk to us a little more. Afterward we would go to the hotel.

But that only added to her confusion. She had no idea why we couldn't just go. The concept of restraining someone's freedom of movement was something she had never encountered. It wasn't in the Yanomama mental inventory, and I couldn't begin to explain it to her. Tears of frustration and anger wet her cheeks.

The two young receptionists watched us with what looked to me like smiles of sympathy—a far cry from the individual whose place they had taken. Then one of them caught my eye. "We're on your side," he said. "We know what's happening." When I asked what he meant, he said, "We were over at the governor's office this morning with the chief. The chief and the public defender were both telling the governor to leave you alone. They said there was no reason to arrest you, they didn't have any problem with you. But the governor said, 'No, I want this guy, I want you to get him.'"

"I think what's going on," said the other, "is that the governor already has plenty of problems with the arms scandal. He didn't need this thing about you and him in the newspaper. The *Diario* goes out all over the world. That's why he's so angry. What he wants them to do is charge you with cohabiting with a minor."

Three hours later the rest of the PTJ returned from lunch. The first thing they did was take Yarima off for questioning again, then after a while they led me upstairs to the chief's office. I sat there while he asked me more questions about my relationship with Yarima. His tone was polite, even kind. His manner seemed to confirm what the two young agents had told us. He obviously wasn't overjoyed to be doing this. In the middle of the interrogation the door opened and a policewoman escorted Yarima in. I could see she had been crying again. She tried to sit down next to me, but the female agent took her arm and directed her into an adjoining room. As Yarima was being led out, her eyes implored me. Why was I letting this happen to her? Why was I not saving her from them? I started to protest to the chief, but he cut me off. "Señor Good, please listen seriously to what I tell you. It has been decided to take the girl to the mission sisters. They will feed her and take care of her. Then they will decide whether to keep her in the mission school or to take her back to her village. As far as you are concerned, we are going to charge you with cohabitation with a minor."

A moment later the door to the adjoining room opened and the woman agent took Yarima out and down the stairs. Yarima looked back at me, her eyes full of fear. That was it. I wasn't going to take it anymore. "No, goddammit," I said, getting up from the chair and shouting at the chief. "She is my wife. You cannot do this. My lawyer is coming, my embassy is coming, the newspapers are coming, too. They know about this. Is this the way you protect Indians around here? If you try to put her in the mission, you are going to have the biggest scandal of your life on your hands. She doesn't even know what's happening to her." The outburst shocked him. This was not a man used to having people yell at him, especially not detainees. "I insist that you at least let me tell her what's happening. She doesn't have any idea what you are doing to her."

The chief thought about this for a moment. It was clearly a delicate political situation for him, and he and the governor knew there was more than a slight chance that some nasty publicity would come of it. Okay, he finally said, I had his permission to go down to the mission and bring her back here. Then we'd talk further.

That was all I had to hear. I raced down the stairs and out the door toward the mission. A block away I saw Yarima standing on the sidewalk with the policewoman. She was sobbing loudly, and I saw she was trembling. She understood only that she was being led away, to her death as far as she knew or to some horror even worse. *"Bushika,"* I said, running up, "it's all right. You can come with me. You don't have to go with her anymore."

"No, they're taking me away from you," she cried. "I know what they are doing. They are taking me away from you." The police-woman was as relieved as I. She had no way to talk to the panicked Yarima, and people had already stopped to stare.

We sat on the police station's hard wooden bench until six-thirty that evening, until they made up their minds what to do with us. We had still had nothing to eat. The chief finally called me into his office and told me that we were free to go back to the hotel for the night. But we were to report to the police station at eight the next morning to continue with the interrogation. Under no circumstances were we to try to leave Puerto Ayacucho. Walking back to the hotel, Yarima and I held hands. Then she put her arm around my waist. After this incredibly traumatic day, she seemed calm at last, and I found myself marveling at her toughness and resilience.

It was almost nighttime when we left that place. When we returned to Irene's big house Kenny asked me why I had cried. I told him it was because of what the Yanomama said to me. He had told me that if I said that I liked Kenny, they would put me in jail until I died an old woman. He said I would never go home again. When I asked him what jail was, he told me it was a big hollow rock. They would put me in there and put another rock on top so I could not see the light. That is where I would stay, forever, until I was dead. When he said that, I thought of my mother and sister. I missed them so much when he said that, and I started to cry. While I cried, he told me I could go back to his village with him and be his wife. If I did that, I would not be put into the rock. He would talk to the Ayacuchoteri pata, and the pata would say yes. But I told the Yanomama that I would not marry him. I had my husband already, I told him. But I was frightened of what he said.

When we got to the police station the next morning, I was livid. I demanded to see the public defender, and when he came in I denounced the interpreter. By the time I was through ranting and raving, they decided there was no alternative but to strike Yarima's statements and dismiss the interpreter. Faced with the necessity of starting the whole thing over again, and of actually confronting an embassy official (the embassy called me while I was talking) and perhaps a lawyer, the chief stepped back. "Señor Good," he said, "we are going to put the whole thing in the hands of the judge."

The day before our hearing was scheduled—less than a week later—the newspapers struck again. But it wasn't De Armas this time. By now the governor had had a chance to place his own stories. SLICES INDIAN GIRL'S EAR OFF BECAUSE SHE LIVED WITH WHITE MAN, one Caracas headline screamed. "With a single stroke," the full-page story began, "the chief of the Yanomama Indians slashed off Yarima's right ear. Around him were the eight hundred members of his tribe . . . condemning her to wander through the forest or to become the slave of some other group." I blanched. "Good took advantage of other Indian girls, too," said a second story, "married or unmarried, reveling in the luxury of having more concubines." "This is no isolated case," declared a supposed authority. "For years indescribable situations have taken place in the Indian communities favored by anthropologists." "Governor General Muller-Rojas personally denounced the North American anthropologist Kenneth Good for raping a minor Indian girl, whose parents cut off her ear as a mark of punishment."

My head was spinning. Each story was more incredible than the last. I had bought Yarima for a few trinkets. I had stolen her. I had dragged her off into the forest. I had forced her to live with me. Her parents had chopped off her ear when they found out about our relationship. The chief of all the Yanomama [a mythical personage] had chopped off her ear, shouting, "This is your punishment for betraying our tribal traditions."

Sitting in front of a youthful judge in his office the next morning, I had the most peculiar sensation. I was looking straight at a jail sentence for cohabitation with a minor. They were going to take Yarima off to a mission. Despite everything I had done to rescue our marriage, these people were going to separate us and consign each of us to a version of hell. If they put Yarima in a mission, the chances of her ever returning to her family were practically nonexistent. For myself I could see nothing at all. Still, I was conscious of feeling neither rage nor anguish, only a mind-consuming numbness, as if my nerve mechanisms had been overloaded and now had shorted out.

"Good morning, Mr. Good." The judge was talking, very pleasantly and informally. "I have considered the case, Mr. Good, and I've reviewed the allegations. I don't think you have a problem with me. As far as I'm concerned there are no legal difficulties with your relationship."

I looked up, not really believing my ears. "Does that mean that she is legally my wife?"

"Yes it does. In terms of the Venezuelan common-law marriage statutes, she is your wife."

"Does that mean that she can't be taken from me?"

"Yes, that's what it means."

"We're free to go?"

"Yes, you're free to go."

The next day I realized there was nothing to do except take Yarima back. I would not be able to get a new permit, which meant there was no way to continue my life upriver. Without an identity card it would be impossible for Yarima to come with me to Caracas. As the judge had said, we were free to go. We were just not free to go together.

I was utterly defeated, after everything. I felt so sorry for Yarima, for all that she had borne. She was still nervous, still tearful, and there was no way I would ever be able to explain why these terrible things had happened to her. One thing was sure: I couldn't let her suffer any more.

The judge was willing to give me permission to return with Yarima upriver, especially since I still had some time left on my old permit. Feeling like death itself, I borrowed money from Irene and chartered a plane.

Yarima was happier than she had been for ages; she seemed light and radiant—I hadn't seen her that way since I had left on my ill-fated trip downriver six months ago. She looked at the plane as it was being fueled and loaded with supplies. There wasn't a hint of fear in her eyes. It was hard to believe that she was the same person who had suffered such paroxysms of terror on the flight just two weeks ago. We stood there silently on the tarmac with Irene and Colonel Borrell, who had come to see us off, waiting as the last supplies were put aboard.

While I shook hands with Borrell, the morning flight from Caracas landed and taxied to a stop not far from us. Among the passengers who disembarked was my old nemesis Chavero, who sauntered over when he saw us. "Where are you going?" he said, his voice dripping malice.

"I'm taking her home," I answered, suppressing an urge to let him know exactly what I thought of him.

"No, I don't think so," he said, the corners of his mouth turning up in a slight sneer. "You're not going anywhere. You have a serious problem. All your upriver permits have just been revoked by the Caracas office."

Before this remark had a chance to register completely, Colonel Borrell stepped forward and walked off with Chavero a little distance. The colonel, I knew, was not a man to take lightly, and I was sure he was giving Chavero some hints about what course of action might be in Chavero's best interests. *"Déjalo,"* I heard. ("Leave him alone.") *"Amigos en Caracas,"* I heard. *"¿Comprendes?"* When they walked back Chavero mumbled, "I never saw you." Then, without looking at me, he continued walking toward the terminal.

Two and a half hours later Yarima and I landed in La Esmeralda. There Juan Eduardo again volunteered to take us upriver. Clearly he had taken a personal interest in this star-crossed affair. In his day he had seen a lot, including the drama of Helena Valero. I wondered as we made our way up the river whether he had ever seen anything quite like this.

How many times over the previous ten years had I motored up the Orinoco? Each time I had been full of anticipation, at first to see the Hasupuweteri and return to my life with them, later to be back with Yarima. Each trip had been marked by emotion—happiness, longing, desire, also anxiety and fear. But in none had I been burdened with this lacerating sadness. It was a sharp pain from which there was no surcease. Much better to suffer physically, I thought. Physical pain you can deal with, you can stand up to it, accommodate to it, even make it your friend. But this feeling invading my heart never stopped. It was corroding my soul.

At my old docking point Juan Eduardo let us out. He and his son waited in the canoe as I watched Yarima pack her basket with the food and goods I had brought. I felt I would give anything just to walk with her to Wawatoi, the inland garden. But it would take a day to get there and another day back, and Juan Eduardo couldn't wait. He needed to make Mavaca by nightfall. I knew that when Yarima was finished packing there would be no more reason to delay. I thought of going in with her anyway, of not going down at all. Wild ideas assaulted me. We could take up our lives again with the Hasupuweteri. The national guard would never get us. If they came, we could escape into the forest. Even if they recruited Yanomama trackers from the mission, it would take forever to find us, and the guard wouldn't be able to wait it out. I had no food or medicine, not even a spare pair of shoes, so it would mean really going native. But I was willing. Why not? Maybe we could hold out a couple of years, until there was a new election or a new governor in Puerto Ayacucho.

But these were daydreams. Even as I imagined us living by ourselves deep in the southern reaches, I knew I couldn't do it. I couldn't do it to her. She had had enough. We walked slowly up from the river to the burned-out clearing, that old familiar sense I had of her moving just behind me on the trail giving me goose bumps. Amid the ruins of the Patahamateri *shapono* and my hut, we stopped. I turned to her, and we embraced. She had said next to nothing the entire trip. She said nothing now, but her hands clenched the back of my shirt. I kissed her on the forehead. "Go," I said, "be careful of the snakes." She looked at me, tears filling her eyes. "Tell *shori* I like him very much. But tell him that this time I will not be back."

Yarima started off down the trail. Before the trees cut us off from each other, she turned and looked at me. Then she disappeared into the jungle.

19

As I took a step backward my foot brushed the maroon cover of a burned notebook. Looking down, I saw I was standing in the middle of my things, the remains of my equipment, my supplies, my notes. I bent and picked up the book. In my head I could hear Juan Eduardo's words the last time we were here: "Ken, look. They're only burned around the sides and down the middle." I opened it. The edges of the first page were singed off, and the middle of the book along the inside of the spine was scorched, obliterating a few phrases on each of the adjoining pages. Slowly I went through the mess, marveling that the journals had held up as they did, not just to the fire, but to almost a month and a half of exposure to the elements. Some of them were gone, but a good number looked as though they could be salvaged. Slowly and carefully I began to gather them up, cradling them to my chest as I walked down the trail to the river and stowed them in the canoe under the bemused gazes of Juan Eduardo and his son.

We stayed at Mavaca that night. There I talked with Father Bórteli, who was sympathetic but also, it seemed to me, relieved. I recalled how he had said to me a number of years earlier, just before he left on a trip to Italy, "Ken, suddenly you get to be forty, and for all your work, for all your sacrifices, you realize you haven't done anything or accomplished anything." He had seemed so depressed that evening. I remembered how he had scolded an elderly nun over some meaningless mistake, not something the gracious Bórteli would ordinarily do. I had thought to myself, The poor man, up here for so long, and after all the years he feels defeated. But Bórteli had come back. I didn't know whether or not he had found renewal in Italy. But the point was that he had returned and taken up his work again.

That night I slept little. I couldn't believe that my years in the Amazon were ending this way. The peculiar feeling I had first experienced in the judge's office was still with me. It wasn't rage or depression or bitterness—I had been on an emotional roller coaster for months—it was more a blankness, a nothingness. But in this void a few thoughts kept repeating and repeating themselves: How could it end like this? How could what Yarima and I had be destroyed? And all for nothing, because of the malevolence of a few cynical individuals.

From Mavaca we continued down to La Esmeralda, and from there I flew to Puerto Ayacucho. At the Hotel Gran Amazonas Irene met me with tears and a hug. I went to the bar for a drink—something I had never done when Yarima was with me—and there looking at me with eyes full of sympathy were the two lady pilots and a couple of other guests whom I had gotten to know. I said nothing. Sympathy was not what I wanted.

It felt strange walking on this trail alone, without Kenny. But I thought to myself that this was the way it must be. I knew I would always remember Kenny, but I could not live like that anymore. Before, when I was a little girl, it was different. But now when he went downriver I had no one to protect me. I knew he would never stop going downriver, and I also knew I did not want to go there with him. It was a frightening place.

As I got farther from the river I walked faster, even though my pack was heavy with all the things Kenny had bought for me. I was afraid that enemy raiders might find me. Also I worried that the Hasupuweteri might not be at Wawatoi. If they were not, I would have to go to Irokai. If they were far away on trek, I did not know if I would be able to find them.

When I got close to Wawatoi I knew they were not there. I could see no tracks on the trail. Then I came to the small clearing outside the garden, and I saw the stick bundle tied up in the tree. When I saw that I knew that someone had died and that many must be sick. They were probably far away, and they would not be coming back until the body was ready for the fire. I thought I would have to sleep many nights in the jungle, and I was very afraid.

The next day I flew out to Caracas, where I found my way to my filmmaker friend Manuel De Pedro's house again. In the tiny extra bedroom I hung a hammock and moved in among the filing cabinets and boxes full of Manuel's personal archaeology. Next to the hammock I put my own cardboard box, the only baggage I had with me. The second bedroom at Manuel's was occupied by another friend of his, a Cuban journalist working in Venezuela who had recently broken up with his wife. Sitting over coffee in Manuel's kitchen, the three of us looked at each other and laughed. Not long before, Manuel's wife had left him, too, moving to California with their two young children. Truly, I thought, this is a house of broken marriages and broken hearts.

I knew I was in a state of shock, too stunned even to take stock of my situation. At times I had the feeling I was floating outside my body, watching myself wander aimlessly around the Santa Eduvigis neighborhood where Manuel lived. Manuel was still making his feature-length film about a group of criollo folksingers who played guitar with a driving rhythm; before long the sound began to drive me out of what little mind I had left. He would try to cheer me up, try to get me to go out to the group's parties and rehearsals, but I wouldn't go. To me they sounded as if someone had wound them up tight and the spring had failed to wind down. Daduh daduh daduh da*duh,* daduh daduh daduh da*duh,* over and over and over. It didn't seem normal that anyone could be so unrelentingly cheerful.

Like Bórteli, Manuel seemed to think that when all was said and done, what had happened to me was for the best. Of course it did have its drama, enough even to make a great movie. The ending of the film, as Manuel saw it, would take place on a big rock in the yard behind his studio. I would sit on the rock as the camera watched me slowly untie the twine that held together my tattered cardboard box. There, as I opened it up, the camera would discover the burned remains of my notebooks—the poignant summation of ten years of work and struggle on the Orinoco. That would be, he thought, quite a finale.

But even in my current state of mind I wouldn't go along with the script. That might be how De Pedro saw my situation, but I didn't see it that way. Or maybe I did see it that way, but that didn't mean I was going to accept it. Neither did I like Manuel's attitude that it was all for the best. Friend or not, he couldn't seem to grasp why I was grieving so profoundly over what had happened. If Yarima had not been an Indian, I thought, if mine had been a more conventional marriage, he wouldn't have any trouble accepting my feelings. If you love someone, then lose them, it is a tragedy. Indian, white—the differences don't make the love any less; they don't alleviate the loss.

Meanwhile the newspapers were calling. The spate of articles on Yarima and me had whetted their appetites—the claims and counterclaims had provided a wonderful tabloid extravaganza. Now they were hungry for a second course. But I refused to meet with any of them, although I did accept a request from the Central University to appear and offer a direct account so that the matter could be cleared up definitively. But even there I wouldn't allow any press in the room. After my experience I was sure that anything I said would come out distorted. I was also positive that if I defended myself in public, the governor and his contacts would fill the headlines with even more blatant and hurtful lies.

Alvaro De Armas called, but I didn't want to talk to him, either. In publishing that article when he did, he had done me the most damage of all. But he managed to squeeze into one of our abbreviated conversations that the newspaper had broken its word to him and that he was sincerely sorry for what had happened. I softened a little and finally agreed to see him.

Alvaro De Armas ran what he called the Gabinete de Crítica y Ensayo, a one-man political/media consulting and publishing firm. The Gabinete was in the De Armas family residence, which took up what looked like half a big block in the exclusive Altamira section of Caracas. There I was received with what I considered impressive formality, passed from one secretary to another through elegantly appointed offices. Thick pile carpeting muted my footsteps, and Victorian-style landscapes and austere aristocrats looked down from the walls onto formidable Spanish colonial furniture. In De Armas's outer room I waited on a heavy, ornately worked love seat.

De Armas himself came out to escort me into his conference room, where we sat at one end of an immense mahogany table so highly polished that it seemed to be made of dark marble. De Armas was a tall, fair, balding man with a broad smile, a charming manner, and a deep, booming voice. Despite his obvious energy, there was an elegant, groomed air about him that I associated with old wealth. Smiling as he talked, he leaned a little to the right to adjust the shoulder holster that nestled under the jacket of his three-piece suit.

De Armas—Alvaro, as he asked me to call him—began by apologizing again for the newspaper mix-up. They had promised, he said, speaking English with a distinguished British accent, that they would wait for his say-so before printing anything. Then they had just gone ahead and done it. He was appalled by the damage it had done me. I should know, he went on, that he and his colleagues were adamantly opposed to General Muller-Rojas, and their intention, if possible, was to have the man removed from his position. They considered him a disaster. "Now," he asked, changing the subject, "what are your own plans? I suppose you'll be going back to the States to finish off your Ph.D?"

"No," I said, surprised a little at how the answer blurted out. "No, I'm not going back to the States. I only want one thing now. I want to get my wife back." Even while I was saying it I could hardly believe my own words. The thought had been gnawing at me for days, but until that moment I had never articulated it, even to myself. I wanted Yarima back. That was all. I had no other plans.

De Armas sat utterly still for a moment and looked at me—a little strangely, I thought. "I understand," he said after a long silence, very slowly, as if he were considering the situation and trying to arrange it in his own mind. "I believe . . . there . . . might . . . possibly . . . be . . . a . . . way"—he was still staring—"to get you up there again. At least for a short time."

My spirits leapt, even though the idea sounded absolutely crazy. I knew Muller-Rojas wasn't about to let me go up. And I was completely, utterly, stone broke; I didn't even have enough money for a bottle of medicine. "Don't worry," said De Armas when I mentioned these things, "matters like that we can always take care of," and he gave a little dismissive wave of his hand. "Why don't you let me consider this situation a little. Come by tomorrow. Maybe we'll have something more concrete to talk about."

The next day I was back in De Armas's office sitting at the polished table. "As I see it," he began, "the problem is that you and your wife aren't formally married. If you had been married in a legal ceremony, you never would have had the problems in the first place. Muller-Rojas wouldn't have been able to touch you."

"Yes," I said, "that may be. But how were we supposed to get married when I couldn't even get her an ID card?"

"I know, but we have a plan to take care of that. What we'll do is arrange with a pilot friend of ours to fly you directly to La Esmeralda, without going through Puerto Ayacucho. I'll take care of all your supplies and equipment, you don't have to worry about that. From La Esmeralda you go upriver and clear a landing pad for a helicopter. Get your wife and wait with her at the landing pad. We are going to fly in and pick you up. We'll have a mobile national identity unit in the helicopter, the kind they use to document people in remote areas. They'll come in and give your wife an ID card on the spot. Then she'll be able to travel. After that the helicopter will drop you off at Río Negro, where we'll have a magistrate marry you. And that will be that. Once you're legally married they won't be able to stop you from bringing her out to Caracas if you want. They won't be able to stop you from living with her in her land. You can even declare her home as your legal residence."

I didn't know exactly what to make of this. But I knew for sure that this was no game De Armas was playing. He had a deadly serious campaign going on against Muller-Rojas, and it was obvious this fit into it somehow, though it wasn't all that clear to me exactly how. The whole previous night I had been puzzling over what he might have in mind. And now that I had heard it, I wasn't positive it was such a great idea for me to get involved. There was no way I was ever going to fathom whatever intricate political maneuverings were going on. Why risk even further complications with the government? I thought. Aren't you in deep enough trouble already? The other side of it, said a second voice, is that if you know one thing in your life, it's that you have to have her back. And what, this voice asked, what other ideas do you have to accomplish that?

The next morning at six A.M. I was at the La Carlota airport with Alvaro. Don't say anything to anyone, he had told me the previous afternoon. And I hadn't, though Manuel must have thought my change in mood was more than a little strange. I had been dragging myself around in a state of profound depression ever since I arrived, and suddenly, this morning, the light was in my eyes again.

This was all happening so fast, I had had almost no time to get things togther, and I would be going in with more or less an empty pack. With what Alvaro had picked up, I'd have enough food and some trade goods, but minimal clothing, almost no medicine, and no antivenom. Oh, well, I thought, let's just pray I get lucky again. I've managed before.

The pilot dropped me at La Esmeralda. Unfortunately Juan Eduardo was ill and not able to take me up. But with his help I was able to hire a Spanish-speaking Ye'kwana motor driver, and by the next morning we had rounded up enough gasoline and were ready to push off. Three weeks earlier I had come down the river with Juan Eduardo, too numbed even to dream I would ever be going up again.

That night we stopped at Mavaca, and the next morning we left, bringing along a Yanomama from the mission who had relatives far upriver and asked if he could hitch a ride with us. I was happy to have him along. If the Hasupuweteri weren't at Wawatoi—their first inland garden—I knew I'd need someone to help me find my way.

The plan Alvaro had laid out was ambitious and complicated. Getting a helicopter into the jungle meant coordinating arrangements with the Defense Ministry and the Interior Ministry, which ran the National Identification Department. The helicopter team would meet me, he said, exactly seven days from the day I went in. I was to find Yarima and bring her to Wawatoi garden, where we had lived with the Hasupuweteri and where I had previously cleared a landing pad for the national guard helicopters during the census operation. Once there I would reclear the pad and wait for them. My timing would have to be precise. They would have the coordinates (I had given them to Alvaro), but if they arrived and there was no clearing, they would have no way to land, and they would not be able to come back.

When we got to the docking point on the river, I asked the motor driver to wait. If the Hasupuweteri were at Wawatoi, I would be able to get there that day, sleep overnight, and come back. If I had to go in to Irokai, their second garden, it would take an extra day, and he'd have to wait two nights. Either way I would return, I told him, or I would send a messenger with a note. By no means should he leave before I gave him a date to pick me up. If the helicopter didn't work out for some reason, I had to have some way of getting out of there.

Leaving all the supplies and food that we couldn't carry comfortably with the Ye'kwana, the mission Yanomama and I headed in to Wawatoi. Walking hard, we arrived by late afternoon, only to find the garden deserted. Examining the hearths and trail growth, I knew that no one had been there for at least a couple of weeks. I was relatively sure they must be at their second garden, but we checked for prints, and my companion found that the freshest trail sign went off not toward Irokai, but toward the east.

Although I had never known the Hasupuweteri to trek in that direction, the mission Yanomama was fairly certain that no one had gone toward the second garden, so we followed the trail, pushing ourselves until after nightfall and making camp in the jungle. Early the next day we were skirting a small hill, watching the ground carefully, when suddenly, without any advance warning, we found ourselves right in the middle of a trek encampment. I was startled, disoriented for a moment. We hadn't heard any voices, hadn't seen anybody, and suddenly the shelters and hearths—and their owners—had materialized around us. The Yanomama were as surprised as we were. The men grabbed their bows and arrows and let out war whoops. We stood very still while they gathered around, watching us carefully while at the same time looking nervously around the area for raiders. We had obviously spooked them at least as much as they had spooked us.

After a moment my companion found his voice. "Don't be afraid, don't be afraid. It's only us. We're friends." As the tension eased and a discussion started up, I noticed that the language these people spoke was a little different, their intonations and pronunciation not quite those of the Orinoco and Siapa Yanomama. My companion was a stranger to them, but they seemed to know quite a bit about me, even though we had never met. They were, it turned out, the Poreweteri, from the Parima highlands far above the Orinoco. They had been hit hard by raids recently; several people had been killed, and their community had split up in panic and fled. This particular group had come to this area because they were related to the Patahamateri through female kinship ties. The Patahamateri, they said, were almost a day's walk farther in. Yes, they had heard about my wife. She was with them. She was living with a man named Shiriwe ("with the one who has already caused you anguish," as they put it, observing the naming etiquette).

I was startled. When I left Yarima three weeks ago she had been on her way to find her brother's group, not the Patahamateri. She never would have gone back with those people who had abused her so badly unless she was under compulsion of some sort. And Shiriwe? I hadn't seen him the last time—for the couple of weeks we were with the Patahamateri he had not showed up. And I was glad he hadn't; after the abduction I didn't know what I might have done to him. But now, according to the Poreweteri, she was living with Shiriwe again. If this was true, it meant that I was going to have to track Yarima down, again, and get her back. I thought back to last time. This wasn't going to be just a simple matter of finding the Hasupuweteri and walking out with Yarima to a nice, clean helicopter pickup—this meant another confrontation, maybe worse than last time.

Thinking over the situation, I decided first to send a note to my motor driver telling him to meet me at the same spot in exactly two months. That would be my backup if I missed the helicopter rendezvous, which suddenly seemed like a pretty good bet. He should leave the supplies on the trail, and I would pick them up later. I knew that if the helicopter didn't make it to Wawatoi, or if I didn't make it, I would have to find a way of getting Yarima downriver and documented myself, then getting us formally married. That would be a little hairy, since we'd have to go out through La Esmeralda and maybe even Puerto Ayacucho. But I felt ready for it. The last time I had been alone, at the mercy of every petty bureaucrat. Now I'd have real support when it came to defending our rights. Besides, from what Alvaro had implied, it was pretty clear that some major event would soon be taking place downriver, that he and his allies were marshaling their forces.

But first, of course, I'd have to find Yarima. That hadn't been easy last time around, when Shiriwe had taken her out into the forest. If he managed the same thing this time, I might be in for a long haul here. But I was not about to let this man take my wife. I didn't care what it took; I wasn't going to leave without her.

Taking one of the Poreweteri with me as a guide, I pushed on into the jungle. I wasn't worried about a confrontation with Shiriwe. I didn't think he would challenge me directly. What I was afraid of was that word of our coming would get there before we did, and that by the time I arrived he would have disappeared, taking Yarima with him.

The Poreweteri and I moved quickly. By late in the day we could hear voices in front of us—the Patahamateri, I was sure. I broke into a jog, hoping to surprise them and get hold of Yarima before anybody had a chance to run. But by the time I made out the encampment shelters I was sure it was already too late. The first person I saw looked at me and said, *"Eou, shori,"* without a trace of surprise. They knew I was coming.

The Patahamateri seemed happy to see me, though there were fewer families than when I was last with them. After I left, they said, the headman Touwe and some of his kinsmen had split from the group and were now making their encampment a little way off. The only Patahamateri not pleased about my arrival were Shiriwe's two brothers and their families, who watched me warily. Shiriwe himself was gone. "Yes, son-in-law," said Yarima's father when I squatted down next to his hammock. "He's taken her off with him again."

By this time I knew exactly what had to be done. And so did everyone else, having been through almost exactly the same scene little more than a month earlier. Sitting around with the men, we talked over the situation. Yes, they said, they thought they could find her. Yes, they would try their best. This time (as last time) the search would be complicated by the fact that the village was on trek. So in addition to the searchers going in different directions, the village was following its own itinerary through the forest. Groups spent the entire day searching, then came back empty-handed, the men looking serious and grim. I went up toward the headwaters, others went downriver. We searched the old gardens and visited neighboring villages to see if Shiriwe and Yarima had shown up in any of these places. Unlike last time, it was now raining quite a bit, so the ground was soft and retained tracks. But still we found few trail signs that looked promising, and what we did find led only to dead ends. Each day it was a tremendous disappointment to see the men walking in without her. The fifth day passed, then the sixth. On the sixth day a Poreweteri showed up in camp with word that the Ye'kwana motor driver had not been on the river when my messenger reached there. He had already left, taking my remaining supplies with him.

If Alvaro had actually succeeded in getting a helicopter, it would be coming into Wawatoi on the seventh day, where it would find nothing—no landing pad and nobody to take out. And now I had no backup, either. I was beginning to feel the first twinges of anxiety about how this might end up. People were saying, "I don't know what they're eating out there, because none of the fruit is ripe." They didn't understand where Shiriwe might have taken her.

At the end of two weeks we had had no luck at all, and the men were rapidly growing tired of the hunt. It seemed clear that Shiriwe must have found some refuge beyond the range of the day-long searches the hunters had been making. Finding Yarima, I realized, would take a more strenuous effort than we had been making. The more I thought about it, the surer I was that if anybody was capable of bringing this to a successful conclusion, it was Touwe the headman.

The next day I sent a message to Touwe at his encampment, asking him to come to see me. During the entire two weeks I had been here we had not spoken, even though he was living only a few minutes away. He was cautious. I knew he was afraid I might be planning some revenge for his having ripped Yarima's ear. He could easily imagine that I harbored ill will toward him. It was much harder for him to conceive that I had no thought of avenging myself. At the same time, I was sure he would welcome a reconciliation, and I was more than willing to take the initiative.

Sometime later I felt a surge of happiness as Touwe walked into camp and got into the hammock next to mine. He did not answer when I told him I was not angry at him anymore, but I could see he was pleased. And when I said I thought he was the only one who might be able to find my wife, and asked if he could help, he beamed. Not only would we be friends again, the idea that I had confidence in him and that I appreciated his skills gave him real pleasure.

He also liked the idea of taking on Shiriwe. Patahamateri was in the process of fissioning, and relations between Touwe's family and Shiriwe's were far from cordial. One of the chief factors in the village split was that Shiriwe's brother had succeeded in taking for himself the wife of an older man, a member of Touwe's lineage, which had angered the headman's entire family. An opportunity to go after Shiriwe was something he welcomed.

"But you can't just go out for a day at a time, like the others have done," I told him when we discussed it. "You'll have to take a machete and a pot and food and matches. You have to be able to stay out long enough to find her. You can't go out in the morning and come back at night. They are too far. But if there is anybody here who can find them, it is you, nobody else."

Young for a headman, Touwe was aggressive and energetic. "Don't worry, *shori*," he said. "I am not coming home until I find her. She's your wife. We will get her back for you." Together with his younger brother and a cousin he set off, after I had supplied them with machetes and matches. As I watched them go I thought to myself, This is my last chance. The other men were already tired. They had made their best efforts and weren't that interested anymore, even with the prospect of my settling with the village again. If Touwe doesn't get them, I thought, what else can I possibly do?

While Touwe was out I sent a message to Yarima's brother. I was sure the Hasupuweteri had heard I was back. But I wanted to invite *shori* specifically. He had visited us last time after I had found Yarima, and his presence had been tremendously helpful, not just for Yarima, but for me. He had a calming influence on her, and to me he was an old friend—much closer than any of the Patahamateri.

For the first three days that Touwe and his relatives were out, speculation in the trek camp ran high. The headman was known as an expert hunter and tracker; many of the people were optimistic he'd find Yarima and be back soon. One old lady told me, "You know, you should really beat her when she comes back. Then she'll know not to run away anymore. Take a hard piece of firewood and hit her on the legs."

"No," I said, "I can't do that," knowing how impossible it was to bridge the gap between my point of view and hers.

"Well," she answered, "if you don't do something like that, then don't complain if she runs away again."

Another day or two passed with no sign of Touwe or Yarima. But *shori* appeared. He had gotten my message and came immediately. It made me feel so much better to have *shori* near me, to have the talk and sympathy of a friend. By the fire at night he brought me up to date on what had been happening among the Hasupuweteri and the other groups that lived in our area: garden news, news of births, deaths, raids, visits, and feasts. He filled me in on the thunderous event that had shaken not only the Hasupuweteri, but the Patahamateri and all the other communities in the region—the death of the great headman Longbeard. There had been a massive funeral ceremony and far-flung mourning. His ashes had been drunk. Longbeard's place as *pata* had now been taken by Koobewe, another good friend of mine, a man who was also Yarima's classificatory brother. For several moons now food had been scarce, he said; many groups were on *wayumi*, almost no one lived near the river anymore. "Why are you back with these people, *shori?*" he asked. "You know you should be living with us."

"Yes," I told him, "I know. But when I came back in I found your sister was here with these people. I had expected her to go to you. I don't know what happened."

Shori had heard that Yarima was with the Patahamateri, but he had only learned about it after she had been back for a time. He didn't know what might have happened to her when she came in from the river. Only she would be able to tell us. It was most likely, he thought, that she had met up with the Patahamateri in the forest, and they wouldn't let her go. "This is what you get for taking her to a different village in the first place," he said, picking up the theme he had started a month ago. "None of this ever would have happened had you stayed with us."

On July 25, 1985, seven days after Touwe's party had left, the headman's cousin walked quickly into camp. It was late in the afternoon, and I was lying in my hammock. The moment I noticed him I searched his face, hoping to read good news there but afraid I would see the same serious expression that every other searcher had come back with. Instead a slight smile touched his features when he saw me looking at him. *"Shori,"* he said, "just wait there. Sit up in your hammock and wait." Then he went by me, walked quickly to his own hammock, and got in, gazing at his wife and two children, whom he had not seen in a week.

I sat there, almost light-headed with anticipation, peering into the shadows he had just walked out of. A minute or two later a little group emerged from the darkness, Touwe first, then his younger brother, and, behind them, Yarima. She looked thin and tired, but not hurt, not traumatized like the previous time. She stood there looking at me for a moment, then came over and squatted next to the fire, warming herself but keeping her distance from me. I sensed her fear. Always, I thought, always they take it out on the women. I knew the entire encampment was watching, waiting to see what I would do. But before I could decide whether I should go over and bring her to the hammock, Yarima made up her own mind. She stood up and walked over by herself. It was a brave thing to do, and her eyes were still wary. Then she saw *shori* in the hammock next to mine, and instantly the tension eased. I could feel it disappear, almost like something tangible. Yarima got into my hammock. "Do not be angry with me," she said. "I am back now."

Later in the evening I went to talk to Touwe's cousin. I was eager to hear what had happened, and I knew that Touwe himself was not likely to tell me much, especially if it involved describing his own exploits (after bringing Yarima back, he had returned immediately to his own encampment). The cousin turned to look at me as I lay down in the hammock strung diagonally to his. "Brother-in-law," he began (he knew why I had come), "this is how it happened. We searched for many days but found nothing. We went south toward the Shukumini ke U. It was there in the land of the Shamatari that we found them, many days to the south. The man did not want to let her go. He complained to us. He insulted my cousin. He held tightly to her arm. Then he cut a club, and my cousin cut a club. His blow did not hurt my cousin. But my cousin hit him hard on the shoulder, and he dropped his club. He hit him with a blow that he could not stand, a hard blow that brought him pain. Then we took your wife from him. My cousin and I walked in front. My brother walked behind. I told your wife that you would not hurt her. I told her not to run away. But she did not want to run. She was afraid that the man would wait for us on the trail and shoot her with an arrow. But I told her not to worry. That man is afraid of my cousin's fierceness."

The next morning I gave most of the trade goods I had with me to the Patahamateri, beyond what I had agreed to pay them. They were happy to get them, but surprised and upset when *shori*, Yarima, and I began packing our things. *Shori* and I had decided several days earlier that we would go to Hasupuweteri, and Yarima had been especially happy to hear this. I knew we had missed the helicopter—if it had ever come—and while I was planning my next step I wanted to be in the safest, most secure surroundings we could manage. I knew that *shori*'s presence was tremendously important to Yarima. He relaxed her and made her feel comfortable. And going back to see her mother and other close relatives would give her even more of a sense of stability, of the essential normalcy of life. "That's the beauty of their kinship relations," I wrote in my journal that night. "That's the significance of them. Our own lives are so filled—with material things, with careers, entertainment, with variety and change, with aspirations and goals. But they have none of this. What they do have are their relatives, that's why family means so much to them."

I knew the Patahamateri would be severely disappointed about our leaving. One of the reasons they had worked so hard to return Yarima to me was the prospect of having us as village mates again. They didn't say much as we made our preparations, but their faces and the occasional glances they gave us were eloquent enough.

Touwe himself was more direct about it. When the three of us stopped at his encampment, he was angry. *"Shori,"* he said, getting out of his hammock, "why are you going away? I found your wife for you. I brought her back. We walked many days over the mountains to get her. It is because of what I did that you have her back. And now you leave."

"I know what you did," I answered. "That is why I am giving you presents." In addition to an assortment of more ordinary trade goods, I had a large steel ax for him, an extremely valuable item. "I want you to know that you will always have presents from me. In the future you will receive many things from me. There is nothing you will lack. But I cannot stay with you. I cannot stay in your village near the place where that man and his brothers live. I cannot live with them. They have abused my wife, and I cannot stay here. Others who live here have also abused her in the past. I cannot live with the Patahamateri."

"Then tell your wife," Touwe said, "that she should not run away anymore. I will not search for her again." And he sat down in his hammock, put his hand over his mouth, and fixed his gaze on the forest.

That evening *shori*, Yarima, and I were back at Wawatoi, waiting for the Hasupuweteri to arrive, as he assured us they would. In our hammock that night Yarima told me what had happened. After I had left her in the burned-out *shapono* above the riverbank, she had walked into Wawatoi, hoping to find her brother. But no one was at the garden. Afraid to be out alone (women almost never are), she had walked in toward Irokai—the Hasupuweteri *shapono* deep in the interior. But on the way there she had met the Patahamateri. She expected the worst, a repeat of what had happened to her the last time she was with Patahamateri alone. But instead, Shiriwe had claimed her. He had been *hushuo,* enraged that I had managed to get Yarima away from him. Now she had fallen right back into his hands. When a Poreweteri runner told him I had come back, he was determined to take her off into the deepest part of the jungle. But it was hard, Yarima said. They had had little to eat. None of the fruits were ripe, and they had only been able to shoot small birds. Without a pot, they tried roasting the peach palm fruit, but the outer husks were extremely tough. When Touwe found them, Shiriwe was already planning to go into a village for food.

The following day the Hasupuweteri began to filter in. In Yanomama fashion they set up their hammocks and went about their business, in which we, the new arrivals, were immediately and effortlessly included. "Yes," they said when they came over to sit in a hammock and talk, "we know what happened to you over there. We heard about it. That was a bad place for you to be. No, we never liked that man who stole her away." Yarima and I had left these people two and a half years earlier under harsh circumstances. Now, suddenly, we were integrated again, almost as if we had never been gone. There they were—Yarima's mother, older now, showing the wrinkles of advancing age . . . my brother-in-law Koobewe, the new headman . . . Yarima's sister and the children Yarima loved so much . . . even Shatakewe, my old enemy. The first day he didn't come near me, but before long we found ourselves getting along together in the normal course of activity. The old antagonism had disappeared. It was all in the past, all forgotten. Maybe, I thought, because I had been through so much since then. When I gave him a swath of red loincloth material I had left in the bottom of my pack, he simply accepted it without question, though he must have wondered why. I didn't tell him how delighted I was to be back.

The next day I mustered the men to clear the helipad. The seven days were long past, but I had not heard a helicopter, nor had there been any word of one flying over the forest. I still had a flicker of hope. I knew that getting the copter upriver was a complicated business and that it might take more time than Alvaro had figured on. Not only did the project have to be coordinated with the Defense and Interior Ministries, which often had disagreements with each other, but even the logistics of it were difficult, as I knew from my census experience. Refueling points had to be set and emergency procedures established. I hoped against hope it might still arrive.

We waited at Wawatoi as one week passed, then a second, until it was obvious nothing was coming. Since the Ye'kwana motor driver had left without waiting for my note, there would be no canoe coming up, either. It occurred to me that maybe I should just stay. We were here with the Hasupuweteri. Yarima was extremely happy to be back with her native village; we had reestablished our life together as husband and wife. But I knew in my heart that as comfortable as I was in the jungle, actually going native was not something I could really do. I had little clothing left. My one pair of sneakers was taped together with my last piece of duct tape. I had no antivenom and no medicine for malaria, dysentery, or hepatitis. I knew that every day I was there I was risking my life. Nor had I anything in the way of supplies, not even a notebook or batteries. I couldn't even work. I had also given away the last of my trade goods. I was now, I realized with a laugh, poorer than the Hasupuweteri. I was dependent on them for food and shelter and had nothing I could give them in return. I reached into my pack and checked the three extra shotgun shells I had left. Three in my pack, two in my pocket, ready at hand—my entire stock of Western technology.

I knew there was no choice. I had to get downriver—*we* had to get downriver, for I was never again going to leave there without Yarima. Once we were out I would get Yarima an identity card, and we could get formally married, just as Alvaro had suggested. Then I would see if I couldn't raise enough funds so that I could continue my research and writing on a more secure basis. But I wanted *shori* to come with us this time. I would like someone, I told him and Koobewe, to represent the village and tell the *nabuh* the truth about my relationship with Yarima. Koobewe was in favor. He was angry when he heard about what had happened to us last time in Puerto Ayacucho, and he wanted to send someone who would describe things accurately. His brother could speak for him in front of the governor. *Shori* thought for a moment, then said yes, even though I could see the idea frightened him. Still, his younger sister had already been there, and she seemed to have survived all right. She hadn't been put in jail, or killed, or eaten. She had even flown in an airplane.

I was very happy to be away from the Patahamateri. I did not know why we ever wanted to live with them. They were not my people. Being with my mother and sister made me very happy. It was good to see my brothers. We went to the garden to sit and talk, and I held my sister's babies, who were like my own children.

When Kenny asked older brother to come with us to Caracasteri, he did not know if he wanted to come. I thought he was a little frightened. He did not know what he was afraid of, except that he heard all the lies that the downriver Yanomama told. But the older men told him to go. They said he would be able to get many trade goods for the village.

The next day *shori*, Yarima, and I packed up what few things we had and left for the river. In Yarima's basket were some plantains, a few *ohina* roots, and half a dozen manioc cakes her older sister

296

had made. Wawatoi garden was nearly depleted, and I knew they'd be leaving soon themselves, either for one of their other gardens or on trek. It was August 1, almost a month and a half since I had left Caracas.

Journal, on the river, August 12:   We have been on the river almost two weeks now. Yarima, *shori,* myself. On August 2 a malaria boat came by. They were going downriver, but there were four people, and they weren't able to take us out. They said they would make sure that someone came up to get us. They also took a letter I wrote to Juan Eduardo. The insects are terrible. No food except piranha and hearts of palm that *shori* climbs for—the cuisine of misery. You can get hungry on the river. It's possible to live in the Amazon, even during seasons of little food, but to do it you have to keep moving. And we are stuck on the river.

By August 15 all three of us were weak from hunger. We left our packs on the river, too exhausted to carry them, and walked back to Wawatoi. The Hasupuweteri were astonished to see us; they thought we had gone down long ago. Koobewe sent some young men down to get our things, then told me that the food at Wawatoi had given out and they were planning to leave the next day for Irokai, where the *ohina* roots were ready to be harvested. The only food left here was the wild honey they had just found (which Yarima, *shori,* and I were already scooping.into our mouths with our fingers).

Two days later we were in Irokai. I had barely managed; it took all the strength I could muster to walk unsupported. The first thing Koobewe did when we arrived was to dig up several pounds of *ocumo* root and boil them in an aluminum pot I had given him in better times. He gave them to me and watched me eat steadily until the entire potful was gone. Then he went off to get more.

On a diet of *ocumo,* varied on occasion with Brazil nuts and more wild honey, I began to recover my strength. Yarima tended me, gathering, cooking, and bringing me water while I lay in my hammock and rested. At night she kept the hearth, making sure the heat never dissipated entirely but warmed the hammocks that she, *shori,* and I had hung in a close head-to-foot triangle around the fire. She and her brother had been just as famished as I on the river, but they had withstood the starvation better and had recovered much faster.

Journal, Irokai, August 26: Tomorrow the three of us are going back to the river. I don't feel up to it yet, but have no choice. If the malaria team comes up, it is almost always between the 1st and the 10th. At least I am strong enough to walk. Yarima and *shori* are thin but seem normally energetic and healthy. I must have lost twenty pounds in the last month. I can see my ribs for the first time since I don't know when. If there were a way to market this diet, I'd be rich. The Yanomama Quick Weight Loss Program. Eat as much *ocumo* root as you want and still lose weight.

On August 29 we got to the river again, but a little too far down for *shori's* comfort—the Konoporepiweteri were less than a day's walk downriver from here, and Hasupuweteri was still at war with them. Moving farther up the Orinoco, we came across the exact spot where my first house had been. That's where we were on September 4, the day I turned forty-three.

Journal, on the river, September 9: We are still waiting. Again there has been almost nothing to eat, some crabs, a few small fish, some days nothing at all. A few days ago we found a stand of cashew trees a little way in. The juicy red fruits were delicious. But we are all emaciated again. I can hardly stand or speak. When I try I sound like Marlon Brando as the Godfather, just before he died. *Shori* and Yarima are holding out better, but they too are famished. I have begun to see the most vivid food hallucinations. I dream I am back in my old hut, eating spaghetti, rice, Knorr's chicken noodle soup, and crackers smeared thick with peanut butter. I can smell the coffee in my coffeepot and hear the music from my shortwave radio.

The next day Yarima and I were picking slowly through a marshy area off to the edge of the river looking for frogs when we heard the buzzing of a motor. We both froze and listened. From where we were it was difficult to see the open river, and we knew they wouldn't spot us. A few minutes earlier *shori* had started up toward the old garden to see if he couldn't find a few tobacco leaves. If he was going to starve, he grumbled, at least he wanted to have tobacco in his mouth while he was doing it.

The buzzing grew louder. Through the grasses I saw a motorboat speeding around the bend, oblivious of our presence. I rushed forward, clambering into the reeds and waving my arms wildly. I tried to shout, and a kind of hoarse croak came out. Splashing in the thigh-deep water, I shouted again and saw the three men in the boat turn their heads. A moment later they made an abrupt U-turn and headed toward us.

20

As the boat drew in I recognized two malaria workers. The third face was familiar, but I couldn't place it. By now Yarima had waded up next to me, still clutching the two frogs she had caught. I knew that *shori* was already racing down the trail to see who was here.

Yarima and I stood there smiling as the third man opened his mouth. "Do you know who I am?" he asked in an angry, threatening tone—an official tone, which under the circumstances seemed wildly out of place.

"No," I answered, my voice a low croak. "Who are you?"

"I am Quijada."

"Yes?"

"Señor Chavero's assistant."

"Oh, yes," I said, recalling his face now from several unpleasant encounters. "Oh, yes. Of course, Quijada."

"You are up here without a permit." His voice had an imperious, insolent edge. "You are here illegally. You have two choices. One is that you can get into this boat with me. The other is that I will send the national guard to arrest you and bring you back."

As weak as I was, I felt a rush of adrenaline. Can you believe this, I thought. We're starving to death here, and the first thing out of this bastard's mouth is that he's going to arrest me!

"You are right," I said, noting that Yarima's smile had frozen on her face. "I do not have a permit. At this moment I do not have a permit. But my permit was still valid when I arrived here, and we have been stranded on the river. You can see our condition. I am here only because I have not been able to get out. I have no boat or motor. You know, I am sure, that there was a malaria boat here three weeks ago. They took my message downriver to send help, but nobody came. We have been abandoned here. So if you think I am here because I want to be, and you can see for yourself what we look like, then you are crazy." I was trying to maintain a stiff, formal tone with this character, but it was already getting away from me. "You want to have the national guard come up here and get us? Fine! I'll welcome them with open arms. I'll welcome anybody who will get us out of here.

"And as far as your boss Chavero is concerned . . ." I took a breath and caught myself. Slow and deliberate was the way to do it with someone like this. Load it with disdain and menace. "As far as your boss Señor Chavero is concerned, the last time I saw him the situation was very different from what it is now. Since then I have been to Caracas. I have established political and legal relationships there and press relationships. Chavero is in serious trouble. Trouble that I would advise you not to get involved in. When I get to Puerto Ayacucho he will have to face a heavy accounting for his actions in this case. My friends and I are going to make this very serious for him." It was mostly bluff, but I knew that if I made it sound threatening enough, he'd back off. Why get involved if he didn't have to?

"Oh," he said, then silence. And then, "If you want to come down with us, of course you can come."

"If I do come with you, I am taking my wife and brother-in-law." I could hear *shori* splashing through the reeds toward us. "They are going, too. Also, if you take us, you have to guarantee that you are going to feed all of us. Is that clear?"

"Oh, yes, of course, of course," he said. "I have plenty of food. I'll feed all of you."

When we got to La Esmeralda I installed Yarima and *shori* at Juan Eduardo's house and called Alvaro on the infirmary's radio. My plan was to go into Puerto Ayacucho myself first, to see if I couldn't short-circuit the kind of problems we had had last time around. Alvaro, it turned out, was away, but his secretary was extremely happy to hear from me. Alvaro, she said, would be overjoyed that I was safe. She didn't know all the details, but she did know that the helicopter they had sent hadn't gotten beyond Puerto Ayacucho. There had been problems between the two ministries, she thought, though she wasn't sure. Anyway, she'd be able to arrange for a plane to pick me up and bring me in.

Landing at the airport in Puerto Ayacucho, I got the best news I had ever heard. Three weeks earlier, it seemed, General Muller-Rojas had been removed as governor. Hearing this, I actually felt a thrill of elation. When I walked into the Hotel Amazonas to see Irene, I was gliding on air.

The next day I sent a plane up to La Esmeralda to get Yarima and *shori*. I didn't go myself—I had arranged a meeting with the new governor, whose secretary told me on the phone that he would be pleased to see me and that he had already spoken with Señor De Armas about my situation. So I missed *shori*'s first experience flying. I could just imagine Yarima, the old hand, keeping him calm and reassured. I wondered if he was crushing *her* legs in a Yano-mama death grip.

When we got into the avión the man who made it fly put the straps around us. Older brother covered his face with his hands when the motor started to roar and the avión ran over the ground so fast. He was so frightened, he could not even look. My poor brother. I knew what he was thinking. The first time I flew in an avión I was sure I was going to die. I will never forget the fear I had. But I had already flown two times, and I liked it now.

We were in the sky a long time before older brother uncovered his eyes. He stared out the window, but all he said was, "So high, so high." I did not say anything. I did not want to make him feel like he was my younger brother. I knew that he would lose his fear, just as I had lost mine.

Two days later Yarima and *shori* had their national identity cards. Even with the change of governor, the two clerks there had still given us problems. I knew Chavero had gotten to them. But this time around Alvaro and Colonel Borrell had contacted the department in Caracas, who informed them that the two Indians were Venezuelan citizens and had every right to national identity cards. Needing an official name for the documents, I christened *shori* "Antonio" ("You can't use his real name," I told the clerks. "It's an insult to use their names"), last name "Armas" in honor of Alvaro. Yarima, though, already a veteran of *nabuh* affairs, decided to use her true name, so her card read,"Armas, Yarima. Birthplace, Territorio Federal Amazonas."

With the identity cards in hand, I booked three tickets on a flight to Caracas. But up to the last moment I was nervous. Despite the new governor, Puerto Ayacucho had become a symbol of problems for me. I couldn't wait to leave it. Once in Caracas, I thought, I'd be able to start all over. I'd get a new permit, approach some of the Venezuelan foundations for support, reestablish contact with Marvin Harris and the University of Florida. I'd reconstruct my journals and data from the scorched notebooks and copies of different segments of my research that I'd left in friends' basements here and there. I'd get myself reequipped and resupplied, then I'd go back in on some kind of stable basis. A more objective observer might have surveyed my finances and prospects and laughed. But I—I couldn't explain it—I felt on top of the world.

A big avión took us from Ayacuchoteri to Caracasteri. It was very different from the little avión. When we were up in the sky it did not make a loud noise—it did not even feel like we were moving. But it flew much, much higher. It flew up to the highest level. The forest was underneath us as far as I could see, and Kenny showed me the shiny paths of rivers and the tiny houses of nabuh villages. Then we flew above the clouds, where everything was white like down. At that time we could not say the word cloud because that was the name of Longbeard's mother. We called the clouds "smoke" instead.

After a time Kenny said we were approaching Caracasteri. When the avión flew lower, we saw a great river. The river was so big that we could not see the other side. Older brother asked Kenny which way was upstream, and Kenny pointed. When older brother asked what was on the other side, Kenny said, "Americateri is on the other side." He said the river was called "Caribe."

When the avión landed we did not walk outside to the house like in Ayacuchoteri. Instead we walked through a long covered way into a very big house where there were more nabuh *than I had ever seen. There were so many of them that they were like the ants that travel through the forest. They were all walking fast in different directions. Older brother and I stayed very near to Kenny so that the crowds of* nabuh *would not carry us away.*

When we stopped there was a big round shiny thing in front of us that began to turn around. Then packs came onto the shiny thing from a black hole in the middle of it. Kenny said that the maquina *brought the packs from the plane and that soon ours would come out of the hole, too. Older brother and I watched carefully. When the hole spat our packs out in front of us, we laughed. We didn't understand at that time how it happened, and it seemed amazing and funny. Older brother reached out and grabbed our packs, just like the* nabuh *were doing. I thought that was a very brave thing.*

Fortunately Alvaro had sent his driver to pick us up. By this time Yarima was addicted to cars and had been since our second or third day in Puerto Ayacucho during our initial trip. She had jumped into the bushes the first time she saw one start up, and that first night she had refused to go outside, where the flame-eyed beasts were roaring through the streets. But once she had satisfied herself they were safe, she wanted to ride everywhere. Even if it was only a couple of blocks, she'd insist on taking a taxi. *Shori,* though, hadn't had a chance to get used to them.

Alvaro's car was a big black Ford Crown Victoria, a Conquistador in Venezuelan nomenclature, the largest luxury automobile sold in the country. *Shori* got in hesitantly, already woozy from the throngs of people and the blaring and honking of hundreds of cars and taxis. Carefully he lowered himself onto the soft plush seating and sat there as we pulled out into traffic, his arms limp at his sides with nervous exhaustion. I saw his eyelids flutter when the windows slid silently up out of the door and closed off the outside world. From somewhere behind his head music suddenly flowed into the air. A cold breeze wafted over him. Doubt is the key problem, I thought, not knowing what's going to happen next. You don't know if this thing might just suddenly zoom off into the sky. And why shouldn't it? The other thing we had just been sitting in had done exactly that.

By this time we were on the freeway into Caracas. *Shori* hadn't said a word, but it seemed to me his breathing was getting faster and shallower. Turning his head slightly to the left, he saw a car pull up and speed past us. He hadn't heard it coming. The thing had just appeared, noiselessly, moving at a velocity even more alarming than our own. He put his head back against the seat. As another car flew by he closed his eyes. I hoped he wasn't about to throw up or lose consciousness. On the other side of me Yarima didn't seem to notice. She was too busy watching with interest as the Conquistador hurtled toward a big hole in the mountain that was rearing up directly in front of us.

Caracas proper is a shocker to many outsiders; the bustle and noise level can seem otherworldly even to the well traveled. Yarima seemed to drink it in, but *shori* stared out the window, his body rigid with fear. Slowly the Conquistador wound its way out of the downtown traffic and climbed the hillside into Altamira. In front of the huge white De Armas complex, the driver pulled up and got out to open the doors. *Shori* looked at the ground, stationary now outside the open door. He got out slowly and stood on the pavement, swaying slightly and watching me as I pushed a white button and talked into the wall, a performance even Yarima wasn't prepared for, judging by her expression. When the wall answered she took a quick step backward, then tentatively raised her hand and touched the small black grill of the intercom speaker. Neither she nor her brother seemed to have noticed the little red light blinking on the video camera that was trained on us from its wall mounting three feet above our heads.

At the top of the spiral stairway that led to the Gabinete were Alvaro and his secretary, Nana, who welcomed us and held out their hands. Yarima and her brother smiled and looked at the outstretched hands, watching as I stuck out my own and clasped Alvaro's and Nana's in turn. They didn't follow my example. Patting *shori* on the shoulder, Alvaro laughed and led us into the conference room, where pastries, coffee, and juice were spread out on the table and the elder Mr. and Mrs. De Armas were waiting to meet us. Noticing that *shori* was walking unsteadily, Alvaro asked if the clothes were making him uncomfortable. Would he prefer to change into a loincloth? When I translated, he said he would, and we went into the outer office to dig one out of the bags. When he came back in, *shori* did look a lot more comfortable, though I knew it wasn't the clothes that were disorienting him. Still, as he squatted on one of the chairs looking through the window wall down onto Caracas and sipping a Coke that Mrs. De Armas had given him, he seemed to be recovering quickly from the first shock of civilization.

Within a week both Yarima and *shori* were going out to dinner with the De Armases and with other friends of mine who were inviting us to some of Caracas's finest restaurants. *Shori* had very quickly proven omnivorous, though Yarima refused to touch any food not closely related to what she had known in the jungle. I watched these scenes fascinated, thinking back to the culture shock I had experienced during my first period among the Hasupuweteri. Even while I was measuring every morsel the Indians were putting into their mouths, I had been wonderfully attached to my own food. Yarima was a little like that. "The lady," Alvaro would say to a waiter in black tie, "will have the fish. But it must be prepared specially. Please have the chef cook it whole with no oil or butter, and it must have absolutely no salt or any other seasoning." The waiter would look at him. "Strict doctor's orders," Alvaro would say. But when the fish came, as often as not it was a species she didn't recognize, and she wouldn't eat it anyway.

Yarima even found it upsetting to be asked what she wanted to eat. It aggravated her that someone would ask something so ridiculous, and instead of answering she'd tell me to make whoever it was stop talking such nonsense. The availability of food in Caracas was too much for either her or *shori* to grasp, and I knew the amazement they exhibited when we went into a supermarket was only the most minor surface reflection of what they were feeling. In the forest each person's entire life is formed around the daily search for sustenance. For a Yanomama, "Are you hungry?" is a question without meaning. You might as well ask someone if he'd care to breathe air. "Would you rather have an *eteweshi* or a peach palm fruit?" is not a sentence any Yanomama had ever uttered. Yet it was exactly the sort of thing our friends were asking all the time. "What do you feel like eating," they'd say, "Chinese or Italian?" and I wouldn't be able to sensibly translate a word.

In the downtown Sabana Grande section of Caracas, Yarima and *shori* began to get used to the vast numbers of people, though I could not get them out of the habit of walking in file behind me. "Walk here beside me," I'd say, taking them by the arm and trying to keep them next to me. But a minute later they'd be in file again. A lifetime's experience of walking behind each other on narrow trails wasn't broken easily. It just didn't feel normal to walk abreast of someone.

Beyond that, I had a tendency to walk too fast. Here, on a level, open sidewalk with no obstacles, my long legs simply moved too quickly, leaving *shori* and Yarima struggling to catch up, even when I purposely kept the pace slow. It was exactly the reverse of the jungle. There you walked with your knees a little bent and your toes a little inward, with a gait adapted to the constant obstacles and the unevenness of the jungle floor. After a decade I had the walk down pretty well, but of course not like the Indians. When they were in a hurry to get somewhere, I was never able to keep up.

But here it was all reversed. All the roles were reversed. Here I was taking care of them. I was the one who understood everything and knew how to do everything. Watching me manage must have been a tremendous experience for *shori* in particular. For the first time I was the one with the competence.

They easily adapted to some things. They quickly got used to wearing clothes, for example, and they weren't surprised at all to see that everyone of these masses of people were also clothed. Every *nabuh* they had ever seen upriver had worn clothes (though one German anthropologist who had been in the Amazon for a short time had affected a penis string). But what did surprise them was how attractive some of the clothes were. And that of course surprised me, to see how very quickly they began noticing, and commenting on, styles and colors. They were both taken with how the *nabuh* used clothing as adornment, an idea that had never occurred to them before. Yarima especially asked me about colors and after a short time wanted to get some skirts and blouses that matched and looked prettier than those I had bought her in Puerto Ayacucho.

Near Alvaro's house was a house where they had many clothes. Nana took me there first. Hanging on the wall there were many beautiful shirts and skirts of all colors. In this place there were piles of pants, blue, red, green, and other colors, too. I knew they must have a maquina *here, like the* maquina *Juan Eduardo's wife had in La Esmeralda.*

When I went in the first time with Nana, she held a blue shirt up to me. Then she held blue pants, but the blue of the pants was darker. She asked me if I liked them. I said, "Si." I had learned to say "yes" in Caracas. Then Nana held up a yellow shirt and a green skirt and asked if I liked them. I said "yes" again, and she laughed.

Nana wanted to buy me something, but I couldn't say which one I liked best. I liked them all. They were all clean and soft and beautiful. So Nana bought the yellow shirt for me. I watched as she gave the woman money, not the shiny money, but the money leaves. It was a beautiful shirt, and I was happy that Nana had taken me there. I planned to get Kenny to go back with me to buy the blue one and the green one.

For the most part neither Yarima nor *shori* asked many questions. Having them with me wasn't at all like showing visiting friends or relatives around a city, where you are constantly pointing out and describing and commenting on one sight or another. This was not just a new and different place; it was a systematic change in life experience. Phenomena their minds had never conceived assaulted their senses in an endless profusion. For the most part they didn't even know how to ask about them, or what questions to ask; they had no frame of reference from which to generate questions.

They also could not shake their fear of police. By now they knew that the men in uniform were police. But even though they were obviously not a different tribe, and even though they were not threatening them, *shori* and Yarima still made sure to keep their distance, pointing out policemen to me on the street and pulling me off in another direction. They were especially shocked to see women police carrying guns. Their own concept of sex role divisions, I knew, was vastly more rigid than ours, and seeing women with guns made them extremely uncomfortable. Skyscrapers and elevators were incomprehensible mysteries that they accepted with amazement, but women carrying weapons was an unsettling distortion of the norm.

At that time I did not understand what police were. It seemed to me that they must live everywhere. We saw them in Ayacuchoteri, and now we saw them in Caracasteri. There were many of them in Caracasteri. I asked Kenny where their village was, and he said they didn't have a village. But that didn't make sense.

I could always see the police from far away because of the clothes they wore. I also saw the wives of the police. They wore the same clothes, and they carried guns, too. I wondered if their children also wore the same clothes and carried guns, but I never saw any. All of them looked very fierce to me, and I didn't like to go near them. I asked Kenny many questions about the police, but I did not understand the things he told me. The reason I didn't understand was that I thought they were a different village of nabuh! *That is what we heard in Hasupuweteri and Patahamateri. Kenny told me that the police were the only people allowed to carry guns in Caracasteri. He said that if he carried his shotgun with him, the police would take it away.*

The one scene of violence we witnessed reinforced their apprehension, though it also fascinated them. As we were walking along the Avenida Real one afternoon, a scuffle broke out on the curb. There, directly in front of us, a broad-shouldered, muscular woman in a tight yellow dress was trying to fight off two policemen who were doing their best to drag her into a police car. As she threw a short, straight punch at one and grabbed the other in a one-arm headlock, I realized it wasn't a woman at all, but a transvestite hooker. She (he) had apparently been plying her trade on the curbside when the two cops drove by and decided to intervene.

We watched as the cops finally got a chokehold on her and wrestled her down into the backseat, all three of them sweating and straining and cursing. Yarima and *shori* didn't need to be told what the cops were doing—they were obviously dragging off the poor person so they could perform some horrible cruelty on her. But they did want to know why the police had picked this particular woman and how she had gotten to be so large and muscular. They had never seen anything like her.

I didn't know where to begin. How to explain a person selling herself for sex? How to explain a man dressing as a woman? Or laws prohibiting it? For that matter, how to explain laws? The Yanomamas' sexual habits are completely standardized, and they don't include homosexuality (I had never witnessed or heard about a single instance in all my years with them). They don't know prostitution, and the idea of transvestism among the naked Yanomama is a laugh. It brought to mind the time a Swiss botanist I met at the Hotel Gran Amazonas years ago had whispered to me that he had seen a transvestite while he was visiting Lizot's village. What could he mean? I thought. Did he see a man wearing a waist string, a woman wearing a penis string? No, he had seen a man wearing a dress. Right out in front of everyone. The botanist was crestfallen when I told him the man hadn't known the difference between men's clothes and women's. He had somehow gotten hold of a dress in a trade, and he was wearing it because the bugs were intolerable, not because he liked pretending he was a girl.

When the city became overwhelming I'd take them to the Parque del Este, Caracas's beautifully landscaped inner-city park, where we could find room to walk and a lush tropical greenery that might not have been exactly Amazonian, but soothed eyes assaulted too long by concrete and asphalt. Our first visit there, though, turned unexpectedly exciting when we crossed a little bridge and looked down into a pond swarming with giant goldfish and other brightly colored scaly specimens. Both *shori* and Yarima leaned over the rail of the bridge and assessed the scene below them with professional interest. "Look at all those fish," *shori* ventured. "Let's catch some and cook them."

"No," I said, "we can't catch them."

"Well," said *shori*, annoyed by my literalness, "what I mean is we can get some fishline and hooks, and then we can catch them."

"No," I said, "even if we had fishline and hooks, we couldn't catch them. People aren't allowed to catch them."

Shori thought about this. "Why not?" he asked.

"You see," I answered, knowing how strange this was going to sound, "the *nabuh* just like to watch them." Yarima and *shori* looked at each other but said nothing.

Fifty yards or so down the same path we arrived at another pond, where several caimans were lolling on the bank. This was different. Fish are one thing, but for Yanomama caiman is the most delectable of dishes. A Yanomama will go very far for the chance of a caiman dinner. "*Shori*," I heard my brother-in-law say. He had taken into account my odd response about the fish, and he didn't exactly know how to put it. "*Shori*, you know we haven't eaten caiman in a very long time." He was eyeing a toothy individual yawning widely just below us. "It would certainly be good to eat caiman again." No response from me. "We could kill this one right here very easily *shori*."

"No," I said. "We can't kill it." I pointed to a guard standing not too far away. "Do you see him? He won't let us kill it."

"I don't mean now," said *shori*, as if it were clear to him that of course the guard wouldn't let us kill it now. "I mean tonight. We can come back here after dark. We can kill it at night and get it back to our house."

"No," I said, though by this time the thought of a caiman dinner didn't seem completely without merit. "No, we can't. The guards are around at night, too."

"What are they doing here then?" said *shori,* really exasperated.

"Well," I said, "it's the same as the fish. People like to look at them."

This was a concept *shori* found bizarre beyond words. Keeping fish around to look at was bad enough. But the idea that somebody might want to watch a caiman for pleasure left him shaking his head. *"Behetiai?!"* he exclaimed. ("Are you joking?!") Then he walked away in disgust, telling Yarima, "These *nabuh* are really stupid. They keep animals to look at." From his tone I was sure he suspected I was lying to him about it.

My plan had been to come out and get myself resupplied and set up with a new permit. There were, I thought, good chances of getting at least some minimal funding from one of the Venezuelan foundations. But though I had made my applications and met with people, nothing seemed to be happening. "Yes, Dr. Good," they'd say (not that I had my doctorate), "there are definite possibilities. But you'll have to speak to the assistant to the director about it, and he's away until the end of the month." (It was the beginning of the month.) "Could you call him on the twenty-ninth? Or better yet, why don't you make it the following Thursday? He'll be so busy when he returns."

Since our arrival we had been staying with Manuel De Pedro. But it was very crowded, and eventually it was just not fair for Manuel anymore. Also, life in the middle of Caracas was not something I felt Yarima and *shori* could sustain for an extended time. It was one thing to be there briefly, experience the world of the *nabuh,* and then go back, quite another to live indefinitely among the noise and stress of a major city. By this time it was already December. The grant process was taking an eternity. It was alive, though for all the movement the foundations were making it was hard to tell what was going on. Whatever happened, it seemed pretty clear we were going to be here for at least another month or two.

Manuel had friends who lived on the mountainside outside of Caracas, and they, it seemed, had an empty guest house we could use. Living out there would have its advantages, the main one being that we wouldn't have to abuse Manuel's hospitality anymore. And I did want to get Yarima and *shori* out of the city. On the mountainside at Turgua, *shori* would be able to build a Yanomama-style shelter. We could cook over a fire. We could have some peace and quiet. At the same time I'd be able to get into Caracas whenever necessary to shepherd along the permit process and the grant applications. At the end of December I decided to move.

When the day came, Alvaro's driver arrived to pick us up, not in the Conquistador, but in a right-hand-drive London taxicab that Alvaro had bought in an impulsive moment while he was studying in England years before and had brought back to Venezuela. It was a curiosity, this taxicab, the only vehicle of its kind in the country, and maybe not, I thought, the best choice to get us up into the rugged mountains where paved roads weren't that common. But Alvaro was using the Ford that day, and his four-wheel drive was in the shop, so we piled our things in the cab and off we went.

The cab was fine for the first part of the trip, but when we got into the steeper areas it started struggling and overheating. The last stretch of dirt road that led to Manuel's friend's place was especially bad. The ruts were full of mud and water from the recent heavy rains, and the taxi strained and slipped and fishtailed. Finally it just stopped altogether and refused to go another inch.

We all got out, watched with great interest by a group of small black children whose families lived on the mountainside and who had been running alongside the cab as it wallowed up the dirt track. The children stared at this strange invasion—Alvaro's driver in his chauffeur's cap, a large *gringo* with a beard, and two jungle Indians, all of them looking mournfully at this comical vehicle that had for some reason delivered them to the backlands of Turgua. This was obviously the most exciting event these kids had seen for quite a while. It put me in mind of when I had dropped out of the sky in a helicopter with the air force crew in their white gloves and mosquito nets in the middle of that uncontacted Yanomama village. The surprise and curiosity factor must have been almost the same.

I marched the remaining quarter mile to the house of Manuel's friend Douglas Branch, an Englishman who, along with his American wife, Hillary, had dropped out of the high-pressure life they had previously led to settle on this mountaintop. When Douglas heard what had happened, we got into his jeep to bring everybody up with the bags. But when he turned the ignition key nothing happened, and when he looked under the hood he found the battery was gone. "It must have been those gents from the lumberyard who were here this morning," he said. "Blighters nicked my battery. But that's all right." And with that he switched the battery from a broken-down car sitting there in his yard, and off we went.

On the slope behind his house, Douglas Branch had a tiny one-room guest house that Yarima and I moved into while *shori* built a Yanomama-type shelter right outside. Thus began our three-month stay in the mountains, where we were shortly joined by a beautiful Doberman Pinscher puppy, given to us by my old friend Carlos Carvallo (whom I had taken upriver with me almost six years earlier, during the time of the malaria epidemic). Yarima promptly named the puppy Wayabito, her pronunciation of Los Guayabitos, the town where Carlos lived. She and I quickly grew attached to the dog, as did *shori*, who had visions of the ferocious hunter such a large and powerful puppy might grow to be.

Carlos also loaned me a motorcycle so I could get into Caracas to look after my permit application and grant requests. Yarima loved the motorcycle. She loved clinging to my back while I scrambled down the Turgua mountainside and raced into the city, where she often stayed with Alvaro's secretary, Nana, who had become her good friend. Meanwhile I fought with secretaries and bureaucrats, gave seminars on Indian life at the Humboldt Foundation (a German-Venezuelan cultural organization named after the great nineteenth-century Amazon explorer Alexander von Humboldt), and assisted on several projects at the Central University's School of Tropical Medicine.

As time passed, my optimism about setting myself up on a decent financial footing began to fade. If nothing at all came through, I would be in desperate circumstances; as it was I had been living on loans from friends. And I couldn't wait forever. Yarima didn't mind life out here. There was much that she was growing to enjoy about the city, and of course we had each other. But *shori* had been out for five months now. He missed the jungle terribly, and he missed his village. Before much more time went by I would have to find a way to take him back.

But any anxiety I was beginning to feel about my financial troubles got put into perspective with a jolt one day when I learned that Harald Herzog had committed suicide in his village near the Rio Bocón. I had heard that Harald was having problems, and the last time I had seen him he had acted strangely, or so it had seemed to me. I had been visiting the Yanomama *shapono* at Platanal when suddenly the Indians began shouting, *"Harati, Harati, Harati!"*

Looking around, I saw Harald marching in through the gate. While the Indians shouted his name, Harald strutted across the *shapono* plaza, turning his head and giving a huge smile to all sides and waving at the people in their hammocks. It was an extraordinary display for someone who had lived among the Yanomama for a year, utterly out of keeping with their behavior norms. But it wasn't just the display that held my attention, it was Harald himself. When I had seen him last his hair had been jet black. Now it had turned steel gray. He looked old, tired, and worn. Later I heard that there was an involvement with a Yanomama woman and terrible problems with her husband. I could imagine some of those possibilities only too well. But even against this background, Harald's death came as a rude shock.

In late January I received a small grant from one of the foundations. It came, they said, from their previous year's funds. If I applied early enough during the present year, they thought they would be able to be more helpful. The money was sufficient to get us all outfitted and back up the Orinoco, but it was nowhere near enough to fund an extended visit. My permit had (finally) come through, too, so from that point of view there were no problems. Not getting the funds I needed was disappointing, but there was no question that we would have to go back, *shori* to stay, Yarima and I to visit. Then the two of us would come back out and try again to raise more money. If it turned out to really be impossible in Venezuela, I'd approach the American foundations. Yarima was ready to come with me to the United States; she had already told me she would like to. She had no idea what my village might be like, but she felt secure about finding out. Compared with the earthshaking contrasts she had already experienced, how much of a change could it be?

21

On February 15, 1986, Alvaro Rotondaro, a lawyer friend who was also a pilot, flew us in to La Esmeralda—Yarima, *shori,* myself, and Wayabito. There we stayed for a few days with Juan Eduardo and his wife while I made arrangements with a Ye'kwana boatman who could take us and our large load of baggage upriver.

When we arrived at our old river camp, *shori* left us to find the Hasupuweteri and bring some of the *huya* down to carry the goods we had brought along. I paid the boatman for the trip up and gave him an additional sum, telling him to come back for us on April 1, as I'd have to get back at that point to begin the grant application procedures again. There was another reason I wanted to go back to Caracas by then, an even more important one. We had just learned that Yarima was pregnant, and this time around I was determined she would have the best prenatal care we could get.

Yarima and I were still in our hammock the next morning when suddenly *shori* materialized out of the forest with the *huya.* To get from Wawatoi so early they had left while it was still dark, waving burning sticks in front of them to light the trail. An hour later the rest of the Hasupuweteri arrived, the whole village coming down to the river from their inland garden to greet us. *Shori* had already shed his clothes, and when the main group arrived Yarima took hers off, too. From all sides came comments on her skirt and blouse and on her hair, which had grown out during her stay with the *nabuh* and looked extremely un-Yanomama—frightening, her sister and friends said in mock horror. Then they sat her down and gave her a haircut, not with the usual long blade of razor grass, but with a pair of new scissors that I fished out of one of the packs.

Back at Wawatoi the Hasupuweteri were building themselves a new *shapono,* and while they were at it I asked them to put up a small house for my supplies and equipment, most of which I planned to give out during our stay. It was good to be back. People were happy to see us, especially since they had heard the usual firm assurances from visiting downriver Yanomama that we had been killed. Like *shori,* they were amazed by Wayabito, who though still a puppy wasn't much smaller than the full-grown village hunting dogs. Everyone was sure he would become the greatest hunter in the forest. I watched at night while *shori* sat in his hammock and told stories of the astounding experiences he had lived through and the wondrous things he had seen among the Caracasteri. His stories were recorded on a tape recorder I gave him for that purpose, but when I listened to them much of what he was saying was hard to understand. As fluent as my Yanomama was, the torrent of analogies and allusions through which *shori* attempted to convey phenomena that had no existence in his listeners' mental universe made his stories all but impenetrable. I knew that I had here the basis of an utterly fascinating linguistic, cultural, and psychological study. But I would need to work closely with an informant—preferably *shori* himself—to transcribe it, translate the literal meaning (which would often seem nonsensical), then determine the connotative meaning. That would be a long process, and *shori* himself would soon be leaving for Mokaritateri, where he had been promised a wife. So the study would have to wait.

The month and a half at Wawatoi passed quickly and pleasantly. Through most of it plantains were abundant and hunting was good. Tensions within the village seemed minimal, and people were relaxed and happy. Once again I took up my studies, adding to my records of the Hasupuweteri's hunting activities and dietary patterns. Having been out for so long and coming back (for a change) to a calm, unstressful situation, I was struck anew by some of the characteristics of life here. I felt like a traveler who has returned home from a long stay abroad. He is home, but at the same time he sees things a little differently; customs, manners, and appearances that in earlier times he took for granted now call themselves to his attention as he compares them in his mind with those of the land he has just left.

The way the Indians moved struck me all over again, the fluid, slow rhythm of their exertions, such a contrast to the frantic pace of Caracas's citizens. I was impressed once more with how good their teeth were, so regular, with no evidence of decay. Now more than ever before I found myself drawn to watching parents interacting with their children, no doubt in part because at the age of forty-three I was myself looking forward to becoming a father. I was touched by the tenderness, by the constant, twenty-four-hour-a-day contact between mothers and children, and by the obvious pleasure the Hasupuweteri fathers took in their daughters as well as their sons. In past years I had studied the Yanomama kinship system closely, but now what attracted me was how a mother's sisters and others related to a child as classificatory mothers actually did behave in such a maternal way toward their "children," just as classificatory "fathers" were so paternal toward theirs. The result was that a child always had close, loving care. Even in cases of a true parent's death, an almost equally close classificatory parent was there to nurture and love the child. Among the Yanomama there were no orphans.

At the end of March Yarima and I left Wawatoi for the Orinoco, taking two *huya* along as carriers. The boatman had promised to return for us on April 1, and I was determined not to miss him. *Shori* had left several weeks earlier for Mokaritateri and his new wife. The rest of Hasupuweteri were unhappy about our leaving, but they accepted it, especially after I explained that with the money I hoped to get in Caracas I would buy them many more of the things they needed. They too would be leaving shortly for a trek. The plantain crop would only last another week or two.

I wanted to go back to Caracasteri with Kenny. I couldn't stay upriver without him. I also wanted to see Irene in Ayacuchoteri and Nana. But the big reason I wanted to go was that Kenny told me the nabuh *doctor in Caracasteri could treat pregnant women. I was still afraid from the time my first baby died. I did not want this one to die also.*

But I was very sad to be leaving my sister and my mother. My mother was old already, and I thought it could be I would never see her again. Her daughter's daughter had already had a baby. The last morning I was sitting at my mother's hearth talking with her and my older sister. The sun was getting high, and Kenny was still in his house with some of the men packing his things. Then he called, "Pei!" and I knew it was time to leave. My mother started to cry. She said, "Go to your husband's village to have your baby. Then come back to me." She was crying while she said this, and my sister and I were crying, too.

I walked quickly down the trail through the gardens, crying while I walked because I was so unhappy. When Kenny caught up to me he gave me the little manashi *chick that older brother had given me as a gift. I had left so fast that I had forgotten it.*

Late the next morning we were at the river where we built a little trek shelter, then watched as the two *huya* who had come with us disappeared back up the trail. The river was low, a bad sign, since we knew that would make it difficult for the boatman to come up. But we settled into our hammocks to wait, hoping that somehow he'd be able to make it the next day regardless, as he had promised. I remembered only too well the last time we were waiting on the river like this. It wasn't an experience I wanted to repeat.

Journal, April 3, fourth day on the river: We finished eating the *klebo* fruits one of the *huya* cut down from the tree for us before they left. The boat has not come. I don't like it. Waiting here by ourselves gives me very bad feelings. The trees were filled with *manashi* birds this morning. I wish I had my shotgun [I had given it to *shori,* thinking that he could put it to better use and that I'd pick up another one in Caracas]. We also ran out of firewood, but we managed to push over a dead tree. Unfortunately it got hung up on a vine. To untangle it I would have had to climb about thirty feet up the bare trunk, which worried me. I can't do that like a Yanomama. They can climb like monkeys, and the women are always sending the men up for honey or fruit or firewood.

When I told Kenny he had to climb up to take the vine from around the tree, he said he didn't think he could go so high. "You have to," I said. "We need it for the fire. If we don't have a fire tonight, the bats will bite us." There were many bats on the river, and they were extremely angry. Kenny said he was afraid the tree might fall on him. "Don't worry," I said. "If it falls on you, I will use it to cremate your body." I said that to make him laugh. But he didn't know if I was making a joke, so I told him that maybe I would not cremate him. Maybe I would float him down the river. I remembered when he was sick with prisi-prisi he used to tell older brother to float him down the river to the padre. "Don't worry," I told him, "I will float you down the river, and then I will walk home by myself."

When Kenny heard that he lifted himself into the tree and started climbing very slowly up the trunk. But he could not climb like a Yanomama, and I thought he would fall, so I shouted at him to come down. He pretended he did not hear me, and he kept climbing. I was very worried he would fall, so I ran into the woods and quickly gathered a pile of firewood, which I put at the foot of the tree so that Kenny could see he didn't have to climb anymore.

When Yarima started teasing me, I thought, What the hell, here goes, and I began to hoist myself up. Needless to say, the moment I was up in the tree she started beseeching me to come down. "You'll fall, you'll fall," she shouted. "Come down. Come down from there." I kept trying to inch up, as if I couldn't hear a thing, but it was really slow going, and finally the only course left was to climb down as gracefully as I could. When I got to the ground she was standing there with a pile of firewood it had taken her about five minutes to gather from the forest.

Journal, April 6, seventh day on river: Little luck fishing. A piranha bit off my large hook; now I have only one left. Without a metal leader it's hard to land them before they cut the line with their teeth. The few we've caught have been about a foot long, maybe four pounds, and they're vicious fighters. They jerk around violently, and all you've got is a line in your hand, no pole, so it's tough to get them in.

For the last couple of days Yarima has been singing to Hesi ke maki, the big rock formation to the south. She says if it hears her chants, the rains will come, which will raise the river, which will bring our boatman.

I have a little Nescao and dried milk left, maybe enough for two days. But Yarima won't touch it. The idea of drinking milk from an animal repulses her. I tried to cut down another *klebo* tree, but my machete is dull and I have no file to sharpen it. I was just beating the trunk to a pulp instead of cutting it. Finally had to stop, much to Yarima's disappointment. My hands are full of blisters.

The morning of April 7 broke with the crack of thunder followed by a brief but violent rainstorm. The river rose a little, which lifted our spirits, but no boat came, and by nightfall we were again depressed as well as hungry. The bloodsucking gnats were so bad that even with a mosquito net each of us had dozens of itching bites that couldn't be scratched for fear of infection. That evening, expecting rain, I put up a plastic cover over the net.

At night Yarima complained of *shitehema nini* pains, stomachache, just as she had before her miscarriage. Frightened, I built up the fire, thinking terrible thoughts. Finally she fell asleep. I knew it was probably just hunger; my own stomach ached badly. But what if it was something else? The next day, I decided, we'd have to find a decent supply of food, even if it meant leaving the river for a while and taking a chance on missing the boat.

The following morning I left a note and a red flag attached to a pole in the river, and Yarima and I went inland toward Wawatoi. On the way we found a large number of *eteweshi* fruit and a real treat, papaya, with its heavy concentration of vitamin C. Returning home with our backs loaded, we came across a band of capuchin monkeys eating *roa* fruit in a tree. They didn't see us, and we stopped to watch as they moved around the branches with their extremely quick, jerky motions. It's a protective trait, no doubt, but it looks comical. Yarima watched them, barely able to keep from laughing. Rarely do you have a chance for an extended close-up observation like this. Seeing her glee at the capuchins' antics, I was happy I didn't have my shotgun with me. Not that monkey meat is one of my favorites, anyway. For a moment we felt a touch of happiness instead of the gloom that was overtaking us down on that bug-ridden river.

That night Yarima prepared a large meal of *eteweshi*, papaya, and a few plantains we had also found, which we devoured with gusto. I was especially glad to see her eat a lot. Her stomach, she said afterward, felt just fine. For a welcome change we settled in for the night feeling full and contented.

We hadn't been in our hammocks for more than ten minutes when a lightning bolt cut the sky over the river, and the air was split almost simultaneously by a huge crash of thunder. Sheets of water sliced down, accompanied by more peals of thunder and flashes of lightning. Yarima was so frightened, she got her dress out of the pack and covered her head with it. Lightning is spooky, the Yanomama think, but thunder truly frightens them. From my hammock I told her not to be afraid, it wouldn't harm her. But between peals we could hear an ominous creaking and moaning, and in a few minutes the whole forest was making a tremendous roaring noise as the wind whipped the giant trees back and forth. I lit our last stub of candle. By its light I saw that the water was overflowing the shallow ditch I had dug around our shelter and was washing across the hearth area, extinguishing our smoldering fire. Frantically I began to scoop it out with my hands when I heard Yarima shout, *"Hei ke!"* ("Here it is!") I listened, then I heard it: a heavy cracking sound directly above us.

A moment later a huge limb crashed to the ground, one of its branches piercing through our roof and snapping a cross stave. It struck less than two feet from where Yarima was standing next to her hammock. Water poured in through the ruined roof. Still holding the dress over her head, Yarima grabbed our bag of tobacco and huddled in a corner where the roof hadn't been damaged while I pushed the branch out, then raced to scoop more water. Just a short time ago we had been told about the two Mokaritateri who had been hit by a falling limb while we were in Caracas. Natiwe, the husband, had broken an arm, which eventually just rotted off at the shoulder. His wife had died of a broken neck. Evil *hekura*, it was said, had pushed the tree over on them.

It poured until nine-thirty, then the rain let up, though not the lightning. Although almost dry under our plastic covering, we worried about the high trees around the camp. I finally drifted off to sleep, and when I opened my eyes, Yarima was standing over me smiling.

Journal, April 16, day 17: I have been worried and angry for days. Angry at that boat driver, who is obviously not coming up, despite the fact that the river is plenty high enough now. Worried about Yarima. Exactly what I didn't want to happen, having her deprived like this, especially in the first trimester. I spent two days hacking at a giant bunch of *yei* fruit. I built a makeshift ladder to get me partway up the tree, then I tied a knife onto a three-foot-long stick and tried to chop it down. The knife wasn't anywhere big enough, and tied to the end of the stick like that, it was next to useless. I almost abandoned the effort three or four times, but with Yarima sitting there waiting there was no choice but to keep at it. When the fruit finally fell, it hit the ladder and almost knocked me out of the tree. The bunch must weigh sixty pounds.

The vampires are unbelievably aggressive. One bit me on the forehead, another got Yarima on the finger. Last night one actually got inside our mosquito net somehow. I cheerfully beat it to death with a shoe. We haven't been sleeping well. Yarima is afraid of raiders; they could come up the bank and be in the camp before we heard a sound. Between the hunger, boredom, bloodsucking gnats, vampires, and trees falling on us, we've both just about had it. For her there are also the ghosts, water monsters, and malevolent shamans to worry about. Both of us would put up with the hardships if we could be sure we were going to get out of here. But I don't think there's a chance of that Ye'kwana coming up. I cannot understand why he didn't at least send somebody else.

On April 18 Yarima and I gave up on the river and went back to Wawatoi, hoping we would find the Hasupuweteri. They were there but about to leave on trek, since they too had run out of food. Although we were unhappy about going with them, without food we had no choice.

The group was heading south toward Ashitoweteri, a community that was related to Hasupuweteri. They had invited the Hasupuweteri to trek in their area and share plantains from the Ashitoweteri gardens. At the usual slow trek rate, it took a week and a half to get there, although the hunting and gathering were fairly good and nobody was suffering from lack of food. Fortunately the Ashitoweteri gardens were abundant with ripe plantains and bananas, so the camp life was happy and enjoyable, with the two groups visiting, trading, and feasting.

At least it would have been enjoyable if Yarima and I hadn't been so anxious to leave. I was beginning to wonder how we were ever going to get out. I knew that if I were alone, I could walk out. I was still weak from malnutrition, but with a little more rest and food I could have done it, although I'd have to follow the longer route along the Orinoquito River to the New Tribes missionaries. None of the Hasupuweteri would have accompanied me down the Orinoco to Platanal or Mavaca. The villages in those areas were traditional enemies.

But though I could have done it by myself, I could not do it with Yarima, who was now three months pregnant. I wouldn't even go out myself in order to come back upriver with a boat to get her. That's the last thing I would do, I thought, leave her up here alone once more.

One day an Ashitoweteri named Hotehawe approached me with a plan. *"Shori,"* he said, "I have visited Mavaca before. I have relatives in Bishaashiteri [a village near the Mavaca mission]. I could walk there to visit them. When I am there I can ask the padre to send a boat for you." This was a tremendous offer. Mavaca wasn't even the nearest mission. Getting there would take a minimum of five or six days, traveling at the fastest pace. Beyond that, to get to Mavaca Hotehawe would have to walk through the territory of villages unfriendly to the Ashitoweteri.

We calculated the timing as best we could. It was now April 26. It would take six days for Hotehawe to get there, perhaps two more before the boat came up. We could expect to be picked up on the fourth of May—if he got through with no problems. I gave Hotehawe a written message for the padre, then watched as he left, his bow and arrows in his hand, his quiver and a folded bark hammock slung over his back. If necessary, he could travel like that almost indefinitely. Even the hammock wasn't essential. Like all Yanomama men, Hotehawe was capable of making a trail hammock out of the inner bark of a *nari nati* tree stripped either with a knife or with his teeth. A few years earlier he would have also taken a fire drill with him, but now he would have a number of matches tucked into his quiver with the arrow points.

The next day Yarima and I left with three young Ashitoweteri carriers. Five days of steady (though easy) travel later, we reached the Orinoco, a little below where we had made camp the last time. Neither Yarima nor I wanted even to see our previous site. The Ashitoweteri *huya* quickly cleared an area and put up a makeshift hut—not much, but considerably more substantial than the trek shelter we had used before. At least it would keep out most of the bugs. Most likely we would only be here a day or two, though predictions in this place had a way of turning out to be disastrously wrong. My main worry was that Hotehawe wouldn't get to Mavaca for some reason, or that he would get there only to find the padre away. If he had problems that forced him to return to Ashitoweteri, I wasn't sure he would even think of walking another five days to the river to tell us that no one was coming.

As soon as darkness fell, though, I found that Hotehawe's progress was not the only worry on my mind. The Ashitoweteri had heard that the Konoporepiweteri were thinking about raiding the Hasupuweteri, their traditional enemies, and we were the only Hasupuweteri in the vicinity. Yarima was very scared, and with the coming of night I felt anxious myself, the first time in all my years here that I had felt this way. I didn't have my shotgun, and being in a house like this was even worse than being out in the open. All they would have to do was come in the doorway and that would be it. At least if we were outside, I thought, I would have a chance to confront them, providing we heard them coming in time. Inside we wouldn't have a chance. I couldn't get to sleep for a while, nor could Yarima. Instead we lay there listening to the jungle sounds. Eventually we nodded off, and in the morning most of our anxieties were gone. There is something about the approach of night that brings out all your insecurities.

Two days later I was taking a swim at a point where a little tributary flowed into the Orinoco when I heard a motor. Almost before I knew it, a big aluminum speedboat roared around the bend, then slowed to a crawl when the occupants saw me. They were obviously surprised to find somebody out in the river like that. As the boat drifted close, four blank faces stared at me, one Yanomama, three white. Then one of the white ones said, "Señor Good?"

"Yes?"

"Padre Bórteli sent us."

They were young doctors, it seemed, doing tropical medicine research at Mavaca mission. Padre Bórteli had sent them with his boat, motor, and gasoline. They could find me and my wife, the padre had said, and they might be able to get the Hasupuweteri to give them blood samples for their study. I listened, but my attention was really focused on their motor, an eighty-five-horsepower Evinrude. I stared at it and laughed. On my old dugout I had had an eight-horsepower motor. The doctors told me it had taken them three and a half hours from Mavaca. The usual trip by dugout was more than a full day.

I knew that the Hasupuweteri were heading back for Wawatoi, so I told the Yanomama with the doctors to see if they had arrived there yet. I was sure they would come down to see the doctors if they had. The next day, a few of the *huya* showed up. They had reached Wawatoi before the main group, and they didn't mind having a little blood extracted, though they weren't happy when they saw the sparse amount of trade goods the doctors were giving out in return. For the next two days I had to hold my eagerness in check as we waited for the rest of the Hasupuweteri to arrive. When they finally did, I watched impatiently as the doctors gave each of the villagers examinations and drew blood. The process took an entire day.

Finally, on May 7, we left. The river was high, and the giant Evinrude roared at the back of the boat. We reached Guajaribo in forty minutes (my personal speed record was two hours), and three hours later we landed at Mavaca. At the mission Bórteli gave us a nice dinner and filled me in on the latest news and gossip. Harald Herzog, he said, had certainly been killed by a shotgun blast, but no one was actually sure if it was a suicide. The Yanomama of his village had said so, but the details of what had happened were cloudy.

That evening I called Alvaro De Armas's office and spoke to Nana, who arranged to have a plane fly in from Puerto Ayacucho to pick us up. The next morning we were off. The moment we landed a thunder shower broke, and we arrived at the Hotel Gran Amazonas wet and bedraggled. But our reception from Irene and Colonel Borrell was as warm as could be. In my journal that night I recorded that Yarima ate baked potatoes and I had "steak, ham, bread, cheese, cake, ice cream, and a Coke. What a feast!" It was a little funny, writing that in my field journal. But I knew that whenever in the future I might look at that entry, I would be reminded of those seventeen days on the Orinoco River thinking of nothing but food, a bath, and a bed. And now I had all three.

Before I went to sleep I called Alvaro. "We are waiting for you with open arms," he said. "I have surprises for you. Kisses and hugs to Yarima. And how is your little 'Kencito'?" By the time I got back to the room Yarima was lying on the bed, naked and fast asleep.

The next day we flew in to Caracas. Alvaro had fixed up a room for Yarima and me downstairs from his offices, where there were also a small kitchen and a bathroom. It was there, he said, that we would live while we were in Caracas.

The next day I began the grant search all over again. It was the usual slow going. I'd wait a week for a meeting, which would go well. Then another meeting would be set up for a week or two weeks later, after which I'd hear that yet another meeting would be necessary. It was a frustrating experience, especially since I was again living on loans from friends, a situation that was stretching my endurance (if not theirs) to the limit.

At least Yarima was getting regular medical attention. One of Alvaro's uncles was a prominent obstetrician who examined her every two weeks himself and arranged additional testing at the maternity clinic he was associated with. Yarima was getting absolutely the best care available, including ultrasound and all the most up-to-date monitoring techniques.

"Would you like to know the sex of the baby?" asked the doctor one day. "If you would rather not, I won't tell you. It's up to you and your wife."

"Sure," I said.

"Yes," said Yarima.

"It's a boy," said the doctor.

Yarima took all this with great calmness, as if there weren't the slightest thing unusual about any of it. This woman, I thought, who had choked with fright to see her own image in a mirror three-quarters of a year ago, was watching her baby move inside her on a television monitor as if it were the most common experience in the world. Not that her reaction was all that strange. When the doctor pointed out fetal outlines and movements, she believed it. I didn't know how the ultrasound imaging worked, either, but I believed it, too.

Toward the eighth month, after one of the imaging sessions, the doctor took me aside and said, "You know, Señor Good, one of the ways we determine fetal normality is by taking measurements. And it is a little hard to say, but at this point it appears to me that your baby's head is slightly larger than it should be in proportion to the legs." He didn't say anything else; he didn't have to in order to send me into a fit of worry. It wasn't just the possibility of an abnormal child that concerned me, though that was horrible enough. It was also that I didn't know what would happen if the child was born with a defect. Among the Yanomama the solution to the birth of an abnormal infant is painfully simple. It is not allowed to live. The Yanomama are not in a position to sustain a child with abnormalities, and their answer is infanticide. So on top of my worries about the baby, I had this added dimension of anxiety. What would we do? What would Yarima do?

Alvaro called up another doctor he knew who was also a well-known obstetrician, and we went for a second opinion. The second doctor assured me that everything was normal. Then when I told him what the first doctor had said, he examined Yarima again, even more carefully this time. Finally he announced that he could find no evidence at all of any kind of abnormality.

As time went by we settled in. Alvaro offered me the use of a Wang word processor on which I could start writing my doctoral dissertation and planning an ethnography on the Yanomama. From my notes and data I began drawing together my formal conclusions about the anthropological questions that had originally led me to the Amazon and that I had been examining since I first moved in among the Hasupuweteri. I had experienced in my own life and had witnessed among those close to me some of the immediate reasons for conflict between individuals and groups within Yanomama villages, conflicts that occasionally led to the breakup of communities (Hasupuweteri and Patahamateri had originally been one, and during my time each of them had split into two). Yet all my records indicated that regardless of the immediate causes of such conflicts, underneath it was the scarcity of game that determined the size and dispersal of communities. And even with small village populations and adequate breathing room between settlements, Yanomama cultivating, hunting, and gathering practices still were not productive enough to allow them a sedentary existence. Their means of subsistence apparently forced them not only to limit the size of their villages, but also to move frequently, and to live part of each year as nomads. Nothing I had seen suggested that the Yanomama were in any way incapable of creating social institutions that would curb violence. On the contrary, they had evolved a host of customs that nurtured community harmony. But their subsistence techniques seemed to have militated against their developing a social organization that would mediate disputes and allow larger numbers to live together.

As I became more absorbed in the work it seemed to me that, apart from my current insolvency, life was going pretty well. After all these years I was finally going to finish my dissertation. Yarima was getting the best of care. We had wonderful friends. I was even confident that eventually we would have some funding.

While I was working on the dissertation and keeping on top of the grant applications, Yarima started learning Spanish. Alvaro had discussed the problem with the staff of a nearby special-education school. Yanomama was an unwritten language, and Yarima had no concept of foreign languages, so she could not be taught Spanish as a second language in the same way visitors or immigrants could be taught. What was necessary was an innovative tutor, and the school recommended a teacher named Yolanda. She immediately became a friend to Yarima, taking her out to places and teaching her Spanish via the sights and sounds they saw all around them in the city. Between Yolanda and Nana, Yarima had the companionship of two warm and understanding women sensitive to the unique challenges she faced in this world so different from her own.

During the day I would work at the computer, then at night Alvaro would call and say he was hungry, where should we go for dinner? So the three of us would go out to a restaurant, sometimes with Nana along, sometimes with other friends. Yarima's eating habits were still a problem. Even now she wouldn't eat anything that didn't closely resemble the usual Yanomama foods (pork was a near cousin to peccary; chicken tasted a lot like *manashi*). In addition I had to work around Yanomama dietary taboos for pregnant women. It was well known, for example, that certain types of fish would attack a baby's throat or liver.

Some days I would take off, and Yarima and I would go to Caracas's Plaza Venezuela with its big, multicolored water fountain. She especially loved the amusement park in Chacaí to where Nana and I took her from time to time. From the ground I could hear her screaming with pleasure as she and Nana rode a boat that swung in a giant but gentle arc fifty feet above the ground.

But despite Yarima's increasing adjustment and the progress I was making on the dissertation, my money anxieties were looming larger every day. After four and a half months it seemed clear that no grants would be forthcoming. I felt I could wait no longer. I was deeply in debt and extremely unhappy about imposing further on my friends. If funding was not available in Venezuela, I knew I would have to start looking in the United States. It had also occurred to me that I could even write a book about my experiences. And the place to do that was also the United States. Alvaro encouraged me and one day told me that some friends of his in New York had made contacts for me there. Pablo and Maria Teresa, a couple I knew slightly, had been in touch with Time-Life. One of Time-Life's writers, they said, was interested in talking to me.

It was early October when I talked to my parents, who immediately offered to send me money for airplane tickets. By the middle of the month I packed all our things and distributed whatever I was not taking to various friends for safekeeping. On October 17 Carlos Carvallo took us to the airport, where Yarima and I boarded a Pan Am flight for New York City. It was five years since I had last been home.

At Kennedy we went through immigration first. Just beyond the big swinging metal doors Pablo and Maria Teresa would be waiting for us. But just as we cleared customs and were picking up our things to leave, another official asked us to step over to a desk at the side of the area. There a woman immigration agent asked to see our passports again. "Yarima Armas," read one. "Kenneth Good," read the other. Looking at Yarima, who was now nine months pregnant, the agent asked why Yarima had come to the United States. I answered that she didn't speak English, but that she was a friend of my family. She had come to the United States to visit and see the sights. The agent looked skeptical. Here, no doubt, was yet another Third World person trying to violate American immigration laws. She looked at Yarima's protruding belly. "Mr. Good," she said, "may I ask if this baby is yours?"

"Madam," I said (my idiomatic English wasn't quite adjusted), "that is a delicate question."

"Just a moment," she said, and walked into the office behind her, leaving me feeling extremely uncomfortable about where this might be leading. A moment later she was back with her supervisor. "This woman," she told him, "has a visitor's visa." Yarima wasn't carrying very large, but at that moment she looked to me like she might be ten months pregnant. "And she doesn't speak any English." She turned to me. "Does she speak Spanish?"

"No," I answered, "she doesn't."

"And she doesn't speak Spanish, either," said the woman to her boss.

"So?" he said. She looked at him, then over at me.

"Okay," she said, "I guess that's that. Have a nice day, Mr. Good." Then, addressing Yarima, "And you have a pleasant stay in the United States."

Outside the doors, Pablo and Maria Teresa greeted us warmly amid the bustle of the arrivals area. Looking around, I had the strangest sensation: I felt as if I were a foreigner. I hadn't heard native American speech—New York speech, no less—for all those years. Even with the crowds everything seemed so organized, so clean. As we said hello the sounds of the place were in my ears. I heard skycaps, people greeting friends and relatives, gyspy cabdrivers who had come inside to hustle fares. "Ey," said a cabbie to a man who had walked out at the same time we did, "Ey, buddy, wanna cab?" After the high-pitched, lickety-split Venezuelan street Spanish, he sounded dignified, almost elegant.

Driving into downtown Manhattan with Pablo and Maria Teresa, Yarima looked at everything, though she didn't say much. Finally she turned to me and observed, "They don't have too many cars here, do they?" I knew what she meant. We were used to Caracas, where cars came barreling at you from every direction, blaring their horns, spewing exhaust, engines rumbling and roaring through nonfunctioning mufflers. You took your life in your hands there. Here traffic seemed so organized. That was the word that kept coming to me—organized. Manhattan was just such an organized place, a relatively subdued place. Not a small town, but not a Caracas, either. It was Caracas with the pollution moderated, Caracas with the chaos tempered. Someone had turned down the volume.

That afternoon at Pablo and Maria Teresa's apartment in the Cuban neighborhood of Union City, New Jersey, I talked by phone to a reporter from Time-Life. He wasn't sure if anyone would be interested in our story, but once I got settled in we should talk.

The next day Yarima and I were on an Amtrak train to Philadelphia. My parents would be waiting at the Thirtieth Street Station to pick us up.

My mother and father were living by then on an historical estate in Havertown called The Grange. Their apartment was in a large brick mansion surrounded by magnificent gardens and paths, all of which had been laid out and built in colonial times. Washington and Lafayette were only two of the Revolutionary figures who had slept there. Surrounded by the ambience of American history, Yarima and I moved in, setting up temporary quarters on a pull-out sofa we brought into the dining room.

Once we were settled, I took Yarima over to the Bryn Mawr Hospital family medicine program for an examination. The hospital was located in Philadelphia's Main Line suburbs and had a first-rate obstetrics unit with a highly trained staff and the most up-to-date equipment. I looked into one of the delivery rooms, with its stirrup bed, monitoring devices, and emergency paraphernalia, and in my mind's eye I saw the stream where the Hasupuweteri women used to go to give birth, squatting over a palm leaf and clutching a tree branch above their heads. I was confident that Yarima would cope well with the hospital experience; she had adjusted already to so much that was new and strange. But as I looked at the delivery table and thought of the stream bank, I wondered just how she would manage it.

I also began making arrangements for us to get married. In Venezuela, where common-law marriage is widespread, a wedding hadn't seemed important, at least not after my permit difficulties were resolved. But here in the United States, if we weren't formally married, there would be problems. Yarima had only a short-term visitor's visa, and I wanted to get permanent residence status for her as soon as I could, something that was possible only if our marital status was formalized. Even more pressing, our baby was due almost any moment, and if we weren't officially man and wife, the hospital procedures and birth records would be unnecessarily complicated.

While a lawyer my brother knew talked to the presiding judge at the county court about our situation, my mother took Yarima shopping for a dress and shoes, with me tagging along to interpret. As I watched the two of them walking together along the crowded 69th Street shopping strip, I realized that my mother was facing these recent events in her life with remarkable equanimity. Her son, whom she had heard from far too infrequently for so many years, had suddenly reappeared from the jungle with a wife—and not just with a wife, but with an Indian wife from the depths of the Amazon, an Indian wife who was on the verge of giving birth to a new grandchild. It could not have been easy for her, yet she had taken us in and was doing her best to help. Together my mother and Yarima picked out dresses, and Yarima tried them on, finally settling on a gray cotton with a large white collar and a pink bow, the ensemble set off by a light beige suit jacket. We then went looking for shoes, a more difficult problem since Yarima's feet were too small for even the smallest women's sizes. After trying several ladies' shoe stores, we ended up at Buster Brown, where fortunately we found a reasonably attractive pair of size twos that went decently with the outfit.

A week later we were married, though the event's solemnity didn't make much of an impression on Yarima. Formal public rites of any sort are sparse in Yanomama life—except for first menses rituals and shaman initiations, there are none. Yarima had never been exposed to the concept of a marriage ceremony or to the idea that

331

two people might not be truly married until a third person had affirmed they were. In her view (as in mine), we had been husband and wife for more than four years already, ever since that day Red had brought her back to me at Wawatoi and she had hung her hammock next to mine. What I told Yarima was that the Pennsylvaniateri *pata* wanted to talk to us about marriage and ask us a few questions.

On the morning of October 22, my father and mother drove us to the Delaware County Courthouse in Media, Pennsylvania, where we met my brother and sister and Pablo and Maria Teresa, who had come in from Union City. District Judge David T. Videon, who was to perform the ceremony, was in his late forties, but he looked a good deal younger. Smiling a welcome at Yarima, he held out his hand to her. She smiled back and shook it, something she often didn't do; the *nabuh* custom still seemed odd to her. In Judge Videon's office we signed the marriage license, Yarima drawing the two circles she had chosen as her mark beneath my scrawled signature. Then we all took our places in a hearing room, under the flags of the United States and the Commonwealth of Pennsylvania, Yarima in her new dress and shoes, I in my safari jacket.

I had been given special permission by the court to serve as interpreter in my own wedding, but until the moment Yarima and I held hands and faced Judge Videon, I hadn't given the slightest thought to what this might entail. "Yarima," the judge began, looking at her, then at me, "Yarima, Ken, marriage is both a contract and a status." From the instant I heard this I knew I was going to have trouble. "Do you agree," he asked, "to enter into this contract, legal marriage, which is an honorable estate? And do you agree to obey the laws of the Commonwealth of Pennsylvania?"

Obey the laws of the Commonwealth of Pennsylvania? I thought. How in the world am I going to translate this? He paused to give me time. "Do you think," I asked Yarima, "that you will like living in Pennsylvaniateri?" "*Awei*," she said. "Yes."

"And do you, Ken," the judge continued, "take Yarima for your lawful wedded wife? Do you promise to love her and comfort her, honor and cherish her, in sickness and in health, for richer or poorer, forsaking all others, until death do you part?"

"Yes," I said. "I do."

"And do you, Yarima, take Ken for your lawful wedded husband? Do you promise to love him and comfort him, honor and cherish him, in sickness and in health, for richer or poorer, forsaking all others, until death do you part?"

The pata said some things, and Kenny told me what they were. First the pata spoke them in Pennsylvania talk, then Kenny spoke them in Yanomama. He told me the pata said we were going to live together the way a husband and wife live together. He told me the pata said that a husband and wife have to like each other and help each other. Then Kenny told me that the pata asked if I wanted him to be my husband, if I would be his wife even if he became sick, and even if he became old, even until we both died. I said, "Tell the pata that I am your wife. Tell him that even if you become sick, I will still be your wife. If you cannot leave our hammock, I will go down to the river and get you water. I will harvest plantains and roast them for you on the fire. Tell the pata that I will gather fruit and honey for you. I will cook your meat. I will care for you and do all these things even when you are very old. Even then I will be your wife."

"I presume," the judge said, "that's a yes?"
"Yes," I said to him, "that's a yes."

Epilogue

Nine days later Yarima gave birth to our son at Bryn Mawr Hospital. I had told her we were going there so the doctors could help her deliver the baby. In the labor room the nurses hooked her up to a fetal monitoring device and told her to lie on her side. She was two centimeters dilated, the obstetrician said; we could expect quite a few hours of labor yet before the delivery. Yarima lay there attached to the device and unhappy about having to stay in one position. After an hour of hard contractions she said, *"A kei waik-iwe"* ("The baby's coming"). "Where are these doctors you said would help?"

Calling the nurses, I told them that Yarima was about to have the baby, and when they said it wasn't possible yet, I got testy. "If she said she's going to have her baby, I'm sure she's going to have it." While they were looking for the doctor, Yarima got up and squatted on the bed, grabbing on to the metal side rails and pushing.

When the doctor came in he was astonished to find her ten centimeters dilated and already in transition. There was barely time to get her into the delivery room before the baby was born, a beautiful boy with almond eyes and a headful of thick black hair, Yanomama hair. I named him David Alexander, though I knew that would mean nothing to Yarima. The Yanomama rarely name their children before they are two or three years old—that is, until the child has proven robust enough to have a good chance at survival. We wanted no circumcision, I told the doctor. I did not tell him why, and he didn't ask about the clothing customs of David's maternal relatives.

That winter we lived with my parents. In January snow came, which amazed Yarima. It was, she thought, like the foam flying off the rapids, but how did it fill the sky, and how did it cover the ground? When I explained, we ran out into the backyard to throw snowballs and start a snowman. Yarima tossed handfuls of the strange white stuff up into the air, laughing with glee. In January too the Time-Life connection worked out. The *People* magazine writer I had originally talked to did his article on us, and in the malls and on the streets people recognized us and came up to introduce themselves, smiling at Yarima and at the beautiful child she always carried in a sling on her side, as the good Yanomama mother she was.

In Caracas we had discovered we could live together happily away from Hasupuweteri, and Philadelphia was no different. We found our happiness in ourselves, though, and in the joy of having David; the adjustment to others did not come easily. Yarima picked up only a few words of English at first. She seemed uninterested in learning the language, and that, of course, made the development of her own relationships very hard. Other aspects of American life, though, she was eager to understand—how money worked, how shopping was accomplished, how we got around. She saw what she considered the essential loneliness of people in our culture, such a poignant contrast to the perpetual companionship of her own. At night we would hear sirens in the distance, and she would talk about the *nabuh* who were sick or hurt or whose house might be burning. In the sirens she believed she could hear them calling out to each other for help.

By July we were able to move to the Scranton area, where a friend of mine owned a big empty house he was in the process of finishing off. There, among the rolling hills and beautiful lakes of northern Pennsylvania, we settled in. Yarima found the cooler nights and days a welcome contrast to the humidity of summer in Philadelphia, and she loved the onset of fall, with its colors and the first cold nights. We slept in sweatshirts and sweatpants under two down quilts, the baby snuggled between us.

We had each other, and we had David. We walked in the wooded hill-and-lake country, we chopped wood for our stoves. We took trips to the malls to buy our necessities and to window-shop. I even located a source for plantains, not easy in Scranton. I also got down to work on my dissertation again while Yarima busied herself with the baby and the house. For all the difficulties of our life, her happy disposition rarely faltered. I watched her prepare Cream of Wheat for David's breakfast, or pick up a bargain at the local mall, or hum a Michael Jackson song she had heard. In spite of the strains of life in an alien place whose inner workings she knew she did not, perhaps could not, know, her inner serenity was unmistakable. She smiled easily and laughed often. But sometimes when she listened on her Walkman to my tapes of village chants and speeches, I would see the tears dropping from her eyes. I knew that she missed her family and friends badly.

In the fall of 1987 our circumstances changed. For one thing, Yarima was pregnant again. For another, we had signed an option agreement with a movie company that had heard about our story. Despite the pregnancy, now that we had the means I knew we had to go back. Yarima was due at the end of March. We could make a long visit, then have the baby in Caracas. Taking David into the jungle, though, would require extra precautions: a Zodiac rubber raft in case something happened to the aluminum boat, special Wyeth Laboratories antivenom, a full array of medicines, baby food, waterproof cases, and maybe most important, a shortwave transmitter with a generator. I wasn't going to take any chances of getting stuck up there again, not this time.

We made the trip in early November, flying into La Esmeralda, then motoring upriver. The Guajaribo rapids, as dangerous as ever, swamped us. Grabbing David, Yarima clambered up on a rock while I struggled to save the boat and supplies. When we finally got to Wawatoi our reunion with the Hasupuweteri was, like everything else in our lives, full of joy and sorrow. Amid all the excitement, Yarima learned that one of her classificatory brothers, Ariwe, had died of malaria, and even while everybody around her was laughing with the pleasure of being reunited, tears were streaming down her cheeks. We were gently scolded for staying away so long but accepted back instantly, as if we had never left. That night Yarima slept naked in a Yanomama hammock, with David tucked in next to her.

I had planned to leave toward the end of February; according to my calculations that would give us about two months in Caracas before the baby was born. But nature had other ideas. On the morning of February 22, Yarima awoke complaining of stomach cramps. It was evident she was in labor. The day started cloudy and darkened steadily. Yarima gathered some palm leaves, intending to take them down to the stream when her time came. Her mother would be with her and her sister; I would be there too with the video camera.

Soon, though, the sky opened, and Yarima decided to give birth in the hut instead of outside in the rain. Just as she was telling me this, she suddenly felt the urge to push—she had only been in labor for a few hours, and it surprised us both. Quickly she spread out the palm leaves in the corner and squatted down. Before getting the camera, I stuck my head out the door to call her mother. Then I looked back, just in time to see my second child enter the world.

Vanessa (as I named her; her Yanomama name would have to wait) weighed just four pounds at birth. Tiny as she was, she seemed healthy and nursed vigorously from the start. But it was another three and a half months before I felt she was strong enough for the trip downriver and a month more before we flew back to the States.

As I write this, David is three and a half years old and Vanessa two. They are, I think, the first and only Yanomama-American children. We live what in many ways is a normal life in Rutherford, New Jersey, near Jersey City State College, where I have come to teach. The children are bright-eyed and active—hyperactive, it sometimes seems, especially at night when Yarima and I are tired. They talk a mile a minute and race around the living room on their push bikes. They watch *Mister Rogers* and *Sesame Street*. David has seen *Pee-wee's Big Adventure* five times and *The Little Mermaid* six. From them Yarima is learning English. I watch as she acculturates herself slowly but surely and wonder what surprises time will bring. The inevitable pressures to learn, to belong, to assimilate the knowledge and ways of the culture, are all weighing on her, pressures I can appreciate better than most. But I know also that there is a reason the Yanomama, alone among the Amazon tribes, have remained so isolated. There is something deep in their makeup that resists change fiercely. Perhaps it is their ultimate security in who they are. Perhaps it is an airtight confidence in their essential superiority to those outside, their conviction that despite the *nabuh*'s technology, despite his wealth, despite the comforts of his life, it is they and not he who define what it means to be human.

Acknowledgments

We would like to express our gratitude to the following people whose help was important to us as this book took shape. Marvin Harris, Gerald Murray, Ellen Simmons, and Raphael Bouganim read the manuscript and provided moral support as well as wise editorial counsel. Our agent, Georges Borchardt, saw the project through its roughest times. His enthusiasm and remarkable professional skill gave it life not once, but twice. At Simon and Schuster we would like to thank Ellen Butts for her attentiveness and competence in managing many of the details involved in bringing the book to completion. Most especially we owe a debt to our editor, Marie Arana-Ward, who combines the qualities of critic and friend with such rare grace.

Index

346

348

trekking patterns of, 222
variations among communities of,
208
violence of, 18, 49, 55–56, 69, 72–
74, 194, 195, 327
See also Hasupuweteri; Patahamateri
Yarakawe, 160–61
Yarima, 13, 53, 64, 79, 103, 104,
115, 128, 147–54, 172, 281, 314
adjustment to married life with,
158–67
anxiety during separations from,
164–66, 178, 180–81, 183–84,
223, 225, 227–29
betrothal to, 120–27, 132–33, 138,
141–43, 145
birth of children of, 334–35, 337
during bouts of malaria, 135–36
in Caracas, 303–14, 325–28, 336–
337
De Armas's help in reuniting with,
283–87
departure from Amazon of, 297–
303
first trip downriver by, 247–58
formal marriage to, 296, 331–33
jealousy about, 194–97

miscarriage of, 186–96, 198,
202
at Patahamateri, 206–10, 212–13,
215–17
pregnancies of, 176–77, 181, 182–
186, 195, 315–31, 336–37
in Puerto Ayacucho, 258–78
raped by Shatakewe, 197–202, 204,
206
rescued by Touwe, 290–93
reunion with, 154, 156–58
and reunion with Hasupuweteri,
293–98
search for, 232–40, 243
Shiriwe and, 238–46, 287–90, 293,
294
in United States, 329–37
Yarimowe ("Longbeard"), 79, 119–
120, 122, 132, 149, 154–57,
165, 176, 183, 248, 291
Yehiopateri, 105, 186
Ye'kwana Indians, 11, 179, 218, 223,
224, 256, 286, 287, 289, 315,
322
Yokami, 71–72, 102
Yorusiwe, 182, 210–11, 213–16,
218–20, 223–25, 236, 243–44,
251